FIFTY KEY THINKERS ON THE HOLOCAUST AND GENOCIDE

This unique volume critically discusses the works of fifty of the most influential scholars involved in the study of the Holocaust and genocide. Studying each scholar's background and influences, the authors examine the ways in which their major works have been received by critics and supporters, and analyse each thinker's contributions to the field. Key figures discussed range from historians and philosophers to theologians, anthropologists, art historians and sociologists, including:

- Hannah Arendt
- Christopher Browning
- Primo Levi
- Raphael Lemkin
- Jacques Sémelin
- Saul Friedländer
- Samantha Power
- Hans Mommsen
- Emil Fackenheim
- Helen Fein
- Adam Jones
- Ben Kiernan

A thoughtful collection of groundbreaking thinkers, this book is an ideal resource for academics, students and all those interested in both the emerging and rapidly evolving field of Genocide Studies and the established field of Holocaust Studies.

Paul R. Bartrop is an Honorary Fellow in the Faculty of Arts and Education at Deakin University, Australia, and head of the Department of History at Bialik College in Melbourne. His publications for Routledge include *The Genocide Studies Reader* with Samuel Totten (2009).

Steven Leonard Jacobs is Associate Professor and Aaron Aronov Chair of Judaic Studies in the Department of Religious Studies at the University of Alabama, USA. His most recent book is *Confronting Genocide: Judaism, Christianity, Islam* (2009).

ALSO AVAILABLE FROM ROUTLEDGE

Fifty Key Political Thinkers, 2nd Edition
Ian Adams and R. W. Dyson
978-0-415-40099-2

Fifty Key Thinkers in International Relations, 2nd Edition
Martin Griffiths, Steve C. Roach and M. Scott Solomon
978-0-415-77571-7

Fifty Key Jewish Thinkers, 2nd Edition
Dan Cohn-Sherbok
978-0-415-77141-2

FIFTY KEY THINKERS ON THE HOLOCAUST AND GENOCIDE

Paul R. Bartrop and
Steven Leonard Jacobs

LONDON AND NEW YORK

First published 2011
by Routledge
2 Park Square, Milton Park, Abingdon, Oxon OX14 4RN

Simultaneously published in the USA and Canada
by Routledge
270 Madison Ave, New York, NY 10016

Routledge is an imprint of the Taylor & Francis Group, an informa business

Typeset in Bembo by Taylor & Francis Books
Printed and bound in Great Britain by TJ International Ltd, Padstow, Cornwall

British Library Cataloguing in Publication Data
A catalogue record for this book is available from the British Library

Library of Congress Cataloging in Publication Data
Bartrop, Paul R. (Paul Robert), 1955–
Fifty key thinkers on the Holocaust and genocide / Paul R. Bartrop and Steven Leonard
Jacobs. – 1st ed.
p. cm. – (Routledge key guides series)
Includes bibliographical references.
1. Holocaust, Jewish (1939–1945)–Moral and ethical aspects. 2. Holocaust, Jewish (1939–
1945)–Social aspects. 3. Holocaust, Jewish (1939–1945)–Psychological aspects. 4. Genocide–
Moral and ethical aspects. 5. Genocide–Social aspects. 6. Genocide–Psychological aspects. 7.
Ethics, Modern–20th century. I. Jacobs, Steven Leonard. II. Title.
D804.3.B3636 2010
940.53'18–dc22
2010006038

ISBN13: 978-0-415-77550-2 (hbk)
ISBN13: 978-0-415-77551-9 (pbk)
ISBN13: 978-0-203-84602-5 (ebk)

Dedicated to the memory of

Donald Anthony Bartrop (1918–74), VX 2496, 2/2 Field
Ambulance, 6th Division,
Second Australian Imperial Force, 1939–46

and

Ralph Albert Jacobs (1921–81), 39-303-349, 385th Medical
Detachment, Military Police Batallion, Army of the
United States, 1941–45

Two men from different continents who fought the same tyranny

CONTENTS

ALPHABETICAL LIST OF
CONTENTS

CHRONOLOGICAL LIST OF
CONTENTS

ABOUT THE AUTHORS

Paul R. Bartrop is an Honorary Fellow in the Faculty of Arts and Education at Deakin University, Melbourne, and Head of History at Bialik College, Melbourne. A graduate of La Trobe University and Monash University, his published works in the areas of Holocaust and Genocide Studies, as author and editor, include *The Genocide Studies Reader* (2009), *Dictionary of Genocide* (2 volumes, 2008); *Teaching about the Holocaust: Essays by University and College Educators* (2004); *Surviving the Camps: Unity in Adversity During the Holocaust* (2000); *False Havens: The British Empire and the Holocaust* (1995); *Australia and the Holocaust, 1933–45* (1994) and *The Dunera Affair: A Documentary Resource Book* (1990). Bartrop is a member of the International Association of Genocide Scholars; the International Committee of the Annual Scholars' Conference on the Holocaust and the Churches; the Editorial Advisory Board of *Genocide Studies and Prevention*; the Editorial Advisory Board of *Holocaust and Genocide Studies*; and a member of the Advisory Board of the Genocide Education Project, California. He is a Past President of the Australian Association of Jewish Studies. He lives in Melbourne.

Steven Leonard Jacobs is the Aaron Aronov Chair of Judaic Studies at the University of Alabama, Tuscaloosa. He was educated at Penn State University and Hebrew Union College – Jewish Institute of Religion, Cincinnati, where he obtained his rabbinic ordination. His published works in the areas of Holocaust and Genocide Studies include *Maven in Blue Jeans: Essays in Honor of Zev Garber* (2009); *Confronting Genocide: Judaism, Christianity, Islam* (2009); *Post-Shoah Dialogues: Re-Thinking Our Texts Together* (2004); *Teaching About the Holocaust: Essays by College and University Educators* (2004); *Dismantling the Big Lie: The Protocols of the Elders of Zion* (2003); *Pioneers of Genocide Studies* (2002); *The Encyclopedia of Genocide* (1999); *The Holocaust Now: Contemporary Christian and*

Jewish Thought (1997); *Rethinking Jewish Faith: The Child of a Survivor Responds* (1994); *Contemporary Christian and Contemporary Jewish Religious Responses to the Shoah* (2 volumes, 1993); and *Raphael Lemkin's Thoughts on Nazi Genocide: Not Guilty?* (1992). Jacobs is editor of the papers of Raphael Lemkin; a member of the Editorial Board of Studies in the Shoah (University Press of America); Educational Consultant to the Center on the Holocaust, Genocide, and Human Rights, Philadelphia; a member of the Board of Advisors of The Aegis Trust for the Prevention of Genocide, England; and a former officer of the International Association of Genocide Scholars.

ACKNOWLEDGEMENTS

In preparing this work we have indeed been fortunate to have enjoyed the help and cooperation of many people along the way. We would like to place on record our gratitude to the following, listed alphabetically: Alex Alvarez, Peter Balakian, Laurence Baron, Omer Bartov, Yehuda Bauer, Donald Bloxham, Christopher Browning, Vahakn Dadrian, Alice Lyons Eckardt, Saul Friedländer, Eve Grimm, Simone Guin, Ted Robert Gurr, Barbara Harff, Alexander Hinton, Herbert Hirsch, Adam Jones, Ellen Kennedy, Berel Lang, Lawrence Langer, Mark Levene, Marcia Sachs Littell, Randi Markusen, Robert Melson, Norman Naimark, Joan Ringelheim, Carol Rittner, John Roth, Richard Rubenstein, Eddie Schubert, Jacques Sémelin, Jordana Silverstein, Robert Skloot, Stephen Wheatcroft and James Young.

INTRODUCTION

The trend in popular culture in recent years has seen an ongoing interest in the compilation of 'best of' lists: the best sports teams, the best movies, the best love songs, the best of Mozart, the best heavyweight champions, and so on. This book does not fall into that category. In fact, the very notion of a listing of the 'best' thinkers on the Holocaust and genocide seems to us an enterprise that breaches the limits of good taste and good sense; in some respects, it could be argued that *all* those who have taken upon themselves the responsibility of trying to make sense of the most evil of human crimes deserve equal respect without distinction for their efforts – save that of the nature and quality of their scholarship. Thus we begin this volume with a fundamental, defining assertion: this book is most decidedly *not* our interpretation of the 'best' writers and scholars on the Holocaust and genocide. Our criteria for the inclusion of the thinkers we have selected are explained below.

That said, we realise, further, that this book will not please everyone. The very idea of such a volume of fifty of the leading scholars of Holocaust and Genocide Studies has already caused controversy among those who know us personally. Some have argued that the twin fields of Holocaust Studies and Genocide Studies are still too nascent to have a recognised canon of authors who are truly 'key thinkers'. Others have told us that the notion of such a book is nothing but crass self-promotion, or hagiography, or academic tree-climbing on the bodies of countless millions of victims. At times we have been told that the list of fifty is too small to be able to encompass all thinkers contributing to the twin fields; one suggestion we received was that this project should in fact be split into two separate books – *Fifty Key Thinkers on the Holocaust* and *Fifty Key Thinkers on Genocide*. A commentator on our original proposal contended that our suggested list for inclusion indicated an avowed bias towards members of the International Association of Genocide Scholars (IAGS) at the expense of the International Network of Genocide Scholars (INoGS), because there was a preponderance of Americans on the list rather than Europeans and others. Another commentator set forth an alternative list of thinkers to ours that included several scholars of Nazi Germany rather than the Holocaust, suggesting to us a lack of understanding on the part of that person as to what Holocaust scholarship is really all about.

On the other hand, many of our colleagues have embraced the project. On at least one occasion, we were actively lobbied by a scholar seeking to be included, this person contending that he was indeed a 'key thinker' in his discipline, and should be recognised as such. Elsewhere, another colleague, aware of his inclusion on account of us having asked him to assist us with some input to his entry, began to include the fact of such recognition in the by-line to his published works. Many we have included have expressed surprise and delight at having their contribution to the development of the field acknowledged as being that of a 'key thinker'.

At no time when the idea for the book was first proposed did we expect there would be such a polarised response within the fields of Holocaust and/or Genocide Studies. A few words need to be offered in order to explain our view on why this has been the case, and why the inclusions we have made are in this volume.

One of the main problems we faced from the outset related to our criteria for inclusion. This conundrum was still occupying us even up to the last weeks prior to our submission of the final manuscript for publication. It was clear, for instance, that the list would *not* focus exclusively on historians or political scientists (despite the bizarre views of one unnamed commentator, who wrote that 'genocide scholars are, in the main, ordinary historians and social scientists, not philosophers or social theorists with elaborate or even interesting views of the world'). The more we reviewed our lists of 'possibles', the more we found that the field has been shaped by thinkers from myriad disciplines. As we reflected on this we came to the conclusion that the *best* approach to take for a book of this kind would be to consider how thinking about the Holocaust and genocide has developed in light of the approaches taken by those various disciplines and scholars.

As a result, we have included thinkers here whose work has been informed by the particular disciplinary area within which they have been writing and working – and who, in turn, have influenced those very disciplines by extending the boundaries of each one's intellectual endeavour. Far from including the work only of leading historians and political scientists – though they are of course included – our list of fifty key thinkers embraces the following areas: critical thought; criminal justice; film studies; poetry; sociology; theology; psychology and social psychology; English literature; art history; anthropology; philosophy; law; social thought; journalism; women's studies; theatre studies; and museum studies. In short, as this is a book relating to *thought*, our task has been to isolate and outline some of the many ways in which thinking about such phenomena as the Holocaust and genocide has taken place by considering those who in our view have been the most influential scholars in the various disciplines to have addressed these topics.

How does one define the term 'key' in this sense? This was another of our concerns and, again, it was one we had to address at an early stage in our deliberations. There are probably tens of thousands of books that have been written that would fit into the general category of 'Holocaust-and-genocide', written by thousands of authors, both scholarly and popular. What makes some 'key' and others not? While any selection will, admittedly, always be idiosyncratic, a careful choice should not be random or subjective or arbitrary. On the contrary, provided a clear-cut set of criteria have been developed and applied consistently, much controversy can be avoided, and even neutralised, as potential critics assess how and why certain authors have been chosen over others. Any selection in a book of this kind will inevitably be subjective, but we have attempted to bring some rigour into the process, so from the outset we adopted three criteria when considering whom to include: first, what is the reputation of the author for accuracy, clarity and originality? Second, has the author maintained an ongoing and sustained scholarly output in the fields of Holocaust and/or Genocide Studies over a lengthy period? And third, has the author's influence on the intellectual development of the field been sufficiently profound that they have broadened the parameters within which the field operates? A further criterion, that of how each scholar has influenced other scholars, was also considered, though all too often this proved difficult to measure other than anecdotally. In our view, the selection in this volume is a testament to how the nature of Holocaust and genocide scholarship has developed – and continues to develop – over time; to the directions it has taken; and to the scholarly areas it now embraces. All those chosen have been included only after a rigorous process of discussion between us, with the selection criteria uppermost in our deliberations. We also thought that any sort of attempt at a 'scientific' calculation, such as (for example) through an investigation of citation indexes, could have proven even more chimerical, as a purely statistical survey would miss a great deal of the informal influence a scholar's work can have.

That said, there are still many whom we wished to have included, but who, for one reason or another, are not in the current selection. We often found it a matter for regret that this selection was not sixty or seventy, or that, as the anonymous commentator suggested, the project was not comprised of two separate volumes instead. Nonetheless, as the difficult decisions presented themselves, we negotiated and discussed, and compromised and argued, until the current list was arrived at. It was, in the fullest sense, a joint enterprise, with input from many others whom we consulted along the way. The list has changed significantly from our original choice of fifty.

As should be apparent, a number of concerns were encountered in establishing the final list of fifty key thinkers, of which three are worthy of deeper discussion.

The first of these relates to the division of the work into the two categories of 'Holocaust' and 'genocide'. This is an ongoing issue generating some degree of discomfort among certain scholars, and the current authors are no exception. The very idea of elevating one experience – the Holocaust (in Hebrew, *Shoah*) – to a distinct status, while all other experiences become subsumed under the heading of 'genocide', smacks of an elitism of horror, which is an anathema to us and has never been intended. Our preference would be that this were a volume with only the word 'genocide' in the title, but the impracticality of this, in a world thoroughly sensitised to the Holocaust as the most extreme manifestation of human evil – and thus, of genocide – would render the title incomplete for many readers through its omission. Quite simply, the term *Holocaust and Genocide* is employed here in order to satisfy a readership that might otherwise overlook the volume if the word Holocaust were missing altogether.

Likewise, the relative proportions of scholars included on the list of fifty – approximately half each for 'Holocaust' and 'genocide' – will, for some, be a matter of controversy. This was our second major issue of concern. However, every way we looked at it, even if the word 'Holocaust' had been omitted from the title, there could be no escaping the facts that (a) the Holocaust has become an iconic case of genocide, and (b) a greater number of works have been written on that event than on any other. Logically, there could be no escaping or avoiding the reality that there exist many more thinkers on the Holocaust than on other genocides. And, given this, an additional issue presented itself: because so much scholarship has taken place on the Holocaust, it has been inevitable that many of the thoughts stimulated by Holocaust scholars have influenced thinkers of other genocides, and that, as a result, Holocaust scholarship has generated work in comparative analysis. Often, therefore, the term 'Holocaust scholar' is not necessarily the most appropriate description of where a specific writer's focus lies, but is, rather, a label of convenience.

The third important issue with which we had to deal related to a concern over the perceived need for balance. We knew this would be a controversial matter, as partisan critics would pick up on what they identified as omissions or biases: too few women, too many Americans, not enough Africans or Latin Americans, too many members of IAGS or not enough of INoGS, too much Holocaust (of which see above), not enough attention paid to colonial genocide, too much (or too little) on the Armenian Genocide, not enough on Cambodia or Rwanda or Bosnia or Darfur, and so on. We were ourselves conscious of these issues, and had to address them as our thoughts evolved. The result was the realisation, perhaps not immediately apparent, that we were examining *ways of thinking* about the Holocaust and genocide, rather than showcasing the breadth of scholars who have engaged with these topics. Our interest is much more one of how such thinking has developed, and what its impact has been, rather than in tracing a series of chronologies or exploring a range of historiographies. Thus, our concern is more one related to the nature of thought than it is to any specific disciplines, geographical regions, case studies or time periods; in like manner, while the well of possible scholars from which we could draw is extremely deep, we selected those for this book on the basis of their thinking, rather than on their gender, age, background, nationality, religion, or their political, organisational or institutional affiliations.

At all times, therefore, our guiding star has been the quest to discern the wellsprings, nature and impacts of thought relative to the Holocaust and genocide. Thought – not biography, not hero-worship, not 'best of', not partisanship – but thought.

In doing so, of course, there are some elements in each entry here that inevitably had to be covered. Foremost among these has been the need to consider at least something of each subject's personal biography. A person's thoughts do not just appear out of nowhere; they are the result of a variety of ongoing inputs among which are family background, education, career developments, personal experiences and human interactions. This is why we begin each entry with a few words on the person's life and career. After each entry, we note the most salient works of each author relative to the Holocaust and/or genocide in order to demonstrate the development of their thinking. A word should also be added here that many contemporary authors are still actively engaged in writing, and as a result new works were appearing even as this book was being prepared. While we have made every effort to be as up to date as possible in drawing attention to their work, all too often publishing events have overtaken us despite our best efforts.

To assist us, we found on occasion that the best way to obtain biographical data was to contact the people themselves (wherever possible) in order to obtain from them a curriculum vitae or other such descriptive material. We also consulted biographical data located on university webpages and in promotional material from publishers. Wherever we could obtain verifiable data, we did so, though the final interpretation of all material, of course, was our own.

It should be reiterated that the Holocaust and genocide, as fields of study, are still only young, and, as such, are still developing. There are areas of investigation yet to be fully explored; notions not yet considered in depth; and ideas still to be given full illumination. While there have been a number of controversies, there are barely any strands of thinking that could yet be termed 'schools', though one debate in the 1980s, between the so-called Functionalists and Intentionalists, could perhaps claim to have spawned two. This dispute, which will appear a number of times here, concerned the origin of the Nazi attempt to annihilate the Jews of Europe. The Functionalists held the view that the push for the Final Solution came from lower ranks within the German bureaucracy, as a response to the chaos of the Nazi form of administration; the Intentionalists argued that there was a master plan to launch the Holocaust that can be tracked back to Hitler's earliest writings.

Equally, there is nothing, until now, that could be termed a 'tradition' in Holocaust or Genocide Studies, making the task of a project such as the one before you that much more difficult to construct. For despite the vast number of superb authors who have written important studies on the Holocaust and/or genocide(s), not many fit all the criteria articulated above (reputation, ongoing and sustained scholarly output and influence on the field to a profound degree). Certainly there are more than fifty; this has already been acknowledged. But within the constraints imposed by the nature of the project, some had to be omitted on this occasion. Perhaps, in a revised edition of this book at some future time, when the contours of the respective fields have developed further (as they surely will), a reformulated list may well see a shift in emphasis, and other names will appear.

A story is told of a man who had a problem. No matter how much he thought about it, he could not resolve it. Why is there so much evil in the world, when we have so many guides, from so many traditions, describing for us the path to goodness? They all give insight, he saw, but the message was not getting through. Generation after generation, year after year, people sought newer and newer ways to do damage to each other. Finally, in desperation, the man went into the wilderness, and prayed – to all the deities he knew, from all the traditions of which he was aware, and he called on all of them by name: 'Show me what to do, and I'll do it; convince me that your way will bring world peace and sanctity for life, and I will follow your lead.' A long silence followed as he waited for an answer. And waited. And waited. Finally, when he was exhausted, and hungry and thirsty to the point of collapse, a small, still voice – he knew not from where – whispered into his ear: 'The answer is within you, my son: *just think about it.*'

This is the task those featured in this book have set themselves; to think about the best ways to expose human evil, to account for it – and hopefully, to encourage others to do the same, in the hope that ultimately a solution will be found.

Paul R. Bartrop, Melbourne, Australia
Steven Leonard Jacobs, Tuscaloosa, Alabama, USA

NOTE: Two points of housekeeping are necessary at the outset: first, where cross-references to authors occur in this book, this will be designated by the person's name appearing in **bold** type; second, 'Major Writings' refers to writings specifically on the Holocaust and/or genocide, and these do not encompass an author's entire bibliography – which in many cases would extend substantially to areas beyond the scope of this study.

A note on further reading

In the preparation of this work we consulted a vast number of books, articles and websites as we strove to learn as much as we could about those being discussed, their lines of thinking and the intellectual milieux in which they worked or are working. As stated above, on occasion the best way to obtain biographical data was to contact the people themselves (wherever possible) in order to obtain from them a curriculum vitae or other such descriptive material. Upon reflection, we found it would have been next to impossible to compile anything like a comprehensive reading guide that would take into account biographical material as well as further and general reading, while at the same time retaining some form of representative integrity within the list.

We therefore concluded that instead of trying to put in *everything* – knowing that we could not do so within the limits imposed by the task – it would be preferable to compile a list of works relative to specific thinkers that would be useful for those seeking to broaden their reading beyond the current volume. It is our hope that the list will thus be of benefit as a starting point; we make no claims as to its inclusiveness.

Of course, each of those profiled in this book have their own listing of their major works in the area of the Holocaust and/or genocide, so their writing does not appear in this list. Also, works by other authors that are referenced within the text itself are cited at the end of each entry.

For reasons of space and convenience, the list of further reading can be found at http://www.routledge.com/books/details/9780415775519.

ALEX ALVAREZ (b. 1963)

Alex Alvarez is a Professor of Criminology at Northern Arizona University, Flagstaff, Arizona, where he has taught since 1990. Born in Biloxi, Mississippi in 1963, in 2001 he was appointed founding Director of the Martin-Springer Institute for Teaching the Holocaust, Tolerance, and Humanitarian Values at NAU. His main areas of study have concerned minorities, crime and criminal justice, and themes related to collective and interpersonal violence, and he has published widely on Native Americans, Latinos and African Americans; fear of crime; sentencing; justifiable and criminal homicide; and genocide. In addition, he has published widely in the areas of genocide, the Holocaust, violence and homicide, and criminological theory. In 2006 he became one of the founding editors of the international journal *Genocide Studies and Prevention*.

One of the very few criminal justice scholars in the field of Holocaust and Genocide Studies, Alvarez has argued forcefully that, whatever else we may say of these mass human tragedies, they are first and foremost *crimes*: against individuals and families, against communities and other groups, and, ultimately, against the nation-state itself (though its practitioners and perpetrators, more often than not, are sanctioned by the state and carried out through its legal, political and military machinery). He has, moreover, addressed how seemingly 'normal' human beings are able to engage in genocidal acts, and the roles of professionals, ideologies and militias in the practice of genocide. As a comparativist, Alvarez understands the Holocaust not as a stand-alone event divorced from other examples of genocide throughout history, but within this larger context.

Alvarez's primary contribution to the field of Genocide Studies, to this point, remains *Governments, Citizens, and Genocide: A Comparative and Interdisciplinary Approach* (2001). Both the title, which presented genocide in the frame of the relationship between governments and their citizens, and the subtitle, which emphasised both the comparative and interdisciplinary nature of Alvarez's undertaking, are of primary importance to his work.

In the book's Introduction, Alvarez argued emphatically that social scientists, and in particular criminologists, have missed the boat in not addressing genocide as an important *political* crime. In so doing, they have diminished the importance and significance of addressing genocide by both governmental officials and the general populace. At the same time, however, he understood the sea change currently taking place as one of positive potential for the future:

> the ways in which genocide is portrayed by social scientists can serve to shape opinion and policy and in turn heighten concern and spur action. The scholarly analysis of genocide may assist in turning the empty rhetoric of 'never again' into a promise and a reality.
>
> (Alvarez, 2001: 2)

After a brief survey of genocide in history – what the term's coiner **Raphael Lemkin** would call 'a new name for an old crime' – Alvarez then pinpointed the contribution of modernity to genocide as it has been practiced in the nineteenth, twentieth and twenty-first centuries: 'What modernity has done is reshape genocide into a more efficient and rational endeavor capable of killing on an industrial scale. The modern age has not created genocide; rather it has altered its nature, application, and efficiency.' (33)

Part of the difficulty of scholarly research has long been the problematics of dealing with **Lemkin**'s original definition and its own complexities of commission and omission. When he first coined the term in 1944, **Lemkin** wrote:

> By 'genocide' we mean the destruction of a nation or ethnic group. ... It is intended ... to signify a coordinated plan of different actions aiming at the destruction of essential foundations of life of national groups, with the aim of annihilating the groups themselves. The objectives of such a plan would be disintegration of the political and social institutions, of culture, language, national feelings, religion, and the economic existence of national groups, and the destruction of the personal security, liberty, health, dignity, and even the lives of the individuals belonging to such groups.
>
> (Lemkin, 1944: 79)

Then, in the United Nations Convention on the Prevention and Punishment of the Crime of Genocide 1948, the definition stated:

> genocide means any of the following acts committed with intent to destroy, in whole or in part, a national, ethnical, racial or religious group, as such:
>
> a) Killing members of the group;
> b) Causing serious bodily or mental harm to members of the group;
> c) Deliberately inflicting on the group conditions of life calculated to bring about its physical destruction in whole or in part;
> d) Imposing measures intended to prevent births within the group;
> e) Forcibly transferring children of the group to another group.

Issues subsequently arose in both instances of what constitutes a group, and a lack of scholarly consensus on this and other such matters has generated divisions within the academy. Yet Alvarez saw and understood what he labeled eight 'definitional commonalities' which, collectively, are a way out of the confusion. In summary, these included the following:

- the recognition that genocide is committed by the state or a similar authority structure;
- that genocides are planned, systematic and ongoing attempts to eliminate a group of people;
- that victims are chosen because of real or imagined membership in a group targeted for destruction;
- that targeted groups are all vulnerable;
- the recognition that genocide appears in various forms and guises, each characterised by different goals and motivations, and that these different goals shape the various strategies and tactics of individual genocides;
- that genocide includes many different types of activities, only one of which is the blatant or immediate murder of a population;
- that an important component common to many definitions is intent; and finally,
- that there is an implicit recognition among scholars that genocide is a crime that must be prevented and punished.

Thus, even though no single clear, universal and unambiguous definition of genocide exists, enough elements are common to most definitions to allow a working understanding of the crime (Alvarez, 2001: 47–53).

For Alvarez, it is these very commonalities that must be communicated outside the academy to politicians and governments, thereby helping to formulate preventive policies. Genocide can be viewed as a rational policy of governments and nation-states who manipulate history and historic myths for their own nefarious ends (Alvarez, 2001: 78–85), so fighting against it must itself be addressed rationally, starting with the accumulation of extensive knowledge and sound social-scientific scholarship.

Having developed the very comparative and interdisciplinary approach that is foundational to the field of Genocide Studies, Alvarez then proceeded, in his subsequent works, to address a number of other significant (and somewhat specialised) issues.

For instance, in asking the question of how it is possible for human beings to become perpetrators, he turned to what are referred to as techniques of neutralisation – central to criminologists' understanding of aberrant behaviour, though far less well-known outside that discipline – as a source of illumination. In 1957 G. M. Sykes and D. Matza identified five such 'techniques of neutralisation' used by juvenile delinquents who engaged in disruptive and anti-social behaviour: (1) denial of responsibility, (2) denial of injury, (3) denial of victim, (4) condemning the condemners, and (5) appeal to higher loyalties. Applying their insights to the specific genocide of the Holocaust, Alvarez showed that these same categories are equally applicable to its perpetrators. He concluded:

> Nevertheless, in spite of residual difficulties experienced by some participants, I believe, overall, that the Techniques of Neutralization shed new light on our understanding of the Holocaust in two significant ways that are worth summarizing.
>
> 1. The techniques illustrate the fact that individuals can engage in genocidal behavior that poses a direct conflict with their belief systems.
> 2. The Techniques of Neutralization identify and describe the specific mechanisms that the participants applied to neutralize internal opposition. Perhaps the most important lesson of the Holocaust remains that 'ordinary' men and women can become active, willing agents of genocide. 'Normal' people can in clear conscience commit the most horrific crimes.
>
> (Alvarez, 1997: 169–71)

Genocides are organised, planned, systematised and carried out by educated professionals. Attempting to understand this particular phenomenon, Alvarez suggested that they do so for one or a number of reasons: professional career advancement, agreement with the genocidal agenda and/or a too-easy manipulation by others such that they acquiesce in doing so. In this regard he cited the case of SS Lieutenant Colonel Adolf Eichmann, responsible for managing the details of the transportation of Jews to the ghettos, concentration and death camps throughout Nazi-occupied Europe. At his trial in Israel in 1961, Eichmann argued initially that he did not hate the Jews, that he had visited Palestine early in his career, and had studied both the Hebrew language and Jewish history – but he had a career-advancing task to perform and did so to the very best of his ability, without any moral qualms whatsoever, as befitted one thoroughly ensconced in a bureaucracy.

Alvarez's recent work on genocide has extended his earlier research and writing. From originally considering the criminality of genocide perpetrators to analysing their social-pathological motivations, he has lately begun investigating the ideological inspirations of those committing the crime. In one such essay he has suggested that the scholarly community has been too easily dismissive of the central role of ideology ('shared beliefs, ideas, and symbols that help us make sense of the world around us') as a potent factor in the perpetration of all genocides, past and present. How to counter its effects (what he calls 'resocialisation') remains a daunting task for all involved in education at every level (Alvarez, 2008).

Even more disturbing, perhaps, is the relationship between militias which essentially exercise a more violent and less organised, quasi-amateurish, paramilitary function, and the perpetration of genocide itself. Recruited from those most easily manipulable by others in positions of authority (military leaders as well as their own community leaders), they perform their dreaded tasks outside the parameters of governmental officialdom, but with both an implicit and explicit understanding of their legitimating value to a genocidally disposed nation-state. Taking as his case studies Arkan's Tigers in the Bosnian genocide and the *Interahamwe* in the Rwandan Genocide, Alvarez has shown their similarities as government-funded and trained militias.

Finally, Alvarez has found a positive new beginning in the International Criminal Court (ICC), the International Criminal Tribunal for the Former Yugoslavia (ICTY) and the International Criminal Tribunal for Rwanda (ICTR), all developments that have built upon the original International Military Tribunal (IMT) held in

Nuremberg between 1945 and 1946, which tried the Nazi leadership at the close of the Second World War. For Alvarez, the significance of such tribunals lies in the fact that government leaders can no longer make claims of ignorance for what others have done under their rule, and, more importantly, that nation-state sovereignty takes a back seat in bringing to trial and punishment those who would violate our common or shared humanity. As he has written:

> In the coming century, police will play an increasingly important role in allowing individual states to fulfil their obligations under international law. It is therefore important for police to understand the historic forces behind this 'new global architecture.' Human rights violations have taken the greatest toll on human life in the twentieth century. Whether or not the mistakes of the twentieth century are repeated in this new century depends in large part upon the role that law enforcement plays in enforcing the new regime of international human rights law.
>
> (Alvarez, 2004: 60)

Alex Alvarez's contributions to the study of the Holocaust and genocide lie within his academic discipline of criminology. In studying criminal justice and criminological theories, his comparative and contextual understandings of these events have enabled him to bring a perspective that transcends the study of both law and sociology. He is thus an important interdisciplinary scholar, who demonstrates an ongoing readiness to engage in debates from within his own and other subject areas, and his comparative and theoretical perspectives have made important and influential contributions to the development of a social science of genocide, expanding the field in what had beforehand been a relatively sparse scholarly literature.

Alvarez's major works

'Adjusting to Genocide: The Techniques of Neutralization and the Holocaust', *Social Science History*, 21, 2 (1997), 139–78.

'Genocide in Bosnia: Turning Neighbors into Killers', *Sociological Imagination*, 36 (1999), 115–23.

Governments, Citizens, and Genocide: A Comparative and Interdisciplinary Approach, Bloomington: Indiana University Press, 2001.

'Justifying Genocide: The Role of Professionals in Legitimizing Mass Killing', *Idea: A Journal of Social Issues*, 6, 1 (2001), at http://www.ideajournal.com.

'Policing and Human Rights in the Post-Holocaust 21st Century', *International Journal of Comparative and Applied Criminal Justice*, 28, 1 (2004), 45–63.

Violence: The Enduring Problem, Thousand Oaks (CA): Sage, 2007.
'Destructive Beliefs: Genocide and the Role of Ideology', in R. Haveman and Alette Smeulers (eds), *Towards a Criminology of International Crimes*, Antwerp: Intersentia, 2008, 213–29.
Genocidal Crimes, New York: Routledge, 2009.

References

Lemkin, Raphael, *Axis Rule in Occupied Europe: Laws of Occupation, Analysis of Government, Proposals for Redress*, Washington: Carnegie Endowment for World Peace, 1944.
Sykes, G. M. and D. Matza, 'Techniques of Neutralization: A Theory of Delinquency', American *Sociological Review*, 22 (1957), 664–70.

HANNAH ARENDT (1906–75)

Political philosopher – though she herself preferred to be identified as a political theorist – Hannah Arendt was one of the most important and controversial thinkers of the twentieth century. She was born in 1906 in Hanover, Germany, but spent her formative years in Königsberg and Berlin. Her parents were middle-class secular Jews, and she was raised with little knowledge of Jewish religious traditions and observances. Her father died when she was only seven years old, and it was her mother who encouraged her to pursue an academic career and make good use of her intellectual gifts. From 1924 to 1929 she studied the New Testament with Rudolf Bultmann and philosophy with Martin Heidegger at the University of Marburg, phenomenology with Edmund Husserl at the University of Freiburg, and existentialism under Karl Jaspers at the University of Heidelberg. Under the direction of Jaspers she received her PhD for a dissertation on the concept of love in Saint Augustine's thoughts and writings. Arrested by the Gestapo and briefly interned in 1933 for her work documenting German anti-Semitism, she fled to France where she remained until the Nazi invasion and occupation of France in 1940. She escaped through the efforts of an American Righteous Gentile, Varian Fry, who managed to rescue a number of intellectuals through his underground activities in Marseille. Arendt arrived in New York in 1941.

During the remaining years of the Second World War she worked as a journalist for the German-Jewish newspaper *Aufbau*, and after the war for the Commission on European Jewish Cultural Reconstruction, under whose auspices she returned to Germany on many occasions. In addition, she worked as an editor at Schocken

Books (New York) and Youth Aliyah, which arranged for surviving Jewish young people to emigrate from Europe to pre-state Palestine. Later she held academic appointments at the University of California, Princeton University, Northwestern University, Yale University, Wesleyan University, the University of Chicago and the New School for Social Research in New York. She died on 4 December 1975.

Her notoriety with regard to the study of the Holocaust rests primarily on two works: *The Origins of Totalitarianism* (1951) and *Eichmann in Jerusalem: A Report on the Banality of Evil* (1963).

The Origins of Totalitarianism, written in the aftermath of the Second World War, is divided into three major analyses: first, anti-Semitism; second, imperialism; and third, totalitarianism. For Arendt, the roots of imperialism and totalitarianism lay not only in their making common cause with anti-Semitism (and thus, racism), but in the fact that Marxism and National Socialism are linked by their use of terror in the service of an ideology that is used to control the masses – and both were thus radically new forms of government. According to scholar Jacob Rogozinski:

> this is one of Arendt's central theses: 'totalitarianism differs in essence from other forms of political oppression with which we are familiar, such as despotism, tyranny, dictatorship.' It is the essence of total domination which is revealed in the camps, and 'nothing can be compared to life in the camps,' neither penal colonies, nor religious persecutions, or ancient slavery; there are so many superficial analogies which lead our judgment astray.
>
> (Rogozinski, 1993: 257)

Extending this, Adam Kirsch has recently noted:

> In *The Origins of Totalitarianism*, she points out that the first step in the Nazis' destruction of the Jews was to make them stateless, in the knowledge that people with no stake in a political community have no claim on the protection of its law.
>
> This is the insight that makes Arendt a thinker for our time, when failed states have again and again become the settings for mass murder. She reveals with remorseless logic why emotional appeals to 'human rights' or 'the international community' so often prove impotent in the face of a humanitarian crisis.
>
> (Kirsch, 2009: 68)

It was this kind of thinking that made Arendt's ideas relevant and applicable at the end of the twentieth century and the beginning of the twenty-first – a time which witnessed the genocides in Rwanda, Bosnia-Herzegovina, and the ongoing genocide in Darfur. The precedent had been successfully established by the Nazis and the Communists, where the terrors of concentration and death camps were used to terrorise populations in the cause of both political and religious agendas, rendering various segments of nation-state populations as superfluous and irrelevant.

Arendt's analysis linked left-wing Marxist Communism and right-wing National Socialism. She saw both as employing the same intellectual mind-set, which was translated into all-too-real operational horror and terror. Within this context, she also identified the centrality of anti-Semitism in both ideologies.

While such thoughts may have galvanised opinion within and among a scholarly readership, Arendt was far more publicly controversial owing to the conclusions she drew when covering the trial in Jerusalem of Nazi SS *Obersturmbannführer* Adolf Eichmann, in particular her analysis of his 'ordinariness' and his seeming inability to think through the consequences of his actions in relation to other human beings. At the same time, she also offered a critique of the members of the various *Judenräte* (the Jewish self-governing councils in both the larger and smaller ghettos under Nazi hegemony), which showed them to be tragically complicit in their own destruction.

As reflected in Arendt's study, Eichmann was, at most, a reasonably intelligent, though hardly introspective, person; a bureaucrat who saw the SS and his role in it as one which provided career advancements. By all accounts, he was *not* an anti-Semite in the classic Nazi mould; he had studied Jewish history, visited Palestine and even attempted to learn Hebrew. Physically, there was nothing distinguishing about either his size or his features. He was, in the final analysis, just an ordinary man, but one who found himself in a situation and role which evidently suited him, regardless of its ultimate consequences: 'The trouble with Eichmann was precisely that so many were like him, and that the many were neither perverted nor sadistic, that they were, and still are, terribly and terrifyingly normal' (Arendt, 1964: 278). For Arendt, the question was how, in fact, he could justify (if indeed his actions required justification) his behaviour. Observing him almost daily in the courtroom and responding to the judges, his defence attorneys and the prosecutors, Arendt came to perceive no insight on his part regarding his behaviour towards other human beings, and she adopted the term 'banal' to describe his ordinariness.

Sadly, as she saw it, it was this very 'banality' that characterised too much of the contemporary human condition. The overwhelming majority of human beings, for her, lack the ability to think about their behaviour, and their lack of self-insight thus lends itself, for some, to their engagement in horrific behaviours without the necessity of either rationalisations or justifications. Eichmann was thus emblematic of too many in too many societies, and, by extension, what continues to be wrong with much of the world.

In a Postscript to the revised and enlarged edition of *Eichmann in Jerusalem* in 1964, Arendt wrote:

> I also can well imagine that an authentic controversy might have arisen over the subtitle of the book; for when I speak of the banality of evil, I do so only on the strictly factual level, pointing to a phenomenon which stared one in the face at the trial. ... He *merely*, to put the matter colloquially, *never realized what he was doing*. It was precisely this lack of imagination which enabled him to sit for months on end facing a German Jew who was conducting the police interrogation, pouring out his heart to the man and explaining again and again how it was that he reached only the rank of lieutenant colonel in the S.S. and that it had not been his fault that he was not promoted. ... He was not stupid. It was sheer thoughtlessness – something by no means identical with stupidity – that predisposed him to become one of the greatest criminals of that period.
>
> (Arendt, 1964: 287–88, emphasis in original)

Beyond her views on Eichmann, Arendt's remarks on the *Judenräte* produced a storm of controversy for which she was somewhat unprepared. But here, too, as she maintained in that same Postscript, the question of Jewish complicity *had* been already raised by others. And, while she disagreed with their conclusions (for example, with regard to evidence of a so-called 'ghetto mentality', an unconscious 'death wish', or even 'self-hatred'), she wrote that her examination of the data presented at the trial itself led her to conclude that those Jews tragically tasked with leadership responsibilities under the Nazis had, for the most part, at least initially unknowingly, participated in their own destruction and the destruction of their fellow Jews. While this particular controversy has diminished somewhat with the passage of time, it still remains one of the unresolved dilemmas of the *Shoah*, and while she was somewhat dismissive of those who attacked her, her conclusion might best be summed up through a quotation she took from a former inmate of Theresienstadt: 'The Jewish people as whole behaved magnificently. Only the leadership failed' (Arendt, 1964: 284).

Arendt's friendship with the novelist Gershom Scholem resulted in an exchange of letters after the publication of *Eichmann in Jerusalem* in which he accused her of evincing no love for the Jewish people (in Hebrew, *ahavat Yisrael*) and of a failure to appreciate the horrific context in which those same leaders had to make their awful decisions. The exchange led, ultimately, to a rupturing of their relationship. In response, Arendt agreed with Scholem regarding his first accusation, at least philosophically:

> You are quite right – I am not moved by any 'love' of this sort, and for two reasons: I have never in my life 'loved' any people or collective – neither the German people, nor the French, nor the American, not the working class or anything of that sort. I indeed love 'only' my friends and the only kind of love I know of and believe in is the love of persons. Secondly, this 'love of the Jews' would appear to me, since I am myself Jewish, as something rather suspect. I cannot love myself or anything which I know is part and parcel of my own person.
>
> (Kohn and Feldman, 1963: 466–67)

With regard to the second charge, that of her failure to understand the historical context and reality of the *Judenräte*, she further clarified her position that the preferred course of action would have been 'the possibility of doing nothing' rather than an attempt at justifying their behaviour or that of others (Kohn and Feldman, 1963: 468).

To sum up the main threads of Hannah Arendt's thinking concerning the Holocaust is no easy task. For most of her adult life – and, some would argue, even prior to adulthood – she remained something of a marginal figure on the periphery of the organised Jewish community and, ultimately, was far more welcomed within the larger academic and intellectual communities wherein she found a home to think and write. As the scholar Steven Aschheim would write of her and Scholem:

> The source of her achievements, conflicts, and limitations lay in the fact that in her great engagement with the wider world, she exemplified the bifurcated Western Jew that she acutely diagnosed and critiqued. Arendt was perhaps the keenest analyst, but also the embodiment, of the experience of German-Jewish intellectuals – their conflicts and convolutions but also their immense creativity. Scholem was interested in Judaism; Arendt,

who knew very little about the body of Judaism itself, was the great explicator of 'Jewishness' and its psychological machinations. She highlighted its ambivalences, multiple loyalties, fissures, breakdowns, and partial reconstitutions.

(Aschheim, 2001: 67)

Arendt remains, however, one of the seminal thinkers and writers on anti-Semitism, Communism, Nazism and the Holocaust, and one whose views cannot be cavalierly dismissed but must be addressed head-on. Her insights were incisive and highly influential (as well as controversial) in their time; how relevant they will remain for future generations of scholars and thinkers, and how applicable they will be to the analysis of post-Holocaust genocides, will await further determination at some future time.

Arendt's major writings

The Origins of Totalitarianism, New York: Schocken Books, 1951.
The Human Condition, Chicago: University of Chicago Press, 1958.
Between Past and Future: Six Exercises in Political Thought, New York: Viking Press, 1961.
Eichmann in Jerusalem: A Report on the Banality of Evil, New York: Viking Press, 1963; revised and enlarged edition, 1964.
On Revolution, New York: Viking Press, 1963.
Men in Dark Times, New York: Harcourt Brace Jovanovich, 1970.
On Violence, New York: Harcourt Brace Jovanovich, 1970.
Crises of the Republic, New York: Harcourt Brace Jovanovich, 1972.

References

Aschheim, Steven E., *Scholem, Arendt, Klemperer: Intimate Chronicles in Turbulent Times*, Bloomington (IN): Indiana University Press, 2001, 67.
Kirsch, Adam, 'Beware of Pity: Hannah Arendt and the Power of the Impersonal', *New Yorker*, 29 January 2009, 68.
Kohn, Jerome and Ron H. Feldman (eds), *The Jewish Writings: Hannah Arendt*, New York: Schocken Books, 1963.
Rogozinski, Jacob, 'Hell on Earth: Hannah Arendt in the Face of Hitler', *Philosophy Today*, 37, 3 (1993), 257–73.

PETER BALAKIAN (b. 1951)

Peter Balakian is an Armenian-American poet, writer and scholar. Born in 1951 in Teaneck, New Jersey, he was raised in Teaneck and

Tenafly, New Jersey. Currently the Donald M. and Constance H. Rebar Professor of the Humanities, and Director of Creative Writing at Colgate University, New York, he was the first Director of Colgate's Center for Ethics and World Societies. A Professor of English at Colgate since 1980, he was a friend and colleague of **Terrence Des Pres** during that scholar's most celebrated period.

Balakian was co-founder and co-editor of the poetry magazine *Graham House Review*, published between 1976 and 1996. Throughout that time he published four books of poetry; *Father Fisheye* (1979), *Sad Days of Light* (1983), *Reply from Wilderness Island* (1988), and *Dyer's Thistle* (1996). Most recently, Balakian has published a selection of his work entitled *June-tree: New and Selected Poems 1974–2000*. His poems have appeared widely in American magazines and journals such as *The Nation, The New Republic, Antaeus, Partisan Review, Poetry, Agni* and *The Kenyon Review*, as well as in a number of anthologies.

As a poet and memoirist, Balakian has not focused solely on genocide, though much of his poetry deals with issues of historical memory and the traumatic past as they pertain to the Armenian Genocide and Armenian culture. One of his most important pieces, *Mandelstam in Armenia, 1930* (first published in 1996), articulates clearly this engagement with history within the context of poetry and trauma as it intersects with the Armenian and, in this case the Russian, past:

> Between arid houses and crooked streets
> a shadow could be your wife or a corpse
> and a mule's hooves sounded like Stalin's
> fat fingers drumming a table.
> In the Caucasus eagles and hawks
> hung in the blue's basilica.
> A swallow flew off a socle
> into the wing of an echo—
> history's caw and chirp and bird shit
> on the tombs in the high grass.
> Oh hairy serrated stems
> poppies flagged like tongues.
> Petals of flat paper
> lined your thumbed-out pockets.
> Anther seeds burned your pen.
> From a cloud of broom a red bee stumbled,
> to your fish-globe brain.

a casket of light kissed the eyebrows of a tree.
Lake Sevan's rippling blue skirt
lapped you. Slime tongues got your eyes.
A half-dead perch slithered your ear.
When the evening air settled
on the creatures of the mountain
the sun was the Virgin's head.
Here, where the bush grew with fresh blood
and ancient thorns, you picked the rose
without scissors. Became an omen.
(Balakian, 2001: 73)

One of Balakian's most widely known poems, *The Oriental Rug*, pursues further the theme of remembrance, and the necessity – and pain – of intergenerational transmission of trauma. Here, in just a few lines, he considers memory of the Armenian Genocide through the metaphor of a hand-woven rug, complete with knots, loops of yarn, wool, colours, and texture. Considering the history of his ancestors' experience (as well as his own), his five-part poem includes such lines as:

Now I undo the loops
of yarn I rested my head on.
Under each flower
a tufted pile loosens.
I feel the wool give way
as if six centuries of feet
had worn it back to the hard
earth floor it was made to cover.
Six centuries of Turkish heels
on my spine-dyed back:
madder, genista, sumac –
one skin color in the soil.
(Balakian, 2001: 47–52)

In Balakian's autobiographical work *Black Dog of Fate: A Memoir* (1997), he reflected in prose what being part of a survivor family was like for him as a young Armenian-American growing up in suburban New Jersey in the 1950s and 1960s. The work was a finely crafted meditation on identity in the face of a past conditioned through the transmitted memory of the experience of genocide – a memory about which little was spoken directly, but which was pervasive and, all too often, stifling. The book related Balakian's journey from dim awareness that 'something' had happened in the family's past, to a full-blown appreciation of his ethnic identity and anger at the fate that had befallen his people. With this work, Balakian entered a new and developing area of genocide reflection, that of inter-generational memoir. As a cutting-edge work, written in a highly sensitive and literary style, *Black Dog of Fate* was named a *New York Times* and *Los Angeles Times* Notable Book for 1997, and was awarded the highly prestigious PEN/Martha Albrand Prize for Memoir in 1998.

Building on the theme of inter-generational memoir, in 1998 Balakian wrote a highly influential essay for the *Chronicle of Higher Education*, in which he considered a number of issues related to the writing of *Black Dog of Fate*, and what the experience of doing so had meant for him as a writer, scholar and human being. Then, in 2004, another essay of self-reflection, also in the *Chronicle of Higher Education*, explored the relationship between humanistic creativity and the reality of genocidal destruction. This essay took readers into Balakian's confidence after he had written a highly acclaimed work of history, *The Burning Tigris: The Armenian Genocide and America's Response* (which was a *New York Times* Notable Book, and for which Balakian was awarded the 2005 **Raphael Lemkin** Prize for the best book in English on human rights and genocide). In the article, Balakian shared with readers the difficulties of writing genocide history as distinct from poetry or memoir, concluding that 'The artistic challenges of locating the events, the characters, and their voices in sensory, human time was an energizing force that kept me writing when the darkness of the subject could have shut me down' (Balakian, 2004: B13). Such a challenge, he contended, has to be met head-on:

> any writer who writes about the worst things human beings can do to each other has to deal, in a personal way, with the weight of those realities. Working in such domains can be depressing and even traumatic. You can feel as if you are living in an alternate universe. (Balakian, 2004: B10)

In Balakian's case, the task was exacerbated by the trauma of survivorship running through his family and the ongoing issue of the Turkish government's denial of the Armenian Genocide, which he had discussed earlier in *Black Dog of Fate* and expressed through his poetry.

The Burning Tigris was a narrative work that recounted the historical contours both of the Armenian Genocide and the United States' response to it. Here, we see the literary artist confronting the realities of factual description, or, as Balakian himself put it,

> One of the challenges for me in crossing genre boundaries was to find the ways I could bring along the appropriate aspects of my craft. In writing a memoir, I found that the past could be opened up by finding images in memory that, like a thread, could unravel into a once-forgotten experience ... [But] in writing *The Burning Tigris*, I had to find a way to allow my own literary process whatever life it could have, within the confines of writing history. Otherwise I could not write the book.
>
> (Balakian, 2004: B10)

The result was a work which took historical writing about the Armenian Genocide to a new level of artistic expression, along the way placing that historical experience into a context which showed an American readership the degree to which the genocide was both relevant and contemporary. As Balakian stated in his Preface:

> In the past decade there has been much focus on and debate about the issue of United States engagement, response, and responsibility for crimes of genocide committed in other parts of the planet. What is the role of the most powerful nation in the world when the ultimate crime is being perpetrated in plain view? Why was there no U.S. activist response to the Holocaust, or to Pol Pot's genocide in Cambodia in 1978, or to the Rwandan genocide in 1994 when in fact the State Department, media, and general public often knew what was happening in those killing fields? Why is U.S. policy evasive, sluggish, resistant to action (of various and creative kinds, not simply or only military intervention), and often tinged with denial? Why has there been so little political will at the top when media coverage and popular knowledge and empathy are often large and dramatic?
>
> (Balakian, 2003: xiii–xiv)

Questions such as these were being taken up in depth, at almost the same time, by other authors such as **Samantha Power**. Balakian's book, for its part, proceeded to cover the American reaction to the Armenian Genocide as an example of how these later responses could have been different, showing that the shock of what the Ottoman Empire was doing to its Armenian population in the early part of the twentieth century was met by a huge outpouring of private aid and public lobbying on behalf of the Armenians. (In this, Balakian's book accompanied a developing stream of other works dealing with the same theme, further underscored by two other books that appeared almost concurrently, by Jay Winter and Merrill D. Peterson.) The popularity of *The Burning Tigris* stimulated further discussion about the US response to the Armenian Genocide, in so doing demonstrating that an otherwise highly specialised historical topic, about which most among the general public previously knew little, could be brought to a wider and literary audience if the right medium – in this case, an attractive and innovative writing style within the genre – was brought to the task.

Despite his success as a writer of history, Balakian is first and foremost a poet and memoirist. Beyond his own poetry – of which no fewer than five volumes have been published – Balakian, as a translator, has also rescued Armenian writers whose work would otherwise have been at risk of being lost to popular memory. Notably, in 1996 he and a colleague, Nevart Yaghlian, translated *Bloody News from My Friend*, by the great Armenian poet and intellectual Atom Yarjanian (1878–1915), known as Siamanto, who lost his life at the outset of the genocide in 1915. Most recently, he has translated, with Aris Sevag, a major memoir of the Armenian Genocide, *Armenian Golgotha* by Grigoris Balakian. A bishop in the Armenian Apostolic Church, Grigoris Balakian was Peter Balakian's great-uncle, and was one of the 250 Armenian intellectuals arrested and deported by the Turkish government on 24 April 1915. The book describes how he lived to tell of what he had witnessed, and rescuing the work has been an important achievement. Beyond this work, Balakian's essays on poetry, culture, art and social thought have appeared in a diverse range of publications. Some of these essays deal with **Primo Levi**, Arshile Gorky and Eghishe Charents, and with issues relating to imagination, trauma and genocide.

A much-decorated writer whose works have been translated into Armenian, Bulgarian, Dutch, German, Greek, Russian and Turkish, Peter Balakian has made a noteworthy contribution to the understanding of genocide and human-rights-related issues among a readership not usually thought of as one that might engage directly in such matters. As a thinker about genocide, he has brought historical memory and issues related to the transmission of trauma into literature, specifically poetry and memoir. Thus, like other writers who have inherited traumatic pasts, Balakian's work has shown the importance of literary imagination in the study of genocide and its aftermath. This has served to develop awareness in a wider audience than that of academic scholarship, and in so doing he has extended the broader compass within which serious reflection about genocide can take place.

Balakian's major writings

'Arshile Gorky and the Armenian Genocide', *Art In America* (February 1996).

(Trans. with Nevart Yaghlian) Siamanto, *Bloody News from My Friend*, Detroit: Wayne State University Press, 1996.

Black Dog of Fate: A Memoir, New York: Basic Books, 1997.

'A Memoir across Generations: Baby-Boom Suburbs, the Armenian Genocide, and Scholarly Corruption in America', *Chronicle of Higher Education*, 12 June 1998, B6–B7.

June-tree: New and Selected Poems 1974–2000, New York: HarperCollins, 2001.

The Burning Tigris: The Armenian Genocide and America's Response, New York: HarperCollins, 2003.

'From Ezra Pound to Theodore Roosevelt: American Intellectual and Cultural Responses to the Armenian Genocide', in Jay Winter (ed.), *America and the Armenian Genocide of 1915*, Cambridge: Cambridge University Press, 2003, 240–53.

(Ed.), *Ambassador Morgenthau's Story*, Detroit: Wayne State University Press, 2003.

'How a Poet Writes History without Going Mad', *Chronicle of Higher Education*, 7 May 2004, B10–B13.

'The Armenian Genocide and the Modern Age', *The Sydney Papers*, 20, 2 (Autumn 2008), 145–62.

'Falling Into a Rug, Some Notes on Imagination and the Artifact', in Matthew Leone (ed.), *Crafting Fiction, Poetry, and Memoir: Talks from the Colgate Writers Conference*, Hamilton (NY): Colgate University Press, 2008.

(Ed. and trans.) Grigoris Balakian, *Armenian Golgotha*, New York: Alfred A. Knopf, 2009.

References

Peterson, Merrill D., *'Starving Armenians:' America and the Armenian Genocide, 1915–1930 and After*, Charlottesville (VA): University of Virginia Press, 2004.

Power, Samantha, *'A Problem from Hell:' America and the Age of Genocide*, New York: Basic Books, 2002.

Winter, Jay (ed.), *America and the Armenian Genocide of 1915*, Cambridge: Cambridge University Press, 2003.

LAWRENCE BARON (b. 1947)

Lawrence Baron is a Professor of Modern Jewish History at San Diego State University, California. Born in 1947 in Chicago, Illinois, Baron earned a PhD in Modern European Intellectual History at the University of Wisconsin-Madison in 1974 under the direction of

Professor George L. Mosse. His dissertation was an intellectual and political biography of Erich Mühsam, a German-Jewish anarchist poet and revolutionary who had been an early critic of the inherent dangers in militarism, nationalism, organised religions, political parties and racism. Arrested the day after the Reichstag Fire (28 February 1933) and murdered in Oranienburg on the Night of the Long Knives (30 June 1934), Mühsam became one of the early Jewish victims of the Third Reich.

Baron's initial teaching position, obtained in 1975, was at St. Lawrence University, Canton, New York. St. Lawrence University, a small college located in a rural environment, at that time had few Jewish professors and only about 50 Jewish students, out of a total enrolment of 2,000. In his second year at SLU, Baron introduced courses on modern Jewish history and the Holocaust; in doing so, he may have been one of the first academics (together with **Harry James Cargas** and one or two others) to initiate teaching of the Holocaust to predominantly non-Jewish classes.

A prolific author, Baron's writing on the Holocaust began soon after he had established himself as a professor at St. Lawrence. Two early projects, in particular, had an impact on the broader field of Holocaust Studies while it was still in its infancy. The first was an oral history of the local response to the opening of a refugee shelter in Oswego, New York, for the only group of Displaced Persons to be offered collective sanctuary in the United States during the Second World War. The standard interpretation of this experience was that the local response mirrored the then national antipathy to Jewish immigration. Baron discovered a much more positive response from the townspeople of Oswego, which he garnered from interviews with them and those who had been interned at the camp. His findings were published in *New York History* in 1983; his writing won the annual Paul Kerr Prize for the best article appearing in the journal that year, and was the basis of a radio documentary (scripted and co-produced by Baron himself) in 1987. This, in turn, won an Ohio State Award for Educational Broadcasting in 1988.

The second of Baron's early projects to attract attention concerned those who saved Jews during the Holocaust, the Righteous Gentiles. His interest lay in what motivated these rescuers. After extensive research, he established a connection with Samuel Oliner, a psychologist then in the throes of assembling an interdisciplinary team to conduct in-depth interviews with rescuers honoured by Yad Vashem, Jews who were rescued by them, and a control group of Gentiles identified by either of the former who did not aid Jews. As a result of this connection, Baron was invited to serve as the historian for Oliner's Altruistic Personality Project in 1983. An important element of this work saw an intensification of Baron's interest in rescuers of Jews during the Holocaust. St. Lawrence University was close to the United States' border with Canada, the country that had liberated most of the Netherlands and to which many Dutch immigrants had moved after the Second World War. As a result, Baron started interviewing Dutch rescuers residing in Canada (and, later, the Netherlands), and eventually encoded all the Altruistic Personality Project's interviews on Dutch rescuers in order to ascertain how being raised in a certain national culture or subculture differentiated these rescuers from those in other countries. His initial conclusions saw the appearance of perhaps the first ever article dealing with how to teach this material, and this was further developed in his chapter on 'The National Context of Rescue' in *The Altruistic Personality: Rescuers of Jews in Nazi Europe*, the publication that emerged from the project. Here, Baron tested the validity of the factors enumerated by **Helen Fein** that decreased or increased the victimisation and survival rates of Jews on a country-by-country basis, considering the motivations and organisational effectiveness of rescue operations in France, Germany, Holland, Italy and Poland. Another contribution to the issue of the 'national' dimension of Dutch rescue appeared in a second volume on altruism, which Baron co-edited with Samuel and Pearl Oliner in 1992 (Baron, 1992: 306–27).

While working on this project Baron inevitably encountered the experience of Dutch Christian Corrie ten Boom, among Gentiles possibly the best-known Christian rescuer of Jews, even though she has been somewhat overlooked within mainstream Holocaust Studies. For Baron, the rescue of Jews by Christian evangelical fundamentalists flew in the face of an earlier scholarly consensus, articulated by such scholars as **Harry James Cargas** and **Franklin H. Littell**, which held that literal readings of the Gospels and proselytising of Jews only led to the vilification of Judaism and their theologically justified genocide. Baron began speaking and writing about Corrie ten Boom, which – owing to her popularity among Christian church groups – saw him begin the work that would come to characterise his best-known contributions to Holocaust scholarship: the study of the meaning of the Holocaust in American popular culture.

Another catalyst for Baron's research on the promotion of Holocaust consciousness was the appearance in 1999 of a highly influential book by historian Peter Novick, *The Holocaust in American Life*. Novick had argued that the Holocaust had been little talked about in the United States in the decades immediately following the end of the Second World War, but Baron maintained that as a child he knew that Hitler had killed Jews in concentration camps and that many of them were gassed and cremated. He considered that his early memories were accurate, and that their veracity had not been constructed retrospectively. While certainly not describing the Holocaust at that time in the same terms he had used as a professional historian since the 1970s, nonetheless he was incensed that Novick could suggest that the Holocaust was neither discussed nor thought about until much later. This prompted two articles that extended the discussion, in the journal *Holocaust and Genocide Studies* in 2003 and 2004, the latter a highly detailed exchange with Novick himself. Baron challenged the standard dating of American Holocaust awareness, and argued that images and interpretations of the Nazi 'Final Solution' were in fact quite prevalent prior to the 1960s. He conceded, however, that they had been filtered through the prevailing intellectual and political paradigms of the Cold War era. One key area of disagreement with Novick was the impact on Americans of both the Nuremberg Trials and atrocity footage from the Holocaust, which, Baron contended, persisted throughout the period.

Baron first began teaching history students about the impact of motion pictures in 1989. As a child, his first source of Holocaust awareness had been film. He had always recalled seeing *The Diary of Anne Frank* (dir. George Stevens, 1959) and watching television footage with his father in the 1950s of the liberation of the Nazi concentration camps. After the release of *Schindler's List* (dir. Steven Spielberg, 1994) he developed an interdisciplinary course on Holocaust cinema with a colleague from the German Department at SDSU. The impact of Spielberg's movie, and its predecessors like the television miniseries *Holocaust* (dir. Marvin J. Chomsky, 1978), convinced him that movies and television probably did more to raise awareness of the Holocaust than college or high-school courses. He realised that such informal Holocaust education was becoming the norm rather than the exception, and that this was leading to an expansion of Holocaust consciousness in American public education. For Baron, it was evident that Holocaust education and perception had been a much greater success than many would otherwise have contended.

Baron's most influential book, *Projecting the Holocaust into the Present* (2005), was prompted by his observation in the first years of the new century that there had not been a major survey on the topic published since the 1980s, when Annette Insdorf and Judith Doneson had published major studies. (His work appeared at the same time as an edited volume by two British scholars, Toby Haggith and Joanna Newman, though each project was undertaken independently of the other.) He was also keenly aware of the oft-quoted argument that the Holocaust was a phenomenon that could not satisfactorily be represented (and, for some, perhaps should not be attempted in any case). As Baron saw it, such arguments seemed out of touch with audience reactions to film in general and Holocaust movies in particular. A series of films released in the 1990s, such as *Korczak* (dir. Andrzej Wajda, 1990), *Europa, Europa* (dir. Agnieszka Holland, 1991), *Schindler's List* and *Life is Beautiful* (dir. Roberto Benigni, 1998), showed Baron that there was a very large segment of society that was receptive to such movies; they touch audiences, he maintained, because they personalise and visualise an event that is difficult to comprehend solely on intellectual or statistical grounds.

Projecting the Holocaust into the Present constituted an appreciation of the power of dialogue, images, narrative and sound to evoke what it was like to have 'been there', to have experienced the events being depicted. Like any narrative form, this entails a willing suspension of disbelief, namely, the realisation that this is not *exactly* what happened, but an approximation that can be assimilated by the viewer and then serve as a spur to learn more about the topic from other kinds of sources. It is necessary to understand that the current period is a post-literate age where the mass media can either be viewed as the enemy – to be dismissed for trivialising the Holocaust – or seen as an ally in generating an emotional attachment and intellectual engagement with a complex but enormously important cataclysm in recent history. Baron's work on Holocaust cinema has opened up the study of children's films on the topic, and of how common Hollywood genres can be recycled and remixed to accommodate Holocaust storylines. He has also explored how changes in media formats, such as television docudramas, and new distribution systems like cable television, videotapes, DVDs and the internet, have altered what types of Holocaust stories get produced and how they are publicised and integrated into the education system. His overriding interest is in assessing the generational changes relating to how the Holocaust is depicted, and how national themes persist through (or are diminished by) the process of globalisation.

As if to underscore Baron's influence as a cutting-edge thinker in this area, in 2006 – the year after the appearance of *Projecting the Holocaust* – he gave the keynote address at Yad Vashem's first sym-posium on Hollywood and the Holocaust. Then, in a short (though important) study of the relationship of film to the study of history, historian Robert Rosenstone went so far as to cite *Projecting the Holocaust* as the basis for his choice of films to discuss in his chapter on Holocaust cinema (Rosenstone, 2006).

Baron's work continues to proceed apace, as the importance of visual literacy becomes more and more pressing and survivor scarcity is starting to have an impact on people's perceptions of what the Holocaust looked like. As of this writing, he is currently working on a new project entitled *The Wandering View: Modern Jewish History in World Cinema.* Although its scope is broader than the Holocaust, he considers the differences to be found in how the Holocaust has been portrayed in a variety of countries, including those whose connection to it would otherwise seem to be remote. He is also continuing his early work on altruism during the Holocaust, this time through an examination of the portrayal of Gentile (or white) rescuers in Holocaust and African-American movies. Further, he has most recently examined the similarities and differences between respective feature films on the Armenian Genocide and the Holocaust.

In a number of ways, for nearly four decades Lawrence Baron has shown himself to be a leading thinker on the Holocaust – first through biography, then through explorations of altruism and rescue, and, most importantly, through his analysis of the role and impact of film and popular culture on memory and education. Simultaneously pioneer and practitioner, Baron's influence on the development of thought and awareness about the Holocaust has been extensive. As a senior member on a number of advisory boards and committees relating to Jewish Studies and the Holocaust, as well as an active participant at scholarly conferences around the world, his influence continues.

Baron's major writings

The Eclectic Anarchism of Erich Mühsam, New York: Revisionist Press, 1976.
'Teaching the Holocaust to Non-Jews', *Shoah*, 2, 2 (Spring 1981), 14–15.
'Haven from the Holocaust: Oswego, New York, 1944–46', *New York History,* 64, 1 (January 1983), 5–34.
'Teaching about the Rescuers of Jews', in Zev Garber (ed.), *Methodology in the Academic Teaching of the Holocaust,* Lanham (MD): University Press of America, 1988, 143–54.
The Altruistic Personality: Rescuers of Jews in Nazi Europe, New York: Free Press, 1988. The primary authors of this volume were Samuel and Pearl Oliner; Baron served as the project's historian, and wrote the chapter 'The Historical Context of Rescue', 13–48.

'The Dutchness of Dutch Rescuers: The National Dimension of Altruism', in Pearl Oliner et al. (eds), *Embracing the Other*, New York: New York University Press, 1992, 306–27.

'Supersessionism without Contempt: The Holocaust Evangelism of Corrie ten Boom', in Donald Dietrich (ed.), *Christian Responses to the Holocaust*, Syracuse (NY): Syracuse University Press, 2003.

'The Holocaust and American Public Memory, 1945–60', *Holocaust and Genocide Studies*, 17, 1 (Spring 2003), 62–88.

Projecting the Holocaust into the Present: The Changing Focus of Contemporary Holocaust Cinema, Lanham (MD): Rowman and Littlefield, 2005.

'What Americans Read When They Read about the Holocaust', in Steven Leonard Jacobs (ed.), *Maven in Blue Jeans: A Festschrift in Honor of Zev Garber*, West Lafayette (IN): Purdue University Press, 2009, 245–54.

'From DPs to Olim: Depicting Jewish Refugees in American Feature Films, 1945–49', in Johannes-Dieter Steinert and Inge Newirth-Weber (eds), *Beyond Camps and Forced Labour: Current International Research on Survivors of Nazi Persecution*, vol. II, Osnabrück (Germany): Secolo, 2009, 749–58.

References

Doneson, Judith E., *The Holocaust in American Film*, Philadelphia: Jewish Publication Society, 1987.

Haggith, Toby and Joanna Newman (eds), *Holocaust and the Moving Image: Representations in Film and Television Since 1933*, London: Wallflower Press, 2005.

Insdorf, Annette, *Indelible Shadows: Film and the Holocaust*, New York: Random House, 1983.

Novick, Peter, *The Holocaust in American Life*, Boston: Houghton Mifflin, 1999.

Novick, Peter and Lawrence Baron, letters to the editor, *Holocaust and Genocide Studies*, 18, 2 (Fall 2004), 358–75.

Rosenstone, Robert, *History on Film/Film on History*, New York: Longman, 2006.

ten Boom, Corrie, *The Hiding Place*, Grand Rapids (MI): Chosen Books, 1971.

OMER BARTOV (b. 1954)

Omer Bartov is the John P. Birkelund Distinguished Professor of European History and German Studies at Brown University, Providence, Rhode Island. A prolific author, he is one of the world's leading authorities on the subject of the Holocaust and the Nazi state, and of the impulses behind genocidal behaviour. Born in Hedera, Israel in 1954, he was educated at Tel Aviv University and St. Antony's College, Oxford. As a youth in Israel he grew up among Holocaust survivors, and in a militarised society where he served as a soldier for four years (including combat service in the aftermath of the Yom Kippur War of 1973), he developed an interest in the scholarly study of war and genocide. Bartov's teaching career began at Tel Aviv University, where he was a member of the History Department between 1983 and 1992. He joined Rutgers University in 1992 as the Raoul Wallenberg Professor in Human Rights and Senior Fellow at the Rutgers Center for Historical Analysis, and was a Professor in the History Department at Rutgers between 1993 and 2000. He joined Brown University in 2000.

From the beginning, Bartov's academic writing was directed towards the study of genocidal behaviour in wartime. His initial research was on the Nazi indoctrination of German soldiers in the *Wehrmacht* under the Third Reich during the war against the Soviet Union, and the crimes committed by the regular soldiery of the Nazi state. These themes formed the main thrust of his first two books, *The Eastern Front, 1941–1945: German Troops and the Barbarization of Warfare* (1985) and *Hitler's Army: Soldiers, Nazis, and War in the Third Reich* (1991).

In *The Eastern Front*, Bartov examined the German army in the war against the Soviet Union. He described the nature of warfare as seen by the German soldier, and analysed the social, educational and political backgrounds of the junior officer echelon. He argued that it was only by considering such personal factors, along with the impacts of Nazi propaganda and indoctrination, that the criminal activities of the German army in Russia could be explained. His analysis pointed towards an interpretation of the extent of army involvement in Nazi ideological crimes, which was previously commonly ascribed only to the SS.

Bartov's second book, *Hitler's Army*, developed these ideas further, challenging the notion that the German army was apolitical. He considered in depth the degree to which the army was riven with Nazi ideology, again through a focus on the Eastern front. Here, however, he went deeper, showing that propaganda and indoctrination motivated the troops not only to fight well, but also to commit crimes against humanity and genocide. Explaining the motivation through an exploration of two interrelated elements – an extreme demonisation of the Soviet enemy and an uncompromising reverence for Adolf Hitler – Bartov showed that most German troops saw the war from a thoroughly ideological perspective, believing it to be part of a struggle for the future of Western civilisation. The book saw considerable success, with translations subsequently appearing in Czech, Polish, French, Hebrew, Italian, German, Spanish and Portuguese.

Given these early works, it seemed a natural progression for Bartov to move towards studying the links between the impact of the First World War on mass consciousness (particularly views regarding death) and the genocidal policies of the Second. Thus, in *Murder in Our Midst: The Holocaust, Industrial Killing, and Representation* (1996), he charted a direct causal link between the emergence of industrialised killing in the trenches during the Great War and the shift in people's awareness of mass killing that took place because of it. And not only that; he traced this trend to the very nature of modernity, as he spelled out in the book's Introduction:

> War, slaughter, and genocide, are of course as old as human civilization itself. Industrial killing, however, is a much newer phenomenon, not only in that its main precondition was the industrialization of human society, but also in the sense that this process of industrialization came to be associated with progress and improvement, hope and optimism, liberty and democracy, science and the rule of law. Industrial killing was not the dark side of modernity, some aberration of a generally salutary process; rather, it was and is inherent to it, a perpetual potential of precisely the same energies and ideas, technologies and ideologies that have brought about the 'great transformation' of humanity.
>
> (Bartov, 1996: 4)

But, he added, 'precisely because modernity means to many of us progress and improvement, we cannot easily come to terms with the idea that it also means mass annihilation'. While this idea has since been taken up by a number of other authors such as Paul R. Bartrop and Alan Kramer, it was Bartov, in this book, who spelled it out for the first time for a general audience (in particular in his Chapter 2, 'The European Imagination in the Age of Total War') as he sought to explore the complex relationship between violence, representation and identity in the twentieth century. *Murder in Our Midst* won Bartov increased recognition through the award of the Fraenkel Prize in Contemporary History from the Institute for Contemporary History and Wiener Library, London. It was in this work that he also introduced what would become another of his interests, in the form of a discussion of the role of cinema in the portrayal of mass death and genocide.

By now, Bartov's reputation as a first-rank historian of Nazi Germany and the Holocaust had for long been established, and his contribution to the development of an understanding of how the

Nazi perpetrators of the Holocaust were able to carry out their crimes frequently saw his name alongside those of such other historians as **Christopher Browning**. Bartov's next book, *Mirrors of Destruction: War, Genocide, and Modern Identity* (2000), went one step further. Here, he examined the relationship between total war, state-organised genocide and the emergence of modern identity – as he summarised it, 'a study in perceptions'. On this occasion, however, his focus was not so much on how perpetrators of genocide have been able to rationalise or justify their activities, as on how perspectives of violence 'have molded European views and redefined individual and collective identities in a process of emulation, mutual reflection, and distortion'. (Bartov, 2000: 1) It was an ambitious book, offering a highly sophisticated analysis of complex interrelationships in German, French and Jewish literature and memory. As such, it dealt almost exclusively with the Holocaust; by extension, however, Bartov could have projected his ideas onto other genocidal experiences should he have chosen to do so. Ultimately, this work extended discussion of the intellectual disposition of modern societies towards genocide, through a consideration of visions of identity and national utopias. Inevitably, such visions are expressed through the histories that are written to explain how each of the nations has understood its past (and thus, how it arrived at its present), so this book also required Bartov to investigate and interpret a number of historiographical traditions, a theme he was to return to in his next major work, *Germany's War and the Holocaust: Disputed Histories* (2003).

Here, he discussed the ways in which the Nazi years could be interpreted through an examination of the histories that have been written trying to understand the impulses and behaviours that characterised life under the Hitler regime. Bartov was inspired to investigate this topic in part by the appearance of two books in the 1990s: Daniel Jonah Goldhagen's *Hitler's Willing Executioners* in 1996 and the contemporary Third Reich diaries of German-Jewish classics professor Victor Klemperer. Bartov's study was again a measured treatment of the interconnections between the Nazis' destructive war, the genocide of the Jews and the subsequent reconstruction of German and Jewish identities in its aftermath. On this occasion, however, he considered his topic from within the labyrinth of historiography that had emerged in recent years, and through careful management of his material he was able to show the degree to which much of the literature proceeded from the wrong premise, was skewed or was otherwise flawed. We see here a Bartov who was pointing to the need for scholars to be more clear-headed when approaching the topics of Nazi Germany and the Holocaust, to ask the right questions, and to seek answers based on objective scholarship rather than preformed selectivity of evidence.

As if to show that this issue of historical representation was not only to be found in the frequently dry world of academia, Bartov moved beyond historiography in his next work, and turned his attention to the ways in which the Holocaust and Jewish identity were portrayed in European, American and Israeli movies. In *The 'Jew' in Cinema: From The Golem to Don't Touch My Holocaust* (2005), Bartov examined the recycling of anti-Semitic stereotypes in film, demonstrating the powerful political, social and cultural impact of these images on popular attitudes throughout the world. Addressing a range of movies, he argued that the representations they make of Jews generally fall into four categories, namely, 'the Jew' as perpetrator, victim, hero and anti-hero. Contextualising his topic with a range of examples taken from film's early days to the present, Bartov considered a number of ways in which fundamental prejudices about Jews have remained deeply embedded in the creative imagination, concluding that some of these attitudes persisted in cinematic depictions throughout the twentieth century.

While engaged on all these projects, Bartov also led a multi-year collaborative project at the Watson Institute for International Studies at Brown University, entitled 'Borderlands: Ethnicity, Identity, and Violence in the Shatter-Zone of Empires since 1848'. This project considered the nature of interethnic relations in the borderlands of Eastern Europe, and was instrumental in changing the direction of Bartov's research. From looking at the broad contours of Nazi policies and their impact, he now considered how genocide actually unfolded on the ground, and how the politics of memory – and erasure of that memory in the minds of the people and through the destruction of the material remains of Jewish culture in the affected areas – was resulting in a permanent loss of historical awareness in local communities. The result was *Erased: Vanishing Traces of Jewish Galicia in Present-Day Ukraine* (2007). Focusing his research on towns and cities in Western Ukraine, Bartov journeyed throughout the region, rescuing the past where he could and identifying the areas in which the Holocaust took place 'on the ground' – and what became of the memory of the experience once the war was over. In this regard his work complemented that of Fr. Patrick Desbois, who at the same time was making a similar journey – not to investigate lost communities, but to describe how the killing itself took place during the Nazi years (Dubois, 2008).

Bartov saw a great need for this to be done, as the Holocaust was not a phenomenon that simply came upon the Jews like an alien force and had no impact on anyone else, but was an event that involved all sectors of society while it was taking place. As he wrote concerning his own voyage to the subject:

> I had to learn – often after already visiting them – the history of individual towns and communities, their moments of glory and demise, their accomplishments and their degradation. I had to imagine how – in these pretty little towns, the vast forests, the rolling hills – people who had lived side by side for generations were transformed into killers and quarry, how a few altruistic souls were drowned in an ocean of hate, greed, and incitement.
>
> (Bartov, 2007: xvi)

Moreover, based on such a private view, Bartov realised that he had to

> rethink the very concept of what we have come to call the Holocaust, or genocide. Because in these little towns, in that corner of the world, this was no distant, neatly organized, bloodless bureaucratic undertaking, but a vast wave of brutal, intimate, and endlessly bloody massacres. Far from meaningless violence, these were often quite meaningful actions, from which many profited politically and economically.
>
> (Bartov, 2007: xvii)

As a result, Bartov produced a work that was at once poignant and informative. Considering the interethnic relationship between the various groups living in these communities before, during and after the war, he was able to demonstrate just how intimate the process of genocidal killing can be, and in so doing he brought to light a number of elements of the Jewish tragedy that might otherwise have been lost.

The experience of writing about lost communities led Bartov to his most recent project, in which he seeks to trace the origins of local mass murder in the complexities of relations between different ethnic and religious groups over a long time span within a single community, the Eastern Galician town of Buczacz. Already this research has seen the appearance of conference presentations and short written pieces, as well as a chapter in *Erased*. With this project, he investigates the dynamic that creates, or prevents, the transformation of a community based on interaction and cooperation into a community of genocide. Composed of a mixed Jewish-Polish-Ukrainian population for centuries, Buczacz saw the eradication of its Jewish inhabitants by Nazi murder squads assisted by local collaborators during the Second World War, and the ethnic cleansing of its Polish population by Ukrainian nationalists. While the main outlines of the Holocaust in East Galicia have recently been reconstructed, Bartov contends that little is known about the nature of the social fabric upon which Nazi policies were enacted, and to which the communities reacted. Bartov's research will help to give a more complete appreciation of this past, through an investigation that will consider the perspective of all groups involved in the event.

In general, Omer Bartov's contribution to the field of historical inquiry of the Holocaust and genocide has been considerable. His work has been pathbreaking in many respects: he has examined, in a manner rarely seen before, the multivariate relationships between war and the Holocaust; the motivation of soldiers and the involvement of the German army in the perpetration of war crimes and genocide; the role of ideology and stereotypes in both warfare and historiography; the links between the age of total war and genocide; the importance of testimonies and local studies in writing the history of the Holocaust and the development of a historical understanding of genocide; and, most recently, the crucial place of Eastern Europe in understanding the Holocaust. As a leading thinker and scholar of the Holocaust and genocide, Omer Bartov is – and will remain – one of the leading academic voices of the late twentieth and early twenty-first centuries.

Bartov's major writings

The Eastern Front 1941–45: German Troops and the Barbarisation of Warfare, Basingstoke, Hampshire (UK): Macmillan/St. Antony's College, Oxford, 1985.

Hitler's Army: Soldiers, Nazis, and War in the Third Reich, New York: Oxford University Press, 1991.

'German Soldiers and the Holocaust: Historiography, Research, and Implications', in Passing into History: Nazism and the Holocaust beyond Memory, in Honor of Saul Friedländer on his Sixty-Fifth Birthday, special issue of History & Memory, 9, 1–2 (Fall 1997), 162–88.

'Antisemitism, the Holocaust, and Reinterpretations of National Socialism', in Michael Berenbaum and Abraham J. Peck (eds), The Holocaust and History: The Known, the Unknown, the Disputed, and the Reexamined, Bloomington (IN): Indiana University Press, 1998, 75–98.

Murder in Our Midst: The Holocaust, Industrial Killing, and Representation, New York: Oxford University Press, 1996.

Mirrors of Destruction: War, Genocide, and Modern Identity, New York: Oxford University Press, 2000.

(Ed.) *The Holocaust: Origins, Implementation, Aftermath,* London: Routledge, 2000.

(Ed. with Phyllis Mack) *In God's Name: Genocide and Religion in the Twentieth Century,* New York: Berghahn Books, 2001.

(Ed. with Atina Grossmann and Mary Nolan) *Crimes of War: Guilt and Denial in the Twentieth Century,* New York: The New Press, 2002.

Germany's War and the Holocaust: Disputed Histories, Ithaca (NY): Cornell University Press, 2003.

'Seeking the Roots of Modern Genocide: On the Macro- and Microhistory of Mass Murder', in Robert Gellately and Ben Kiernan (eds), *The Specter of Genocide: Mass Murder in Historical Perspective,* Cambridge: Cambridge University Press, 2003, pp. 75–96.

The 'Jew' in Cinema: from The Golem to Don't Touch My Holocaust, Bloomington (IN): Indiana University Press, 2005.

Erased: Vanishing Traces of Jewish Galicia in Present-Day Ukraine, Princeton (NJ): Princeton University Press, 2007.

'Interethnic Relations in the Holocaust as Seen Through Postwar Testimonies: Buczacz, East Galicia, 1941–44', in Doris L. Bergen (ed.), *Lessons and Legacies,* vol. VII, *From Generation to Generation,* Evanston (IL): Northwestern University Press, 2008, 101–24.

'White Spaces and Black Holes: Eastern Galicia's Past and Present', in Ray Brandon and Wendy Lower (eds), *The Shoah in Ukraine: History, Testimony, Memorialization,* Bloomington (IN): Indiana University Press, 2008, 318–53.

'Eastern Europe as the Site of Genocide', *Journal of Modern History,* 80, 3 (September 2008), 557–93.

References

Bartrop, Paul R., 'The Relationship between War and Genocide in the Twentieth Century: A Consideration', *Journal of Genocide Research,* 4, 4 (December 2002), 519–32.

Dubois, Fr. Patrick, *The Holocaust by Bullets: A Priest's Journey to Uncover the Truth behind the Murder of 1.5 Million Jews,* New York: Palgrave Macmillan, 2008.

Goldhagen, Daniel Jonah, *Hitler's Willing Executioners: Ordinary Germans and the Holocaust,* New York: Random House, 1996.

Klemperer, Victor, *I Will Bear Witness: A Diary of the Nazi Years, 1933–1941,* New York: Random House, 1998.

Klemperer, Victor, *I Will Bear Witness: A Diary of the Nazi Years, 1942–1945,* New York: Random House, 1999.

Kramer, Alan, *Dynamic of Destruction: Culture and Mass Killing in the First World War,* Oxford: Oxford University Press, 2007.

YEHUDA BAUER (b. 1926)

Yehuda Bauer is one of the world's foremost scholars of the Holocaust. Currently Professor Emeritus at the Hebrew University of Jerusalem, he was formerly the Director of the Institute of Contemporary Jewry and Professor of Holocaust Studies, and Director of the International Centre for Holocaust Studies at Yad Vashem, Israel's Holocaust Martyrs' and Heroes' Remembrance Authority. An Israeli born in Prague, Czechoslovakia in 1926, he came from a family with a committed Zionist background. During the 1930s his father sought to enter Palestine, then under the British Mandate. He was successful in obtaining entry permits in 1939, and the family arrived on 15 March 1939 – the same day the Nazis invaded Czechoslovakia.

As a young man, Bauer became a member of the Palmach, the front-line troops of the Haganah (the unofficial Jewish army fighting for independence during the Mandate). During this time he also began his studies at Cardiff University, Wales, though as a Palmachnik (Palmach soldier) he returned to Palestine in 1948 in order to fight during Israel's War of Independence. After the war he continued his studies, graduating in History.

Upon his return to Israel, he commenced advanced work at the Hebrew University of Jerusalem, and received his doctorate in 1960 (while living and working at Kibbutz Shoval, in the Negev). In 1961, Bauer commenced his academic teaching life with a position at the Institute for Contemporary Jewry at the Hebrew University, and became one of the early scholars of the new field of what became known as Holocaust Studies. He served as Chairman of the Department of Holocaust Studies at Hebrew University, and quickly became a leading voice on the Holocaust, anti-Semitism and the Jewish resistance movement during the Holocaust years. Throughout his career he has served as visiting professor in a number of settings in the United States and Europe, as well as travelling extensively throughout the world as an eminent scholar. Among his many academic activities, he has acted as the historical advisor to the film *Shoah* (dir. Claude Lanzmann, 1985); served on the editorial board of Yad Vashem's *Encyclopaedia of the Holocaust* (1990); served as an academic advisor to the International Task Force for Holocaust Education, Remembrance, and Research; acted as a senior advisor to the Swedish government's International Forum on Genocide Prevention; and is a founding member of an informal Academic Advisory Group on Genocide Prevention conducted by a number of scholars from around the world.

As a historian of the Holocaust, Bauer has broken new ground in numerous areas, as well as having challenged those with whose approach he has disagreed. Three key areas (among many) may be considered here: Jewish resistance during the Holocaust; the issue of Jewish collaboration *via* the *Judenräte* (Jewish councils set up by the Nazis); and the so-called Intentionalist/Functionalist debate over how the Holocaust unfolded.

In the first of these, Bauer has offered a major reconsideration of the dynamics of Jewish ghetto and partisan resistance against the Nazis, holding that resistance – he uses the Hebrew term *Amidah* – encompassed not only physical opposition, but any activity that reinforced dignity and humanity. As he stated in his 2001 volume *Rethinking the Holocaust*, a compendium and enhancement of many of his thoughts on the Holocaust and genocide, *Amidah* embraces

> both armed and unarmed actions and excludes passive resistance, although that term is almost a *non sequitur*, because one cannot really resist passively. When one refuses to budge in the face of brutal force, one does not resist passively; one resists without using force, and that is not the same thing.
>
> (Bauer, 2001: 120)

Bauer's interest here focuses on the oft-mentioned issue of perceived Jewish passivity in the face of the Nazi assault, in which the Jews have sometimes been referred to as having gone to their deaths as 'sheep to the slaughter'. For Bauer, the question of active resistance requires further research, but, on balance, he has disputed the popular view that most Jews went to their deaths passively. Given the options available to Jews in Nazi-occupied Europe, together with the conditions under which they had to try to survive, he considers that what is surprising is not the dearth of resistance, but, on the contrary, how extensive it actually was.

Where unarmed resistance is concerned, the act of clinging to the trappings of a 'normal' – even a 'civilised' – life represented a determination that the Nazis would not be successful in their aim to debase Jewish society and thereby gain a moral, as well as a physical, victory over the Jews. Leading a 'normal' life in the ghettos through the creation of libraries, conducting weddings, organising schools, and the like, was often the only resistance option open to the Jews.

In Bauer's work regarding the *Judenräte*, the Nazi-instituted Jewish councils set up in the ghettos with the intention of administering local Jewish communities on behalf of the Nazis, a number of difficult questions are asked. Two positions present themselves within the literature: first, that many of those who served in the *Judenräte* found themselves having to serve their Nazi masters and at the same time trying to act as a buffer between their overlords and their fellow Jews; or, second, that they were complicit in their own demise, and in the demise of the community which they had a responsibility to safeguard. Bauer asks whether or not the actions of those in charge of the *Judenräte* could have led to the survival of more Jews, and, while recognising the appalling dilemma faced by these leaders, concludes that what matters more than casting blame – for no-one could have prevented the Nazis from carrying out their murderous plans – was the effort that was put into trying to keep at least some Jews alive despite those plans. No-one knows whether more Jews would have survived without Jewish participation in the *Judenräte*, but Bauer holds that with more research on the question of complicity or collaboration in the ghettos a conclusion based on the balance of probabilities might be reached at some time in the future – based on the vital premise that only the Nazis could have stopped the Holocaust, and that only they could have prevented the deaths of most of the victims.

Finally, in the current analysis – and it must be pointed out that the vast corpus of Bauer's output over several decades has led him into many other fields within the scholarly study of the Holocaust – consideration can be given to his views on the so-called Intentionalist/Functionalist debate of the 1980s (see the Introduction to this volume). Critical to the views of the Intentionalists are Hitler's many public speeches vilifying the Jews and promising them harm, as well as his own writing in his book *Mein Kampf.* The most famous of these expressions was his speech of 30 January 1939 to the German *Reichstag*, where he freely affirmed that if 'international Jewry' would be the cause of another world war 'then the result would not be the Bolshevisation of the earth and with it the victory of Jewry, it will be the annihilation of the Jewish race in Europe'. Intentionalists also argue that with the invasion of the Soviet Union in June 1941, and the Wannsee Conference of January 1942, Hitler was able finally to carry out his long-sought programme. For those calling themselves Functionalists, the Holocaust was *not* the result of a planned, carefully organised and orchestrated agenda springing from Adolf Hitler's overwhelming anti-Semitism, but, rather, an evolving and sometimes even chaotic programme of death and destruction which really began to assert itself after the invasion of Soviet Russia in June 1941, prior to which it was done by low-level bureaucrats in a somewhat haphazard and inefficient manner. Functionalists view the Nazi hierarchy as one of competing vested interests and power centres, with Hitler not in control.

Bauer holds that Hitler was the key figure in causing the Holocaust, and that at some point in the latter half of 1941 he gave a series of orders for the genocide of the entire Jewish people. He does not concede, however, that this was a long-held goal of the Nazis or the *Führer* himself. As he sees it, the perspectives of both the Intentionalists and the Functionalists are unsatisfactory. He is more comfortable with a synthesis of the two schools: it is true, he argues, that 'structures do not explain why bureaucrats sent people to their deaths' (Bauer, 2001: 30), but it is just as true that 'the intentionalist school … has a hard time proving Hitler's intentions toward the Jews in the 1920s and early 1930s, because he never really said what he would do with the Jews, except for uttering endless streams of gutter invectives'. Certainly, Bauer does not consider that there was a master plan for genocide going back as far as the time when Hitler wrote *Mein Kampf.* By the same token, he finds it difficult to concede that the decisions for the Holocaust were taken on the initiative of less senior members of Hitler's government, as though the *Führer* or his inner circle were unaware of it.

A further issue into which Bauer has brought an authoritative voice concerns the passionate debate in the literature that ensued after the publication of *Hitler's Willing Executioners*, a 1996 book by Harvard University political scientist Daniel Goldhagen. Goldhagen's argument was that ordinary Germans permitted themselves to be transformed by the Nazis into genocidal killers of Jews because of cultural characteristics within German society that allowed for a specific type of what he termed 'eliminationist antisemitism'. The furore that erupted in light of this assertion was nothing short of massive. The most frequent criticism levelled at Goldhagen was that he was labelling German society in the 1930s and 1940s with the taint of an innate anti-Semitism, which, for many, shifted responsibility away from the Nazis in order to condemn all Germans for the Holocaust (see Littell, 1997; Shandley, 1998).

Bauer appreciates Goldhagen's attempt to provide an answer to the question of why the Holocaust happened (something he considers many scholars have been either unable or unwilling to do), and acknowledges that in attempting this Goldhagen has placed anti-Semitism centre stage in his analysis. Bauer deems the thesis to be simplistic, however, as 'Goldhagen ignores the social and economic traumas that afflicted German society in the wake of World War I' (Bauer, 2001: 96). He is thus critical of Goldhagen for only selecting evidence favourable to his thesis, and for tailoring his arguments to fit a preconceived position. Just one example of this will suffice as an illustration:

> in the 1930s some 50,000 Jews were living in mixed German-Jewish marriages, so at least 50,000 Germans, and presumably parts of their families, had familial contact with Jews. ... In a society where eliminationist norms were universal and in which Jews were rejected even after they had converted [to Christianity], or so he [Goldhagen] argues, the rise of this extreme form of assimilation of Jews would not have been possible.
>
> (Bauer, 2001: 99)

Thus, although there are certain attractions for Bauer in the fact that Goldhagen has attempted a causal analysis of why the Holocaust happened, he is far from convinced that Goldhagen is saying anything that is new or unchallengeable.

One of the areas in which scholars have sometimes been critical of Bauer has been his perspective on the so-called uniqueness of the Holocaust, a point of critique in which many have missed the core of his argument. Bauer does not refer to the Holocaust as 'unique'; indeed, he rejects that word, preferring to use the more defensible term 'unprecedented'. As he sees it, the Holocaust was an extreme example of genocide: it was unique in the same way that all historical events are unique unto themselves, though even when comparing it to other events it had specific characteristics that had never happened before. These were, in summary form:

1. the ideological motivation of the killings, unlike other genocides in which ulterior motives based on physical acquisition (of land or loot) can be traced;
2. the totality of the Nazis' aims, according to which *every* Jew in the world, without exception, was the intended target;
3. the breadth of the Nazis' scope, which transcended borders and spread across all lands occupied and yet-to-be occupied by the Nazis and their allies and/or supporters; and
4. the nature of the Nazi concentration camp system, in which mass imprisonment, ritualised degradation, and, ultimately, purpose-built factories for the killing of huge numbers of people were developed for the first time in human history.

In Bauer's view, none of these four features had ever before been a characteristic of what could be considered genocide. Because of this, he argues, the Holocaust's 'unprecedentedness' renders it of universal importance, as he told a special session of the German Bundestag in a speech in 1998:

> The Holocaust has assumed the role of universal symbol for all evil because it presents the most extreme form of genocide, because it contains elements that are without precedent, because that tragedy was a Jewish one and because the Jews – although they are neither better nor worse than others and although their sufferings were neither greater nor lesser than those of others – represent one of the sources of modern civilization.
>
> (Bauer, 2001: 270)

Bauer's overall analysis thus holds the Holocaust to be the most extreme form of genocide, on a continuum that ends with the *Shoah* as its ultimate point. It is the definitive yardstick against which all anti-human activities should be measured, and as a result of it having taken place society can never again be the same as it was.

As one of the most prominent scholars of the Holocaust, Yehuda Bauer has enlightened, provoked and expanded the boundaries within which discussion can take place. The thinking which motivates much of his analytical approach rests on a quest for understanding, and in this he has proven himself to be both a first-rate historian and an inspirational educator.

Bauer's major writings

Flight and Rescue: Brichah, New York: Random House, 1970.

They Chose Life: Jewish Resistance in the Holocaust, New York: American Jewish Committee, 1973.

My Brother's Keeper: A History of the American Jewish Joint Distribution Committee, Philadelphia: The Jewish Publication Society of America, 1974.

The Holocaust in Historical Perspective, Seattle: University of Washington Press, 1978.

The Jewish Emergence from Powerlessness, Toronto: University of Toronto Press, 1979.

American Jewry and the Holocaust: The American Jewish Joint Distribution Committee, Detroit: Wayne State University Press, 1981.

(Ed. with Nathan Rotenstreich) *The Holocaust as Historical Experience: Essays and a Discussion*, New York: Holmes and Meier, 1981.

A History of the Holocaust, New York: Franklin Watts, 1982; revised edition, 2001.

Out of the Ashes: The Impact of American Jews on Post-Holocaust European Jewry, Oxford: Pergamon Press, 1989.

Jewish Reactions to the Holocaust, Tel Aviv: Ministry of Defence, 1989.
Jews for Sale? Nazi–Jewish Negotiations, New Haven: Yale University Press, 1994.
Rethinking the Holocaust, New Haven: Yale University Press, 2001.
The Death of the Shtetl, New Haven: Yale University Press, 2009.

References

Goldhagen, Daniel Jonah, *Hitler's Willing Executioners: Ordinary Germans and the Holocaust*, New York: Random House, 1996.
Littell, Franklin H. (ed.), *Hyping the Holocaust: Scholars Answer Goldhagen*, Merion Station (PA): Merion Westfield Press International, 1997.
Shandley, Robert R. (ed.), *Unwilling Germans? The Goldhagen Debate*, Minneapolis: University of Minnesota Press, 1998.

ZYGMUNT BAUMAN (b. 1925)

Zygmunt Bauman is an Emeritus Professor of Sociology at the University of Leeds, in the United Kingdom. He has been one of the most significant thinkers in his field across the past five decades, and one whose influence has extended far beyond sociology, not only in Europe but throughout the world. His focused attention on the ambiguities of modernity, and in particular his concerns regarding the Holocaust, rank him as one of a relatively small (though growing) group of important theoreticians to address the meaning of this event, along with its present and future implications. Bauman's book *Modernity and the Holocaust* (1989) was, and remains, one of the very few sociological texts to address the Holocaust. Indeed, the chapter titles themselves – 'Modernity, Racism, Extermination', 'The Uniqueness and Normality of the Holocaust', 'Soliciting the Co-operation of the Victims', 'The Ethics of Obedience (Reading Milgram)', 'Towards a Sociological Theory of Morality' and 'Rationality and Shame' – are themselves signposts indicative of his thinking and concerns, regarding not only the Holocaust as a group event, but the morality (or absence thereof) surrounding it.

Bauman was born in 1925 in Poznań, Poland, to secular Jewish parents. During the Second World War, he and his family fled the Nazis, escaping to the Soviet Union. He served in the Polish First Army (as a political education instructor under Soviet direction), and fought in the Battles of Kolberg and Berlin, for which he was awarded the Military Cross of Valour. In the post-war period (1945–53), he held a similar position in the Polish army as a political officer with the Corps for Domestic Security, rising to the rank of major. In 1954 he became a lecturer at the University of Warsaw, where he remained until 1968, but as communist Poland became increasingly anti-Semitic in the late 1960s he moved to Israel to teach at Tel Aviv University. In 1971 he accepted an appointment to teach at the University of Leeds, where he remained until his retirement. Although his early work related to analysis of class issues, Bauman has become best known for his analysis of the links between modernity and the Holocaust. It was his book *Modernity and the Holocaust* that brought Bauman's ideas to their widest audience, producing his most profound influence within the field of modern critical thought. In the book's Preface, he laid out quite clearly his essential position regarding the Holocaust. Here, he outlined his critique not only of the discipline of sociology generally, but of those who relegated the Holocaust to being a specifically 'Jewish' story:

> My complacency, and that of my fellow sociologists, was greatly helped (though not excused) by certain ways in which the memory of the Holocaust has been appropriated and deployed. It has been all-too-often sedimented in the public mind as a tragedy that occurred to the Jews and the Jews alone, and hence, as far as all others were concerned, called for regret, commiseration, perhaps apology, but not much more than that. ... Just how much and how perilously the significance of the Holocaust had been reduced to that of a private trauma and grievance of one nation was brought to me recently in a flash, by a learned and thoughtful friend of mine. I complained to him that I had not found in sociology much evidence of universally important conclusions drawn from the Holocaust experience. 'Is it not amazing,' my friend replied, 'considering how many Jewish sociologists there are?'
>
> (Bauman, 1989, viii–ix)

Thus, from the outset, he chided not only the discipline and his colleagues for their complacency in failing to address the Holocaust, but some Jews and non-Jews for their 'privatisation' of it, a critique which has not lessened in the years since the end of the Second World War.

For Bauman, the Holocaust was *'born and executed in our modern rational society, at the high stage of our civilization and at the peak of human cultural achievement, and for this reason it is a problem of that society, civilization, and culture'* (Bauman, 1989: x, emphasis in original).

It is the very modernity of the event which Bauman addressed, and, in so doing, he charted the issues elaborated upon in the book overall:

> *The purpose of the various investigations of the present study is not to add to specialist knowledge and to enrich certain marginal preoccupations of social scientists, but to open up the findings of the specialists to the general use of social science, to interpret them in a way that shows their relevance to the main themes of sociological inquiry, to feed them back into the mainstream of our discipline,* and thus to lift them up from their present marginal status into the central area of social theory and sociological practice.
>
> (Bauman, 1989: xi, emphasis in original)

Further sharpening his understanding of the modernity of the Holocaust, he noted that:

> *the Holocaust was an outcome of a unique encounter between factors by themselves quite ordinary and common; and that the possibility of such an encounter could be blamed to a very large extent on the emancipation of the political state, with its monopoly of means of violence and its audacious engineering ambitions, from social control — following the step-by-step dismantling of all non-political power resources and institutions of social self-management.*
>
> (Bauman, 1989: xiii, emphasis in original)

Bauman therefore attributed to the modern nation-state, in the aftermath of the European Enlightenment, with its loosening of its ties to Catholic (and, to a lesser extent, Protestant) Christianity and its vaunting of intellect and scientism over moral constraint, initially benignly perceived 'progress' as putting in place those modernist factors — state-sanctioned violence and non-state powerlessness — which opened the door to the Holocaust, factors which continue to be very much in evidence in the world of the twenty-first century.

Bauman's fundamental argument was that the Holocaust was not simply an event in Jewish history, nor was it a regression to some form of earlier Dark Age. It was, instead, a phenomenon that was deeply connected to modernity itself. Bureaucracy; specialisation and the general division of labour within the modern world; classifications on racial and ethnic lines; the elevation of law and order as civic virtues — all of these played important roles in bringing the Holocaust to fruition. With this in mind, he argued further that because of the centrality of these features to contemporary society, the lessons of the Holocaust have yet to be properly internalised.

None of the eight chapters comprising *Modernity and the Holocaust* shies away from controversy. Chapter 1, 'Sociology after the Holocaust', seriously critiques sociology as an intellectual and academic discipline for the failure of its practitioners to identify in the event not only its very modernity but its wider implications beyond the tragedy of its victim peoples. Chapters 2 and 3, 'Modernity, Racism, Extermination I' and 'Modernity, Racism, Extermination II', place under a micro- scope the 'dark factors' of the modern nation-state: the preoccupation with sacrosanct boundaries and thus the breakdown of the historically traditional order of societies; the rise not only of science and scientific reasoning but social engineering as well in the rationalised name of progress; the emergence of racism as a latent form of communal antagonism; and the relationship between the latter and genocidal practice. Chapter 4, 'The Uniqueness and Normality of the Holocaust', suggests that neither factor can be fully understood without reference to the technological achievements of the twentieth century, as well as the cultural context of Western civilisation. Chapter 5, 'Soliciting the Cooperation of the Victims', is Bauman's response to the thesis pre- sented by political theorist **Hannah Arendt** in her study *Eichmann in Jerusalem: A Report on the Banality of Evil* (1963) that in performing the tasks required of them by their Nazi overlords, the various *Judenräte* (self-governing Jewish councils) participated, albeit unwillingly, in their own demise. Bauman, in turn, sees in this process of forced cooperation a further example of the process of dehumanisation in modern society, what he calls 'a paradigm of modern bureaucratic rationality' and 'a textbook of scientific management'. Chapter 6, 'The Ethics of Obedience (Reading Milgram)', addresses not only the work of Stanley Milgram, but also that of Philip Zimbardo and his Stanford Prison Experiment, where, in 1971, twenty-four seemingly normal college students were assigned roles as either 'prisoners' or 'guards' and too quickly adapted to their respective roles. This chapter is Bauman's commentary and reflections upon both Milgram and Zimbardo, and offers them legitimacy despite the ongoing con- troversies surrounding them. Chapter 7, 'Towards a Sociological Theory of Morality', is, as its title suggests, a theoretical rethinking of morality and its constraints within a sociological context and whether such is even possible in a modern nation-state, while stopping short of a fully explicated theoretical construction. Chapter 8, 'Afterthought: Rationality and Shame', concludes with the positive (and, therefore, optimistic) statement '*It does not matter how many people chose moral duty*

over the rationality of self-preservation – what does matter is that some did'
(Bauman, 1989: 207, emphasis in original)

In an Afterword to the book published in the 2000 edition, Bauman added to his original perspectives by reminding his readers of how little human beings have progressed since the Holocaust. Here, he considered

> the most terrifying, and still most topical, aspect of the 'Holocaust experience:' that in our modern society people who are neither morally corrupt nor prejudiced may also still partake with vigour and dedication in the destruction of targeted categories of human beings; and that their participation, far from calling for the mobilization of their moral or any other convictions, demands on the contrary their suspension, obliteration and irrelevance.
>
> This is by far the most important lesson of the Holocaust which needs to be learned and remembered.
>
> (Bauman, 2000: 250)

In the late 1980s and early 1990s Bauman published a number of other books that dealt with the relationship between modernity, bureaucracy, rationality and social exclusion. In *Modernity and Ambivalence* (1991), for example, Bauman addressed the different approaches modern societies adopt towards the stranger in their midst. Showing how a certain ambivalence characterises some attitudes towards the strange or foreign (for instance, in attractions to different styles of food, clothing or tourist destinations), he identified that the stranger – essentially on account of his or her foreignness – is always the object of fear, the person external to 'normal' society who, through their very existence, is a constant threat that must be brought under control. The Jews, in Bauman's view, have fitted this bill in Europe and elsewhere throughout the modern period.

Thus, in Zygmunt Bauman we see an intellectual at work who has confronted the Holocaust within the parameters of his own academic discipline, and, in doing so, has drawn important conclusions which warrant further examination. Clearly, his most important consideration in this regard has been that the confluence of a number of factors to produce the Holocaust could have only come about in the so-called modern period, and that as a result, with the additional dimensions of both bureaucratic precision and technological expertise and efficiency, more than six million Jews and more than five million others were murdered in less than six years between September 1939 and May 1945.

Bauman's major writings

Freedom, Philadelphia: Open University Press, 1988.
Modernity and the Holocaust, Ithaca (NY): Cornell University Press, 1989; revised and expanded edition, 2000.
Paradoxes of Assimilation, New Brunswick (NJ): Transaction Publishers, 1990.
Modernity and Ambivalence, Ithaca (NY): Cornell University Press, 1991.
Mortality, Immortality and Other Life Strategies, Cambridge: Polity 1992.
Alone Again: Ethics after Certainty, London: Demos, 1994.
Globalization: The Human Consequences, New York: Columbia University Press, 1998.
Community: Seeking Safety in an Insecure World, Cambridge: Polity, 2001.
Society under Siege, Cambridge: Polity, 2002.
Wasted Lives: Modernity and Its Outcasts, Cambridge: Polity, 2004.
Does Ethics Have a Chance in a World of Consumers?, Cambridge (MA): Harvard University Press, 2008.

References

Milgram, Stanley, *Obedience to Authority: An Experimental View*, New York: Harper and Row, 1973.
Zimbardo, Philip, *The Lucifer Effect: Understanding how Good People Turn Evil*, New York: Random House, 2007.

DONALD BLOXHAM (b. 1973)

Donald Bloxham is Professor of Modern History at the University of Edinburgh, Scotland, where he has been teaching since 2002. Born in Birmingham, England, in 1973, he received his PhD in History from the University of Southampton in 1998. As the youngest full Professor of History in the United Kingdom, Bloxham is the winner of several prizes and honours for his work, including most recently a 2006 Philip Leverhulme Prize, a 2007 University of Edinburgh Chancellor's Award, and the 2007 **Raphael Lemkin** Award for Genocide Scholarship. During 2007–8 he held the prestigious position of J. B. and Maurice C. Shapiro Senior Scholar-in-Residence Fellow at the United States Holocaust Memorial Museum.

In a relatively short time, Bloxham has achieved much as a scholar of genocide (defined broadly), as well as of the Holocaust and the Armenian Genocide (specifically). From the outset, he appeared to gravitate towards issues related to the Holocaust and genocide. As an undergraduate he was moved by the events taking place in Yugoslavia during the early 1990s, and the Rwandan Genocide, which took place during his final undergraduate year, coincided with a year-long special subject on the Holocaust he was then undertaking. This subject was then being taught by a medieval historian, Colin Richmond, before the Holocaust was a popular or even mainstream subject of tuition in the UK, on what might even have been the first ever UK course to have the Holocaust as its main focus (Bloxham, personal correspondence, 19 June 2008). This conjunction of factors was very significant in shaping his interests. Further, the end of the Cold War had brought with it all manner of optimism about the role human rights and international law could play in regulating international affairs, which helps to explain why Bloxham's doctorate, and the subject of his first book, concerned the legal reckoning with Nazi criminality after the Second World War.

In *Genocide on Trial: War Crimes Trials and the Formation of Holocaust History and Memory* (2001), Bloxham addressed the origins of contemporary understandings of the preconceptions and purposes of the International Military Tribunal (IMT) at Nuremberg after the Second World War. His study was among the most comprehensive and authoritative studies of the war crimes trials yet written, in that he did not limit himself to only looking at the IMT, but, rather, extended his examination to the other Allied war crimes trials that followed that of the major Nazi leaders in 1945–46. He concluded that these trials did little to resolve how the general public, especially in Britain, viewed Nazi criminality, nor did they aid in the process of closure after the war. This was hardly helped by the British government's policy of premature releases of prominent war criminals during the Cold War. In short, *Genocide on Trial* questioned the effectiveness of the war crimes trials, arguing that the flawed judicial processes they exhibited were detrimental to the achievement of the aims that had motivated their appearance in the first place.

As Bloxham viewed it, *Genocide on Trial* addressed the most significant moment in the development of international humanitarian law, namely, the Nuremberg Trials, and concluded that there can be no legal 'quick fix' for profound societal problems such as those unleashed by the war. Unique in the scholarship on the years 1945–58, the book considered not only the Nuremberg Trials but also cases from wider American, British and French trial programmes, and assessed them, in accordance with Allied aims, as an intrinsic part of Germany's post-war re-education. Confrontation with the greatest Nazi crime, the Final Solution, was a particular focus. Bloxham's subsequent work in the area, in the form of a number of major scholarly articles, has focused on refuting the claims that are frequently made by legal scholars and political scientists about the significant role played by contemporary international criminal courts in making genocidal societies confront their past, leading to reconciliation. His later work, indeed, argued that such trials are often little more than a fig leaf for the continued pursuit of self-interest by hegemonic elements of the 'international community'. It is apparent that Bloxham's formative intellectual years, cutting as they did across such episodes as Bosnia and Rwanda, played an important role in shaping his approach to his scholarship. His work on war crimes trials has revolved around the question: can war crimes trials reform societies tainted by mass atrocity? Events in Yugoslavia, Rwanda and Iraq have lent immediacy to this question for scholars and policy-makers, and as a result Bloxham has been particularly interested in the role of the perpetrators of genocide and the culture of impunity – or at least, external ineffectiveness – that can accompany their actions.

Considering this further, Bloxham's research interests increasingly concerned the perpetration, punishment and representation of genocide, war crimes and other mass atrocities. He began to contemplate the Armenian Genocide of 1915–23 within its historical context as one of the most contentious issues in modern history. In *The Great Game of Genocide: Imperialism, Nationalism and the Destruction of the Ottoman Armenians* (2005), for which he won the 2007 **Raphael Lemkin** Award for Genocide Scholarship, Bloxham reflected on the varied interactions that took place throughout the Ottoman Empire in the period before and during the genocide. While noting that modern Turkish nationalist scholarship portrays the deportation of the Ottoman Armenians during the First World War as an act of military necessity provoked by Armenian insurgency, with any ensuing deaths attributable to wartime circumstances, he also recognised that Armenian accounts, on the contrary, focus on demonstrating the long-standing criminal intent of the Ottoman regime, depicting the wartime destruction as a logical extension of years of repressive state policy. Bloxham's work confirmed that the process of destruction was indeed orchestrated centrally by the Young Turk regime, and was certainly genocidal. Beyond this, however, his study deployed a wide range of sources and historical perspectives to illustrate the fundamental inadequacy of many other aspects of both interpretations.

Bloxham's book charted the emergence of a Young Turk policy of deportation and murder in the contexts of Ottoman territorial decline, Muslim refugee movement into the shrinking empire, European encroachments on Ottoman internal sovereignty, and the opening year of the war. Further contextualising his study, he also saw a need to consider the interaction of Russia and Britain with the Ottoman Empire from the mid-nineteenth century onwards. The diplomatic cold war between Russia and Britain known as 'The Great Game', centring on a struggle for hegemony in Central Asia, influenced the course of Ottoman reform during the second half of the century, as the battle for influence over the Christian minorities shaped the mind-sets of future Ottoman leaders, who feared that foreign intervention portended further territorial diminution of the ailing empire. The resentment of external intervention was illustrated in two explosions. In 1895, European pressure for Christian reforms was met with the slaughter of 100,000 Armenians. Then, during the First World War, the explosion was fully genocidal. Nevertheless, however vicious it was, Ottoman policy frequently developed reactively, shaped by wartime events in the Russian and Persian border regions and the Mediterranean. There was no single 'decision' for genocide as such. A variety of smaller triggers were the key to a process of 'cumulative policy radicalisation' that paved the way for the genocide to follow in 1915. Thinking about the decision for genocide in this way placed Bloxham on the Armenian Genocide into a similar category to **Christopher Browning** on the Holocaust – namely, as one who had a commitment to searching for a distinct genesis of the programme of mass murder leading to genocide, rather than simply running with the assumption that it began as if by remote control.

The Great Game of Genocide was, in Bloxham's words, 'not intended as a restatement' of the events of 1915 and beyond. Rather, his purpose was

> to chart the relationship between external intervention in state-minority relations from the mid-nineteenth century, through response to the genocide itself and the post-war division of the Near East, to the latter-day acceptance of the denial agenda of the modern Republic of Turkey. Most important, I try to show that these stories are not distinct: great power involvement in Ottoman internal affairs was a key element in exacerbating the Ottoman-Armenian dynamic towards genocide while Turkish sensitivity about external intervention on behalf of the Armenians – whether directed towards reforms before 1914 or independence after 1918 – was a vital contributory factor to the emergence of denial.
>
> (Bloxham, 2005a: 5)

Bloxham was thus most interested in tracing the international dimensions of the Armenian Genocide, seeking the ways in which linkages could be made between what was happening in Turkey and how these events were (a) part of larger world and regional developments, and (b) themselves influenced by these external stimuli.

Lest it be thought that Bloxham's work settled on the Armenian Genocide, it should be emphasised that he continued to examine the Holocaust and other cases of genocide, as well. In two books – first, written with fellow historian Tony Kushner, *The Holocaust: Critical Historical Approaches* (2005b), then another in his own right, *Genocide, the World Wars, and the Unweaving of Europe* (2008) – Bloxham sought to build on his examination of the Armenian Genocide. In these works he was not concerned with the crude equation of one event with another, but instead with the ways in which both may be seen within the context of the wider geopolitical and ideological develop-ments of the late nineteenth century through the mid-twentieth century. As he saw it, it is impossible to understand the 'final solution of the Jewish question' outside of the context of a Europe in which so many violent 'solutions' to other ethno-national 'questions' had been initiated in the preceding two or three generations. The collapse of the old European dynastic empires; their replacement by new forms of empire (of both the Nazi and Soviet variety); and the way in which new ideologies sought to reshape the demography of the newly con-tested territory in eastern, east-central and southeastern Europe and the Caucasus and Anatolia – all these things were vital to understanding the hyper-extreme violence of Germany during the Second World War, and for Bloxham the dynamic forces accompanying modernisation thus carried within them the awful potential that could be realised in genocide.

New projects built further upon this theme. In 2009 Bloxham released his latest work, *The Final Solution: A Genocide*, which was an attempt to consider what light the study of genocide generically, and particular instances thereof, cast on the Holocaust, as well as vice versa. In some aspects, such as the consideration of the orchestration of genocide, the book took a comparative approach, examining the Holocaust alongside the crimes of Stalinism, the Rwandan Genocide and the Armenian Genocide. Overall, however, he eschewed a fully comparative analysis, preferring instead a study based more on con-textual and correlative considerations, on patterns and interlinkages between different cases of genocide and ethnic cleansing.

Bloxham's interest in the connections between different episodes of mass state and societal violence, as they occur in relation to each other over time, has led to a large ongoing project with University of Southampton genocide scholar **Mark Levene**. This ten-volume monograph series, entitled Zones of Violence, is to be published by Oxford University Press. Each volume is authored by an area-studies specialist, and examines a region of the globe that has been subject to repeat instances of genocide and related violence in modern history. Further cementing his place in the new scholarship of genocide at the highest level is another major work currently in train, the *Oxford Handbook of Genocide*, on which he is working with Sydney University genocide scholar and historian A. Dirk Moses.

In a short career to date, Donald Bloxham's influence in the field of Genocide Studies has been substantial. His early work on law and punishment relative to war crimes and genocide trials has led some to contend that he is too sceptical as to their value; certainly, while a supporter of such justice in principle, he is quite doubtful about the capacity of international criminal law to do what so many of its advocates claim for it. Thus far, he holds, little concrete evidence has come forward in subsequent studies to rebut his main claims about these trials. His interpretation of the genesis of the Armenian Genocide has been important in that it has led to additional questions being asked about what inspired that event when it did. Also, the ways in which he has tried to relocate the Holocaust into broader patterns of European history have, again, led to new questions being asked and new directions in scholarship thereby being generated. Bloxham's ideas on a number of topics related to genocide and the Holocaust are at the cutting edge of contemporary scholarship, and, barely a decade on from his student years, his authority as a leading thinker in both fields is already assured.

Bloxham's major writings

Genocide on Trial: War Crimes Trials and the Formation of Holocaust History and Memory, Oxford: Oxford University Press, 2001.

'The Armenian Genocide of 1915–16: Cumulative Radicalisation and the Development of a Destruction Policy', *Past and Present*, 181, 1 (2003), 141–91.

(Ed. with Ben Flanagan) *Remembering Belsen: Eyewitnesses Record the Liberation*, London: Vallentine Mitchell, 2004.

The Great Game of Genocide: Imperialism, Nationalism and the Destruction of the Ottoman Armenians, Oxford: Oxford University Press, 2005a.

(with Tony Kushner) *The Holocaust: Critical Historical Approaches*, Manchester: Manchester University Press, 2005b.

'Beyond "Realism" and Legalism: A Historical Perspective on the Limits of International Humanitarian Law', *European Review*, 14, 4 (2006), 457–70.

Genocide, The World Wars, and the Unweaving of Europe, London: Vallentine Mitchell, 2008.

'Organized Mass Murder: Structure, Participation and Motivation in Comparative Perspective', *Holocaust and Genocide Studies*, 22, 2 (Fall 2008), 203–45.

'The Organisation of Genocide: Perpetration in Comparative Perspective', in Olaf Jensen and Claus-Christian W. Szejnmann (eds), *Ordinary People as Mass Murderers: Perpetrators in Comparative Perspectives*, London: Palgrave Macmillan, 2008, 185–200.

The Final Solution: A Genocide, Oxford: Oxford University Press, 2009.

CHRISTOPHER BROWNING (b. 1944)

Christopher Browning is an American historian of the Holocaust. Born in 1944, he taught at Pacific Lutheran University, Tacoma, Washington, from 1974 to 1999, eventually becoming a Distinguished Professor. In 1999 he moved to the University of North Carolina at Chapel Hill as Frank Porter Graham Professor of History, and in the spring of that year he gave the George Macaulay Trevelyan Lectures at Cambridge University, which in 2000 were published as a book under the title *Nazi Policy, Jewish Workers, German Killers*. In the spring of 2001 he delivered the inaugural George Mosse Lectures at the University of Wisconsin-Madison, and these, too, were published, as *Collected Memories: Holocaust History and Postwar Testimony*.

Browning's primary early interest in the area led him to investigate the role played by the German civil service in the formation of policies leading to or carrying out the Holocaust. His first book, in 1978, was *The Final Solution and the German Foreign Office*, in which he considered the relationship between anti-Semitic ideology and the implementation of Nazi foreign policy. Most of his research took place in the political archives of the German Foreign Office, located in Bonn; he also examined other German records providing insights into how Nazi bureaucrats had carried out the Final Solution. This led Browning into a series of intellectual confrontations known as the *Historikerstreit*, then taking place among historians of the Third Reich. In this struggle, scholars found themselves pitted on opposing sides, as either Functionalists or Intentionalists. The Functionalists were led by the German historians **Hans Mommsen** and Martin Broszat, who argued that the Holocaust was an evolving and sometimes even bureaucratically chaotic programme of death and destruction which only began to assert itself after the invasion of Soviet Russia in June 1941. The Functionalists viewed the Nazi hierarchy as one of competing vested interests and power centres, with Hitler not in supreme control. The Intentionalists, on the other hand, included among their number authors such as **Lucy S. Dawidowicz** and Eberhard Jäckel, and argued that the Holocaust was primarily centred on the person of Adolf Hitler, his anti-Semitism and his commitment to bringing to realisation a world free of Jews.

Browning stood somewhere between these two poles. While he agreed that there was a good deal of improvisation in the formation of Nazi policy towards the Jews, he could not accept the arguments of Broszat, **Mommsen** and others regarding Hitler. This designated Browning as what might be called a 'moderate functionalist'. As a result, he published a short article (Browning, 1981: 97–109), for which he attracted considerable notice within the academy. Notably, he was contacted by Yad Vashem, Israel's Holocaust museum and research centre, with a view to taking part in a projected multi-volume comprehensive history of the Holocaust. Browning's area of responsibility would involve researching and writing on the origins of the Final Solution. As he was to relate some time later, 'my research for that work allowed me to continue writing and publishing shorter pieces in two related areas: a gradual refinement of my arguments over the decision-making process that led to the Final Solution on the one hand, and a variety of case studies of the perpetrators on the other' (Browning, 2004a: 35–36).

One of these – a book published in 1992 entitled *Ordinary Men* – was a study of German Reserve Police Battalion 101, deployed by the Nazis to round up Polish Jews in 1942 for massacre and/or deportation to the death camps. In this study, Browning utilised the post-war court records of 210 former members of the battalion in order to ascertain what motivated this unit, numbering around five hundred, who, in a period of some 16 months, murdered up to 38,000 men, women and children in cold blood, while arranging the deportation of 45,000 more, mainly to Treblinka. Browning's chilling conclusion was that these men – ordinary, middle-aged men of working-class background from Hamburg, who had been drafted but found unfit for combat duty – were neither Nazi fanatics nor socio-pathological misfits. Within their cohort, he argued that the men of Reserve Police Battalion 101 killed as a result of peer pressure and a fundamental obedience to authority. The broader implication of his study was that people do not have to be maladjusted individuals or political fanatics in order to commit mass murder, but that, rather, group pressure and comradeship plays an important role when it comes to obeying even the most horrific orders.

The release of *Ordinary Men* caused considerable consternation among those who had preferred to believe that there was something demonic in the Nazis that led them to committing atrocities during the Holocaust; it also received substantial praise from a majority of Holocaust experts. Browning was, however, castigated by Harvard University scholar Daniel Goldhagen, whose alternative position – that an innate German anti-Semitic culture caused the Holocaust – polarised the argument of why it was that the Germans were so prepared to unleash the Holocaust on the Jews of Europe. Goldhagen's own contribution to the discussion – a controversial book produced in 1996 entitled *Hitler's Willing Executioners* – was seen as the most logical response to *Ordinary Men*, though many scholars of the Holocaust thought it was a poor attempt at a rebuttal that did little to shake Browning's essential position (Littell, 1997; Shandley, 1998).

As a result of his rapidly escalating image as a leading scholar of the *Shoah*, Browning was engaged in a number of high-profile legal cases during the 1990s as an expert witness on the veracity of the Holocaust. In this capacity, he was called upon to testify in the cases of Heinrich Wagner in Australia, Radislav Grujicic and Serge Kisluk in Canada, and Simon Serafimovich and Andrei Sawoniuk in the United Kingdom. In addition, he served as an expert witness in the cases of *Crown v. Ernst Zündel* in Toronto in 1988, and *David Irving v. Penguin Books and Deborah Lipstadt* in London in 2000. Where these two cases were concerned, the key issue related to the question of Holocaust denial and, in both, the popular perception was that the Holocaust itself was on trial. The role of the expert witness, on this reading, was to 'prove' that it really happened so as to throw out the arguments of the other side. In the Irving case in particular, those engaging Browning also employed a battery of other leading historians – Robert Jan van Pelt, Peter Longerich, Richard Evans and Hajo Funke – the better to establish beyond a reasonable doubt that the truth of the Holocaust could be established in a court of law. This was successfully argued in both cases, further strengthening Browning's stature as one of the world's foremost scholars of the Holocaust.

Browning's work in the field culminated in 2004 with the appearance of his long-awaited study *The Origins of the Final Solution: The Evolution of Nazi Jewish Policy, September 1939–March 1942*. This was the volume commissioned by Yad Vashem two decades earlier, and, in so far as a comprehensive study can ever be written about such a topic, it was definitive. Here, he again asked whether the Nazis always meant to kill the Jews, or whether their actions simply evolved gradually, radicalising over time when other solutions to the

'Jewish question' became unworkable. Browning's response was a much more detailed study than anything he had produced before, and in a systematic analysis he worked through a number of pre-existing controversial issues. These included the argument that prior to 1939 Hitler's intention had been to drive the Reich's Jews out of the country through emigration, but that the conquest of Poland in September of that year forced a shift in tactics from emigration to expulsion – whether to Madagascar, or the *Generalgouvernement* or, later, through forced removal into the territories that would be conquered in the Soviet Union.

A second key argument was that the Nazi 'Final Solution to the Jewish Question' – *Die Endlösung der Judenfrage* – evolved slowly as the bureaucrats sought ways to respond to the policy challenge laid before them by their political leaders. The notion of expulsion developed into one in which the Jewish population could be reduced, as they would be worked and starved to death after having been removed from lands coveted for ethnic German resettlement. As Browning showed, however, the Nazi *Einsatzgruppen* (mobile killing squads, of which Reserve Police Battalion 101 formed part) moved in brutally as the German combat soldiers conquered more territory within the Soviet Union, their intention being to wage war on the communist government and all those perceived to be its supporters (including, principally, the Jews). With this in mind, the Jews were now transformed into an enemy that was both racial and political, and had to be eradicated completely. The 'solutions' of emigration and expulsion were in fact no solutions at all; only the Jews' utter destruction, for all time, could be countenanced if the glorious future mapped out by National Socialism was to be realised.

Following on from this, Browning's third major argument was that the timing of the decision to completely annihilate the Jews of Europe thus took place some time in the summer of 1941, as the Nazis saw the ease with which they were destroying the Jewish population of the Soviet Union, and concluded that the process that had now started could – and should – be extended Europe-wide. The Wannsee Conference of January 1942, which has often been wrongly touted as the place where the Final Solution was decided, therefore played very little role in Browning's conception; the crucial decisions had already been taken, in an improvised manner, back in the summer of 1941. All that remained was the rationalisation and, if possible, simplification of the policy already decided – a process that had already begun to take place before Wannsee, but which received a huge boost as a result of that meeting.

Browning's study concluded in March 1942. At that point, the majority of Europe's Jews were still alive, and the Final Solution had not yet reached its apogee in the six death camps that the Nazis established in Poland. With this book, Browning had taken his brief literally – that is, to seek out the origin of the Final Solution, not its realisation. His earlier studies on the other hand, in particular *Ordinary Men*, showed how it was implemented.

Since the publication of *The Origins of the Final Solution*, Browning's research has continued along the lines established earlier in his career, and early 2010 saw the appearance of *Remembering Survival: Inside a Nazi Slave-Labor Camp*, a case study of the Jewish factory slave labour camps in Starachowice, in central Poland. As it was with his work on Reserve Police Battalion 101, this research is based on a wide range of testimonial literature, in this case, some 265 accounts by survivors of the camps. It is a remarkable story of survival for those who lived to recount the brutalities of the Nazi work camps there. Drawing on the rich testimony of survivors, Browning examined the experiences and survival strategies of the Jewish prisoners, alongside the policies and personnel of the Nazi guards.

Through asking questions of 'how', 'when' and 'why', and then painstakingly working through vast amounts of documentary material in order to answer them, Christopher Browning has established himself as one of the leading Holocaust scholars of the later twentieth century. His work has influenced a large number of younger historians through the stimulation of additional questions that had hitherto previously only received scant attention. When Browning began his academic life, he tells us, 'I was unusual for being both a non-Jew and a non-German in a field in which most active scholars were either Jews (American or Israeli) or Germans' (Browning, 2004a: 47). Owing largely to his efforts, he is now 'comforted that it is no longer unusual for a non-German, non-Jew to study the Holocaust' (Browning, 2004a: 48). His work as a researcher, writer and teacher has been of obvious importance, but it is also this bigger picture – namely, his influence and the legacy he will leave to the broad area of Holocaust scholarship – that must also be placed high among his achievements.

Browning's major writings

The Final Solution and the German Foreign Office: A Study of Referat D III of Abteilung Deutschland, 1940–1943, New York: Holmes and Meier, 1978.
'Zur Genesis der "Endlösung." Eine Antwort an Martin Broszat', *Vierteljarhshefte für Zeitgeschichte*, 29, 1 (1981), 97–109.

Fateful Months: Essays on the Emergence of the Final Solution, New York: Holmes and Meier, 1985.

Ordinary Men: Reserve Police Battalion 101 and the Final Solution in Poland, New York: HarperCollins, 1992a.

The Path to Genocide: Essays on Launching the Final Solution, Cambridge: Cambridge University Press, 1992b.

'Daniel Goldhagen's Willing Executioners', *History & Memory*, 9, 11 (Spring/Summer 1996), 88–108.

'Ordinary Germans or Ordinary Men? A Reply to the Critics', in Michael Berenbaum and Abraham J. Peck (eds), *The Holocaust and History: The Known, the Unknown, the Disputed, and the Reexamined*, Bloomington: Indiana University Press, 1998, 252–65.

Nazi Policy, Jewish Workers, German Killers, New York: Cambridge University Press, 2000.

Collected Memories: Holocaust History and Postwar Testimony, Madison (WI): University of Wisconsin Press, 2003.

'Writing and Teaching Holocaust History: A Personal Perspective', in Samuel Totten, Paul R. Bartrop and Steven Leonard Jacobs (eds), *Teaching about the Holocaust: Essays by College and University Teachers*, Westport (CT): Praeger, 2004a, 31–49.

(with contributions by Jürgen Matthäus) *The Origins of the Final Solution: The Evolution of Nazi Jewish Policy, September 1939–March 1942*, Lincoln (NE): University of Nebraska Press, 2004b.

Remembering Survival: Inside a Nazi Slave-Labor Camp, New York: Norton, 2010.

References

Goldhagen, Daniel Jonah, *Hitler's Willing Executioners: Ordinary Germans and the Holocaust*, New York: Random House, 1996.

Littell, Franklin H. (ed.), *Hyping the Holocaust: Scholars Answer Goldhagen*, Merion Station (PA): Merion Westfield Press International, 1997.

Shandley, Robert R. (ed.), *Unwilling Germans? The Goldhagen Debate*, Minneapolis: University of Minnesota Press, 1998.

HARRY JAMES CARGAS (1932–98)

Harry James Cargas was a Professor of Literature at Webster University in St. Louis, Missouri, and one of the leading Catholic voices examining Christian–Jewish relations in light of the Holocaust. His work transcended the world of the classroom and the lecture circuit. Through the pen, through radio and television, and through inter-faith dialogue, Cargas spread his message widely. In 35 books, 2,600 printed articles of all kinds (ranging from commentaries on religion, to the Holocaust, to baseball, and innumerable other topics in between), through speaking appearances at over 200 universities around the world, and across the airwaves via a radio talk show he ran on Missouri Public Radio for 24 years, Cargas reached an audience that was simultaneously diverse, discerning and receptive.

Born in 1932 to an American mother of Polish descent and a Greek immigrant father, and raised in a tough neighbourhood in Detroit, he began (and quit) his university studies four times, working instead at various jobs around the United States: at the Dodge auto factory in Detroit, at a copper smelter in Montana, as a short-order cook in Indiana, as a bouncer in a bar and then as a truck driver, both in Michigan, as an athletic director in a boys' school in New York, and as a wrestling coach in New Jersey. From time to time he also held down temporary teaching positions and writing assignments as a reporter with local newspapers (Cargas, 1997a: 34). In all this time he rarely thought about Jews, and even less about the Christian–Jewish relationship. It took almost until the onset of early middle age, in fact, before he even encountered the word 'Holocaust', and that by accident, in a magazine excerpt of **Elie Wiesel**'s *Night* that he read one evening in his living room.

Turning his attention to the Holocaust was at first no easy matter. With practically no background in the history of the topic, Cargas read as much as he could find on the Nazi persecution of the Jews. It was while doing this that he had, as he put it, 'another shocking, surprising illumination': when reading a Holocaust survivor's account one day in a library, he was confronted by

> the crashing realization that probably every Jew killed in the Holocaust was murdered by a baptized Christian. There would be almost no exception, not necessarily a practicing Catholic or Lutheran or whatever, but one who had at least received the watery sacrament as a child.
>
> (Cargas, 1997a: 35)

Cargas henceforth found it increasingly difficult to reconcile his Catholic Christianity with the reality of the Holocaust and those who were its perpetrators. He had not been born a Catholic, but had converted to Catholicism at the age of nineteen. Now, he was to begin a sincere questioning of what had become a vital part of his very existence.

His encounter with the Holocaust shook him to such an extent that he asked: 'Am I a fool to be an active member of a church which proclaims love as its motivating energy when historically … ? I let the question hang. I'm not even sure how to ask it' (Cargas, 1989: 17). It was his search for an answer that led him to make the statement that would define all of his subsequent work:

> To call myself a Roman Catholic is to describe my spiritual development incompletely. It is more honest for me to say at this time in my life that I am a post-Auschwitz Catholic, in the wider context of Western Christianity. The Holocaust is, in my judgement, the greatest tragedy for Christians since the crucifixion. In the first instance, Jesus died; in the latter, Christianity may be said to have died. In the case of Christ, the Christian believes in a resurrection. Will there be, can there be, a resurrection for Christianity? That is the question that obsesses me. Am I a part of a religious body which in fact is a fossil rather than a living entity? Can one be a Christian today, given the death camps which, in major part, were conceived, built and operated by people who called themselves Christians and some of whom – records prove, their own words prove – took pride in this work?
>
> (Cargas, 1989: 15–16)

The more Cargas reflected on the matter, the more the questions multiplied:

> accordingly, to identify myself as a Roman Catholic, in the shadow of recent history, is inaccurate, incomplete, even mis-leading. Culturally, of course, I am that, but spiritually I put on the mantle of a post-Auschwitz Catholic. It is in this concept that all my work – indeed my life – is now rooted.
>
> (Cargas, 1989: 16)

Such enlightenment led Cargas on a quest which reconsidered what Christianity meant now that its fundamentals had been challenged so radically. Christianity had failed during the *Shoah*; by its ongoing refusal to come to terms with that failure, the Church demonstrated that it did not recognise a need for repentance. But there was more to it than that. One of the features of Cargas's writing that made him such a commanding voice was an ability to offer practical suggestions for the future alongside criticism about past and present. His most important contribution, first put as early as 1979 and repeated many times after that, was a list of sixteen proposals which, if adopted, would establish a proper foundation for Christian–Jewish reconciliation:

1. The Catholic Church should excommunicate Adolf Hitler;
2. The Christian liturgical calendar should include an annual memorial service for the Jewish victims of the Holocaust;
3. Christians must publicly and officially admit the errors of their teachers where they were wrong concerning Jews;
4. The Christian Church must insist on the essential Jewishness of Christianity;
5. Jesus should be recognised as a link between Jews and Christians;
6. The Church's teachings on the subject of evil need to be re-evaluated;
7. Traditional Christian theologies of history must be re-examined;
8. The Vatican's historical archives for the twentieth century need to be opened to historians;
9. Chairs of Judaic Studies ought to be established at more Christian colleges and universities;
10. Consideration should be given to redefining the notion of inspiration in Christian scripture;
11. Christians must find new terminology for what are now designated as Old Testament and New Testament;
12. The Christian Sabbath should be changed to Saturday;
13. Catholics must demand an encyclical letter which deals specifically with the sins of anti-Semitism and with the sins of Christians in their actions toward Jews;
14. The heavy Christian emphasis on missionising should be re-directed toward perfecting individual Christian lives;
15. Christians need to 'get on our knees and repent our sins against the Jewish people'; and finally,
16. The Vatican should recognise Israel.

(Jacobs, 1985: 33–43)

These sixteen points would remain intact until Cargas's death in 1998.

Cargas aroused further notice as he challenged the Vatican to do something constructive in the area of Christian–Jewish relations. In 1988 he issued what he referred to as 'My Papal Encyclical'. In view of the fact that the Vatican did not at that time 'appear to be making enough significant steps' in the area of repentance for the wrongs done by Catholics to Jews during the *Shoah*, he argued that 'it is time that we required the publication of an up-to-date encyclical concerning the vital issue of Catholic–Jewish relationships' (Cargas, 1989: 190). Cargas thereupon produced 'Seeking Reconciliation', a series of declarations rather than mere suggestions. The appearance ten years later of the Vatican statement *We Remember: A Reflection on the Shoah* would to a large degree embody the spirit (if not the full content) of Cargas's 'encyclical'.

Being a 'post-Auschwitz Catholic' meant, in the first place, that one acknowledged the inadequacies of the Church during the *Shoah*, and faced up to the responsibility of individual Catholics who participated in it. Second, it meant that one would henceforth seek atonement for the Church's past sins toward God's first Covenant people. And finally, it meant that one would henceforth undertake to work, in a practical sense, for reconciliation between Catholics and Jews. Only then could one address the question of how best to serve God through the medium of the Church. Cargas's hope was that every professing Catholic would achieve this realisation, and that, because of it, the doctrinal foundation of the Church would itself undergo change.

When all was said and done, Cargas was prepared to ask hard questions of his own faith; to expect answers; and to propose actions when none were forthcoming. As he wrote in 1989:

> I think that contemporary Christian theology has neglected to attempt to deal with the Holocaust in any meaningful way and consequently it has failed us all. ... [V]ery probably every killer was baptized in the Christian faith. Every one. Why aren't our theologians dealing with that?
>
> Is history the revelation of God's plan for humanity as has been traditionally taught by the Church? Then how does this massacre of Christ's own people, of God's chosen, fit into this schema? What kind of a God is it to whom we are asked to dedicate our allegiance?
>
> (Cargas, 1989: 63–64)

Even asking questions of this kind was illustrative of Cargas's thought processes, and shows how far removed he was from mainstream Catholicism in the 1970s and 1980s.

Cargas also sought to learn where others stood, and he engaged in a series of dialogues with scholars, clergy and laity for the purpose of opening up discussion. In 1992 he republished (and expanded) an earlier discourse with one of the *Shoah*'s leading voices, in *Conversations with Elie Wiesel*. A year later came the highly acclaimed

Voices from the Holocaust (1993), a series of conversations conducted between Cargas and a number of leading thinkers in the area. These included such notables as Simon Wiesenthal, Jan Karski, Leo Eitinger, **Emil Fackenheim** and, again, **Elie Wiesel**.

Even after his death his influence was felt in the area of dialogue: first, through the completion of a project that had been dear to his heart for some time, *Holocaust Scholars Write to the Vatican* (1998); and second, through the appearance of his thirty-fifth (and last) book, another edited volume entitled *Problems Unique to the Holocaust* (1999) – problems of a theological and moral nature, still yet to be resolved despite the considerable distance the Church had travelled since Cargas first began his quest nearly three decades earlier.

Harry James Cargas was, in short, one of the most important lay Catholic voices in Christian–Jewish relations in the second half of the twentieth century. In general terms, his work can be evaluated in the following ways. First, he was a scholar of Christian thought who found it extremely difficult to reconcile the Church's past with his own spiritual present; he managed to do so by a rigorous and emotionally painful confrontation with that past, and an acknowledgement that only through full repentance could a meaningful future be established. Second, he taught that others should imitate him in this quest if the religion overall was to have any credibility as a faith system. Third, he was an activist who strongly believed in letting his behaviour speak with the same degree of exertion as his pen. And finally, he was a man of broad interests and abilities, who was equally adept at appearing as a guest in a pulpit or on a *bimah*, in a classroom or in a bullpen; a man who could *do* his theology as well as *write* it, and who took a genuine Christian interest in his fellow human beings.

Cargas's major writings

A Christian Response to the Holocaust, Denver: Stonehenge Books, 1981.

When God and Man Failed: Non Jewish Views of the Holocaust, New York: Macmillan, 1981.

Reflections of a Post-Auschwitz Christian, Detroit: Wayne State University Press, 1989.

Shadows of Auschwitz: A Christian Response to the Holocaust, New York: Crossroad, 1990.

Conversations with Elie Wiesel, New York: Justice Books, 1992.

(Ed.) *Voices from the Holocaust*, Lexington: University Press of Kentucky, 1993.

Telling the Tale: A Tribute to Elie Wiesel, St. Louis: Time Being Books, 1993.

'In the Name of the Father', in Carol Rittner and John K. Roth (eds), *From the Unthinkable to the Unavoidable: American Christian and Jewish Scholars Encounter the Holocaust*, Westport (CT): Praeger, 1997a, 33–39.

The Unnecessary Problem of Edith Stein, Lanham (MD): University Press of America, 1997b.

(Ed.) *Holocaust Scholars Write to the Vatican*, Westport (CT): Greenwood Press, 1998.

(Ed.) *Problems Unique to the Holocaust*, Lexington: University Press of Kentucky, 1999.

Reference

Jacobs, Steven L., 'Harry James Cargas: Appreciation and Response', *Journal of Reform Judaism*, 32, 2 (Spring 1985), 33–43.

ISRAEL W. CHARNY (b. 1931)

Israel W. Charny is an American-born Israeli psychotherapist, and a doyen in the field of Genocide Studies. His foundational scholarship has been insightful regarding the minds not only of the perpetrators but also of the deniers. His work has helped chart both the present and future directions of the broad field of Genocide Studies. Born in Philadelphia in 1932, he received his PhD in clinical psychology from the University of Rochester (New York) in 1957. Upon moving to Israel later that year, Charny was Professor of Psychology and Family Therapy at the Hebrew University Jerusalem, and then taught in the School of Social Work at Tel Aviv University between 1973 and his retirement in 1992.

For Charny, the passion of his Jewish concerns regarding the Holocaust, compounded by the death of his mother from cancer at an early age, has broadened to include his ongoing work as a clinical practitioner in his own field, as well as an ever-larger concern not only with Jews collectively, but with all victim peoples who have experienced the horrors of genocide. His writings have not been without serious critique and rebuttal, and his own personal journey not without its confrontations.

Originally appearing in his landmark study *How Can We Commit the Unthinkable? Genocide, the Human Cancer* (1982), Charny's Genocide Early Warning System, which he lists as one of his most personally fulfilling initiatives, 'identifies ten major early warning processes that define a series of natural psychocultural processes with which all groups (and individuals) … may be turned by society toward support of life, or … toward momentums of increasing violence toward human life, culminating in genocide'. He identified these as the following:

1. The Valuing of Human Life
2. Concern with the Quality of Human Experience
3. The Valuing of Power
4. Machinery for Managing Escalations of Threat
5. Orientation toward Force for Self-Defense and Solution of Conflicts
6. Overt Violence and Destructiveness
7. Dehumanization of a Potential Victim Target Group
8. Perception of Victim Groups as Dangerous
9. Availability of Victim Group
10. Legitimization of Victimization by Leadership Individuals and Institutions.

(Charny, 1999: 253–61)

Though unsuccessful either nationally or internationally in getting such a 'genocide radar system' established, due both to a lack of adequate funding and multi-level political and academic opposition, Charny's efforts in attempting to create a Genocide Early Warning System were to some degree complemented by the work of **Franklin H. Littell** in the United States and Kumar Rupesinghe from Sri Lanka. The approach Charny proposed, moreover, remains vital (and viable) to any assessments of present and future genocides.

In 1982, together with Nobel Laureate **Elie Wiesel**, Charny successfully hosted a conference in Israel addressing both the Holocaust and other genocides, with a very small number of papers on the Armenian Genocide (in Charny's words, 'the first major genocide of the twentieth century'). Despite intense political pressure from the government of Turkey (and, disturbingly, Israel), the conference was held with approximately 300 in attendance, and resulted in a volume he co-edited with Shamai Davidson, *The Book of the International Conference on the Holocaust and Genocide: Book One: The Conference Program and Crisis* (1983), which included all of the papers presented. On this conference, Charny wrote later:

few people knew that the Conference probably cost me the tenure that I never achieved at Tel Aviv University where the then-rector (and then in later years president) of the university was deeply embarrassed by the fact that the Israeli press supported me overwhelmingly for having maintained the Conference in the face of government pressure to close it down, while simultaneously criticizing him for having withdrawn both his participation and the university's participation from the Conference.

(Charny, 2002: 444)

Earlier, in 1981, Charny had created in Jerusalem the Institute on the Holocaust and Genocide, 'to create tools for other genocide scholars and to inspire and facilitate scholars in their initiatives in this terribly difficult area of human experience' (Charny, 2002: 453). A major accomplishment of this stance, from 1985 to 1995, was the newsletter *Internet on the Holocaust and Genocide: An International Information Exchange*, which saw the production of fifty-six regular issues and eight Special Issues, addressing such topics as the UN Whitaker Report on updating the 1948 Convention on the Prevention and Punishment of the Crime of Genocide; the important work of such scholars as **Barbara Harff**, **Ted Robert Gurr** and **R. J. Rummel**; global genocide education; the Holocaust; the Armenian Genocide; and ongoing threats to minorities throughout the world. In 1995 editorship of the newsletter passed to Colin Tatz of Macquarie University, Australia, where it was renamed the *International Network on the Holocaust and Genocide*.

As both a practicing psychotherapist and a scholar of genocide, Charny has explored the nexus between the two with an extensive list of relevant publications. This nexus may best be seen and understood in his work *Fascism and Democracy in the Human Mind: A Bridge between Mind and Society* (2006), which he would label before its publication as the culminating work of his scholarly career.

Obviously opting for the 'democratic mind' as the paradigm to be preferred over that of the 'fascistic mind', Charny articulated that both are part of the individual human psyche, with either or both at times dominating the other. The former is open to new ideas, tolerant of those ideas and persons with which the individual disagrees, and able to live with contradictions and disharmonies. The latter, on the other hand, is closed to new and other ways of thinking, intolerant of other ideas and persons, unable to live with contradictions and disharmonies. The former translates these ideals into behavioural activities that affirm life; the latter in behavioural modalities which destroy life, the ultimate of which is genocide itself. In linking the individual ways in which the human mind is organised and structured to those of society as a whole (and, by extension, nation-states in their relationships to each other), Charny attempted to present a new bridge-building theoretical model, the pragmatic, educational, and political goal of which was to raise a generation opposed to genocide.

By further extension, living and working as he does in the State of Israel, Charny has also addressed the horrific violence manifested in the phenomenon of suicide bombing in which innocent Israeli Jews (and innocent Israeli Muslims and Christians as well as foreign visitors) have been victims in recent years. The subtitle of his study *Fighting Suicide Bombing* (2007) – 'A Worldwide Campaign for Life' – says much about his response to this ongoing tragedy not only in Israel itself, but in Iraq, Russia, Lebanon, Sri Lanka, Kenya, India, Indonesia and Pakistan, among other places. The last chapter of this work ('A Proposal for a "Worldwide Campaign for Life" by the Leaders of Many Religions and Other World Leaders and Heroes') further fleshes out his idea in very real terms by calling upon those leaders in positions of authority to reject suicide bombing (which he considers to be genocidal by implication), and to bring those to account who recruit others to perform such heinous acts.

Charny's current and ongoing project, in which he has been attempting to both understand the psychology of Holocaust and genocide deniers and countering the speciousness of their arguments, is itself a major contribution to Genocide Studies. Originally presented as a conference paper in 1995, he developed his thinking such that by 2001 he had produced a major article on the subject (Charny, 2001). Here, after first articulating five 'thinking defense mechanisms' by which people are able to engage in denial (innocence and self-righteousness; scientificism in the service of confusion; practicality, pragmatism and political realism; idea-linkable distortion and time-sequence confusion; and indirection, definitionalism and maddening), Charny addressed the relationship between 'innocent' and 'malevolent' denial. He broadened the scope whereby the phenomenon may be understood by suggesting two 'continua': (1) Continuum of Malevolence of Denial of Known Genocides: 'Innocent Denial' to Malevolence; and (2) Continuum of Celebration of Violence and Denials of Known Genocides: 'Moral Innocence' and Disavowals of Violence to Celebration of Violence.

Such work has led Charny to produce a number of further papers exploring the issue. His 'Twelve Ways to Deny a Genocide' (originally entitled 'Templates for Gross Denial of a Known Genocide: A Manual', addressing specifically the Holocaust and the Armenian Genocide), may best be understood as a fuller listing of the very topics he has considered previously on this issue. The list of denial strategies reads as follows:

1. Question and minimise the statistics.
2. Attack the motivations of the truth-tellers.
3. Claim that the deaths were inadvertent.
4. Emphasise the strangeness of the victims.
5. Rationalise the deaths as the result of tribal conflict.
6. Blame 'out of control' forces for committing the killings.
7. Avoid antagonising the genocidists, who might walk out of 'the peace process.'
8. Justify denial in favor of current economic interests.
9. Claim that the victims are receiving good treatment.
10. Claim that what is going on doesn't fit the definition of genocide.
11. Blame the victims.
12. Say that peace and reconciliation are more important than blaming people for genocide.

(Charny, 1999: 168)

With the publication of the two-volume *Encyclopedia of Genocide* in 1999, Charny continued his goal of 'seeking to develop basic resources for this field of knowledge' and his hope that it would 'serve as catalyst for much more productive work on the study and the prevention of genocide' (Charny, 2002: 466). This has since proven to be the case, as the field has recently seen the publication of other key reference works such as Leslie Alan Horvitz and Christopher Catherwood's *Encyclopedia of War Crimes and Genocide* (2006), Dinah Shelton's *Encyclopedia of Genocide and Crimes Against Humanity* (2004) and Samuel Totten and Paul R. Bartrop's *Dictionary of Genocide* (2008). Mention must also be made that the official journal of the International Association of Genocide Scholars, *Genocide Studies and Prevention*, was first produced during Charny's presidency of that organisation, further underscoring his vision for the future and the viability of Genocide Studies.

Collectively, Israel Charny's considerable output and influence have made him one of the leaders in the still-emerging field of genocide studies. His professional perspective, that of a scholar of psychology and practitioner of psychotherapy, has contributed enormously to our understanding of why human beings engage in harmful behaviour, commit genocide and deny its reality.

Charny's major writings

'Teaching the Violence of the Holocaust: A Challenge to Educating Potential Future Oppressors and Victims for Nonviolence', *Jewish Education*, 38 (1968), 15–24.

'Normal Man as Genocider', *Voices: The Art and Science of Psychotherapy*, 7, 2 (1971), 68–79.

'A Contribution to the Psychology of Genocide: Sacrificing Others to the Death We Fear Ourselves', *Israel Yearbook of Human Rights*, Tel Aviv: Tel Aviv University, 1980, 139–54.

(with Chanan Rapaport) *How Can We Commit the Unthinkable? Genocide, the Human Cancer*, Boulder (CO): Westview Press, 1982.

(Ed. with Shamai Davidson), *The Book of the International Conference on the Holocaust and Genocide: Book One: The Conference Program and Crisis*, Tel Aviv: Institute of the International Conference on the Holocaust and Genocide, 1983.

Toward the Understanding and Prevention of Genocide, Boulder (CO): Westview Press, 1984.

'Genocide and Mass Destruction: Doing Harm to Others as a Missing Dimension in Psychopathology', *Psychiatry*, 49, 2 (1986), 144–57.

(Ed.) *Genocide: A Critical Bibliographic Review*, New York: Facts on File, 1988.

(Ed.) *Genocide: A Critical Bibliographic Review*, vol. 2, New York: Facts on File, 1991.

(Ed.) *The Widening Circle of Genocide* (vol. 3 in the series *Genocide: a Critical Bibliographic Review*), New Brunswick (NJ): Transaction Publishers, 1994.

(Ed.) *Encyclopedia of Genocide* (2 vols), Santa Barbara (CA): ABC-Clio, 1999.

'Innocent Denials of Known Genocides: A Further Contribution to a Psychology of Denial of Genocide', *Human Rights Review*, 1, 3 (2000), 15–39.

'The Psychological Satisfaction of Denials of the Holocaust or Other Genocides by Non-Extremists or Bigots, and Even by Known Scholars', *Idea: A Journal of Social Issues*, 6, 1 (17 July 2001), at http://www.ideajournal.com/articles.php?id = 27.

'A Passion for Life and Rage at the Wasting of Life', in Samuel Totten and Steven Leonard Jacobs (eds), *Pioneers of Genocide Studies*, New Brunswick (NJ): Transaction Publishers, 2002, 429–78.

'A Classification of Denials of the Holocaust and Other Genocides', *Journal of Genocide Research*, 5, 1 (2003), 11–34.

Fascism and Democracy in the Human Mind: A Bridge between Mind and Society, Lincoln (NE): University of Nebraska Press, 2006.

Fighting Suicide Bombing: A Worldwide Campaign for Life, Westport (CT): Praeger, 2007.

References

Horvitz, Leslie Alan, and Christopher Catherwood, *Encyclopedia of War Crimes and Genocide*, New York and London: Facts on File, 2006.

Shelton, Dinah (ed.), *Encyclopedia of Genocide and Crimes against Humanity* (3 vols), New York: Macmillan, 2004.

Totten, Samuel and Paul R. Bartrop, *Dictionary of Genocide* (2 vols), Westport (CT): Greenwood Press, 2008.

ROBERT CONQUEST (b. 1917)

Robert Conquest is an American-based British historian of the USSR. Born in 1917, he was educated at Winchester College, then Magdalen College, Oxford, where he read Politics, Philosophy and Economics. During his student days he spent a year in France (studying at the University of Grenoble) and Bulgaria; returning to Oxford, he was attracted to communism, and joined the British Communist Party in 1937. He undertook a doctorate in Soviet history, but later moved away from communism upon becoming aware of its destructive capacities under Stalin.

Upon the outbreak of the Second World War he joined the British army, serving with the Oxford and Buckinghamshire Light Infantry. After demobilisation, he joined the British Foreign Office, where he remained for the next ten years. In 1948 he became a member of the Foreign Office's Information Research Department, working in the area of counter-Soviet propaganda. He left in 1956, turning his hand to freelance writing and editing. His first published works were about the Soviet Union.

It was during the early 1960s that Conquest attracted notice as an authority on the Soviet Union, but his breakthrough came in 1968 with the appearance of *The Great Terror: Stalin's Purge of the Thirties*. This was generally acknowledged as the first wide-ranging examination of the subject. Owing to the Cold War environment within which the book was written, it was of necessity based only on materials available in the West, or Soviet materials that were already in the public domain. Conquest attacked Stalin's regime as one that was brutally destructive, his calculations estimating that, when taken together, the political purges and the famines perpetrated in the name of building socialism were responsible for the deaths of millions of people.

Conquest's criticism of Stalin as a mass political murderer led to him developing an influential role over those who were critical of the excesses of Soviet communism. Moreover, Conquest was equally condemnatory of Stalin's predecessor Lenin, which disturbed those who had previously been prepared to accept that Stalin was evil but that Lenin was less so. Conquest showed, on the contrary, that Lenin, in fact, was just as bad, and that Stalin was simply in a better position to carry out the programme Lenin had already plotted.

Earlier, in 1960, Conquest had produced a short book entitled *The Soviet Deportation of Nationalities*. This was reissued in a different format ten years later as *The Nation Killers: The Soviet Deportation of*

Nationalities, and extended Conquest's remit: from being a critic of Stalin's murderous internal political policies, he now showed Stalin as a leader possessed of an aptitude for genocide, or at least ethnic cleansing. The book described the forced deportation, at Stalin's orders, of the entire population of eight small national groups from the Caucasus before and during the Second World War. He calculated that some 1.6 million people were forcibly removed, with an estimated 600,000 killed owing to Soviet actions, exposure, starvation and cold. The pretext for these removals was that the people involved – Volga Germans, Kalmyks, Chechens, Ingush, Karachai, Balkars, Meskhetians and Crimean Tatars – were potentially or in reality disloyal, and that security concerns forced the Soviets' hand. In a scenario being played out at the same time in Nazi Europe, the deportees were transported in cattle trucks, over enormous distances. Having arrived at their eventual destinations, the deportees were often simply unloaded onto the bare earth and told to begin building their new homes, with little food and, all too frequently, next to nothing in the way of building materials. In a classic case of ethnic cleansing, it then became Soviet policy to act as if these people had never existed in the first place; within their ancestral territories, the Soviets arranged for the settlement of other peoples on the land they had formerly occupied.

As Conquest saw it, the fate of these small nations was 'no accidental vagary'. It was, rather,

> A test case, a declaration of overriding intent, of the view taken by the new type of state, not merely of hostile political ideas but actually of hostile cultures or races. It was part and parcel of an entire attitude to the rights of small nations under Communist Party rule, of which the basic principle had been established in Lenin's time and earlier.
>
> (Conquest, 1970: 7)

Conquest's writing on the USSR during the 1960s and 1970s consisted essentially of historical descriptions of the brutality and oppressiveness of the Soviet system. Where issues relating to mass murder and/or genocide were concerned, his major works were *The Great Terror* and *The Nation Killers*, though a third study on the theme of persecution, *Kolyma: The Arctic Death Camps* (1978), was a key study of what was considered to be the worst of the camps in the Soviet gulag. Conquest explained how prisoners were categorised, and the ways in which they found the means to stay alive in this most extreme of environments. He utilised his study of Kolyma in order to demonstrate the degree to which the casualty rates in the Soviet concentration camps matched those of other regimes at the same time, notwithstanding the fact that the prisoners he was examining were sent there for so-called political reasons rather than for racial extermination. Altogether, estimates have shown that several million Soviet citizens died in these camps, from overwork, exposure, starvation, disease, brutality and shooting, and Conquest argued that the death rate at Kolyma was by far the worst.

In 1986, Conquest published *The Harvest of Sorrow: Soviet Collectivisation and the Terror-Famine*. This work dealt with that period of Soviet history in the 1930s known in Ukrainian as the *Holodomor*, during which millions of peasants (mainly, though not only, Ukrainians) died of starvation or through deportation to labour camps. The Soviet aim of feeding the proletarian revolution at the expense of the peasantry through the redistribution of food from the country to the cities had a devastating effect, resulting in the death of millions. In the drive to collectivise agriculture, the independence of agricultural producers – even of smallholders who made a modest profit from their harvests – was to be destroyed totally. The systematic nature of this destruction was massive. Independent land-owning peasants (commonly referred to as *kulaks* by the communists), were targeted in two major campaigns in 1930 and 1931, which saw the seizure of about 1,800,000 *kulaks* (and, by the end of 1933, another 400,000). The key aspect of the communist strategy was the *kulaks'* resettlement; by removing them from the land and placing them on communal farms substantial distances from their original districts, a transformation could be effected both in agricultural practices and demography. Privation, cold, disease and violent treatment by the communists during these forced population transfers saw a death toll in the hundreds of thousands, but this did not deter the government from its so-called dekulakisation programme; nor did the massive disruption this programme caused to agricultural production. Perhaps six million peasants starved to death due to Stalin's campaigns. By the middle of the 1930s, the full collectivisation of agriculture had taken place throughout the Soviet Union, and the rural peasantry was no longer identifiable in the form it had been just two decades earlier.

Conquest's study showed the degree to which the famine penetrated Ukrainian society, and there was little in his argument that could deny the Soviets' destructive intent. As he wrote of the early 1930s:

> the Ukraine and the Ukrainian Cossack and other areas to its east – a great stretch of territory with some forty million

inhabitants – was like one vast Belsen. A quarter of the rural population, men, women and children, lay dead or dying, the rest in various stages of debilitation with no strength to bury their families or neighbours. At the same time (as at Belsen), well-fed squads of police or party officials supervised the victims.

This was the climax of the 'revolution from above', as Stalin put it, in which he and his associates crushed two elements seen as irremediably hostile to the regime: the peasantry of the USSR as a whole, and the Ukrainian nation.

(Conquest, 1986: 3)

Many of Conquest's critics in the West rejected his argument that Stalin's action was wholly unnecessary and a betrayal of what the Soviets said they stood for, preferring to consider the destruction as a necessary step in building the socialist state. Moreover, it was held by some that his position lacked subtlety, and that his contentions were far more geared towards popular appeal at a time of Cold War tensions. For present purposes, however, the suggestion that Stalin's campaign had genocidal motives has since been much more a matter of contention. Among Ukrainian nationalists and their supporters, for instance, the massive death toll caused through the famine was a clear case of Stalin attempting to destroy Ukrainian national identity, requiring no further comment. Indeed, Conquest would reaffirm his basic position in another work five years later: 'It was a fight to the death against the peasantry – and, blended with it, against the Ukrainian nationality. When Stalin was engaged in a fight to the death, there was always plenty of death to go round' (Conquest, 1991: 164). Because a wide reading public associated the 'famine-as-genocide' argument with Conquest's work, and his ideas on the subject were influential in conditioning attitudes towards that event, he ensured his place as a cutting-edge thinker on the impact of state-directed famine as an agent of genocide.

Careful study of the motives behind the 'dekulakisation' programme, however, has shown that this was not necessarily the case. Two other British historians, R. W. Davies and Stephen Wheatcroft, addressed this issue in their 2004 study of the famine, *The Years of Hunger: Soviet Agriculture 1931–1933*. Their conclusion, summarised by Stephen Wheatcroft in late 2007, was that

the famine in 1932/33 was the culmination of a series of factors over a lengthy period that began with the urban food crises of 1928–30 that led the regime to impose severe grain procurements and radical land transformation (Collectivization). The urban food shortages of this early period were not relieved by these measures, although the fine weather of 1930 brought a good harvest which provided some temporary relief. Unfortunately the government exported the large amount of grain that it collected from the 1930 harvest instead of replenishing its reserve stocks, and so was poorly prepared to face the drought of 1931 and the equally poor harvest of 1932. In these desperate circumstances, with famine already present in the cities the government increased the severity of its grain procurements which forced the main burden of the famine onto the rural areas and eventually onto Ukraine. We estimate that about 6 million people died from the famine in the 1930–33 period throughout all the USSR. A disproportionately high proportion of these, probably as many as 3 million, died in Ukraine. This was a consequence of severe supply problems, bad decisions and inadequate responses. It was not the consequence of deliberate murder or genocide.

(Wheatcroft, personal correspondence, 30 November 2007)

While this is a somewhat clear-cut statement of the matter, Wheatcroft drew readers' attention to what some might have seen as an unsettling admission from Conquest himself. Advocates of the 'mass murder' or 'genocide' allegation who rely on Conquest's work as a support for their contention should, he wrote,

be made aware that Dr Robert Conquest no longer supports this claim. After reading a draft of our book in which we criticised the Conquest thesis of a deliberate cause of the famine, Conquest wrote to us stating that he would like us to point out that it was no longer his opinion that 'Stalin purposely inflicted the 1933 famine. No. What I argue is that with resulting famine imminent, he should have prevented it, but put "Soviet interest" other than feeding the starving first – thus consciously abetting it.'

(Wheatcroft, personal correspdonence, 30 November 2007)

This was a startling disclosure, highlighting the rigour with which Conquest continued his ongoing reflections about the Soviet period and Stalin's excesses. If the period known as the Great Hunger, fur-thermore, could not be put down to genocide or mass murder, but, rather, to wilful negligence, it painted Stalin's crimes in an altogether different light. It would not exonerate Stalin, but it would lead to a different set of charges from those levelled against him by his opponents. The disavowal, once it began to be known, damaged Conquest's reputation among those scholars who had earlier been prepared to accept his position.

Conquest further explored whether or not his ideas still stood the test of time in 1990, in a twentieth-year anniversary reconsideration of his book on the Great Purges, *The Great Terror: A Reassessment.* This was in large part prompted by the full opening of the Soviet archives towards the end of communist rule in the USSR, and in light of the newly available evidence Conquest reaffirmed the con-clusions he had originally reached in 1968. His most recent volumes, at the end of a scholarly life exposing the massive human-rights excesses of the Soviet Union, are further reflections of the horrors of the system it created (Conquest, 2000; Conquest, 2004). These seek to understand not just what happened during the Soviet eruption, but why so many in the West were taken in by it, for so long.

Robert Conquest was one of the first scholars to address seriously the issue of Stalin's crimes within the context of genocide or ethnic cleansing. An eminent and controversial historian, his considerable literary output has shown him to be a champion of scholarly thought and one who values evidence in order to draw his conclusions. His goal is one of learning the lessons of the twentieth century in order to survive the twenty-first, and in view of the century now left behind, Conquest's major contribution must reside in the value he places on the free exchange of ideas and the safeguards against tyranny they can promote.

Conquest's major writings

Soviet Deportation of Nationalities, New York: Macmillan/St. Martin's Press, 1960.
Soviet Nationalities Policy in Practice, London: The Bodley Head, 1967.
The Great Terror: Stalin's Purge of the Thirties, New York: Macmillan, 1968.
The Nation Killers: The Soviet Deportation of Nationalities, New York: Macmillan, 1970.
Kolyma: The Arctic Death Camps, London: Macmillan, 1978.
Inside Stalin's Secret Police: NKVD Politics, 1936–1939, Stanford (CA): Hoover Institution Press, 1985.
The Harvest of Sorrow: Soviet Collectivization and the Terror-Famine, New York: Oxford University Press, 1986.
Stalin and the Kirov Murder, New York: Oxford University Press, 1990a.
The Great Terror: A Reassessment, Oxford: Oxford University Press, 1990b.
Stalin: Breaker of Nations, London: Weidenfeld and Nicolson, 1991.

Reflections on a Ravaged Century, New York: Norton, 2000.
The Dragons of Expectation: Reality and Delusion in the Course of History,
New York: Norton, 2004.

Reference

Davies, R. W. and Stephen G. Wheatcroft, *The Years of Hunger: Soviet
Agriculture 1931–1933*, London: Palgrave-Macmillan, 2004.

VAHAKN N. DADRIAN (b. 1926)

Vahakn N. Dadrian is a Professor of Sociology, and one of the early
scholars of the academic study of genocide. A specialist on the
Armenian Genocide of 1915–23, his many contributions to the
investigation of that event, through multilingual original research in a
number of archival collections throughout the world, has stamped
him as one of the foremost thinkers on the nature of the Armenian
Genocide and how it was carried out.

Born in Istanbul, Turkey in 1926, to a family that had seen many
members wiped out by the Ottoman Turks during the First World
War, Dadrian's early educational training was diverse. He studied
mathematics at the University of Berlin, history at the University of
Vienna and, later, international law at the University of Zürich. He
obtained his PhD in Sociology at the University of Chicago in 1954,
after migrating to the United States. His early work was in mainstream sociology, particularly in the area of dominant group–minority
relations in heterogeneous social systems. Through this, he considered
the phenomenon of social conflict, concluding that it was more or
less endemic in such intergroup relationships. This, coupled with a
close reading of some of the key works on the Armenian Genocide
(in both Armenian and English), led him towards the scholarly study
of that event as well as the wellsprings of genocide itself.

After teaching at the State University of New York Geneseo from
1970 to 1991, he retired from active teaching in order to conduct
research full-time on the Armenian Genocide. For several years he
was engaged as Director of a large Genocide Study Project sponsored
by the H. F. Guggenheim Foundation, the first major publication of
which was to be his most important work, *The History of the Armenian
Genocide: Ethnic Conflict from the Balkans to Anatolia to the Caucasus*
(1995). A much-decorated scholar, in 1998 Dadrian was made a
member of the Academy of Sciences of the Republic of Armenia and
awarded an honorary doctorate from the Academy for his research in

the field of Armenian Genocide Studies. In 2005 he received the first ever Lifetime Achievement Award from the International Association of Genocide Scholars, and was chosen as a recipient of the Ellis Island Medal of Honor. He is currently the Director of Genocide Research at the Zoryan Institute, an international centre devoted to the research and documentation of contemporary issues related to the history, politics, society and culture of Armenia and Armenians around the world.

Dadrian's research on the Armenian Genocide is based on his outstanding facility for languages. Fluent in Armenian, German, English, French, Turkish and Ottoman Turkish, he has undertaken research in a range of repositories that few individuals, acting alone, have been able to. Where the Armenian Genocide is concerned, he adopts the highest standards of veracity for the sources he consults, as he wrote in a personal reflection in 2002:

> my framework of analysis as envisaged for the task of documenting the Armenian Genocide revolves around four elements: (1) reliable, (2) explicit, (3) incontestable, and (4) verifiable. Material that is deficient in any of these elements will have to be discounted strictly for methodological considerations.
>
> (Dadrian, 2002: 243)

What this has led to is a form of study that seeks to rescue a history that might otherwise have been lost (or at least hidden) from general view, especially through the translation, analysis and publication of documentary evidence of a wide variety of elements of the genocide between 1915 and 1923, together with events on either side of those dates.

While Dadrian's work focuses on the Armenian case, his work on the broader nature of genocide has also been influential. In one of his first statements on the subject, in 1975, he produced a definition of genocide that many would in subsequent years hold to be definitive:

> Genocide is the successful attempt by a dominant group, vested with formal authority and/or with preponderant access to the overall resources of power, to reduce by coercion or lethal violence the number of a minority group whose ultimate extermination is held desirable and useful and whose respective vulnerability is a major factor in contributing to the decision for genocide.
>
> (Dadrian, 1975: 202)

In later works Dadrian has extended his authority over the general topic of genocide, considering such cases as the Holocaust, Native Americans and Rwanda, as well as in comparative analysis and in the development of his theoretical perspectives of genocide relative to perpetrator motivations and behaviour.

It is in his work on the Armenian Genocide, however, that Dadrian has made the greatest contribution to the field of Genocide Studies. In a series of articles during the 1980s, for example, he considered the role of a number of major actors in the Turkish processes of destruction, such as physicians, the military, the so-called Special Organisation (comprised largely of prisoners released from Turkish jails and given the task of killing Armenians), as well, of course, as the politicians of the Committee of Union and Progress (the so-called Young Turks) who ran the government. Later, in 1996, he investigated the role of Ottoman Turkey's wartime ally Germany in the genocide, and in his examination of the subject, *German Responsibility in the Armenian Genocide: A Review of the Historical Evidence of German Complicity* (1996), he concluded that there was active German participation in the Ottoman destruction of the Armenians.

To complete the profile of Dadrian's attempt at rescuing the history of the Armenian Genocide, he has in recent times been examining the legal processes against Turkish officers charged with it in 1919, particularly their international dimensions. In addition, he has also engaged in work exposing and countering Turkish denial of the Armenian Genocide; this activity culminated in the book *The Key Elements in the Turkish Denial of the Armenian Genocide: A Case Study of Distortion and Falsification* (1999).

Undoubtedly, Dadrian's magnum opus is the major study of the genocide itself to which reference was made earlier, *The History of the Armenian Genocide: Ethnic Conflict from the Balkans to Anatolia to the Caucasus* (1995). A work of substantial detail, it was both a distillation of all he had written over the previous two decades, and an extension of it. The very first words of Dadrian's Preface summarised his intentions:

> The present study has two principal goals: 1) to examine the World War I Armenian genocide through the vast corpus of official Ottoman-Turkish documents, as well as those of Imperial Germany and Imperial Austria, Turkey's wartime political and military allies; 2) to subject that genocide to a critical analysis from a historical perspective.
>
> (Dadrian, 1995: xv)

Through a painstaking narrative development, Dadrian described the background, initiation and unfolding of the genocide, and placed it within a conceptual framework of genocide theory. In this way he showed the extent to which the Turkish campaign of annihilation of the Armenian population was an obvious case of genocide, according to clear-cut social-science and legal criteria. Again, he made extensive use of sources from a wide variety of archival collections in a number of countries, and relied on his exceptional facility for reading original sources in their unadulterated form, without third-party translation, in Turkish, Armenian, German, French and English. His adherence to the sources, in fact, made his work an Armenian counterpart to that of **Raul Hilberg** on the Holocaust, and in the final section of the book – Part IX, 'A Review of the Armenian Genocide in a Comparative Perspective' – Dadrian made use of the research of scholars such as **Hilberg** for the purpose of further illustrating the saliency of the Armenian case as the great precedent of all twentieth-century genocides.

The History of the Armenian Genocide presented the event as a historical process in which a domestic conflict escalated dramatically, exacerbated by the tests of the global war crisis. The book was perhaps the most closely researched work on its topic up to that time, considering not only the detailed context in which the Genocide took place, but also the international politics surrounding it. In view of his approach, Dadrian's work was innovative within the scholarly literature on the Armenian Genocide, yet despite its title, the implementation of the Genocide itself occupied only a small part of the book. Dadrian amassed a great deal of evidence in order to demonstrate the slow build up of Turkish animosity towards the Armenians, and how this received a radical boost as a result of Turkey's entry into the First World War, and in this way he was able to ensure that his readers received a full grasp of why the Genocide occurred.

In overall terms, Dadrian's major theoretical approach to genocide is a critique of how power, when unchecked, can develop destructive characteristics that ultimately result in persecution leading to its ultimate expression. Indeed, this is exactly the point he draws from the Armenian situation at the end of the Ottoman phase of Turkish history:

> the most striking lesson to be derived from the reality of the Armenian Genocide is the paramount fact that both its perpetration and its ensuing denial is a function of one and the same condition, namely, overwhelming power. It is a kind of power

that is sustained before, during, and in the aftermath of the crime vis-à-vis a relatively weak and, therefore, vulnerable victim group. Denial is seen here as the logical extension of the very same conditions and processes that produced the genocide itself.

(Dadrian, 2002: 247)

What this translates to, in Dadrian's view, is a situation in which conflict between a potential perpetrator and a potential victim, coupled with a critical disparity in their respective power positions and the opportunity for the potential perpetrators to put their ideology into action, will be resolved through a resort to massive lethal violence after a number of preliminary steps of preparation and radicalisation take place (Dadrian, 2002: 248). It is only through the exercise of overwhelming power, moreover, that this can be carried out to its ultimate conclusion.

In a much-quoted endorsement, genocide scholar Roger Smith has written of Dadrian in the following terms:

> In the 1970s, Vahakn N. Dadrian helped to create the field of the Comparative Study of Genocide, bringing to his work an inter-disciplinary perspective that joined sociology, history and law, enriched further by his ability to draw upon half a dozen languages. He is also the foremost scholar of the Armenian Genocide, having devoted more than 30 years to research on virtually every aspect of it.
>
> (http://www.zoryaninstitute.org/Genocide/
> genocide_bio_dadrian.htm)

To this can be added the observation that his work has been translated into many different languages (including Turkish), and that his theoretical approaches on genocide have been absorbed by many within the field. A working scholar, still active in his eighties, Dadrian's thinking about the nature of genocide, and in particular its Armenian variant, has been both profound and influential, as it remains today.

Dadrian's major writings

'A Typology of Genocide', *International Review of Sociology*, 5, 2 (1975), 201–12.
'The Naim-Andonian Documents on the World War I Destruction of Ottoman Armenians: The Anatomy of a Genocide', *International Journal of Middle East Studies*, 18, 3 (August 1986), 311–60.

'The Role of Turkish Physicians in the World War I Genocide of the Armenians', *Holocaust and Genocide Studies*, 1, 2 (1986), 169–92.

'Genocide as a Problem of National and International Law: The World War I Armenian Case and Its Contemporary Legal Ramifications', *Yale Journal of International Law*, 14, 2 (Summer 1989), 1–134.

'The Documentation of the World War I Armenian Massacres in the Proceedings of the Turkish Military Tribunal', *International Journal of Middle East Studies*, 23, 4 (November 1991), 549–76.

'The Role of the Turkish Military in the Destruction of the Ottoman Armenians: A Study in Historical Continuities', *Journal of Political and Military Sociology*, 20, 2 (Winter 1992), 257–88.

'The Role of the Special Organisation in the Armenian Genocide during the First World War', in Panikos Panayi (ed.), *Minorities in Wartime*, Providence (RI): Berghahn Books, 1993, 50–82.

'The Secret Young Turk Ittihadist Conference and the Decision for the World War I Genocide of the Armenians', *Holocaust and Genocide Studies*, 7, 2 (1993), 173–201.

Haykakan Tsekhaspanut'iune Khorhtaranayin ev Patmagitakan Knnarkumnerov (The Treatment of the Ottoman Genocide by the Ottoman Parliament and its Historical Analysis), Watertown (MA): Baikar, 1995.

Jenosid Ulusal ve Uluslararasi Hukuk Sorunu Olarak: 1915 Ermeni Olay ve Hukuki Sonuçlar (Genocide as a Problem of National and International Law: The World War I Armenian Case and its Contemporary Legal Ramifications), Istanbul: Belge Uluslararas Yaynclk, 1995.

The History of the Armenian Genocide: Ethnic Conflict from the Balkans to Anatolia to the Caucasus, Providence (RI): Berghahn Books, 1995.

'The Comparative Aspects of the Armenian and Jewish Cases of Genocide: A Sociohistorical Perspective', in Alan S. Rosenbaum (ed.), *Is the Holocaust Unique?*, Boulder (CO): Westview Press, 1996, 101–35.

German Responsibility in the Armenian Genocide: A Review of the Historical Evidence of German Complicity, Watertown (MA): Blue Crane Books, 1996.

'The Armenian Genocide and the Legal and Political Issues in the Failure to Prevent or to Punish the Crime', *University of West Los Angeles Law Review*, 29 (1998), 43–78.

The Key Elements in the Turkish Denial of the Armenian Genocide: A Case Study of Distortion and Falsification, Cambridge (MA) and Toronto: Zoryan Institute, 1999.

Warrant for Genocide: Key Elements of Turko-Armenian Conflict, New Brunswick (NJ): Transaction Publishers, 1999.

'The Quest for Scholarship in My Pathos for the Armenian Tragedy and Its Victims', in Samuel Totten and Steven Leonard Jacobs (eds), *Pioneers of Genocide Studies*, New Brunswick (NJ): Transaction Publishers, 2002, 235–51.

'The Armenian Genocide: An Interpretation', in Jay Winter (ed.), *America and the Armenian Genocide of 1915*, Cambridge: Cambridge University Press, 2003, 52–100.

'Patterns of Twentieth Century Genocides: the Armenian, Jewish and Rwandan Cases', *Journal of Genocide Research*, 6, 4 (December 2004), 487–522.

'The Prefiguration of Some Aspects of the Holocaust in the Armenian Genocide (Revisiting the Comparative Perspective)', *Genocide Studies and Prevention*, 3, 1 (April 2008), 99–109.

LUCY S. DAWIDOWICZ (1915–90)

Lucy Schildkret Dawidowicz was a historian of the Holocaust, and the originator of the notion that Adolf Hitler and the Nazis waged a war against the Jewish people that was concurrent with the military war against the Allies. Born in 1915 to secular Jewish parents in New York, her interests in poetry and literature led her to Columbia University for an MA degree, which she never completed. Concerned about the fate of the Jews in Europe, she switched her interest to Jewish History at the suggestion of one of her teachers at the Sholom Aleichem Middle School, New York, Jacob Shatzky, a founder of the American branch of the Polish Jewish Scientific Institute (later renamed the Institute for Jewish Research but known by its acronym, YIVO). Her pursuit took her to Vilna, Lithuania, in 1938, where she studied until August 1939. This visit would later result in her first important book, *The Golden Tradition: Jewish Life and Thought in Eastern Europe* (1967), a documentary collection with a lengthy introductory essay written as a tribute to the world extinguished by Nazi brutality. From 1940 to 1946 she worked in the New York offices of YIVO, and in 1946 she travelled to Germany where she worked as a refugee aid worker with the American Jewish Joint Distribution Committee. Between 1948 and 1969 she undertook research for the American Jewish Committee, rising to the position of Research Director. In 1969 she left the AJC to teach Holocaust Studies at Yeshiva University, where she remained until her retirement.

Her most important work was *The War against the Jews, 1933–1945* (1975), which was later supplemented by a collection of documents entitled *A Holocaust Reader* (1976). In her introductory essay to *The War against the Jews*, 'The Subject – Definitions and Contours', she raised four questions that frame the entire book and which remain, even today, at the heart of Holocaust research:

1. How could it have happened?
2. How was it possible for a modern state to carry out the systematic murder of a whole people for no reason other than that they were Jews?

3. How was it possible for a whole people to allow itself to be destroyed?
4. How was it possible for the world to stand by without halting the destruction?

(Dawidowicz, 1975: xiii)

Her answer – that the extermination and annihilation of the Jews was the centre of the overall Nazi agenda – was one from which she never wavered. For Dawidowicz,

> The 'Jewish question' was, at bottom, a euphemism whose verbal neutrality concealed the user's impatience with the singularity of this people that did not appear to conform to the new political demands of the state. ... *'The Final Solution of the Jewish Question' in the National Socialist conception was not just another anti-Semitic undertaking, but a metahistorical program devised with an eschatological perspective* ... The Final Solution transcended the bounds of modern historical experience. Never before in modern history had one people made the killing of another the fulfillment of an ideology, in whose pursuit means were identical with ends. ... The German state, deciding that the Jews should not live, arrogated to itself the judgment as to whether a whole people had the right to existence, a judgment that no man and no state have the right to make.

(Dawidowicz, 1975: xiv–xv, emphasis added)

The Holocaust remained for Dawidowicz – and, she believed, for the Jewish people as a whole – at the very heart of existence. She revisited this notion and confirmed it further a decade later, in her Preface to *The Jewish Presence* (1977): 'The specter of the Holocaust continues to haunt Jews everywhere and to define their priorities. The imperative is Jewish survival, above all, the security of Israel. Anti-Semitism has not ceased to cast its shadow, especially in an atmosphere of brightness' (Dawidowicz, 1977: x).

In addition to 'telling the story', what set *The War against the Jews* apart from other one-volume histories were her two appendices: (A) 'The Fate of the Jews in Hitler's Europe', and (B) 'The Final Solution in Figures'. As she noted:

> Appendix A, 'The Fate of the Jews in Hitler's Europe,' is an attempt to put on record the essential bare facts about the Jews in each European country. Each country is considered individually

and its wartime status described. A sketch of that country's prewar Jewish population follows, and then the course of the Final Solution in the country is briefly recounted. It was my intention here to provide, in a kind of historical shorthand, a summary account of the fate of the European Jews during World War II and, at the same time, within the limits of the presentation, to enable the reader to distinguish those political, historical, social, and geographic factors that accounted for the different treatment accorded to the Jews in various countries.

(Dawidowicz, 1975: xviii)

She then briefly summarised the respective fates of the Jews of France, Belgium, Luxembourg, the Netherlands, Italy, Norway, Denmark, Finland, Germany and Austria, Czechoslovakia, the Protectorate of Bohemia and Moravia, Slovakia, Hungary, Rumania, Bulgaria, Yugoslavia, Greece, Poland and the Soviet Union.

Her accounting in Appendix B – 'Estimated Number of Jews Killed in the Final Solution' – put the total at 5,933,900, and was divided into four columns: (1) Country (she numbers 21 in her list), (2) Estimated Pre-Final Solution Population (total 8,861,800), (3) Estimated Jewish Population Annihilated (5,933,900), and (4) Percentage of Jewish Population Loss (from 11 per cent in Russia to 90 per cent in Poland, the Baltic countries and Germany/Austria). In approximately fifty pages she thus cogently summarised the key elements of her much larger text of more than 350 pages.

Dawidowicz's approach was careful and methodical, as she considered many of the social, political and economic dimensions of German life before and during the Holocaust. The first part of the book detailed the origins and growth of the phenomenon of Nazi anti-Semitism, and how the Nazi campaign to destroy the Jews of Europe drew inspiration from deep wells of centuries-old Jew-hatred. The second part, entitled 'The Holocaust', described how the plight of the Jews – already made untenable owing to confinement in barbaric conditions in Nazi-imposed ghettos – worsened with the acceleration of the war crisis from mid-1941 onwards, and how anti-Semitic violence thereafter intensified the longer the war lasted. She described how the nature of existence for those living in camps and ghettos was intended to wear them down, until a vast number succumbed through general hardship, mistreatment, disease, starvation and exposure. The most telling element of the work, however, related to her argument that the Nazis waged a war against the Jews that was no less real than that against the Allies, only employing different means.

A spin-off from this study was a collection of edited documents entitled *A Holocaust Reader* (1976). It was divided into two parts, together with a running narrative of comments from the editor herself. Part One, 'The Final Solution', dealt with the Nazi plan to exterminate Europe's Jews, and included anti-Semitic Nazi legislation, minutes from meetings, and various orders. Part Two, 'The Holocaust', considered Jewish life in Germany during the pre-war years between 1933 and 1939; the ghettos in Eastern Europe; and the deportations of Jews during the Holocaust years. The nature of the documents ranged from personal accounts to official government records of all sorts, and Dawidowicz, in keeping with her approach in *The Destruction of the European Jews*, covered a broad spectrum of document types and topics.

Immediately after this, she published a collection of essays, *The Jewish Presence: Essays on Identity and History* (1977). This book was based on a series of essays she had written over the course of the previous few years, in which she had disseminated her ideas about a variety of historical and contemporary topics. The majority of these had earlier been published in what was at that time a Jewish monthly magazine with an orientation towards the political left, *Commentary*. Many of her ideas were controversial, but as an essayist she did not baulk when faced with an argument; indeed, she would face a number of opponents in her writing. Looking at the nature of Dawidowicz's arguments, Neal Kozodoy, the editor of *Commentary* between 1995 and 2009, argued in her favour that 'the unyielding emphasis which Mrs Dawidowicz, in common now with other traditional historians of the period, placed on the role of human agency and personal will, as opposed to impersonal historical or institutional "forces," in the execution of Nazi ideas, remains fully validated' (Kozodoy, 1992: 36). In 1992, shortly after her death, Kozodoy collected more of Dawidowicz's *Commentary* essays, and published them, posthumously, as *What Is the Use of Jewish History? Essays by Lucy S. Dawidowicz*. This contained more of her thoughts on such subjects as the Jews in America, modern Jewish identity, Holocaust denial, and the impact of the Holocaust on the Jewish future.

Casting her net beyond the writing of disparate essays, in 1981 she began examining the issue of the centrality of the Holocaust from the perspective of other national groups and non-Jewish historians. The six essays comprising *The Holocaust and the Historians* (1981) looked at how the event has been treated by British, American, German, Russian, Polish and Jewish historians. While recognising that the 'Jewish story' is not at the heart of other national narratives, and that those scholars who choose to address it would not necessarily share the same 'empathy and moral concern' (Dawidowicz, 1981: 2), the question remained for her 'why so many contemporary historians have neglected a subject that has, in intellectual circles, raised fundamental questions about Western civilization and Christian morality' (Dawidowicz, 1981: 3). *The Holocaust and the Historians* contained harsh critiques of many contemporary historians, as Dawidowicz examined several existing theories of the event. One of her major concerns lay in her observation that the Holocaust had, up to that time, been either a subject of relative neglect (by historians in the English-speaking world), benign denial (in the case of the then-USSR and Poland), or exculpation (as part of a longer German historiographical tradition). She laid down a challenge that has certainly been picked up in the three decades since it was penned:

> Despite the historians' neglect, courses in the history of the Holocaust, its literature, and its theological implications have proliferated, especially in those colleges and universities with substantial Jewish enrollments. These courses often function as a Jewish equivalent to Black Studies, that is, as ethnic gratification rather than bona fide academic offerings. Actually, just a few history departments have incorporated the history of the Holocaust into their curricula of modern European history. Only when the Holocaust is accepted as a suitable subject for such study and is not regarded merely as an adjunct of ethnic studies will it have attained its proper academic recognition.
>
> (Kozodoy, 1992: 35)

It is perhaps a testament to Dawidowicz's pugnacity that the path she forecast has in fact been travelled by the academy, and that core education on the Holocaust not only proliferates in universities in the Western world today, but that it is also mandated throughout the secondary education sectors of many states and countries.

In his obituary for Dawidowicz, Neal Kozodoy wrote of her 'obligation to her murdered kin, the Jews of Europe', and her 'compulsion to set down a record already seen by her as slipping away in forgetfulness and selective distortion' (Kozodoy, 1992: 35). Here, he was tapping into a very rich part of Dawidowicz's life journey. She recounted part of this in *From That Place and Time: A Memoir, 1938–1947* (1989), describing the vibrancy of Jewish life in Eastern Europe, the horrors of the war, and relations with survivors and perpetrators afterwards. The book simultaneously presented the seminal moments in modern Jewish history and the formative moments in the life of its author.

After her death, Kozodoy further observed of Dawidowicz that:

> She was truly obsessed with the memory of the dead – or rather, with the memory of the living who had disappeared, not only from the earth but from the history books, our designated preservers of memory. ... Through the project of establishing a true and faithful record of the living and the dead, through the project of guarding that record from distortion and defilement, Lucy Dawidowicz meant to assume her own activist share of responsibility for Jewish history.
>
> (Kozodoy, 1992: 37)

He also noted that she was particularly exercised by those who argued not only for the complicity of various Jewish groups in their own demise, but also their passivity in the face of their own destruction:

> She for her part categorically repudiated the share of collective passivity, let alone of collusion. The irrefutable point, she demonstrated again and again, was that just as the trapped and encircled European Jews had been innocent of provoking, so they were powerless to repeal, the total, unrelenting fury loosed upon them. During the war the point, for someone like her, had been to commit every moral and spiritual resource to the Allied effort to defeat the fury by dint of countervailing arms. After the war, the point (for her) was not only to understand the fury but to render upon it a definitive historical judgment – and in this way, for the victims, to raise up a memorial.
>
> (Kozodoy, 1992: 36)

Lucy Dawidowicz concerned herself with a number of historical issues. These included painstakingly constructing the actual record based upon the documentary evidence, letting the accuracy of the record serve as its own memorial and keeping the memory of the victims alive, and refuting those on both the political right and left who she truly believed distorted that record for other purposes. She also contested what she regarded as the baseless charges of complicity and passivity (potentially to be misinterpreted as 'cowardice'); rejected the idea of impersonal forces in place of human choice; and addressed Jewish concerns with anti-Semitism, framed by the full awareness of the Holocaust. All these issues remain at the forefront of Holocaust history and historiography two decades after her death, not only within the academy but also throughout Jewish communities. In such light, they mark her as a strong and feisty advocate of historical truth and of the Jewish people.

Dawidowicz's major works

The Golden Tradition: Jewish Life and Thought in Eastern Europe, Boston: Beacon Press, 1967.

The War against the Jews, 1933–1945, New York: Holt, Rinehart and Winston, 1975.

(Ed.) The Holocaust Reader, New York: Behrman House, 1976.

The Jewish Presence: Essays on Identity and History, New York: Holt, Rinehart and Winston, 1977.

The Holocaust and the Historians, Cambridge (MA): Harvard University Press, 1981.

From That Place and Time: A Memoir, 1938–1947, New York: Norton, 1989.

What is the Use of Jewish History? Essays by Lucy S. Dawidowicz (ed., Neal Kozodoy), New York: Schocken Books, 1992.

Reference

Kozodoy, Neal, 'In Memoriam: Lucy S. Dawidowicz', Commentary (May 1992), 35–37.

TERRENCE DES PRES (1939–86)

Terrence Des Pres was an American Professor of English Literature best known for his theories on the survival of concentration camp prisoners under the Nazis and Soviets. Born in Illinois in 1939 and raised in Missouri, for 15 years prior to his sudden early death at the age of 47 he held the Crawshaw Chair in English Literature at Colgate University, Hamilton, New York. An author, poet and political activist with an often-troubled humanitarian conscience, in 1976 Des Pres published The Survivor: An Anatomy of Life in the Death Camps. This looked at the question of survival from the point of view of the survivors themselves, making an in-depth investigation of accounts written by former concentration camp prisoners. The book rapidly became a bestseller. It was soon republished in a cheap paperback edition, and lengthy excerpts were reproduced in feature magazines throughout the English-speaking world.

Until then, analysis of prisoner behaviour had largely been dominated by the writings of psychologist (and former prisoner of

Buchenwald and Dachau) Bruno Bettelheim and those who agreed with him. The prevailing view was that survival in the concentration camp was essentially a random occurrence, in which the actions of the prisoners themselves counted for little. Bettelheim's key argument regarding prisoner behaviour, for example, held that the Nazis had instituted a highly complex camp regime designed to break the prisoners' will to resist Nazi directives, the major effect of which would produce changes in the prisoners' own psychological perceptions of themselves; thus, the longer they remained incarcerated, the more they came to identify with the goals of their persecutors, along the way regressing to a state of childlike helplessness and dependence.

In contrast, Des Pres argued that prisoners struggled at every turn to find ways of staying alive in the camps, despite the conditions under which they were compelled to exist. In developing his position, Des Pres introduced a new term, 'excremental assault', to help explain the debasements to which prisoners were treated as a means of reducing their sense of self-worth. He showed how prisoners were systematically subjected to their own personal filth, denied the use of adequate sanitary conditions, fed a diet in which diarrhoea was commonplace, surrounded by diseases; prisoners soiling themselves was a common experience. They were, under such circumstances, literally assaulted by their own excrement, in what were very often rituals of degradation that had been carefully thought out in advance by the guards. This policy, which aimed at the complete humiliation and debasement of the prisoners, often led them to so revile themselves that they gave up wanting to live. Such spiritual destruction, especially in the wartime Nazi camps, became an end in itself – particularly as the SS guards were able to compare their superior status and clean clothes with the ragged, starving and filthy prisoners under their unchallengeable rule. The process also served the purpose of dehumanising the prisoners in the eyes of the SS, making the task of extermination easier and more palatable. 'Excremental assault', therefore, served a twofold purpose: to destroy the inner souls and self-esteem of those forced to endure it, and to elevate the status of the guards in their own eyes, while at the same time reducing any misgivings they may have had towards the destruction of those whom they saw living in their own filth. For Des Pres, the calculated nature of this strategy only served to make the horrendous situation even more morally appalling and cruel. Des Pres's message here was one focusing on a positive affirmation of the human spirit, regardless of the degradation and violence to which the prisoners were subjected on a daily basis.

The Survivor was based exclusively on the published accounts of Nazi concentration camp and Soviet gulag survivors themselves. Des Pres built his picture of life in the camps this way in order to allow the former inmates to tell their own story, and in so doing he advanced the position of survivor testimony as a specific genre of memoir literature. While fiction had an important part to play in creating a mood or developing an imagined narrative – what Des Pres referred to as 'an ideal lucidity' – it was survivor testimony that really cut to the heart of what might be referred to as the reality of the extreme situation:

> To come from fiction to documents is to move ... to the dense anguish of men and women telling as straightforwardly as they know how the story of what they saw and endured in the passage through the concentration camps. Their testimony is given in memory, told in pain and often clumsily, with little thought for style or rhetorical device. The experience they describe, further-more, resists the tendency to fictionalize which informs most remembering.
>
> (Des Pres, 1976: 29)

For Des Pres, there is thus a certain dimension of truth in survivor testimony which is absent elsewhere. Once the dry statistical data of a prisoner's incarceration are known – the 'why' and 'where' elements of a prisoner's life, which generally differ from one person to another – the contours of the camp experience appear remarkably uniform:

> the world survivors speak of has been so rigidly shaped by necessity, and so completely shared ... that from one report to the next the degree of consistency is unusually high. The facts lie embedded in a fixed configuration; fixed, we may come to believe, by the nature of existence when life is circumscribed by death.
>
> (Des Pres, 1976: 29)

Therefore, survivors aim to tell their stories in as clear a manner as possible, the better to be able to convey the essence of what they went through.

Basing himself on this material, Des Pres concluded that 'survival is an experience with a definite structure, neither random nor regressive nor amoral' (Des Pres, 1976: v). He argued against the mistaken notion that a 'state of nature' prevailed in the concentration camps, or that a war of all against all necessarily erupts as soon as constraints are removed. For otherwise, primary aspects of the camp experience – group formation, 'organizing,' sharing and the giving of gifts – are evidence amounting to proof that in man social instincts operate with the authority and momentum of life itself, and never more forcefully than when survival is the issue.

(Des Pres, 1976: 197)

By utilising testimonial literature, he believed he could portray 'a world ruled by death, but also a world of actual living conditions, of *ways of life* which are the basis and achievement of life in extremity' (Des Pres, 1976: v, emphasis in original). In short, Des Pres held that life in the Nazi concentration camps and Soviet gulags was intensely social, and depended on such fundamental elements of human behaviour as the maintenance of a sense of dignity and conscience, on helping and sharing activities between individuals and groups, and on forms of collective resistance at every level of the camp experience.

In a major confrontation with Bruno Bettelheim three years after the appearance of *The Survivor* – during which time Bettelheim refused to accept that Des Pres's arguments about a positive prisoner society had any validity – Des Pres put forth the view that, while 'to defeat Auschwitz was plainly not possible', nonetheless 'from the beginning a group of prisoners had organized themselves to try' (Des Pres, 1979: 624). This indicated, in his view, the degree to which concentration camp inmates refused to bend before the SS onslaught. Moreover – and this was the crux of his argument both before and after his showdown with Bettelheim in 1979:

What counted for survivors was finding *ways to live* in places like Auschwitz, then endure the death marches, and then, in places like Belsen and Dachau, hold themselves together in body and spirit against sickness, against extreme exhaustion and starvation *until* the Allies arrived. How ordinary men and women, with no resources but themselves, were able to do this *is* a 'main question' [in contrast to Bettelheim's criticisms], and even provisional answers can give us invaluable information about man *in extremis*.

(Des Pres, 1979: 624, emphasis in original)

He identified this type of behaviour as 'positive coping'.

As a poet and humanist, Des Pres had a distinctive perspective on concentration camp survival. He defined this as 'the capacity of men and women to live beneath the pressure of protracted crisis, to sustain terrible damage in mind and body and yet to be there, sane, alive, still human' (Des Pres, 1976: v). The major concern here was thus with life, and how people managed to sustain it in an environment dedicated to its destruction. Des Pres considered those who survived in such conditions as heroic, and thereby challenged the Western literary and cultural tradition which otherwise considers warriors and martyrs – that is, those who are extra-human – as the real heroes. For Des Pres, ordinary humans who, by simply surviving, defied an entire system bent on their annihilation, were heroic beyond anything Western literature or folk culture could conceive.

Yet his concern was not with survival for survival's sake. Staying alive without compromising one's morality or inner integrity was what made concentration camp survivors heroic; as Des Pres wrote, the ideal was 'To come through; to keep a living soul in a living body' (Des Pres, 1976: 6). And what was this push for survival? From whence did it come? In the case of the Holocaust, Des Pres held that the contrast between life and death in the camps was as profound as that between an affirmation of goodness on the one hand, and a demonic principle on the other. The death camps of the Third Reich were, for Des Pres, the ultimate expression of the demonic:

> What went on in the killing centers was highly organized and very dependable indeed: routines were established, and different methods of killing were experimented with; solid bureaucratic systems implemented the extermination process at every stage of its operation, and large numbers of men and women went daily about their jobs fully aware that the entire aim and final product of this modernized factory system was death.
>
> (Des Pres, 1991: 55)

Dedicating themselves to the production of death rendered the Nazis, in Des Pres's view, as a party committed to 'a demonic principle of the first degree' (Des Pres, 1991: 55). They viewed life's primary obligation as the cultivation and achievement of mass death. The singularity of the Holocaust was the world's most obnoxious event, for

> Unlike any example of genocide I can think of from the thick history of mankind's inhumanity … the destruction of the European Jews had no rational motive whatsoever, neither

political nor plunder, neither military strategy nor the moment's blind expediency. Jews did not obstruct Hitler's war aims, nor were they in any sense a threat to national security. This was genocide for the sake of genocide.

(Des Pres, 1991: 55–56)

Little wonder, then, that in the concentration camps 'spiritual damage sustained without capitulation' equates to 'absolute power which turns out to be less than absolute' (Des Pres, 1991: 62). For Des Pres, this is at the core of everything.

The debate between Terrence Des Pres and Bruno Bettelheim over prisoner behaviour in the concentration camps breathed new life into questions about survivorship, which had been long stagnant owing to Bettelheim's previous dominance over the field. Des Pres was responsible for stimulating a major transformation in the nature of scholarship in this area, and, since the appearance of *The Survivor*, an entire literature addressing issues of survival in extremity – in which both Bettelheim and Des Pres are acknowledged – has emerged.

In addition to his groundbreaking work concerning prisoner behaviour in Nazi concentration camps and Soviet gulags, Terrence Des Pres was also active with regard to other issues in Genocide Studies, ranging from advocacy of the veracity of the Armenian Genocide of 1915–23 to a discussion on mass killing at Treblinka, to literary approaches to understanding totalitarianism, to reflections on how death is represented in literature. Unfortunately, these aspects of his work were little known outside of a narrow circle, and his meditations on such matters were always subordinate to his pathbreaking – indeed, field-transforming – studies of life and death (but above all, life) in the Nazi and Soviet concentration camps.

Des Pres's major writings

'The Survivor: On the Ethos of Survival in Extremity', *Encounter*, 37, 3 (September 1971), 3–19.

The Survivor: An Anatomy of Life in the Death Camps, New York: Oxford University Press, 1976.

'The Bettelheim Problem', *Social Research*, 46, 4 (Winter 1979), 619–47.

'Holocaust Laughter?', in Berel Lang (ed.), *Writing and the Holocaust*, New York: Holmes and Meier, 1988.

Praises and Dispraises: Poetry and Politics, the 20th Century, New York: Viking, 1988.

Writing into the World: Essays, 1973–1978, New York: Viking Penguin, 1991.

References

Bettelheim, Bruno, 'Individual and Mass Behavior in Extreme Situations', *Journal of Abnormal and Social Psychology*, 38, 4 (October 1943), 417–52.

Bettelheim, Bruno, *The Informed Heart: Autonomy in a Mass Age*, Glencoe (IL): Free Press, 1960.

Bettelheim, Bruno, *Surviving, and Other Essays*, London: Thames and Hudson, 1979.

A. ROY ECKARDT AND ALICE LYONS ECKARDT (1918–98)

It is rare when a husband and wife contribute significantly, both together and independently, to enlarge our understanding of a given field of academic endeavour and inquiry. Such was the case, however, with A. Roy Eckardt and Alice Lyons Eckardt, both former faculty members at Lehigh University, Pennsylvania. (One thinks, too, of **Barbara Harff** and **Ted Robert Gurr**, also included in this volume.)

A. Roy Eckardt was born in 1918 in Brooklyn, New York, and died in Coopersburg, Pennsylvania, in 1998. After a number of short-term positions, he taught at Lehigh University from 1951 until his retirement in 1980. Alice Lyons Eckardt was born in 1923, also in Brooklyn, and taught at Lehigh University between 1972 and 1987. Together, Roy and Alice Eckardt formed a dynamic team, making a significant contribution to the nature of how Christian anti-Semitism can be approached in a post-Auschwitz environment.

What initially animated Roy Eckardt's doctoral work was not the Holocaust, but rather the 'why' of anti-Semitism within the overall structure of Christianity itself. Eckardt had studied at Union Theological Seminary with such giants of Christian thought as Paul Tillich and Reinhold Niebuhr. He argued that the Christian affirmation of Jesus as the Christ did *not* exclude Jews from the salvation of God, and that their own Covenant was not diminished or superseded. Two years earlier, in an article entitled 'The Theology of the Jewish Question', he had already dealt with the 'temptation' of anti-Semitism within (and seemingly inherent in) Christianity itself. From this initial concern, moving towards addressing the Holocaust in its totality was something of a logical progression. It remained so throughout the rest of his life, as did his struggle to define a Protestant and Catholic Christianity freed of both anti-Semitism and super-cessionism, and the building of bridges between Jews and Christians seriously investing themselves in a dialogical relationship.

Already by 1965, the Eckardts had come to the unalterable conclusion that two thousand years of Christian antipathy towards the Jews had provided a fertile environment in which German National Socialism could thrive and flourish, drawing upon seeds already well planted and nurtured in the past. Summing up many of their early thoughts on the matter, they wrote later that 'it was the anti-Jewish problematic within Christian teaching and the history of Christianity that finally led us, perhaps inexorably, to the Holocaust' (Eckardt and Eckardt, 1978: 227). It was in 1965 that Roy arranged a symposium in the *Journal of Bible and Religion* (of which he was editor), the official organ of the American Academy of Religion, soliciting contributions from biblical scholars Samuel Sandmel, Malcolm L. Diamond and Manfred Vogel. Eckardt's own provocative contribution, 'Can There Be a Jewish–Christian Relationship?', illustrated the central ideas and emphases that were to populate much of his writing, particularly with regard to the interconnectivity between anti-Semitism and the Holocaust.

One of the key points in Eckardt's essay showed him to be most concerned to address the 1965 Roman Catholic document *Nostra Aetate* (Latin: *In Our Time*), which exonerated the Jewish people for any role in the death of Jesus while at the same time repudiating anti-Semitism as inimical to the Church itself. It heralded a sea change in both Jewish–Catholic, and, later, Jewish–Protestant relations, but for Roy Eckardt its lack of self-reflection was telling:

> Yet in vain does one search the draft ... for even the slightest mark of Christian contrition, for even a single word of recognition that the church of Jesus Christ has been a knowing and willing participant in the centuries-long demonry of antisemitism.
>
> (A. Roy Eckardt, 1965: 124)

Not one to be shy when confronting the enormity of anti-Semitism and the Holocaust, he went even further:

> in the present instance, while the voices are voices which would foster understanding, the hands are hands which have clasped death: the death of Christendom, the 'death of God,' and the deaths of six million Jews. How admirable of us now to exonerate the Jewish people for all their reputed transgression! Could there be a more damning judgment upon the church of our century than this one – that not until after the day of Auschwitz did Christians see fit to fabricate a correction for the record?
>
> (A. Roy Eckardt, 1965: 124)

Two years later, in 1967, he published a reflection that marked him as a major figure not only in Jewish–Christian relations but in post-Holocaust thought as well: *Elder and Younger Brothers: The Encounter of Jews and Christians*. Here, Eckardt re-presented his contention that Christian anti-Semitism paved the way for Nazism, but, more importantly, he argued that such behaviour represented paganism's war against God and the Gentile world's war against Jesus Christ. In an important Appendix entitled 'Again, Silence in the Churches', Eckardt introduced his co-author, Alice Lyons Eckardt, and together they condemned the lack of public voice of all of Christendom in response to the threat to Israel's very existence in the 1967 Arab–Israel War:

> We submit, in sum, that the overwhelming moral force of the case for Israel makes it impossible either to explain or to justify the new silence of the churches through the contention that the evidence is either lacking or equivocal. Accordingly, we are led to seek other reasons for the silence.
>
> (Eckardt and Eckardt, 1967: 169)

Sadly and tragically, they found it in the Arab peoples' conviction, shared by many Christians as well, 'that Israel deserves to die'. They concluded:

> The moral tragedy is that the only tangible way open to us to atone for our historic crimes against original Israel is by assuming a special responsibility for the rights and welfare of Jews. The present refusal to bear this obligation may well reflect the Christian community's wish to exonerate itself from culpability for the long years of antisemitism.
>
> Karl Barth once said: 'In order to be chosen we must, for good or ill, either be Jews or else be heart and soul on the side of the Jews.' It almost seems that the entire history of Christianity, including the churches' current response to the Middle Eastern crisis, has been an attempt to make Barth's words as irrelevant as is humanly possible. Writing as Christians who oppose that attempt, we say to our Jewish brothers: we too have been shocked by this new silence. And we are greatly saddened. But we have not been surprised. The causes of the silence lie deep in the Christian soul. Therefore we can only mourn and pray and hope.
>
> (Eckardt and Eckardt, 1967: 176–77)

In 1974, Alice Eckardt published her first piece on the *Shoah*. In 'The Holocaust: Christian and Jewish Responses', published in the

Journal of the American Academy of Religion, she laid the groundwork for her own subsequent writing (Alice L. Eckardt, 1974: 453–69). Here, she asserted that 'Christianity had failed to grasp the crucial nature of the questions raised by the Holocaust for its own theology and future, just as it generally has refused to admit any responsibility for the death camps' (Alice L. Eckardt, 1974: 453). These were themes to which she would return in ensuing publications.

In a reflective piece written in 1979 dealing with the Christian approach to Yom Hashoah, the Jewish Holocaust Memorial Day, she wrote: 'I am convinced that no Christian service should be without a penitential confession of Christian failings and culpability. Since every confession of sin and repentance are part of every Christian worship, to omit a specific confession on this occasion would be a continuation of earlier sin' (Alice L. Eckardt, 1979: 1). She then enumerated six *mitzvot* (Hebrew: divine obligations) on the part of those constructing such liturgies:

1. Do not 'Christianize' the Holocaust.
2. Do not turn the Holocaust experience into a demonstration of the truth of the Christian gospel.
3. Do not use readings from Jewish sources and then criticize, refute, or reinterpret them to fit Christian views.
4. Do not attempt to strip the Holocaust of its terrifying and awesome character.
5. Remember the total abandonment Jews experienced.
6. Finally, do not allow a Yom Hashoah service to become a one-time occurrence.

(Alice L. Eckardt, 1979: 1–4)

In a similar vein, she later enumerated six 'commandments' that all Christians should follow:

1. Remember the Holocaust not as a dead past but as a burning challenge to our present conscience; as 'true history,' simultaneously past, present, and future.
2. Remember in pain.
3. Remember in dread.
4. Remember in solidarity.
5. Remember in compassion.
6. Remember in love.

(Alice L. Eckardt, 1981: 37–41)

As early appointees to the US presidential commission tasked with developing a rationale for the construction of a United States Holocaust Memorial Museum, in 1979 Roy and Alice Eckardt travelled with a group of colleagues to Poland, the Soviet Union, Denmark and Israel, and in 1981 they reported on their trip. Most importantly, they raised the question 'What are some of the lessons and the consequences that our experience may bring to the morphology of a living memorial in this country?' Answering their own question, they concluded:

1. Somehow the witness of such a place as Nes Amim [a Christian community in the western Galilee which has the goal of educating Chrstians about Judaism and Israel], and the axis for which it stands, ought to become integral to the life of our memorial.
2. An American memorial to the victims of the Holocaust ought to reflect the distinctive treatment of the universalist-particularist dilemma that is coming to prevail more and more with the ethos of our country.
3. A unique way is open for the Washington memorial to focus true universalism.
4. Those who know something about the character of antisemitism are entirely aware that strictly Jewish insistence upon the particularity of the Holocaust, however truthful, becomes that much more raw material for the ever-ready antisemites.
5. Reinhold Niebuhr taught us that self-righteousness is the most stubborn and ravishing sin that can infect any human collectivity.
6. The pearl of greatest price is a wholehearted American effort to witness to the truth, the truth of the Holocaust of the Jews.
   (Eckardt and Eckardt, 1981: 103–14)

As Christian theologians, the Eckardts later turned their eyes towards the necessity of a 'restructured and revitalized theology', and demanded of their community that

> The church needs to put an end to all teachings of superiority and claims to exclusive possession of the means of salvation. ... The church must cease once and for all its presentation of the Jewish people as the enemies of God and the children of Satan, as well as the murderers of God, for the issue is far more than a religious one ... we must stop asserting that the cross constitutes the ultimate in human suffering ... the Holocaust not only exposed the extent of the church's anti-Jewish theology, but

it also revealed the shallowness of its devotion to its own love ethic.

(Eckardt and Eckardt, 1982a: 111–25)

In the same vein, Roy also wrote that 'Forgiveness for God may be possible if he can still somehow manage to leave his gifts at the altar and go and be reconciled with his human children. He has sinned against life, and life can only be vindicated through life. God has one chance left – *kiveyakhol*? – to be saved. He must do two things: seek human forgiveness, and act to redeem himself' (A. Roy Eckardt, 1982: 61). Some of these same sentiments would be further echoed and enlarged upon by Alice in a major article in 1986, published in the prestigious journal *Holocaust and Genocide Studies* (Alice L. Eckardt, 1986).

As a corollary to these theological issues, Roy also concerned himself with matters related to the resurrection of the Christ-figure, nowhere better illustrated than in a series of questions he asked in 1989:

- How can the resurrection of Jesus be proclaimed as a special act of God without the Christian triumphalism that paved the way to Belzec and Sobibor?
- Is not the resurrection in and of itself a form of Christian supercessionism?
- How can the Christian church escape supercessionism and triumphalism while continuing to proclaim as a realised fact the resurrection of Jesus Christ?
- In its claim that the resurrection of Jesus concretely means God's triumph over death, is not the church inevitably implying its own triumph over non-Christian faith?
- In the resurrection does not God (reputedly) confirm the Christian gospel in the sense of a definitive embodiment of objective truth?
- Does not the resurrection appear as a divinely wrought displacement event?
- Is it possible, or how is it possible, to proclaim Jesus' resurrection in a nontriumphalist way?

(A. Roy Eckardt, 1989: 321)

To really drive the point home, he framed his comments with the equally provocative question, 'Is the Christian message morally credible?' (A. Roy Eckardt, 1989: 318).

Subsequent to Roy's death in 1998, Alice continued to write with the verve with which the two began their collaboration, including revising and enlarging what may very well be their most important contribution to post-Holocaust Christian thought, *Long Night's Journey into Day: Life and Faith after the Holocaust* (1982). In that work, the Eckardts addressed such difficult issues as human and demonic culpability for the Holocaust; God's own guilt for what transpired; and the possibilities of forgiveness. In so doing, they provocatively challenged the central idea of Christian tragedy, namely, the crucifixion of the Christ-figure, and argued that the Holocaust may very well supplant it as the ultimate example of God-forsakenness.

Collaboratively and individually, A. Roy Eckardt and Alice Lyons Eckardt were among the most important voices in the Christian world for three decades, confronting the members of their faith community not only with the historical and theological reality of the Holocaust, but the anti-Semitic precedents within Christianity itself. Throughout a lengthy and fruitful scholarly partnership, they attempted to reconstruct a faith meaningful to themselves and others, and to build bridges between the Christian community and the wounded Jewish people.

Major writings

NOTE: It can be difficult to separate the work of the Eckardts into areas of discrete authorship, as their collaboration took many forms – some of which were informal as to attribution. The following, however, should serve as a guide to their various activities, jointly and independently.

A. Roy Eckardt

'Can There Be a Jewish–Christian Relationship?' *Journal of Bible and Religion*, 33, 2 (1965), 122–30.

Elder and Younger Brothers: The Encounter of Jews and Christians, New York: Charles Scribner's Sons, 1967.

Your People, My People: The Meeting of Jews and Christians, New York: Quadrangle Books, 1974.

'The Holocaust and the Enigma of Uniqueness: A Philosophical Effort at Practical Clarification', *Annals of the American Academy of Political and Social Science*, 450 (1980), 165–78.

'Yom Ha-Shoah Commandments: A Christian Declaration', *Midstream*, XXVII, 4 (1981), 37–41.

'Ha'Shoah as Christian Revolution: Toward the Liberation of Righteousness', *Quarterly Review*, 2, 4 (1982), 52–67.

'Power and Powerlessness: The Jewish Experience', in Israel W. Charny (ed.), *Toward the Understanding and Prevention of Genocide: Proceedings of the*

International Conference on the Holocaust and Genocide, Boulder (CO): Westview Press, 1984, 183–96.

Jews and Christians: The Contemporary Meeting, Bloomington: Indiana University Press, 1986.

'Is There a Way Out of the Christian Crime? The Philosophic Question of the Holocaust', *Holocaust and Genocide Studies*, 1, 1 (1986), 121–26.

'The Holocaust, the Church Struggle, and some Christian Reflections', in Richard Libowitz (ed.), *Faith and Freedom: A Tribute to Franklin H. Littell*, Oxford: Pergamon Press, 1987, 31–44.

'The *Kristallnacht* Pogrom: Christian Perspectives Then and Now', *Mosaic*, 5 (1989), 42–74.

'The *Shoah* and the Affirmation of the Resurrection of Jesus: A Revisionist Marginal Note', in Alan L. Berger (ed.), *Bearing Witness to the Holocaust, 1939–1989*, Lewiston (NY): The Edwin Mellen Press, 1991, 313–31.

Collecting Myself: A Writer's Retrospective, Atlanta: Scholars Press, 1993.

On the Way to Death: Essays toward a Comic Vision, New Brunswick (NJ): Transaction Publishers, 1996.

Alice L. Eckardt

Encounter with Israel: A Challenge to Conscience, New York: Association Press, 1970.

'The Holocaust: Christian and Jewish Responses', *Journal of the American Academy of Religion*, XLII, 3 (1974), 453–69.

'In Consideration of Christian Yom Hashoah Liturgies', *Shoah: A Review of Holocaust Studies and Commemorations*, 1, 4 (1979), 1–4.

'Yom Ha-Shoah Commandments: A Christian Declaration', *Midstream*, XXVII, 4 (1981), 37–41.

'Post-Holocaust Theology: A Journey Out of the Kingdom of Night', *Holocaust and Genocide Studies*, 1, 2 (1986), 229–40.

(Ed.) *Burning Memory: Times of Testing and Reckoning*, Oxford: Pergamon Press, 1993.

A. Roy and Alice L. Eckardt

'Again, Silence in the Churches', in A. Roy Eckardt, *Elder and Younger Brothers: The Encounter of Jews and Christians*, New York: Charles Scribner's Sons, 1967.

'Studying the Holocaust's Impact Today: Some Dilemmas of Language and Method', *Judaism*, 27, 2 (1978), 222–32.

'Travail of a Presidential Commission Confronting the Enigma of the Holocaust', *Encounter*, XLII, 2 (1981), 103–14.

'After the Holocaust: Some Christian Considerations', in Norma H. Thompson and Bruce K. Cole (eds), *The Future of Jewish–Christian Relations*, Schenectady (NY): Character Research Press, 1982a, 111–25.

Long Night's Journey into Day: Life and Faith after the Holocaust, Detroit: Wayne State University Press, 1982b.
Long Night's Journey into Day: A Revised Retrospective on the Holocaust, Detroit: Wayne State University Press, 1988.

EMIL L. FACKENHEIM (1916–2003)

Emil Ludwig Fackenheim was a Jewish philosopher and rabbi, and a scholar of the relationship between God and man in the aftermath of the Holocaust. Born in 1916 in Halle, Germany, he witnessed the final flickerings of the *Haskalah*, the encounter between Judaism and the eighteenth-century Enlightenment. He studied at Halle University, and enrolled at the *Haskalah*-oriented *Hochschule für die Wissenschaft des Judentums* in Berlin. After studying under Rabbi Dr Leo Baeck, the acknowledged leader of German Jewry at that time, he was ordained a reform rabbi in 1938, but was interned at Sachsenhausen concentration camp for three months in the aftermath of the *Kristallnacht* pogrom of 9–10 November 1938. In 1939, he and his family escaped to Scotland, but owing to the outbreak of the Second World War they were transported to Canada and interned as enemy aliens. While serving as a rabbi in Hamilton, Ontario, he received his PhD in medieval Arabic philosophy in 1945 from the University of Toronto, joining its faculty in 1948. He remained there until his retirement in 1984. Moving to Israel that same year, he died there in 2003.

According to professor of religion Louis Greenspan, the following two sentences from Fackenheim's reflections *To Mend the World: Foundations of Future Jewish Thought* (1982) 'explain very well the maxim that has guided all his studies':

> There has come into existence in our time a hermeneutical teaching that begins with the acceptance of historical situatedness. It confronts the problem of recovery of the past – the past itself and the word of the past, human and divine – when the past itself is in one situation and we who seek access to it are in another.
>
> (Greenspan and Nicholson, 1992: 6–7)

Indeed, Fackenheim's *oeuvre* may very well be understood as his ongoing attempt to assess the relevant validity of German idealistic philosophy and bring it into conversation with the intellectual richness of the Jewish religious tradition, while reassessing both in the aftermath of the Holocaust. The fact that he is considered among the giants of post-Holocaust philosophy is an affirmation of the soundness of his project.

The imperative that drove Fackenheim's thought was the search for an answer to the vexing question, 'Where was God at Auschwitz?' While there could be no immediately rational explanation, he felt, at least one fundamental truth stood out as a result of the Jewish people's experience. An ongoing Jewish commitment to survival 'denied Hitler a posthumous victory', and, along with this, only a strong Israel could prevent the Jews from vanishing as a people. Thus, in 1968, Fackenheim first introduced what became his most well-known theological notion, the idea of a '614th commandment' stemming from the Holocaust. Here he built on the rabbinic tradition of 613 *mitzvot* (divine commandments) to be found in the Bible. These are divided among the positive ('You shall', of which there are 248) and the negative ('You shall not', of which there are 365). Later, he developed the idea more fully, such that his new commandment read:

> Jews are forbidden to hand Hitler posthumous victories. They are commanded to survive as Jews, lest the Jewish people perish. They are commanded to remember the victims of Auschwitz lest their memory perish. They are forbidden to despair of man and his world, and to escape into either criticism or other-worldliness, lest they cooperate in delivering the world over to the forces of Auschwitz. Finally, they are forbidden to despair of the God of Israel, lest Judaism perish.
>
> (Fackenheim, 1970: 45)

Ultimately, 'A Jew may not respond to Hitler's attempt to destroy Judaism, by himself cooperating in its destruction. In ancient times, the unthinkable Jewish sin was idolatry. Today, it is to respond to Hitler by doing his work' (Fackenheim, 1970: 46).

For traditionally observant Jews, who regard the 613 *mitzvot* as sacrosanct and immutable, Fackenheim's elevation of post-Holocaust Judaic moral responsibility is problematic. Indeed, he addressed this himself in a lecture entitled 'Faith in God and Man after Auschwitz: Theological Implications', delivered in April 2002. Why a 614th commandment, he asked, and why not (as with the Protestant theologian **A. Roy Eckardt**), in order to stress its importance, an 11th? First, he said, in Jewish tradition there are 613 commandments, sufficient for all situations, future as well as past, but the tradition could not anticipate Hitler: the Holocaust was unpredictable, even for *torah-she'-be'al-pe* (the Oral Torah). Second, why a commandment that names an enemy, when Jewish tradition avoids names, say of Titus or Hadrian, and avoids others with the words *yimach sh'mo*, 'may his name be wiped out'? Earlier enemies had found Jewish 'sins' in *behaviour* – stubborn politics in Roman antiquity, stubborn faith in the Middle Ages – but the enemy Hitler found Jewish 'sin *in birth*', and set out methodically to 'solve' a so-called problem (http://www.holocaust-trc.org/fackenheim.htm).

For other Jews, even the non-Orthodox, reconstructing Jewish life in the aftermath of the Holocaust, and basing one's religious responsibilities upon it, accords the event an almost meta-historical status but an insufficient rationale for a viable modern Jewish religious life. That is to say, that the Holocaust or *Shoah* is in and of itself *not a sufficiently positive reason to commit oneself to a Jewish religious life or to sustain a positive and observant religious community*. Nor should it be a bludgeon with which to beat unobservant Jews into submission or Gentiles into guilt, nor non-Zionists into Zionists. Thus, for instance, Steven Leonard Jacobs has argued that after the Holocaust all Jews have become Zionists despite the complex realities of the Middle East and the ongoing Israeli–Arab/Palestinian conflicts. In this critique, no Jew alive after the *Shoah* can morally, ethically or religiously refrain from calling him or herself a Zionist, regardless of where he or she chooses to live. Indeed, if anything, the reverse is now the case: after the *Shoah* all Jews have become Zionists de facto by virtue of their continuing Jewish existence and Jewish affirmations (Jacobs, 1994: 82).

Despite this, acceptance of the moral mandate of this 614th commandment does have implications for Jews. It muted Fackenheim's criticisms of the State of Israel regarding both the Palestinians and the surrounding Arab states, and alarmed those in the American Jewish community viewing intermarriage and conversion to other religions as sounding the death knell of continuing Jewish existence. Taken to its extreme, however, it has hardened responses to anti-Semitism within some Diaspora Jewish communities to the point where too many see enemies where they do not exist, while failing to identify legitimate threats. (An example would be those who deny any legitimate criticism of Israel's government and military policies as the work of anti-Semites, including labelling Jewish critics as 'self-hating Jews'.) Finally, it also lent support positively for those for whom *Yom Ha-Shoah* (Holocaust Remembrance Day) is a central event in the Jewish calendar, but negatively to those inside the various Jewish communities who continue to exploit both its memory and fear of repetition for their own organisational and/or other agendas.

Among the critiques of Fackenheim's argument was the oft-repeated comment that he was calling on Jews to remain Jewish on account of a negative force rather than for the intrinsic values of Judaism itself. One of the most articulate of these came from Rabbi Harold M. Schulweis, of Valley Beth Shalom (Encino, California). In a lecture in 1999 Schulweis asserted:

> We abuse the Holocaust when it becomes a cudgel against others who have their claims of suffering. The *Shoah* must not be misused in the contest of one-downmanship with other victims of brutality. It does not credit our uniqueness; it only is perceived as callousness. That is not the informed heart of our memory to enter the 21st century with a new heart and a new spirit. For decades the justification for our fidelity to Judaism has leaned entirely on the *Shoah*. The *Shoah* has become our instant *raison d'être*, the short-cut answer to the penetrating questions of our children: 'Why should I not marry out of the faith? Why should I join a synagogue? Why should I support Israel? Why should I be Jewish?' We have relied on a singular imperative: 'Thou shalt not give Hitler a posthumous victory.' That answer will not work. To live in spite, to say 'no' to Hitler, is a far cry from living 'yes' to Judaism.
>
> (http://www.jewishpublicaffairs.org/publications/
> schulweis.html)

Schulweis was not the only one to take issue with Fackenheim over this issue, as others also saw the need to try to attract young Jews through reference to Judaism's moral goodness rather than simply staying Jewish notwithstanding the Jewish past.

A less controversial matter for Fackenheim was the question of the uniqueness of the Holocaust. Because all historical events are at the same time similar and different, Fackenheim preferred the term 'unprecedented' (as does historian **Yehuda Bauer**), and reminded readers in the Preface to his new edition of *God's Presence in History* (1997) that

1. The Holocaust is a *novum* [new, singular event] in history and, within the Jewish faith, is irreducible to evils perpetrated by Pharaoh or Amalek, the Spanish Inquisition or the Cossacks' Chmelnitzki, or even the enemies of Jerusalem – Nebukadnezzar, Vespasian, Titus, Hadrian.
2. No meaning, redemptive or other, religious or secular will ever be found in the Holocaust.

3. His [Hitler's] victories did not end with his death.
4. This prohibition is a '614th commandment.'

(Fackenheim, 1997: x–xi)

Asked in an interview published posthumously in 2005 – his last interview, as it turned out – Fackenheim dealt once more with the issue of Holocaust uniqueness, this time focusing on the simple matter of Hitler's intention:

> Now of course, what is so unique about the Holocaust? Number one: it's just numbers. But you know, who goes by numbers? The Russians lost 10 million people and so on. But the important thing was that whereas the Nazis thought there were too many Poles, too many Czechs, Jews must not exist at all. That's a quantum jump. Even one Jew is enough. Jews must be wiped out. And of course, if Hitler had won the war there wouldn't have been a Jew left, nowhere in the world.

(Thorpe, 2005)

For Fackenheim, the Holocaust was ever-present. In *Encounters between Judaism and Modern Philosophy: A Preface to Future Jewish Thought* (1973), he noted:

> Ever since the Nazi Holocaust it is Western civilization that is on trial. And ever since the rebirth of the Jewish people in its ancient land the age-old image of this people as a dead people or a nonpeople has become as absurd factually as, morally and spiritually, it already was.

(Fackenheim, 1973: 5)

Thus, even concerning himself with the widest possible implications of the Holocaust, Fackenheim did not limit himself to the event as a Jewish tragedy only, but saw it as the central crime of the West, the result of centuries of falsely stereotyping the Jewish people. Considering the discipline of Philosophy in its relationship to the Holocaust, Greenspan and Nicholson similarly observe, 'in confronting philosophy with the Holocaust, [Fackenheim] reminds philosophy of its own shallowness, of issues that it has to address' (Greenspan and Nicholson, 1992: 12). In working through these issues Fackenheim produced *To Mend the World: Foundations of Future Jewish Thought* (1982), wherein he confronted such philosophical thinkers as Franz Rosenzweig, Baruch Spinoza, Georg Wilhelm

Friedrich Hegel and Martin Heidegger, as well as Judaism itself, in an attempt to answer the question 'how Jewish (also Christian and philosophical) thought can both expose itself to the Holocaust and survive' (Fackenheim, 1982: 24; see also Morgan 1996 and Morgan, 1987).

Finally, as almost all who have made an attempt at assessing Fackenheim's writing and thinking have correctly noted, it is the centrality of the historical experience – his own as well as that of the Jewish people generally – in its relationship to Jewish thought which has been his ultimate philosophical confrontation, thus making the 'lived experience' foundational to both present and future, shaping indelibly what is and what will be. It is no accident, therefore, that both *To Mend the World* and *Encounters between Judaism and Modern Philosophy* have the word 'Future' in their subtitles. For Emil Fackenheim, changed not only by his own experience of the Holocaust but also that of the Jewish people as a whole – and a Western world yet to fully confront it as well – both the present and future have been irrevocably altered.

Fackenheim's major writings

Quest for Past and Future: Essays in Jewish Theology, Westport (CT): Greenwood Press, 1968.

God's Presence in History: Jewish Affirmations and Philosophical Reflections, New York: New York University Press, 1970.

The Human Condition after Auschwitz: A Jewish Testimony a Generation After, Syracuse (NY): Syracuse University Press, 1971.

Encounters between Judaism and Modern Philosophy: A Preface to Future Jewish Thought, New York: Schocken Books, 1973.

From Bergen-Belsen to Jerusalem: Contemporary Implications of the Holocaust, Jerusalem: Cultural Department, World Jewish Congress, 1975.

An Epitaph for German Judaism: From Halle to Jerusalem, Madison (WI): University of Wisconsin Press, 1977.

The Jewish Return into History: Reflections in the Age of Auschwitz and a New Jerusalem, New York: Schocken Books, 1978.

To Mend the World: Foundations of Future Jewish Thought, New York: Schocken Books, 1982.

'The Spectrum of Resistance During the Holocaust: An Essay in Description and Definition', *Modern Judaism*, 2, 2 (1982), 113–30.

'Concerning Authentic and Unauthentic Responses to the Holocaust', *Holocaust and Genocide Studies*, 1, 1 (1986), 101–20.

The Jewish Bible after the Holocaust: A Re-reading, Manchester: Manchester University Press, 1990.

God's Presence in History: Jewish Affirmations and Philosophical Reflections, new edition, Northvale (NJ): Jason Aronson, 1997.

References

Greenspan, Louis and Graeme Nicholson (eds), *Fackenheim: German Philosophy and Jewish Thought*, Toronto: University of Toronto Press, 1992.

Jacobs, Steven Leonard, *Rethinking Jewish Faith: The Child of a Survivor Responds*, Albany (NY): State University of New York Press, 1994.

Morgan, Michael L. (ed.), *The Jewish Thought of Emil Fackenheim: A Reader*, Detroit: Wayne State University Press, 1987.

Morgan, Michael L. (ed.), *Jewish Philosophers and Jewish Philosophy*, Bloomington: Indiana University Press, 1996.

Thorpe, Samuel, 'Emil Fackenheim: The Last Interview', *Habitus: A Diaspora Journal*, 2005, at http://www.habitusmag.com.

HELEN FEIN (b. 1934)

Helen Fein is a sociologist who has specialised in the study of genocide, human rights, collective violence and other issues. She is Executive Director of the Institute for the Study of Genocide at John Jay College of Criminal Justice, City University of New York, and a Research Associate at the Belfer Center for Science and International Affairs in the Kennedy School of Government, Harvard University. Born in New York in 1934, she has taught at the State University of New York, New Paltz and City College, New York. Fein was one of the founders, and the first president, of the Association (later International Association) of Genocide Scholars (1995–97).

Having an early interest in theories of non-violence, she entered the general field of the study of oppression through her PhD dissertation topic at Columbia University, later published as *Imperial Crime and Punishment: The Jallianwala Bagh Massacre and British Judgment, 1919–1920* (1977). This was an examination of the massacre of nearly 400 Indian men, women and children (with another 1,500 wounded) in the northern Indian city of Amritsar on 13 April 1919, when British Indian army soldiers under the command of Brigadier-General Reginald Dyer opened fire on an unarmed gathering. The official inquiry that took place after the massacre whitewashed Dyer's actions, and Fein's book, focusing on the massacre, was a historical-sociological investigation of how groups condone, legitimate and authorise violence towards other groups – the kind of violence that would otherwise be punished as criminal if committed against their own members. By looking closely at the origins of such violence, she concluded that it is related to certain types of power structures that make such crimes more likely.

Fein's interest in violence and the nature of the societies that condone it led two years later to an important study of the Holocaust, *Accounting for Genocide: National Responses and Jewish Victimization during the Holocaust* (1979). While that event was garnering more and more attention during the 1970s, not a lot of work had yet been done on sociological approaches to the topic. Yet it was precisely this treatment that was needed in order to assist the historical understandings then developing as the decade went on. As scholarship into the Holocaust proceeded there appeared to be a lacuna in analysing the social phenomena that occurred in Europe prior to, during and after the event. Fein's study attempted to fill that gap. Combining historical and sociological methods of analysis and interpretation, and supported by considerable detail, she confronted the broad issues that until then had been raised only briefly. She analysed the rates of Jewish survival according to the states in which the Holocaust was carried out, and sought explanations for why there were different rates in different countries, trying to understand these differences in terms of varied national responses to persecution. Rather than focusing on the success of the Nazi programme of destruction, as much scholarship had done so far, Fein examined a number of sectors within the societies in question in order to reach a conclusion regarding their moral accountability either in resisting the Nazis or in assisting them. Fein focused not only on the Nazi campaign against the Jews, but extended her study also to other racial victims such as the Roma. This pioneering work began also to develop a theoretical approach towards understanding twentieth-century genocide, and made a huge contribution to the field through the introduction of a simple phrase with an important meaning: the universe of obligation.

This significant concept she defined as 'that circle of people with reciprocal obligations to protect each other' (Fein, 1979: 4), 'toward whom obligations are owed, to whom the rules apply, and whose injuries call for expiation by the community' (Fein, 1979: 33). Fein explained her position clearly:

> Within any polity, the dominant group defines the boundaries of the universe of obligation and sanctions violations legally. Injuries to or violations of rights of persons within the universe are offenses against the collective conscience that provoke the need for sanctions against the perpetrators in order to maintain the group's solidarity. ... Violations of (or collective violence against) those outside the boundaries do not provoke such a need;

instead, such violence is likely to be explained as a just punishment for their offenses.

(Fein, 1979: 33)

To illustrate her point, she concluded that 'resistance to legal and physical violence against the Jews as Jews would depend upon their inclusion within the universe of obligation' (Fein, 1979: 33).

Considering the universe of obligation to be the outer limits of the common conscience – the place where we find those whom we are obligated to protect and to whom we are accountable – Fein introduced a new model by which scholars could approach some of the central issues relating to the formation of an in-group/out-group dynamic. By this means, she was able to discern which groups were more easily stigmatised and thus able to be excluded from society, and, therefore, how some people could become victims of violence (and genocide) and others not. She was thus able to show how an operational definition of community could be created, through demonstrating that communities often expand and contract to include or exclude members – and that this expansion or contraction involves not only circumstances, but real moral and ethical choices about how to view 'others'. While *Accounting for Genocide* was thus a first-rate piece of historical analysis, it was also a contribution that broke new ground concerning the sociology of genocide, and was recognised as such by Fein's peers through her winning the inaugural Sorokin Award of the American Sociological Association in 1979.

From the later 1970s Fein was, as she put it herself, 'increasingly preoccupied with genocide after the Holocaust' (Fein, 2002: 224), leading her onto paths she might once not have foreseen. One of these was to bring her to the forefront of Genocide Studies, as she sought ways to understand better the UN Convention on Genocide and how it could be applied in the modern world. The result, a long article for the International Sociological Association's journal *Current Sociology* (1990), was republished soon thereafter as a short monograph, *Genocide: A Sociological Perspective* (1993).

This work was an analysis of the sociology and history of genocide that asked when and why such eruptions of deliberate violence occurred. Fein analysed the origin of genocide as a concept, and summarised the various controversies that had up to that point taken place about definitions, explanations and comparisons. Here, she was attempting to bring a sociological understanding to the study of genocide, and to make genocide an object of concern for the discipline. Written with academic distance and objectivity, the study was a dispassionate analysis of the phenomenon of genocide that ranged across the breadth of social scientific scholarship. Fein offered a critical review of the literature as it had developed up to then, and proposed a vision of where research might be taken in the future. The original article in *Current Sociology* drew considerable attention from within the field, and was awarded the first annual prize by the PIOOM Foundation (an international research institute on human rights based in the Netherlands); the subsequent book, now available to a broader audience, was received with acclamation in many sectors worldwide.

In a memoir published in 2002, Fein drew the conclusion that from this point on her work was to move in several directions:

> (a) an explanation of violations of life-integrity or gross violations of human rights, (b) new directions in genocide studies, including genocide by attrition and gender, and (c) strategic studies and mobilization to show that genocide can be prevented. In the latter, I have reached out to a larger community, forging bonds with people in different fields, especially human rights.
>
> (Fein, 2002: 229)

Further, she noted, she also worked towards the 'institutionalisation' of the study of genocide 'in mainstream academic life'. The Institute for the Study of Genocide, with which Fein was later to be closely involved, had already been established in New York in 1982, but her initial efforts within Sociology were not altogether successful. Other colleagues with a similar vision, however, encouraged Fein to persevere, leading to a meeting of minds at an academic conference on the Holocaust in Berlin in 1993, where genocide scholars **Robert Melson, Israel Charny** and Roger Smith prevailed upon Fein to preside over the formation of a new organisation, the Association of Genocide Scholars. Other initiatives, frequently at Fein's behest or with her support, followed through the American Sociological Association, as the study of genocide began to move more and more into the mainstream of sociological inquiry.

One of her major concerns was also that of genocide prevention, and while her work in the 1980s and 1990s was peppered with reports and academic articles, it might be said that a study published in the second half of the first decade of the new millennium was the culmination of all her work in the area. In *Human Rights and Wrongs: Slavery, Terror, Genocide* (2007), Fein examined the major threats to the world as they had developed over previous decades, investigating atrocities such as terror, torture, sex trafficking, terror states and slavery, whether perpetrated by states or by non-state actors. From this, her readers could develop a better understanding of why such cruelty had occurred so frequently throughout the twentieth century, and why it had been so difficult to bring it to an end. As with the work of scholars such as **Rudolph J. Rummel**, Fein also discussed the place of democracy as a force in fostering and preserving human rights, highlighting the positive links between human rights, social equality and freedom. Further, she sought to explain why the international community had not been effective in stopping the culture of violence and destruction that had so come to characterise the period.

While connecting theory with practical examples taken from case studies of Islamic states, India, Thailand, Israel, Algeria, Argentina, Iraq and Guatemala, Fein saw that it was important to show also how the United States was as much a part of the problem as of the solution. The failure of the United States to provide moral leadership, and its complicity and participation in some of the worst abuses, exposed human rights at one of their most vulnerable points. The USA had played a leading role in drafting many of the pioneering pieces of human-rights legislation during the early years of the Cold War, but continually failed to follow through on its avowed commitments. In this, her work echoed that of **Samantha Power**, though her analysis was conveyed in a style tailored more for a scholarly than a popular audience. Of course, American foreign policy, despite its many shortcomings, was far from responsible for all the major atrocities or human-rights violations of the twentieth century, a point she made clear.

Human Rights and Wrongs synthesised much of the scholarly literature on genocide, and pointed out how it was that ethnic hatred, religious extremism, heightened nationalism and power struggles all built towards the century's immense disregard for human life. Fein employed her skills as a sociologist to explain these gross human-rights violations in terms of an integrated theory of how life can be given value, and provided insight into the motives and rationale for why genocide and terror have remained dominant features of modern society.

Since the start of the crisis in Darfur in 2003, another element of Fein's work has often been cited by authors keen to find a way to describe the events in that region. Here, they have built on her analysis of the earlier catastrophe in Sudan between 1983 and 1993 (Fein, 1997: 11–45) in which she introduced the term 'genocide by attrition'. According to this theory, a group is singled out for political and civil discrimination, separated from the dominant groups in society, and has its right to life threatened through concentration and forced displacement together with systematic deprivation of food, water, and sanitary and medical facilities. These measures, along with the frequent imposition of overcrowded living quarters, often lead to death through disease and starvation. Three prime examples of this, as Fein saw it, had been the Warsaw Ghetto (1939–43), Cambodia (1975–79) and Sudan (1983–93). In each of these cases, the targeted populations officially fell outside 'the universe of obligation', as defined by the government or dominant sector of society in the position of classifying 'the other'.

Since 1987, as Research Director, then Executive Director, of the Institute for the Study of Genocide, Helen Fein has been able to continue promoting scholarship on the causes, consequences and prevention of genocide. She has employed the sociological imagination as a tool in order to examine how humans produce collective evil and collective good. Her pioneering work concerning the 'universe of obligation' has seen her explore in depth how it is that the denial of political and civil rights can lead to more dangerous situations for those outside that universe, resulting in the stripping away of a group's rights, resources, land, jobs and businesses, followed by segregation or isolation and concentration prior to the ultimate step, removal. As one of the most distinguished thinkers in the field of Genocide Studies, she has also been a significant influence in bringing together scholars from across the globe to discuss and share ideas and research within the field, and has set a high standard of excellence for herself – and for all others – in conducting research about genocide.

Fein's major writings

Imperial Crime and Punishment: The Jallianwala Bagh Massacre and British Judgment, 1919–1920, Honolulu: University Press of Hawaii, 1977.

'A Formula for Genocide: Comparison of the Turkish Genocide (1915) and the German Holocaust (1939–45)', *Comparative Studies in Sociology*, 1 (1978), 271–94.

Accounting for Genocide: National Responses and Jewish Victimization during the Holocaust, New York: Free Press, 1979.

'Is Sociology Aware of Genocide? Recognition of Genocide in Introductory Sociology Texts in the U.S. 1947–77', *Humanity and Sociology*, August 1979, 177–93.

(Ed.) *The Persisting Question: Social Contexts and Sociological Perspectives on Modern Antisemitism*, Berlin: de Gruyter, 1987.

Congregational Sponsors of Indochinese Refugees in the US, 1979–1981: Helping Beyond Borders, Rutherford (NJ): Fairleigh Dickinson University Press, 1987.

Lives at Risk: A Study of Life-Integrity Violations in 50 States in 1987, Based on the Amnesty International 1988 Report, New York: Institute for the Study of Genocide, 1988.

'Genocide: A Sociological Perspective', *Current Sociology*, 38, 1 (Spring 1990), 1–126.

(Ed.) *Genocide Watch*, New Haven (CT): Yale University Press, 1992.

'Accounting for Genocide after 1945: Theories and Some Findings', *International Journal of Group Rights*, vol. 1, no. 1 (1993), pp. 79–106.

'Discriminating Genocide from War Crimes: Vietnam and Afghanistan Reconsidered', *Denver Journal of International Law*, 22, 1 (Fall 1993), 29–62.

'Revolutionary and Antirevolutionary Genocides: A Comparison of State Murders in Democratic Kampuchea (1975–79) and in Indonesia (1965–66)', *Comparative Studies in Society and History*, 35, 4 (October 1993), 794–821.

(Ed. with Joyce Freedman-Apsel) *Teaching about Genocide: A Guidebook for College Teachers*, Ottawa: Human Rights Internet, 1993; revised edition, Washington DC, American Sociological Association, 2002.

Genocide: A Sociological Perspective, London: Sage, 1993.

(Ed.) *The Prevention of Genocide: Rwanda and Yugoslavia Reconsidered*, New York: Institute for the Study of Genocide, 1994.

'Genocide, Terror, Life-Integrity and War Crimes: The Case for Discrimination', in George J. Andreopoulos (ed.), *Genocide: The Conceptual and Historical Dimensions*, Philadelphia: University of Pennsylvania Press, 1994, pp. 95–107.

'Genocide by Attrition, 1939–93: The Warsaw Ghetto, Cambodia, and Sudan: Links between Human Rights, Health, and Mass Death', *Health and Human Rights*, 2, 2 (1997), 1–45.

'The Three P's of Genocide Prevention: With Application to a Genocide Foretold', in Neil Reimer (ed.), *Protection Against Genocide: Mission Impossible?* New York: Praeger, 1999, 41–66.

(Ed. with Orlanda Brugnola and Louise Spirer) *Ever Again? Evaluating the United Nations Genocide Convention on its 50th Anniversary and Proposals to Activate the Convention*, New York: Institute for the Study of Genocide, 1999.

'Genocide and Gender: The Uses of Women and Group Identity', *Journal of Genocide Research*, 1, 1 (June 1999), 43–63.

'Civil Wars and Genocide: Paths and Circles', *Human Rights Review*, 1, 3 (April–June 2000), 49–61.

'From Social Action to Social Theory and Back: Paths and Circles', in Samuel Totten and Steven Leonard Jacobs (eds), *Pioneers of Genocide Studies*, New Brunswick (NJ): Transaction Publishers, 2002, 219–33.

Human Rights and Wrongs: Slavery, Terror, Genocide, Boulder (CO): Paradigm Publishers, 2007.

STEPHEN C. FEINSTEIN (1943–2008)

Stephen C. Feinstein was a Professor of History (and, later, Professor Emeritus) at the University of Wisconsin-River Falls between 1969 and 1999, prior to becoming adjunct professor and director of the Center for Holocaust and Genocide Studies at the University of

Minnesota-Twin Cities. Born in Philadelphia in 1943, in 1971 he earned his PhD in eighteenth-century Russian history from New York University. At Wisconsin he taught a wide range of courses, and served as Chairman of the History Department between 1991 and 1997. He often conducted study tours to the Soviet Union and China, giving him an opportunity not only to teach in vastly different environments, but also to expand his own understandings of the art, culture and history of the places he was visiting.

Throughout the 1970s and 1980s, Feinstein was actively involved in campaigns in support of Soviet Jews, and his efforts enabled many new immigrants to resettle in the Midwest. He threw himself physically into his work, not only in securing visas and other permits, but also in welcoming immigrants, arranging accommodation and attempting to secure employment. And, as a practitioner of the humanity he taught, Feinstein did not limit his activities just to the rescue of Jews from the Soviet Union, as threatened people from other countries would discover in subsequent years.

From 1975 onwards, Feinstein taught the history of the Holocaust, developing a scholarly interest in artistic representations of that event. He took every opportunity to write and speak about it, to whatever audience he had before him. His belief in the sanctity of humanity under all conditions was broadened over time into the study of the broader phenomenon of genocide, as his understanding grew of the significance of the interconnections between the Holocaust and other examples of genocide such as that against the people of Armenia between 1915 and 1923.

In 1999, Feinstein moved to the University of Minnesota-Twin Cities (Minneapolis), to become Director of the University's Center for Holocaust and Genocide Studies. (He has already been acting director since 1997.) Over time, he built the Center into a premier educational, research and outreach institution, of high international repute. As one keen to raise consciousness about the questions that concerned him, Feinstein brought issues relating to human rights, the Holocaust, genocide and Jewish history to the university community. He developed academic courses and research activities on the history of the Holocaust, the Armenian Genocide, the treatment of Native Americans, the genocide in Rwanda and the ongoing crisis in Darfur. He was an energetic promoter of the cause of humanitarian education. Largely due to his efforts, the university not only achieved its Center for Holocaust and Genocide Studies, but also an endowed chair in Jewish history, a chair devoted to issues of atrocity crimes, human rights and Armenian history and culture, and an endowed lecture series. The Center's website, constructed during Feinstein's tenure as director, provides a rare showcase for the history and art of Jewish and Armenian culture, as well as the history of these and a number of other genocides.

As a key thinker on the Holocaust and genocide, however, it was Feinstein's interest in, and contribution to, the problems of artistic representation that established his unique position in the field.

Feinstein entered the world of art history when working in his earlier field of Russian and Soviet studies. In particular, he developed an interest in Soviet dissident art of the 1970s, while on a sabbatical at Tel Aviv University in 1984–85. Against this general background, he was invited by the Minnesota Museum of American Art in 1994 to serve as curator for a travelling exhibition it was developing on the art of the Holocaust, to be entitled 'Witness and Legacy: Contemporary Art about the Holocaust'. The exhibition was to coincide with the fiftieth anniversary of the liberation of Auschwitz; ultimately, it would travel throughout the United States, touring some seventeen museums and galleries between 1995 and 2002. At first, it was Feinstein's reputation as an expert in Holocaust history, more than his expertise in art, which led to the invitation to act as curator. Having done so, however, it stimulated a new area of academic interest that was to remain with Feinstein for the rest of his life.

Then, in 1999, Feinstein reprised his role as curator, this time of a 7,000-square-foot exhibition at the University of Minnesota's Nash Gallery, entitled 'Absence/Presence: The Artistic Memory of the Holocaust and Genocide'. The catalogue and explanatory notes accompanying this exhibition were published as a book of essays under the same title, under Feinstein's editorship. These essays considered how the trauma of the Holocaust can be represented, and in what ways art mixes with theory. The book was an important insight into how Feinstein's own thinking worked, and covered such issues as the politics of representation, the position of art relative to the Holocaust after 60 years, German and American Jewish art in light of the Holocaust, and, in Feinstein's own contribution, 'Toward a Post-Holocaust Theology in Art: The Search for the Absent and Present God', a discussion of religious issues and the quest for meaning. Overall, the book was a searching inquiry into how art has represented the Holocaust in any sort of adequate capacity, addressing a number of important issues.

'Witness and Legacy' and 'Absence/Presence' were two of what would eventually be six major exhibitions on the theme of art in the Holocaust and/or genocide for which Feinstein was the curator.

One of the areas concerning Feinstein's handling of art history relative to the Holocaust was the unfortunate necessity of art to vie with photography in representations of the Holocaust, though this was, in his view, a challenge that could be met:

> Artists in every country have been struggling with issues of representation, how to depict repetitive tropes of victimization: the watch towers, barbed wire fences, yellow stars, concentration camp uniforms, and mounds of corpses. Of course, these images are all taken from reality. But artists have to compete with the photographic record on this account, and they usually lose if the question is creating some sort of 'authentic' and durable image. Yet artists have been dealing with the Holocaust even before it happened. What I sometimes refer to as the 'scent of Fascism' can be seen in the drawings, paintings, photomontages and collages of George Grosz, Otto Dix, Hannah Hoch, John Heartfield, and others.
>
> (Feinstein, 2004: 57)

He later extended this list through reference to artists such as Marc Chagall, Ben Shahn and Ron B. Kitaj, among others. The issue was always one of how to try to make sense of the inexplicable. 'The Nazis,' Feinstein wrote, 'used an attack on art as a prelude to attacks on the imagination and then on the actual victims.' With this in mind, almost since the very beginning of the Third Reich, 'artists have tried to grapple with the subject':

> Art about the Holocaust, therefore, is nothing new, nor is the territory of the Shoah sacred space, despite warnings from survivors and philosophers. If artists can simply capture the shadow of the Shoah, that may be sufficient, as Christian artists have hardly captured the image of Golgotha.
>
> (Feinstein, 1999a: 155–56)

Feinstein then sought to find a way to create a typology of Holocaust art, which in his view was simultaneously complex and relatively simple: complex, because a great deal of art is Holocaust-influenced though not dealing directly with Holocaust themes; simple, because all that is required is to 'divide artists into survivors, the second generation, and those who were only indirectly or obliquely touched by the event as outsiders, whose work may justify a classification as empathizers' (Feinstein, 1999a: 156). (The term 'empathizers' was used by Feinstein on a number of occasions throughout his work; it is a term he coined to explain those without a direct personal or family relationship to the Holocaust, but who have been touched by it nonetheless.) And as if to demonstrate further that the worlds of art, literature and memoir were not hermetically sealed – in other words, that representation and creativity could be compatible across a number of different genres – he sought to trace inspirational linkages where they could be found. In an important essay dealing with the influence on American art of the work of survivor-author **Primo Levi**, Feinstein wrote that

> Representation of the Holocaust through the visual arts is an ongoing and a difficult subject for artists. Entering the world of the Holocaust, especially for those who were not in the camps, provides the same barrier that novelists and even some historians face – the need to interpret, but not falsify information and narratives about the event. ... For the artist, ... visually representational works are completed in smaller spaces [than written works], do not contain a total narrative as a written work, and leave it to the viewer to complete the metaphor.
>
> (Feinstein, 2001a: 169)

The twin tasks of inspiration and representation thus present problems for the artist, but they can certainly be (and have been) surmounted. In his work on the representation of horror and memory through art, Feinstein's thinking in many respects complemented that of his contemporary, **James E. Young**, regarding museums and memorials. Feinstein's lasting contribution to the field has been to show the vast number of ways in which art is a viable means of approaching the Holocaust, and, indeed, of even deriving a measure of understanding from it.

As he broadened his interests, Feinstein was not content to focus only on the Holocaust, and in 1999 he produced an essay examining the art of genocides other than that with which he had the deepest familiarity. In 'Art of the Holocaust and Genocide: Some Points of Convergence', he recognised that artistic representation of the former had a longer tradition, but observed that this was beginning to turn the other way. The failures of international intervention in the 1990s to prevent genocide and ethnic cleansing in Bosnia, Rwanda, East Timor and Kosovo had led to the stimulation of artistic expression on the theme of atrocity, leading Feinstein to conclude that 'Silence is clearly not the answer for artists' (Feinstein, 1999b: 233). In his highly detailed article, Feinstein then proceeded to outline the work of a number of artists from a variety of backgrounds, all of whom have taken genocide (in particular, in Armenia and Bosnia) as their theme. As he concluded, none of this presumes that 'art has the power to heal'. Art projects such as those he identified, however, have 'the power to inform and provide for an element of discovery, and perhaps understanding, by a viewing public not expecting to be moved in a political direction by art' (Feinstein, 1999b: 246). One of the ways in which he could encourage this was through the 'Voice to Vision' project, which helps survivors of the Holocaust and other genocides to share their experiences through art. Pioneered by Feinstein, it was developed through the collaboration of an interdisciplinary visual research team that includes participants from the Art Department and the Center for Holocaust and Genocide Studies at the University of Minnesota, as well as participants from surrounding communities.

Stephen C. Feinstein was a scholar imbued with a profound belief in the value of research and education to enhance respect for life. At the time of his sudden death in March 2008, he was generally considered to be a visionary within the field of Holocaust and Genocide Studies. He sought to foster scholarly research and increase public knowledge about the history and politics of ethnic and national conflict, the Holocaust and genocide. Committed to the idea that people can live together regardless of their differences, Feinstein's universalistic worldview was that individuals and groups could get along if enough people tried to make it happen. As a thinker, he showed that the road to understanding human evil can take another form than just through contemplation of the written word, and in so doing he made a contribution that extended the boundaries of inquiry and awareness.

Feinstein's major writings

(Ed.) *Witness and Legacy: Contemporary Art About the Holocaust*, Minneapolis: Lerner Publications, 1994.

Absence/Presence: The Artistic Memory of the Holocaust and Genocide, Minneapolis: Center for Holocaust and Genocide Studies, University of Minnesota, 1998.

'Art after Auschwitz', in Harry James Cargas (ed.), *Problems Unique to the Holocaust*, Lexington: University Press of Kentucky, 1999a, 152–68.

'Art of the Holocaust and Contemporary Genocide: Toward a Point of Convergence', *Journal of Genocide Research*, 1, 2 (1999b), 233–56.

'Art after Auschwitz: Jozef Szajna's Theatre of Panic', in F. C. Decoste and Bernard Schwartz (eds), *The Holocaust's Ghost: Writings on Art, Politics, Law and Education*, Edmonton (Alberta): University of Alberta Press, 2000, 109–23.

'Primo Levi and His Work as a Source for Artistic Representation', in Roberta S. Kremer (ed.), *Memory and Mastery: Primo Levi as Writer and Witness*, Albany (NY): State University of New York Press, 2001a, 133–72.

Samuel Bak: Working Through the Past, Paintings 1946–2000, St. Petersburg (FL): Florida Holocaust Museum, 2001b.

Fritz Hirschberger: The Sur-Rational Paintings, Minneapolis: Center for Holocaust and Genocide Studies, University of Minnesota, 2002.

'What are the Results? Reflections on Working in Holocaust Education', in Samuel Totten, Paul R. Bartrop and Steven Leonard Jacobs (eds), *Teaching about the Holocaust: Essays by College and University Teachers*, Westport (CT): Praeger, 2004, 51–63.

SAUL FRIEDLÄNDER (b. 1932)

Since 1988 Saul Friedländer has been the 1939 Club Professor of Holocaust and History at the University of California, Los Angeles. Through much of that time, until his retirement, he was also a Professor of History at Tel Aviv University. Born in Prague in 1932, he was raised in France. As a Jewish child during the Nazi occupation, he survived by having been hidden in a Catholic boarding school in Montlucon, near Vichy. In order not to be discovered, he was presented as a Christian child; his parents, meanwhile, attempted to flee to Switzerland. Arrested by Vichy French police, they were deported to Auschwitz while their son, unknowingly, continued to live in the Catholic school. He only learned of their fate after the war.

In June 1948 Friedländer emigrated from France to Israel on the Irgun ship *Altalena*. After finishing high school, he served in the Israeli army. Between 1953 and 1955 he studied Political Science in Paris, and in 1963 he received his PhD from the Graduate Institute of International Studies in Geneva, where he would teach until 1988.

Friedländer's first major studies related to the Catholic Church, in which he had an interest owing to his wartime experience. In *Pius XII and the Third Reich: A Documentation* (1966), he considered the highly controversial question of Pope Pius XII's enigmatic posture regarding the Nazi persecution of the Jews. Working through a large number of documents from German Foreign Office sources, and placing this documentary material within its appropriate historical context, Friedländer composed a picture of Pius's pro-German bias and near-fanatical anti-communism. While drawing readers' attention to these two features of Pius's reign, he conceded that the creation of a direct link between these and the Pope's silence during the Holocaust was not possible until the Vatican began to augment the available documents through opening its own archives.

What Friedländer could do, however, was focus on the efforts of one highly placed Catholic who tried to do something to stop the Holocaust. In *Kurt Gerstein: The Ambiguity of Good* (1969), he examined the actions of Kurt Gerstein, an SS officer who witnessed Nazi actions against Jews at the extermination camps of Bełzec and Treblinka. Shocked by what he saw, he tried to inform public opinion about what the Nazis were doing through contacts in the Swedish diplomatic service and through the Roman Catholic Church. Friedländer's book examined the motives underpinning Gerstein's behaviour; a devout Catholic, he was also an officer in charge of disinfection techniques, and thus an important cog in the Nazi machinery of death. From the day he first learned of the Nazi gassings, however, he sought to find ways of informing the world of what was happening. At the same time, he was unable to tip his hand by exhibiting any lack of enthusiasm for the Nazi killing processes. Based on a wide array of documents, Friedländer's book showed a tortured soul who was ultimately unable to effect any change in a system he detested.

Friedländer's main thinking on the Holocaust developed during the intensely rich period of controversy in the 1980s known in Germany as the *Historikerstreit* – a time when German historians, in particular, engaged in often heated debates about the way the Holocaust should be interpreted historically. The debate drew in other historians from around the world, including **Yehuda Bauer** and **Christopher Browning**. Friedländer also weighed in with his own contributions.

Advocating an Intentionalist perspective on the origins of the Holocaust, he qualified his views with the argument that there was no intention to exterminate the Jews of Europe before 1941. Along with **Browning**, Friedländer holds a perspective best described as 'moderate Intentionalist'. This did not prevent him taking issue with one of the leading German actors in the *Historikerstreit*, Martin Broszat, who called for the 'historicisation' of the Third Reich rather than the ongoing 'demonisation' of the period that had characterised much of the scholarship up to that point. The debate between Broszat and Friedländer was carried out through an energetic correspondence conducted between 1987 and 1989. In 1990, this correspondence was edited by Peter Baldwin and published in book form as *Reworking the Past: Hitler, The Holocaust, and the Historians' Debate* (Brozsat and Friedländer, 1990: 102–32).

In 1979 Friedländer wrote a memoir of his childhood years, *When Memory Comes*. This was a very different kind of history, in which he plumbed the depths of his recollections as a boy between the ages of 7 and 12, interspersed with his reflections on these same times as an adult in 1977. Here, we can see the origin of Friedländer's intensity as a historian, as he discussed the pain of family separation, being raised in an alien (Catholic) environment, eventually learning the fate of his family, and his emigration to Israel – another alien environment, though one that was less frightening. Above all, a close reading of this book shows us just how far Friedländer saw Nazism as a force dedicated to destruction, a horrific event for which normal language is unsuited. The struggle to come to grips with his own history motivated Friedländer to try to find a way to understand the nature of Germany in the Nazi era, and ultimately led him to become one of the most influential scholars on the history of the Holocaust.

By 1992 Friedländer had already established himself as an important thinker and teacher of the Holocaust, but in that year he produced an edited volume that reflected deeply his interest in searching for meaning. In *Probing the Limits of Representation: Nazism and the 'Final Solution'* (1992), Friedländer included essays from a number of leading scholars of the Holocaust, including **Christopher Browning** and **Berel Lang**, among many others of high repute. He outlined the parameters of his assignment in his Introduction:

> This project evokes some doubts which are not easily dispelled. Can the extermination of the Jews of Europe be the object of theoretical discussions? Is it not unacceptable to debate formal and abstract issues in relation to this catastrophe? It would be if these abstract issues were not directly related to the way contemporary culture reshapes the image of this past. Present memory of Nazism and its crimes is directly influenced by global intellectual shifts intrinsically linked to the questions raised in this volume. The necessity of such discussion is thus clear; it will be evident, moreover, that none of the contributors has forgotten the horror behind the words.
>
> (Friedländer, 1992: 1)

These thoughts set Friedländer up for what was to follow, a stinging critique of those who would say that the Holocaust is unapproachable:

> The extermination of the Jews of Europe is as accessible to both representation and interpretation as any other historical event.

125

But we are dealing with an event which tests our traditional conceptual and representational categories, an 'event at the limits.'

What turns the 'Final Solution' into an event at the limits is the very fact that it is the most radical form of genocide encountered in history: the willful, systematic, industrially organized, largely successful attempt totally to exterminate an entire human group within twentieth-century Western society.

(Friedländer, 1992: 2–3)

As if to reinforce his point, Friedländer followed up this book with another collection a year later. In *Memory, History, and the Extermination of the Jews of Europe* (1993), he brought together a range of essays he had written between 1985 and 1992, during which time the collapse of communism had shed new light on the nature of totalitarianism and persecution. Here, he was mainly concerned about the relationship between memory and history, that is, how the evolution of attitudes towards the Nazi period and the Holocaust had undergone change over time within German and Jewish memory, and why it was that individual memories and collective recollection of the past appeared to be divergent. In particular, he was conscious that:

we are confronted with an insoluble choice between the *inadequacy* of traditional historiographical representation and the need to establish as reliable a narration as possible. At the same time we must comply with the most rigorous requirements of scholarship in order to keep records of events which are constantly challenged by a negationist trend.

(Friedländer, 1993: x, emphasis in original)

He would soon put his words into practice in the most telling of ways, with the publication of two major works that would have a profound impact on the nature of Holocaust scholarship.

The first of these, *Nazi Germany and the Jews, 1933–1939* (1997), was intended as Friedländer's response to the assertions made by his opponents, in particular Martin Broszat. It took the form of a definitive history of Nazi policies prior to the Holocaust, and in June 1999 he was awarded a prestigious MacArthur Foundation 'genius' grant for having 'transformed our understanding of this period by weaving into a coherent whole the perspectives of the participants: ordinary Germans, party activists, military and political figures and, most

importantly, victims and survivors' (http://www.research.ucla.edu/chal/
99/highlights/article02.htm). In this work, Friedländer employed
newly available documents in order to draw an intimate picture of
German-Jewish society before the outbreak of the Second World
War, at a time in which some form of 'normality' still prevailed
despite the increasingly anti-Semitic measures imposed by the Nazi
regime. He related methodically how each anti-Jewish measure led to
the next, then the next, and so on, noting that all the while there was
not the slightest hint that any sort of 'final solution' was in the offing.
As he rightly observed, Hitler's main goal in the late 1930s was for-
cible Jewish emigration rather than annihilation, and he found no
evidence of any plan for extermination prior to Germany's invasion
of the Soviet Union in mid-1941. While considering the ways in
which early Nazi anti-Semitic measures developed, the book also
looked at the nature of the Jewish community, seeking to learn why
it was that there was so little resistance to Nazi legislation. He showed
clearly that relatively few Jews saw any reason for panic in the face of
the Nazi actions, and that emigration was consequently very slow in
developing a momentum. Moreover, there was little opposition to
the regime voiced from any of the sources that might be expected to
raise objections: the Protestant and Catholic Churches, universities,
the press and even the labour movement were either muzzled or
voluntarily remained silent (when not enthusiastically supporting the
regime).

Friedländer used the MacArthur Foundation 'genius' grant as seed
money to assist in the research phase of what would be a follow-up
study that would take the story up to the end of the Second World
War, and cover the period 1939–45. The result – an 870-page
volume entitled *The Years of Extermination: Nazi Germany and the Jews,
1939–1945* (2007) – would ultimately win Friedländer the 2008
Pulitzer Prize for General Non-Fiction.

Friedländer noted that the 'history of the Holocaust' – he used the
designation in quotation marks –

> cannot be limited only to a recounting of German policies,
> decisions, and measures that led to this most systematic and sus-
> tained of genocides; it must include the reactions (and at times
> the initiatives) of the surrounding world and the attitudes of the
> victims, for the fundamental reason that the events we call the
> Holocaust represent a totality defined by this very convergence of
> distinct elements.

> (Friedländer, 2007: xv)

As a result, his history is in many respects as much a history of everyday life under Nazi persecution as it is of Nazi actions and programmes. That said, Friedländer recognised that this convergence was not something that should be dealt with flippantly; indeed, 'No single framework can encompass the diverse and converging strands of such a history' (Friedländer, 2007: xvi). His solution was thus to focus

> on the centrality of ideological-cultural factors as the prime movers of Nazi policies in regard to the Jewish issue, depending of course on circumstances, institutional dynamics, and essentially, for the period dealt with here, on the evolution of the war.
>
> (Friedländer, 2007: xvii)

The Years of Extermination was a book that skilfully interwove individual testimony into the broader picture. The personal accounts Friedländer employed built a picture of how Jews in Europe (and particularly in the Third Reich) viewed their impending fate only by increments – and, for those who were not direct targets of the Nazis, how the events swirling around them were greeted by an attitude of indifference, if not always active cooperation. What Friedländer managed to develop in this volume was an obvious extension to his earlier examination of the pre-war years, making an otherwise complex story manageable, and it is here that his skills – and his contribution to scholarship – shone through.

Overall, it can be said that Saul Friedländer is the academic equivalent of **Elie Wiesel** and **Primo Levi**, namely, a survivor-scholar whose contribution to the field of Holocaust Studies is both vast and multi-faceted. As a historian, he has been a thinker who has mastered the skill of synthesising considerable amounts of original material, and also in building on the research of others. In addition, he has consistently advocated that any history of the Holocaust must include the human voices of those who experienced it in their flesh – the victims themselves. While official documents are of course vital, and the bedrock for subjects of study such as the Holocaust, Friedländer's technique has been exemplary in bringing the human dimension into consideration. Without this, he has unswervingly argued, the story will always be incomplete. As a thinker about the Holocaust, therefore, Freidländer is not so much a visionary as a guardian, one who has spent an academic lifetime keeping alive the human dimension of the victims rather than focusing only on the process that led to their victimhood.

Friedländer's major writings

Pius XII and the Third Reich: A Documentation, New York: Knopf, 1966.

Prelude to Downfall: Hitler and the United States 1939–1941, London: Chatto and Windus, 1967.

Kurt Gerstein: The Ambiguity of Good, New York: Knopf, 1969.

L'Antisémitisme nazi: histoire d'une psychose collective, Paris: Editions du Seuil, 1971.

Some Aspects of the Historical Significance of the Holocaust, Jerusalem: Institute of Contemporary Jewry, Hebrew University of Jerusalem, 1977.

History and Psychoanalysis: An Inquiry Into the Possibilities and Limits of Psychohistory, New York: Holmes and Meier, 1978.

When Memory Comes, New York: Farrar, Straus and Giroux, 1979.

Reflections of Nazism: An Essay on Kitsch and Death, New York: Harper and Row, 1984.

Visions of Apocalypse: End or Rebirth?, New York: Holmes and Meier, 1985.

(Ed.) *Probing the Limits of Representation: Nazism and the 'Final Solution,'* Cambridge (MA): Harvard University Press, 1992.

Memory, History, and the Extermination of the Jews of Europe, Bloomington (IN): Indiana University Press, 1993.

Nazi Germany and the Jews, 1933–1939, New York: HarperCollins, 1997.

The Years of Extermination: Nazi Germany and the Jews, 1939–1945, New York: HarperCollins, 2007.

References

Brozsat, Martin and Saul Friedländer, 'A Controversy about the Historicization of National Socialism', in Peter Baldwin (ed.), *Reworking the Past: Hitler, The Holocaust, and the Historians' Debate*, Boston: Beacon Press, 1990, 102–32.

BARBARA HARFF AND TED ROBERT GURR (b. 1942)

Just as **A. Roy Eckardt** and **Alice Lyons Eckardt** in respect of the Holocaust, Barbara Harff and Ted Robert Gurr have made important contributions to genocide scholarship both together and in their own right. Harff is a former Professor of Political Science at the United States Naval Academy, Annapolis, Maryland. She is best known for her rigorous statistical methodologies examining various genocides, as well as her coinage of the word 'politicide' to describe mass political killings in view of the failure of the 1948 United Nations Convention on Genocide to include such destruction within its definition. Gurr is currently Distinguished University Professor Emeritus at the University of Maryland, a political scientist and an internationally recognised authority on the causes and management of political conflict, instability and ethnic conflict.

Harff was born in 1942 in Kassel, Germany. After migrating to the United States she obtained her PhD in political science from Northwestern University, Illinois. Gurr was born in Spokane, Washington in 1936, and received his PhD in international relations from New York University.

Harff's initial interest in the Holocaust came as a result of her having read Gerhard Schoenberner's *The Yellow Star: The Persecution of the Jews in Europe, 1933–1945*, in 1960. Over time, the more she reflected on what she read, the more personally uneasy she became regarding the behaviour of her country towards minorities during the Third Reich. She became distressed by the failure of law to protect those rendered vulnerable, and her first visit to the site of the Auschwitz extermination camp, in 1983, furthered her journey towards issues of human rights and social responsibility in the context of genocide.

These seminal experiences led Harff to start compiling massive amounts of data regarding genocide, accompanied by her own increasing dissatisfaction with the inadequacy of the term itself. Ultimately, this led her to coin a new term, 'politicide', which she defined as:

> The promotion, execution and/or implied consent of sustained policies by governing elites or their agents – or in the case of civil war either of the contending authorities – that result in the death of a substantial portion of a communal, political, or politicized communal group. ... In genocides, the victimized groups are defined primarily in terms of their communal characteristics. In politicides, by contrast, groups are defined primarily in terms of political opposition to the regime and dominant groups.
>
> (Harff, 2002: 106)

Harff, seeing how unacceptable was the omission of political groups from the UN Convention on Genocide in light of such politically driven atrocities as those of the Khmer Rouge in Cambodia, made political groups the centrepiece of her definition. She agreed that questions of motive and intent are necessary to any assessment of genocide and politicide (often difficult to discern and not always easy to uncover), but concluded that 'true genocides are rare'; most cases are, in fact, politicides (Harff, 2002: 106; see also Harff, 2005: 57–61). Bringing together her concerns with both the specificity of the *Shoah* and genocide more broadly, she developed a 'structural model [Very

High, High, Medium, and Low] ... to assess the risks of future episodes in 25 countries' – engaging in armed conflict in 2001. These risks were based upon such factors as (1) prior geno/politicides, (2) upheaval since 1986, (3) risk factors (minority elites, exclusionary ideology, type of regime, trade openness), and (4) possible target group(s). Among those rated 'very high' were Afghanistan, Burundi, Rwanda, Congo, Sierra Leone, Algeria, Philippines, Columbia and Israel (Harff, 2003: 57–73).

She also drew an important distinction between what she labelled 'accelerator events' and 'trigger events', using the easily discernible analogy that 'triggers are the equivalent of a match thrown onto a combustible pile, whereas accelerators are the gasoline poured on the pile making it combustible' (Harff, 1998: 73.) Further, she argued that current weaknesses in the data collection process were caused by the failure of most analysts 'to give reliable assessments of whether, where, and when we can expect different types of crises to occur' and the lack of any 'established systematic early warning system', arguing that such information be made readily available in the public arena (Harff, 1998: 110).

Throughout her writing Harff has advocated strongly for humanitarian intervention, though never as a first option. In 1995 she wrote, 'I favor humanitarian intervention as a last resort to correct massive abuses of human rights, that is, to protect people from genocide and political mass murder' (Harff, 1995: 23–24). She drew a critical distinction, however, between rescue operations, which open borders and the possibility of emigration, and interventions, which enable populations in conflict to remain in residence. Such interventions 'must combine precise policy goals, clear strategic objectives, and tactics that are suited to the desired end-state of the military involvement' (Harff, 1992b: 2). In addressing the situations in Bosnia and Somalia in 1992, for example, she noted that

> the international community has at its disposal a wide variety of interventionist possibilities, ranging from the issuing of early-warning assessments, to mediation and arbitration with nation-state perpetrators, to condemnation, to the withdrawal of diplomatic recognition, to 'limited shows of force,' to 'selective applications of force,' to 'collective military intervention,' and, finally, to establishing 'internationally sponsored trusteeships, rebuild civil administration and basic services, provide material and technical assistance, supervise free elections' to nation-states torn apart by genocides and/or politicides.
>
> (Harff, 1992b: 5–6)

In articulating the ramifications of such interventions, Harff has not been above challenging the otherwise sacrosanct notion of state sovereignty, and asserting that concerns for human life must of necessity trump concerns relating to nation-state boundaries.

Harff's husband Ted Robert Gurr is one of the world's leading authorities on the identification of minorities at risk. In 1968, after the assassinations of Dr Martin Luther King and Robert Kennedy, he was asked by US President Lyndon Johnson to join the national Commission on the Causes and Prevention of Violence. That assignment saw him co-author a widely disseminated report, *Violence in America: Historical and Comparative Perspectives* (1969). In 1970, his book *Why Men Rebel* received the American Political Science Association Woodrow Wilson Prize as the best book of that year. For Gurr, 'to understand violent conflict within societies, it is essential to begin by understanding people's shared grievances and beliefs, and that to defuse violence it is necessary to alleviate some of those grievances' (Gurr, 1970: 2).

Gurr was also one of the early scholars to raise questions about the implications of resource scarcity and economic decline and their neglect by political analysts, and pressed for the need for much more empirical research on these topics (Gurr, 1985: 51–75). Further, he addressed such questions as the rise of coercive states, contending that they maintain their hold on their populations through military and police activity fostering and maintaining elite political cultures that utilise coercion to maintain their power, and that such states remain potentially violent towards sub-populations (Gurr, 1988: 45–65).

As president of the International Studies Association in 1993–94, he was approached by US Vice President Al Gore to help establish the White House State Failure Task Force (later renamed the Political Instability Task Force), and for more than 10 years thereafter he remained a senior consultant providing global risk assessments of impending intrastate conflicts. He continued to serve in this capacity under George W. Bush and Barack Obama.

In an important study concerning population vulnerability published in 1994, he divided the world into six regions and looked at 190 countries, finding 120 of them with minorities at risk (embracing 292 minority populations), totalling more than 988,701,000 persons (Gurr, 1994: 347–77). Based on this information, he later concluded that the 'international community [must] accept a common obligation to protect collective rights within such an emergent system', while not imposing 'cultural standards or political agendas on other peoples' (Gurr, 1995: 212).

Six years before this study, Gurr, together with James R. Scarritt of the University of Colorado at Boulder, had studied '261 non-sovereign peoples who are both numerically significant and accorded separate and unequal treatment. ... [M]ost are outnumbered by other groups within the jurisdiction they inhabit. More precisely, they are *differentially treated communal groups*' (Gurr and Scarritt, 1989: 375–405, emphasis in original). The authors divided the world into eight regions and examined 126 countries, finding 99 of them with minorities at risk (embracing 261 minority populations), totalling more than 913,812,000 persons. Thus, revisiting the same scenario only 6 years later, and using the same methodological tools and increasing the data base as to the number of countries studied, Gurr identified an increase of approximately 9.2 per cent in populations at risk.

As founding director of the Minorities at Risk Project at the University of Maryland's Center for International Development and Conflict Management, Gurr's major interest concerned the predictive value of data regarding nation-state instability, and he addressed this with his colleague Will H. Moore in 1990. Using a theoretical model based on deprivation and resource mobilisation, they examined fifty-eight cases of armed rebellion, and, working backwards to the 1980s, attempted to determine if their model had any predictive value. Their conclusion was that their model *did* in fact help explain those groups which would rebel as well as those that would not (Gurr and Moore, 1990: 1079–103).

Elsewhere, Gurr also suggested that ethnic warfare may actually be waning, which, if true, would be 'one of the signal accomplishments of the first post-Cold War decade'. In his view, 'Today, class, ethnicity, and faith are the three main alternative sources of mass movements, and class-based and religious movements may well drain away some of the popular support that now energizes ethnic political movements' (Gurr, 2000b: 63–64). This could suggest that the genocides of the future may posit differences other than those heretofore seen.

Together, Harff and Gurr have worked closely to develop and enhance an understanding of genocide, politicide and conflict resolution, collaborating on a number of important publications. In one such study, they argued that:

> our definitions are not victim-centered. Although the intrinsic characteristics of the victims are important, what is crucial are the characteristics and purposes of the state ... whether an episode of mass killing is a genocide or a politicide depends on the combination of the state's objectives, the motives of its ruling elite, the

prevailing ideology, and the power relations within its authority structure.

(Harff and Gurr, 1988: 360)

Developing this, they constructed a typology of two kinds of genocide (hegemonial and xenophobic) and four kinds of politicides (retributive, repressive, revolutionary and repressive/hegemonial), leading them to a specific agenda:

1. the need to complete 'the search for episodes which meet our criteria and to compile background material on them',
2. the advance of 'a detailed comparative analysis of coded information on each episode',
3. 'the further development and testing of theoretical explanations of the cases and processes of geno/politicide', and, most importantly,
4. the use of 'this kind of data base to assess the likelihood that communal minorities now involved in conflicts are at risk of victimization in future episodes of genocide and politicide'.

(Harff and Gurr, 1988: 370–71)

They have also worked together on a risk-assessment model of conflict, and have assembled what they regard as international background, internal background and intervening conditions, all of which become part of the analytical model necessary for predicting potential genocides and/or politicides:

1. *International Background Conditions*: shifting global alliances, reaction to political upheaval, international economic status of the regime;
2. *Internal Background Conditions*: strength of group identities in heterogeneous societies, degree of factionalisation within a communal group, a history of the governing elite's reliance on coercion to seize and maintain power, duration and strength of democratic experience;
3. *Intervening Conditions*: a governing elite's commitment to an ideology that excludes categories of people defined in terms of class, belief or ethnicity from the universe of obligations, fragmentation/ competition within the governing elite, state security agencies that operate with few legal or institutional restraints, charismatic leadership that generates mass followership, economic hardship that results in differential treatment for disadvantaged groups.

(Harff and Gurr, 1998: 561–62)

A number of factors have driven the work of these two scholars. Barbara Harff has made an important contribution to the way in which quantitative research on genocide prevention is undertaken. The value of her work lies not only in the accumulation and assessment of vast quantities of data regarding countries in internal conflict, the delineation of the various factors responsible for that conflict, and the examination even more closely of the vulnerable sub-populations at risk of genocide and/or politicide; it is also in her recognition of the moral necessity of attempting to establish solid early warning systems, grounded in both analysis and theoretical understanding. Likewise, Ted Robert Gurr's concerns, relating to the collection and analysis of empirical data, rigorous methodological work, theoretical and predictive writing, and concern for potentially victimised minority populations, have marked his seminal contributions to the development of an understanding of a world at risk of continued violence and unending horror.

Between them, Harff and Gurr have offered vital insights into the ways in which quantitative social-science methods can be employed in a predictive capacity to identify vulnerable populations, and their contribution to the field of Genocide Studies has thus been profound and highly influential.

Major writings

NOTE: It can be difficult to separate the work of Harff and Gurr into areas of discrete authorship, as their collaboration took many forms – some of which were informal as to attribution. The following, however, should serve as a guide to their various activities, independently and jointly.

Barbara Harff

Genocide and Human Rights: International Legal and Political Issues, Denver: University of Denver Monograph Series in World Affairs, 1984.

'The Etiology of Genocide', in Michael N. Dobkowski and Isidore Walliman (eds), *The Age of Genocide*, Westport (CT): Greenwood Press, 1987a, 41–59.

'Empathy for Victims of Massive Human Rights Violations and Support for Government Intervention: A Comparative Study of American and Australian Attitudes', *Political Psychology*, 8, 1 (1987b), 1–20.

'Recognizing Genocides', in Helen Fein (ed.), *Genocide Watch*, New Haven (CT): Yale University Press, 1992a, pp. 27–41.

'Bosnia and Somalia: The Strategic, Legal and Moral Aspects of Humanitarian Intervention', in *Report from the Institute for Philosophy and*

Public Policy, College Park (MD): University of Maryland, Institute for Philosophy and Public Policy, Fall 1992b, 1–7.

'Rescuing Endangered Peoples: Missed Opportunities', *Social Research*, 62 (Spring 1995), 23–40.

'An Early Warning of Potential Genocide: The Cases of Rwanda, Burundi, Bosnia and Abkhazia', in Ted Robert Gurr and Barbara Harff (eds), *Early Warning of Communal Conflicts and Humanitarian Crises*, Tokyo: United Nations University Press, 1996.

'Early Warning of Humanitarian Crises: Sequential Models and the Role of Accelerators', in John L. Davies and Ted Robert Gurr (eds), *Preventive Measures: Building Risk Assessment and Crisis Early Warning Systems*, Totowa (NJ): Rowman and Littlefield, 1998, 73.

'A German-born Genocide Scholar', in Samuel Totten and Steven Leonard Jacobs (eds), *Pioneers of Genocide Studies*, New Brunswick (NJ): Transaction Publishers, 2002, 97–112.

'No Lessons Learned from the Holocaust? Assessing Risks of Genocide and Political Mass Murder since 1955', *American Political Science Review*, 97, 1 (2003), 57–73.

'Assessing Risks of Genocide and Politicide', in Monty G. Marshall and Ted Robert Gurr (eds), *Peace and Conflict 2005*, College Park (MD): Center for International Development and Conflict Management, 2005, 57–61.

Ted Robert Gurr

(with Hugh Davis Graham) *Violence in America: Historical and Comparative Perspectives*, Washington DC: US Government Printing Office, 1969.

Why Men Rebel, Princeton (NJ): Princeton University Press, 1970.

'On the Political Consequences of Scarcity and Economic Decline', *International Studies Quarterly*, 29 (1985), 51–75.

'War, Revolution, and the Growth of the Coercive State', *Comparative Political Studies* (1988), 45–65.

(with James R. Scarritt) 'Minorities at Risk: A Global Survey', *Human Rights Quarterly*, 11, 3 (1989), 375–405.

(with Will H. Moore) 'Ethnopolitical Rebellion: A Cross-Sectional Analysis of the 1980s with Risk Assessment for the 1990s', *American Journal of Political Science*, 41, 4 (1990), 1079–103.

Minorities at Risk: A Global View of Ethnopolitical Conflict, Washington DC: US Institute of Peace Press, 1993.

'Peoples against States: Ethnopolitical Conflict and the Changing World System', *International Studies Quarterly*, 38 (1994), 347–77.

'Communal Conflicts and Global Security', *Current History*, 94, 592 (1995), 212–17.

(Ed. with John L. Davies) *Preventive Measures: Building Risk Assessment and Crisis Early Warning Systems*, Lanham (MD): Rowman and Littlefield, 1998.

Peoples versus States: Minorities at Risk in the New Century, Washington DC: US Institute of Peace Press, 2000a.

'Ethnic Warfare on the Wane', *Foreign Affairs*, 79, 3 (2000b), 63–64.

(Ed. with Deepa Khosla and Monty G. Marshall) *Peace and Conflict 2001*, College Park (MD): Center for International Development and Conflict Management, 2001.

(Ed. with Monty G. Marshall) *Peace and Conflict 2003*, College Park (MD): Center for International Development and Conflict Management, 2003.

(Ed. with Monty G. Marshall) *Peace and Conflict 2005*, College Park (MD): Center for International Development and Conflict Management, 2005.

(Ed. with Joseph Hewitt and Jonathan Wilkenfeld) *Peace and Conflict 2008*, Boulder (CO): Paradigm Publishers, 2007.

(Ed. with Joseph Hewitt and Jonathan Wilkenfeld) *Peace and Conflict 2010*, Boulder (CO): Paradigm Publishers, 2009.

Barbara Harff and Ted Robert Gurr

'Toward Empirical Theory of Genocides and Politicides: Identification and Measurement of Cases since 1945', *International Studies Quarterly,* 32 (1988), 359–71.

Ethnic Conflict in World Politics, Boulder (CO): Westview Press, 1994; second edition revised, 2003.

'Victims of the State: Genocides, Politicides, and Group Repression from 1945 to 1995', in Albert J. Jongman (ed.), *Contemporary Genocides: Causes, Cases, Consequences*, Leiden: Interdisciplinary Research Program on Root Causes of Human Rights Violations (PIOOM), Department of Political Sciences, University of Leiden, 1996a, 33–58.

(Ed.) *Early Warnings of Communal Conflicts and Genocide: Linking Empirical Research to International Responses*, Tokyo: United Nations University Press, 1996b.

'A Systematic Early Warning of Humanitarian Emergencies', *Journal of Peace Research*, 35 (September 1998), 551–80.

RAUL HILBERG (1926–2007)

Raul Hilberg, one of the earliest major scholars of the Holocaust, was an Austrian-born American political scientist. His examination of the evolution and execution of the Nazi programme of Jewish annihilation, *The Destruction of the European Jews* (1961), detailed for the first time the manner in which mass murder under the Nazis became possible. The work was a groundbreaking piece of research which effectively set in train the academic study of the Holocaust throughout the English-speaking world.

Hilberg was born to a Jewish family in Vienna in 1926. In April 1939 the family fled Nazi persecution, transiting through France and Cuba before reaching the United States. The Hilbergs settled in New York, where Raul attended Brooklyn College. After the United

States entered the Second World War, Hilberg was drafted into the US army. As a native speaker of German, he was seconded to the War Documentation Department, charged with examining Nazi (and other) archives. It was this that prompted his initial research into the Nazi destruction of the Jews. After the war Hilberg returned to academic study, completing a PhD under the direction of Franz Neumann at Columbia University. He obtained an academic position at the University of Vermont in 1955 (after a year teaching at the University of Puerto Rico), and spent the rest of his academic life there.

The Destruction of the European Jews, Hilberg's best-known scholarly work, was also his biggest in terms of size and influence. It was not easy for him to find a publisher, as there were still many in the United States in the late 1950s and early 1960s who were reluctant to confront precisely what had happened in the Third Reich. He offered the manuscript to a number of mainstream academic publishers, most of whom rejected it on the grounds that at over 1,200 pages long it was too unwieldy, or that as a work of scholarship it was based too exclusively on German documents. Eventually he was successful in attracting the attention of Quadrangle Books, then a small Chicago publisher. It began with a tiny print run, but the book's sheer size and authority meant that it could not remain hidden for long. Appearing at precisely the same time as the capture and trial of Adolf Eichmann, the book began to spark the interest of specialists within the academy – including **Hannah Arendt**, who employed it extensively in her own work on Eichmann (Arendt, 1963) – as well as among a broader readership. While recognition of Hilberg's achievement was far from immediate, the appearance of *The Destruction of the European Jews* nonetheless marked an important passage in the historiography of what, later in the decade, came to be called the Holocaust.

Hilberg's main thrust was that the Holocaust was the result of a huge bureaucratic machine with thousands of participants, not the fulfilment of a preconceived plan by Hitler. Responsibility, from this perspective, was diffused out to a wide variety of agencies, as innumerable instructions from a multitude of government offices were forwarded, formally and informally, to a range of actors. These included not only Nazis enforcing policy directives, but also train timetablers, procurement agents and concentration camp designers, among others. Hilberg thereby established a model, supported by a painstaking devotion to tens of thousands of Nazi documents, of how the bureaucratic machinery of the Nazi state had made the murder of millions of Jews possible. Instead of focusing on leaders, Hilberg showed how the Nazi programme was the product of a system that evolved over time. Each step in this process was more extreme: in a classic taxonomy of genocide, Hilberg identified that the Jews were first defined as enemies of the state, then discriminated against and disenfranchised, then had their property expropriated, were moved into ghettos, and, finally, were transported to their deaths.

Hilberg's book attracted criticism for more than just its size. His methodology, for example, was not seen to be sufficiently sympathetic to Hitler's targets, the Jews, for not only did Hilberg place his emphasis on the perpetrators rather than the victims; he also showed that Nazi-imposed institutions such as the *Judenräte* (Jewish councils) led some Jews to be complicit in their own demise. He was further criticised for not taking into account the wide variety of *Judenrat* responses to Nazism, and for downgrading the impact and extent of Jewish resistance.

Overall, however, this emphasis was not what Hilberg wished his study to pursue. Not examining the suffering of the Jews was deliberate; he preferred to examine the means whereby the Nazis could achieve their objective of wiping out a complete group of people numbering millions. He was not interested in questions relating to the historical background of European or Nazi anti-Semitism. As he wrote in the very first paragraph of his Preface, 'this is not a book about the Jews. It is a book about the people who destroyed the Jews' (Hilberg, 1961: v). When critics attacked his book, therefore, they were in fact often condemning him for a book he had not written, rather than for the one before them.

As the field of Holocaust Studies developed over the next 15 to 20 years Hilberg's pioneering contribution came to be recognised more widely. Over time, the work was regarded as a seminal study of the process of the Nazi Final Solution. His fidelity to the documents accompanied him through all his work, acting as the ultimate guidance for the conclusions he drew, and his influence grew steadily among succeeding generations of Holocaust scholars. Not only Hilberg's model, but in many instances also his very terminology – such as, for example, his reference to the principal actors in the Holocaust as perpetrators, victims and bystanders – has since been employed widely.

The Destruction of the European Jews, which was produced as a single volume on double-columned pages, was reissued twice more in expanded editions of three volumes (in 1985 and 2003), further reinforcing Hilberg's place as one of the most pioneering and original thinkers regarding the process of Nazi destruction of Jews during the Holocaust. His influence was profound in reinforcing the work of other historians of Nazism, such as **Hans Mommsen** and Martin Broszat, as the so-called Functionalist school of thought was developing. In the United States, Hilberg's work had a significant impact on the intellectual development of **Christopher Browning**, who extended the former's approach regarding Nazism's murderous bureaucratic machine. **Browning**, following Hilberg, also relied heavily on the use of Nazi documents in reaching his conclusions (Browning, 2007).

So committed was Hilberg to the importance of using original sources in historical writing that in a much later work he evaluated the varied types of material scholars have available from which to rescue the history of the Holocaust. In *Sources of Holocaust Research: An Analysis* (2001), he attempted to develop an accessible means whereby scholars could amalgamate data and draw conclusions about the nature of the Third Reich. Survivor testimonies, contemporary government memoranda, diary entries, letters of all kinds, newspaper accounts: these and many other sources of Holocaust history were analysed, with the intention both of alerting readers to their diversity, and of showing some of the ways in which such material can be employed. Looking at his own work, he asked himself the question:

> what is the nature of my sources? They are not identical to the subject matter. They have their own history and qualities, which are different from the actions they depict and which require a separate approach.
>
> (Hilberg, 2001: 7–8)

As he showed, engaging in such work is not always easy. Moreover, he insisted that documents could be as significant for what they do not say as for what they explicitly describe. Overall, he demonstrated that different types of documents can be utilised as accurate sources for the writing of history. He showed the ways in which *all* material, even the most fragmentary, can be employed so as to recreate a reliable record of what happened during the Holocaust.

In 1979, Hilberg, together with Stanislaw Staron (Professor of Political Science at the University of Vermont) and Josef Kermisz (Director of Archives at Yad Vashem, Jerusalem) published *The Warsaw Diary of Adam Czerniakow: Prelude to Doom*, which was Czerniakow's record of day-to-day life as the head of the *Judenrat* in the Nazi-occupied city. In a 45-page Introduction, Hilberg and Staron outlined clearly the nature of the *Judenrat*, where it fitted into the Nazi administrative arrangements for Warsaw's Jews, and what Czerniakow's role was within it. Once more, Hilberg showed his familiarity with documentary resources. In the translation of the diary itself, he provided a careful set of explanatory notes. Overall, the project took about six years, after which Hilberg could look back with satisfaction on having rescued an important part of Holocaust history for the general public which might otherwise have been closed off in the archives at Yad Vashem. Hilberg's work became an indispensable addition to the literature in English that had appeared by the 1970s regarding life in other places such as the Warsaw Ghetto.

By the 1990s, Hilberg's readers were beginning to wonder whether he had anything left to say that could come close to matching *The Destruction of the European Jews*. While this massive work was the definitive statement of his authority, he nonetheless saw a need to supplement it with an investigation of the people behind the process he had so thoroughly delineated earlier. The result was *Perpetrators, Victims, Bystanders: The Jewish Catastrophe, 1933–1945*, which appeared in 1992. Here, he put forth his views on the 'who', rather than the 'how' of the Holocaust, and, as with his treatment of the multifarious nature of documents, he showed that those involved in the Holocaust (defined at its broadest) were many and varied. While this might seem like a given, it had not yet been treated thoroughly until Hilberg articulated the notion in his typically painstaking and careful manner. As he identified the issue, the Jewish catastrophe was an event 'that was experienced by a variety of perpetrators, a multitude of victims, and a host of bystanders. ... Each saw what had happened from its own, special perspective, and each harbored a separate set of attitudes and reactions' (Hilberg, 1992: ix). It was to an investigation of these responses that Hilberg devoted his attention in this volume, in a project that took several years of research and writing.

In 1996 Hilberg produced his memoir, *The Politics of Memory: The Journey of a Holocaust Historian*. This was a sometimes passionate account of the testing ordeals that befell him as he strove to advance his career, establish himself in the area of Holocaust Studies and fend off those who did not agree with his conclusions. Less a vindication of his work than an explanation of how it came to take the shape it did, this book gave an insight into the man behind the writing, and showed just how difficult it was for him to find acceptance in a field that was still nascent even as he wrote.

A few years before his death, Hilberg laid out for younger scholars the challenge that lay before them:

> In its advanced stages, Holocaust research has given rise to specializations and subspecializations. As the subject is divided into microcomponents, similarities and distinctions may be seen with greater acuity, but there is not finality. Findings are always subject to correction and reformulation. That is in the nature of the empirical enterprise. Since historiography is also an art form, there is inevitably a striving for perfection. Yet the reality of the events is elusive, as it must be, and the unremitting effort continues for the small incremental gains, no matter what their cost, lest all be relinquished and forgotten.
>
> (Hilberg, 2001: 204)

It was simultaneously a statement of what needed to be done, and how far Holocaust research had come since Hilberg first began his work – largely, it might be said, as a result of his own efforts.

In 1979, Raul Hilberg was appointed by President Jimmy Carter to the President's Commission on the Holocaust. A much-decorated scholar, he was also honoured by the German government through the award of that country's Order of Merit, the highest award that can be paid to a non-German. When Hilberg died in 2007, he was mourned by generations of students and colleagues who acknowledged his immense contribution to the establishment of a field of study which had not existed prior to his pioneering endeavours.

Hilberg's major writings

The Destruction of the European Jews, Chicago: Quadrangle Books, 1961.

(Ed.) *Documents of Destruction: Germany and Jewry, 1933–1945*, Chicago: Quadrangle Books, 1971.

(Ed. with Stanislaw Staron and Josef Kermisz) *The Warsaw Diary of Adam Czerniakow: Prelude to Doom*, New York: Stein and Day, 1979.

The Holocaust Today, Syracuse (NY): Syracuse University Press, 1988.

Perpetrators, Victims, Bystanders: The Jewish Catastrophe, 1933–1945, New York: Aaron Asher Books, 1992.

The Politics of Memory: The Journey of a Holocaust Historian, Chicago: Ivan R. Dee, 1996.

Sources of Holocaust Research: An Analysis, Chicago: Ivan R. Dee, 2001.

References

Arendt, Hannah, *Eichmann in Jerusalem: A Report on the Banality of Evil*, New York: Viking, 1963.

Browning, Christopher, *The Origins of the Final Solution: The Evolution of Nazi Jewish Policy, September 1939–March 1942*, Lincoln (NE): University of Nebraska Press, 2007.

ALEXANDER LABAN HINTON (b. 1963)

Alex Hinton is a Professor in the Department of Anthropology and Global Affairs at Rutgers University, New Jersey, and founding director, since 2007, of its Center for the Study of Genocide and Human Rights. Born in 1963 in Palo Alto, California, Hinton obtained his PhD in Anthropology from Emory University, Atlanta. He is one of only a few anthropologists who have consistently addressed the question of genocide, along the way criticising the discipline of Anthropology itself for failing to consider the topic. His ethnographic fieldwork in Cambodia has led him to concern himself with such issues as human rights and transitional justice, political rights and terrorism, and genocide and related issues (globalisation; modernity; culture and mind; and self, memory and emotion).

Hinton initially became interested in the academic study of genocide as a by-product of a different study on which he was engaged as a graduate student, undertaking fieldwork research in Cambodia. When talking with his host community, he learned of the tragic human impact the events of the Pol Pot years (1975–79) were still having two decades later. It was the experience of such discussions that led him to put aside his earlier project and begin to examine the reasons behind the killing that took place during the Khmer Rouge period.

Already in 1998, in an important article entitled 'A Head for an Eye: Revenge in the Cambodian Genocide', Hinton made the claim that 'While social scientists in other fields have addressed this question, anthropology has remained largely silent on the origins of large-scale genocide' (Hinton, 1998a: 352). He noted that 'anthropology stands poised to begin making a significant contribution to the comparative study of genocide. In recent years, the number of anthropological analyses of political violence has greatly proliferated as anthropologists have attempted to explain the origins of conflicts' (Hinton, 1998a: 352). His faith in the future of his discipline stems, in large measure, from the foci of his work: doing ethnographic fieldwork, having developed the descriptive, methodological and analytic tools with which to do so; addressing all aspects of a group's cultural realities, including its physical culture; and doing so repeatedly from a comparative perspective.

In *Genocide: An Anthropological Reader*, and *Annihilating Difference: The Anthropology of Genocide*, both of which he edited in 2002, Hinton tackled much more pointedly the question of the failure of Anthropology and other social sciences to address the pressing issue of genocide. Hinton suggested possible reasons for its hesitancy, for instance that the topic of genocide threatened the concept of cultural relativity and the claim to dispassionate understanding; that anthropologists participated in the Second World War and Vietnam, but shied away from this politically volatile issue; and, finally, that Anthropology is predisposed to focus on small-scale political processes to the neglect of large-scale politically violent societies and processes (Hinton, 2002b: 3). He also suggested, as have others, that the discipline of Anthropology has often been bound up with a colonialist, and to a lesser degree post-colonialist, Western perspective, which privileges modernity and which essentialises differences. As he expressed it:

> There is a deep and complex relationship between genocide and modernity, which is bound by tropes of 'progress,' programs of social engineering, the reification of group difference (often in terms of racial categories), capitalism and the pursuit of profit, bureaucratic distanciation, the rise of the nation-state and its highly increased centralization of power, technologies of mass murder, and crises of identity and search for meaning in a world of upheaval. Moreover, to ignore this relationship is to overlook a deeply troubling implication – that some of the processes that help generate genocide are operative in our everyday lives.
>
> (Hinton, 2005: 5)

At the same time, Hinton was equally concerned with the construction of what he calls 'an anthropology of genocide', believing full well that the perspectives of his own field can contribute much to our ongoing investigations of this phenomenon. In his view, 'genocide is always a local process and therefore may be analyzed and understood in important ways through the ethnohistorical lens of anthropology' (Hinton, 2002a: 3). Developing this, he continued:

> I believe we may legitimately delineate the domain of 'an anthropology of genocide' as encompassing those cases in which

a perpetrator group attempts, intentionally and over a sustained period of time, to annihilate another social or political community from the face of the earth.

(Hinton, 2002a: 6)

Equally, because of Anthropology's combination of 'macro-level analysis' and 'local level understandings', it remains poised to contribute significantly to our understanding of the phenomenon of genocide in the future (Hinton, 2002b: 3, 10).

Central to Hinton's own understanding and contribution, therefore, is how he conceptualises the very notion of genocide as, ultimately, a social-cultural construct of any given society building upon its own historical foundations. To that end, he stresses the intermixing of the past, present and future, noting that:

Genocide usually takes place when the state is going through a period of social, economic, or political upheaval. In many cases, a genocidal regime gains popular support and power by promising to revitalize the country. Unfortunately, such promises of renewal usually accentuate structural divisions in the state by blaming a victim group for the country's woes and legitimating violence directed toward such sources of 'contamination.'

... genocidal regimes always blend the old with the new in such a way as to make their lethal ideologies effective and seem reasonable to people. Thus genocidal regimes usually co-opt preexisting cultural knowledge, dressing it up in new ideological guises that maintain familiar and compelling resonances while legitimating new structures of domination and violence against victim groups.

(Hinton, 2005: 29)

This recognition, not only of social, economic and political forces, but also of historical ones, all of which must align for there to be genocide, is an important one, even if all-too-often overlooked by practitioners of disciplines other than History itself. That is to say, the role of the past is every bit as much a contributory factor as any other in the construction and perpetuation of genocide, and requires of those who study the various genocides a 'look back' every bit as much as a 'look to the present'.

Additionally, Hinton sees the actual practice of genocide as what he labels a two-step (or two-stage) process, embracing priming and activation. The former he defines as 'the process by which various primers [contributory factors] coalesce, making genocide more or less likely, though by no means an inevitable outcome'. Once in place, the latter then becomes 'a series of direct and indirect, more or less organized pushes from above [the genocidally predisposed regime] that begins to trigger the "charge" that has been primed' (Hinton, 2002a: 14). The metaphor is fully appropriate as long as one thinks of the priming and activating of an explosive charge powerful enough to extend far beyond the moment of its detonation – once perpetrated, genocide's lasting effects and long-range implications last far longer than the moment of impact, no matter how long the moment. For example, the genocidal moment of the Holocaust (specifically 1939–45), even taking into account a 2,000-year Western historical anti-Semitic priming before implementation, finds its impact continuing not only with those survivors who are still alive but with their offspring as well.

The central focus of Hinton's research has been to argue that it is impossible to understand genocide without taking into account its cultural dimensions, while recognising that it cannot by itself explain genocidal phenomena. In this regard, the cultural dimensions of genocide are manifold, ranging from the local knowledge that is incorporated into genocidal ideologies (thereby giving them resonance to perpetrators) to cultural patterning of violence (as opposed to being dismissed as 'irrational' or 'savage', violence almost always has a cultural patterning since the perpetrators are cultural beings), to the local construction of group identity and difference. Hinton's work has also sought to explore perpetrator motivation in a manner that, rather than focusing on one level (for example, that of psychology), explores how genocidal violence is motivated by the synergies of various levels, ranging from the emotional and locally meaningful resonance of ideological knowledge (what Hinton identifies as 'ontological resonance') to the construction and assertion of self-group identity through the act of violence itself. His arguments reach the point where he considers that genocide is tied to modernity itself, in important ways.

Most recently, Hinton has been focusing on the aftermaths of genocide with a particular focus on post-genocide justice instruments. This is the topic of another edited volume, *Transitional Justice: Global Mechanisms and Local Realities after Genocide and Mass Violence* (2010). His work was recognised by the American Anthropological Association, which awarded him the 2009 Robert B. Textor and Family Prize for Excellence in Anticipatory Anthropology.

Overall, Hinton's efforts have not only been important for his own discipline as he directly challenges his own colleagues to get involved in the conversation – indeed, his two early collections of essays are the direct result of those efforts – but, in so doing, he has opened up to those who are not anthropologists an additional world of theoretical and practical insight towards a fuller and more complete understanding of genocide.

Building on Hinton's efforts, it can be argued that the field of Anthropology can make a significant contribution to a broader comprehension of genocide. Hinton's work has introduced the process of genocidal priming and activation, examining how it unfolds in both genocidal and non-genocidal situations. Concepts like 'primes' and 'accelerators', however, are macro-level explanatory ideas that must be rooted to the complex local realities in which genocide takes place. Anthropology therefore has the potential to shed considerable light on genocide by exploring how the dynamics of mass violence are influenced by local understandings and sociocultural dynamics (for instance, cultural change, ritualised behaviour, symbolism, revitalisation movements, schismogenesis, the construction of identity, thick description, the localisation of transnational flows of knowledge, intergroup boundary formation and social relations, conflict resolution, the interplay of structure/agency and power/knowledge, the cultural patterning of violence, literature on genocide), all of which illustrate some of the crucial and distinct ways in which anthropological insights can illuminate the genocidal process and its aftermath, ranging from the impact of modernity to the construction of difference, to local strategies for coping with trauma and suffering (Hinton, 2002b: 16).

Alexander Laban Hinton's influence on the field of Holocaust and Genocide Studies can be categorised in three ways: first, through the introduction of anthropological insights into the field of Holocaust and Genocide Studies, where there has otherwise been little work done previously employing this discipline; second, through his development of the notion of the centrality of the cultural dimension of genocide to the genocidal process; and third, through his examination of perpetrator motivation in a non-reductive, multi-factorial and locally meaningful manner. His overall contribution can thus be subsumed under the broader argument that genocide cannot be fully understood unless scholars take local understandings into account when considering perpetrator motivations, victim responses and bystander reactions.

Hinton's major writings

'Agents of Death: Explaining the Cambodian Genocide in Terms of Psychosocial Dissonance', *American Anthropologist*, 98, 4 (1996), 818–31.

'A Head for an Eye: Revenge in the Cambodian Genocide', *American Ethnologist*, 25, 3 (1998a), 352–77.

'Why Did You Kill? Anthropology, Genocide, and the Goldhagen Controversy', *Anthropology Today*, 14, 3 (1998b), 9–15.

'Purity and Contamination in the Cambodian Genocide', in Judy Ledgerwood (ed.), *Cambodia Emerges from the Past: Eight Essays*, DeKalb (IL): Northern Illinois University Press, 2001, 60–90.

(Ed.) *Annihilating Difference: The Anthropology of Genocide*, Berkeley (CA): University of California Press, 2002a.

(Ed.) *Genocide: An Anthropological Reader*, Malden (UK): Blackwell, 2002b.

Why Did They Kill? Cambodia and the Shadow of Genocide, Berkeley (CA): University of California Press, 2005.

'Genocide and Modernity', in Conerly Casey and Robert B. Edgerton (eds), *A Companion to Psychological Anthropology: Modernity and Psychocultural Change*, Maldern (MA): Blackwell, 2005, 419–35.

'Savages, Subjects, and Sovereigns: Conjunctions of Modernity, Genocide, and Colonialism', in A. Dirk Moses (ed.), *Empire, Colony, Genocide: Conquest, Occupation, and Subaltern Resistance in World History*, New York: Berghahn Books, 2008, 440–59.

'Truth, Representation and the Politics of Memory after Genocide', in Alexandra Kent and David Chandler (eds), *People of Virtue: Reconfiguring Religion, Power and Morality in Cambodia Today*, Copenhagen: NIAS Press, 2008, 62–81.

(Ed. with Kevin Lewis O'Neill) *Genocide: Truth, Memory, and Representation*, Durham (NC): Duke University Press, 2009.

(Ed.) *Transitional Justice: Global Mechanisms and Local Realities after Genocide and Mass Violence*, New Brunswick (NJ): Rutgers University Press, 2010.

HERBERT HIRSCH (b. 1941)

Herbert Hirsch is a Professor of Political Science at Virginia Commonwealth University, Richmond. Born in New York in 1941, he undertook graduate study at Villanova University, Pennsylvania and the University of Kentucky. Soon after the completion of his doctorate he published his first book, *Poverty and Politicization: Political Socialization in an American Sub-Culture* (1971) and joined the faculty at the University of Texas at Austin, where he taught political science. In 1981 he moved to Virginia Commonwealth University, where he has remained ever since.

While Hirsch's teaching always embraced a number of standard areas in political science (introductory classes on American government, political socialisation, the politics of race, class and ethnicity, legislative politics, and the like), from an early time he had an interest in such matters as repression, violence in society, the question of power and its abuse, and human rights in the international system. It seemed to be a natural progression that he would gravitate from these areas towards the study of genocide (at a time when it was not yet common for scholars to do so), and in 1983, at the American Political Science Association meeting in Chicago, Hirsch organised a panel specifically on that subject. Little interest was shown by those attending the conference (a fact not helped by the scheduling of the panel on the last session of the last day), but Hirsch was determined that awareness-raising about genocide was not something that should be put into the 'too-hard' basket. With this in mind, he later became one of the founding members of the Association (now International Association) of Genocide Scholars, established at an inaugural meeting held at the College of William and Mary, Williamsburg, Virginia in 1994.

While Hirsch had already been engaging in research and teaching about violence and social pathology for some time, it was really through his realisation of the impact of memory on such matters that he was able to develop his ideas and communicate them to a wider reading audience. The more he considered the social psychology of those committing genocide, the more he came to the conclusion that public memory played an important role in motivating people to commit what others would consider to be unspeakable horrors. It was as a result of this realisation that he commenced a major project investigating just how far the argument could be taken, and the result – a book that appeared in 1995 entitled *Genocide and the Politics of Memory: Studying Death to Preserve Life* – was an important contribution to an area that had hitherto been little considered by political scientists or social psychologists.

Hirsch's argument, put simply, was that memory, with regard to those regimes harbouring a potential for genocidal or lesser violence, can be (and has been) manipulated to serve political ends. Violence and mass murder are thus not spontaneous or collateral, but deliberate instruments intended to achieve specific political outcomes. The role of memory in this schema, for Hirsch, is profound. Hence,

> Generations pass on memories, making them part of the historical record, by using language to transmit their particular version of events to the next generation through the process of socialization. These processes contribute to the formation of an individual's identity or sense of self, which may, in turn, influence the decisions a person will make when confronted with a crisis or an order to commit an act that might, in most circumstances, be

considered morally questionable – such as an order to march elderly men, women and children to a ditch and kill them.

(Hirsch, 1995: 3–4)

Hirsch's role, as he saw it, was to explore the impacts that can take place when individual memories are manipulated by the state – and not how collective memories are shaped. At base is a single, simple question: Why are people seemingly so prepared to continue killing their fellow human beings, when they know where such actions will lead? As Hirsch himself put it, 'Are we destined to play out succeeding scenarios of memory and destruction? In short, why is there no change if we have so many memories of so many destructive acts?' (Hirsch, 1995: 35).

In a later essay, Hirsch reinforced this general notion with an eloquent statement that encapsulated his whole position:

> [The memory of] the primal impulses to kill each other in large numbers for reasons of racial, religious, ethnic, or national hatred, … appears to run so deep that it is not erased, replaced, or controlled by the attempt to impose a veneer of civilization. People continue to behave and to kill for the same reasons, and the memory of these attachments to ethnic, religious, racial, national, or regional territory continue as prime motivations. The species can only hope to ameliorate this condition if we look deeper into the importance of those memories and attempt to understand in greater depth the relationship between memory and politics.
>
> (Hirsch, 2002b: 123)

As a way into such an understanding, Hirsch investigated the writing of a number of earlier scholars whose work considered the role of memory. **Primo Levi**, for instance, who combined his personal experience as a Holocaust survivor with that of a philosopher on the human condition, was employed by Hirsch as one whose role was 'to tell unconscious humanity what it does not wish to hear and to live a life … that might force confrontation with the guilt of indifference and might compel historians to incorporate the survivor's memory and vision into contemporary human chronology' (Hirsch, 1995: 44).

Hirsch also considered the debate over survivorship between Bruno Bettelheim and **Terrence Des Pres** as one which sheds light on the meaning of memory. While providing a solid summary of the debate, Hirsch also analysed each author's argument from the perspective of its political dimension, concluding that it is in the 'politics of their analyses that they reveal the basic reasons for their respective views' – that is, that Bettelheim sees survivorship from the viewpoint of one who has grounded his thinking in the notion that personal discipline guaranteed survival, and that those who were not 'tough' in their confrontation with the Nazis were bound to succumb, while **Des Pres** takes the opposite view, namely, that politics is victimisation, and that the will to survive is paramount; the reasons for survival are less relevant than the human impulse to survive for its own sake. Hirsch showed that both authors relied on memory in order to explain their positions, just as the Nazi (and, for **Des Pres**, also the Soviet) state relied on memory in order to establish political hegemony and public acquiescence to their murderous policies. Affirmations of life, as well as their negations, thus depend upon memory and the way it is utilised both by individuals and by governments.

Hirsch concluded *Genocide and the Politics of Memory* by arguing that genocide could be prevented if a series of steps – both long and short term – were taken. In the short term, he held that the most important thing was to stop the killing; only then could additional matters, such as reconciliation and peace-building, take place. In order to achieve this, he advanced three positions: first, some sort of a mechanism should be created in order to bring together the UN Genocide Convention, existing laws of war, and international legislation covering crimes against humanity; second, a serious attempt should be made to develop a genuine 'Genocide Early Warning' system, together with the establishment of workable interventionist regimes; and third, a procedure should be developed internationally to negate the culture of impunity that had so far let the perpetrators of genocide escape justice (Hirsch, 1995: Chapter 14).

Ultimately, *Genocide and the Politics of Memory* was a major contribution to the study of genocide. Hirsch was dealing with one of the most vexing of topics for genocide scholars, namely, what motivates people to kill their fellow human beings when no personal animus exists. That political activity plays a crucial part in this is, perhaps, a given, but pointing out how memory maintains and develops a hold over that political activity was Hirsch's singular achievement.

Acknowledgement of this, however, was not sufficient for Hirsch. Recognising the dominant position of memory was one thing, but Hirsch called for memory to be accompanied by political action:

If it is not, if we continue to dissemble and allow policymakers to slouch toward settlements that entail the ratification of genocide as a means to achieve political goals, the world will have welshed on its promise of 'never again.' It is important to remember that the consequences of inaction are often more devastating than the results of positive action to resolve suffering.

(Hirsch, 1995: 216)

Henceforth, Hirsch began to devote himself almost exclusively to raising awareness about the urgency of national and international action to prevent genocide, and across a number of conference presentations and published articles he called for such action at every opportunity.

This call was emphasised in Hirsch's next book, *Anti-Genocide: Building an American Movement to Prevent Genocide*, which was published in 2002. This re-examined some of the conclusions with which he ended *Genocide and the Politics of Memory*, but took them further. Here, he argued once more for the creation of mechanisms and institutions to contain genocidal violence in the short term, and eventually shift, if possible, human behaviour away from recourse to violence when seeking to achieve desired political ends.

The book considered how to build what Hirsch described as a 'politics of prevention'. His specific focus was on the United States; here, he wrote, a political movement needs to be built in order to support such a push internationally. He considered this to be the short-term political objective. The second part of his anti-genocide solution – the attempt to control genocidal behaviour in the longer term – would depend on changing the ways in which human beings view each other. This, he argued, could be achieved by creating a new ethic of life-enhancing behaviour based on the ideology of universal human rights; it could be passed on from generation to generation through the process of re-educating human beings to move away from hatred and violence as solutions to their problems.

Hirsch contended that models already existed for the development of a political movement capable of bringing about change, citing such examples as the Civil Rights Movement of the 1950s and 1960s and the peace movement of the Vietnam War era. While taking these as paradigms for action, he then considered just how much Americans already know about genocide, and how far they might be prepared to do something to stop it; considering further the American response to such genocidal outbreaks as Bosnia, Rwanda, Kosovo and East Timor, he noted that the failures of both the Clinton and Bush administrations were clearly politically motivated, with an eye to public opinion and vote-catching (or vote-losing) potential.

He followed this up in the book's final section with the core of his formulations: a policy that could be created to try to prevent the repetition of genocide in the modern world. It was here that he proposed a new policy direction for United States foreign relations – what he referred to as 'the practicality of morality' – and how to structure a political movement (or 'ethic') that would prevent genocide in the future.

Hirsch situated his discussion in the realities of post–Cold War United States policy, but also in the aftermath of the terrorist attacks in the United States on 11 September 2001. Considering the 'War on Terror' that followed, Hirsch postulated that a 'War on Genocide' could be fought by governments using similar tools. Defensive movements required to protect populations from terror could be adapted to protect populations from attack by genocidal regimes:

> The focus here is to make it difficult for the terrorists to complete their acts successfully. A main example is increased security at, for example, airports. Similarly with genocide, 'anti-genocide' might involve the creation of the early warning system that has been discussed ...
>
> (Hirsch, 2002a: 182)

On a pessimistic note, however, Hirsch recognised that this was unlikely to be successful. Looking at the world around him, he noted that he was 'writing a book to advocate something that I believe may be highly unlikely to take place' – even though 'I want it to happen and hope that my pessimism will not become a self-fulfilling prophecy' (Hirsch, 2002a: xi).

Herbert Hirsch's commitment to stopping genocide, whether through the actions of nation-states or as a result of international action, remained undimmed throughout the first decade of the twenty-first century, even as new horrors arose after 2003 in Darfur, Sudan. In 2006 he became one of the founder editors of a new international journal, *Genocide Studies and Prevention*, which rapidly assumed the role of a premier publication in the field. As a pioneer of the academic study of genocide, and a keen student of human behaviour as reflected through politics, Hirsch has remained one of the leading figures in Genocide Studies, and is a scholar whose opinion is sought and respected by those seeking to draw conclusions about the nature and potential of government in the years following the end of the Cold War.

Hirsch's major writings

Poverty and Politicization: Political Socialization in an American Sub-Culture, New York: Free Press, 1971.

'Why People Kill: Conditions for Participation in Mass Murder', *International Journal of Group Tensions*, 15, 1–4 (1985), 41–57.

'Nazi Education: A Case of Political Socialization', *Educational Forum*, 52, 4 (Fall 1988a), 65–76.

(Ed. with Jack Spiro) *Persistent Prejudice: Perspectives on Anti-Semitism*, Fairfax (VA): George Mason University Press, 1988b.

'Trivializing Human Experience: Social Science Methods and Genocide Scholarship', *Armenian Review*, 42, 4 (1989), 71–81.

Genocide and the Politics of Memory: Studying Death to Preserve Life, Chapel Hill (NC): University of North Carolina Press, 1995.

Anti-Genocide: Building an American Movement to Prevent Genocide, Westport (CT): Praeger, 2002a.

'Studying Genocide to Protect Life', in Samuel Totten and Steven Leonard Jacobs (eds), *Pioneers of Genocide Studies*, New Brunswick (NJ): Transaction Publishers, 2002b, 113–27.

ADAM JONES (b. 1963)

Adam Jones is a Professor of Political Science at the University of British Columbia Okanagan, Kelowna, Canada, with broad research interests in areas such as Comparative Genocide Studies, gender and politics, and media and democratisation. Born in Singapore in 1963, Jones holds a PhD in Political Science from the University of British Columbia. Between 2000 and 2005 he was a Professor-Researcher at the Center for Research and Teaching in Economics (CIDE) in Mexico City, prior to appointment as an Associate Research Fellow in the Genocide Studies Program at Yale University (2005–7). In 2007 he took up his present position at UBC Okanagan.

As a youth Jones developed an interest in human-rights issues, and in his late teens picked up a second-hand paperback copy of **Leo Kuper**'s *Genocide: Its Political Use in the Twentieth Century*. Although he later admitted that 'it was not until another couple of decades that I got around to reading it', nonetheless the die was cast; this, coupled with a long-term interest from childhood in modern history and conflict, including the Holocaust, saw Jones gravitate almost seamlessly towards the serious study of violence and ethnic conflict. In the 1980s he worked as an activist on a number of Central American human-rights issues, which included the Guatemalan Genocide. Then, in the 1990s, he addressed himself to themes relating to gender and ethnic conflict in the Balkans. Motivated by the twin crises in Kosovo and East Timor in 1999, Jones established the Gendercide Watch website (http://www.gendercide.org) in that same year, and began systematically to explore genocide from a comparative perspective.

Building on the term 'gendercide', introduced by American professor of philosophy Mary Anne Warren in 1985, Jones developed a new approach to the study of genocide by examining the reality and impact of gender-selective mass murders in history. *Gendercide and Genocide* (2004a) was a systematic exploration of the targeting of non-combatant 'battle-age' males in various wartime and peacetime contexts. In the book's introductory essay, first published in the *Journal of Genocide Research* in 2000, Jones argued that the population group most consistently targeted for mass killing and state-backed oppression throughout history has been non-combatant men of roughly 15 to 55 years of age. Such males, he contended, are typically seen as 'the group posing the greatest danger to the conquering force'. Jones's article also examined the use of what he termed 'gendercidal institutions' – such as female infanticide, witch-hunts, military conscription and forced labour – against both women and men. Another of his essays in the book, 'Gender and Genocide in Rwanda', applied the theory to a specific case study. Overall, Jones contended that the gender variable, inclusively approached (that is, in such a way as to incorporate men and masculinities as well as women and femininities), offers powerful analytical purchase on genocidal dynamics, and useful strategies of humanitarian intervention. His argument was contentious, in that it left him vulnerable to the criticism that he was seeking to displace an emphasis on genocide by discussing a new construct, 'gendercide'. For his part, however, he viewed this as a form and variant of genocide, useful in isolating the workings of the gender variable to produce both genocidal perpetration and victimisation.

Jones was to develop his interpretation of gendercide as it applied to genocidal destruction in a major text published in 2006, *Genocide: A Comprehensive Introduction*. As an example of the gendercidal targeting of males, Jones explored the genocidal massacre at Srebrenica, Bosnia, in July 1995, in which Bosnian Serb General Ratko Mladic led a ten-day campaign to take over the city and subject it to the process known as 'ethnic cleansing'. As the campaign was getting underway, thousands of Srebrenica's men and boys fled the city in order to seek refuge in Muslim-controlled areas beyond the hills. The women, children and very elderly men were for the most part loaded onto Serb-chartered buses and evacuated to a no-man's land between Serb and Muslim lines, from where they were rescued. Upon taking the city, Mladic's men began hunting down the 'battle-age' Muslim men. Capturing them in small groups, the Serbs concentrated them in larger numbers in fields, sportsgrounds, schools and factories, where the best estimates have settled on a figure of up to 8,000 slaughtered. Srebrenica has become a symbol of the brutality of the Serb war against Bosnia's Muslims, as well as of the UN's failure to stand up to genocide – especially given the fact that the 'safe zone' created by the UN was not defended, while the Dutch peacekeepers were helpless to stop the Serb assault.

Jones considered that 'the war in Bosnia offers one of the most vivid modern instances of gendercide ... [in which] the gender variable interacted with those of *age* and *community prominence* to produce a genocidal outcome' (Jones, 2006: 216, emphasis in original). The Serb strategy, as he saw it, had a deliberate aim, established in an earlier precedent:

> As in Armenia in 1915, with community males murdered or incarcerated, Serb soldiers and paramilitaries were better able to inflict atrocities on remaining community members. Women, especially younger ones, were special targets. They were subject to rape, often repeatedly, often by gangs, and often in the presence of a father or husband. ... It was in the Bosnian context that the term 'genocidal rape' was minted, stressing the centrality of sexual assaults on women in the broader campaign of 'cleansing.' It should be noted that men and adolescent boys were also sexually assaulted and tortured on a large scale in detention facilities such as Omarska and Trnopolje.
>
> (Jones, 2006: 217–18)

Thus, for Jones, genocide can possess a gender-persecution dimension that is more than just an adjunct to the crime; in numerous instances, it is an integral part of the crime of genocide itself.

In a volume entitled *Genocide, War Crimes and the West: History and Complicity* (2004b), Jones had earlier assembled a collection of writings detailing the history of Western responsibility for mass atrocities and state-based terror. The book showed the ways in which Western governments have run the full gauntlet of relationships where genocide has been concerned: as opponents, as bystanders, as accomplices and as perpetrators, from the dawn of the modern liberal-democratic state through to the post-9/11 environment. The book addressed war crimes, genocide and crimes against humanity with regard to the role of the West, more frequently held up as the exemplar of how 'good global citizens' should behave when confronted by such phenomena.

While Jones was concerned to expose Western hypocrisy, inaction and, all too often, perpetration with regard to genocide, it was in his 2006 book *Genocide: A Comprehensive Introduction* that he really made his mark as a genocide educator of the first rank. His book was the most wide-ranging and interdisciplinary textbook on genocide yet published. It was designed as a text for undergraduate and graduate students, as well as a primer for non-specialists and general readers interested in learning about what Jones described as 'one of humanity's most enduring blights'. He not only discussed genocide as a historical phenomenon and a legal concept; he also explored the roles of imperialism, war and social revolution as its most important stimuli, illustrating his arguments with a number of thoroughly examined case studies. His study explored genocide from a social-science perspective, covering Psychology, Sociology, Anthropology, Political Science, International Relations and Gender Studies. The book's final section considered what Jones referred to as 'The Future of Genocide'. Here, he looked at historical memory and genocide denial, initiatives for truth, justice and redress, and strategies of intervention and prevention.

Beyond these major contributions, Jones has also pursued other areas of investigation – for example, in emphasising the role of Western countries in perpetrating genocide in colonial and post-colonial contexts, and the structural and institutional forms that genocide can take, beyond a time-bound political–military context. Together with Nicholas Robins, he has also developed the concept of 'subaltern genocide', that is, the use of genocidal strategies by oppressed groups against their oppressors (Jones and Robins, 2009).

Jones's most recent project has seen the compilation of a large number of short reflective pieces from leading scholars and activists in the field of Genocide Studies, who consider the stimuli that influenced their initial engagement with genocide and crimes against humanity. *Evoking Genocide: Scholars and Activists Describe the Works That Shaped Their Lives* (2009) shows that those involved in the field have been inspired by many things: books and stories, films, songs, drawings, documents, monuments, sculptures, personal testimonies, and even a Lego set. Among those included by Jones in this collection are such diverse authors from around the world as **Raphael Lemkin**, Ward Churchill, **William Schabas**, Benjamin Lieberman, Ani Kalayjian,

Paul R. Bartrop, Joseph Robert White, Jack Nusan Porter, Michael Hayse, **Robert Skloot**, Steven Leonard Jacobs, **John K. Roth**, Henry Maitles, Dominik J. Schaller, **Jacques Sémelin**, Donna-Lee Frieze, Simone Gigliotti, **Stephen C. Feinstein**, G. Jan Colijn, **Hannah Arendt**, Lee Ann Fujii, Victoria Sanford, R. Charli Carpenter, **Alex Hinton**, Eric Reeves and Jones himself.

Overall, Adam Jones can be seen as one of an emerging generation of genocide scholars who are opening up fresh areas for analysis. These include gender issues, the role of subaltern actors as genocidal perpetrators, and the legacies of Western colonialism. Thinkers such as Jones are in the process of adding to the ways in which the study of genocide can be approached, enhancing the field through raising new questions – all of which of necessity require academic treatment given that so much of the detailed narrative work on specific case studies is either being done or has already been done by other scholars.

Jones's major writings

'Gender and Ethnic Conflict in ex-Yugoslavia', *Ethnic and Racial Studies*, 17, 1 (January 1994), 115–34.
'Gendercide and Genocide', *Journal of Genocide Research*, 2, 2 (June 2000), 185–211.
'Gender and Genocide in Rwanda', *Journal of Genocide Research*, 4, 1 (2002a), 65–94.
'Problems of Genocide-Gendercide Studies and Future Agendas: A Comparative Approach', *Journal of Genocide Research*, 4, 1 (2002b), 127–36.
(Ed.) *Gendercide and Genocide*, Nashville (TN): Vanderbilt University Press, 2004a.
(Ed.) *Genocide, War Crimes and the West: History and Complicity*, London: Zed Books, 2004b.
Genocide: A Comprehensive Introduction, London: Routledge, 2006.
(Ed.) *Genocide* (4 vols), London: Sage Publications, 2008a.
Crimes Against Humanity: A Beginner's Guide, Oxford: Oneworld, 2008b.
(Ed. with Nicholas Robins) *Genocides by the Oppressed: Subaltern Genocide in Theory and Practice*. Bloomington (IN): Indiana University Press, 2009.
(Ed.) *Evoking Genocide: Scholars and Activists Describe the Works That Shaped Their Lives*, Toronto: Key Publishing House, 2009.

Reference

Warren, Mary Anne, *Gendercide: The Implications of Sex Selection*, Lanham (MD), Rowman and Littlefield, 1985.

BEN KIERNAN (b. 1953)

Benedict (Ben) Kiernan is the Whitney Griswold Professor of History and Director of the Genocide Studies Program at Yale University. Born in 1953 in Melbourne, Australia, he received his PhD from Monash University in 1983, before moving to Yale in 1990. In 1994 he founded the Cambodian Genocide Program at the Yale Center for International and Area Studies, and in 1998 Yale's Comparative Genocide Studies Program. In 2000 he convened Yale's East Timor Project, bringing a scholarly appreciation to coverage of atrocities in that country under Indonesian occupation.

In 1975, while still a student, Kiernan made his first visit to Cambodia, after which he learned the Khmer language and began to immerse himself in Cambodian culture. His very early work on the Khmer Rouge was inconclusive as to their capacity for extreme violence, and errors of interpretation led him to believe initially that communism could have been a force for positive change in what was previously a feudal country with massive problems of corruption and underdevelopment. In some instances, his early analyses were far from accurate, but in this he was not alone: several commentators held hopes for a positive new future for Cambodia. Kiernan was quick to alter his views after he began interviewing refugees from Cambodia in 1978, and began to carry out extensive research on the Cambodian situation. Beforehand, there were some who even criticised him for being pro–Khmer Rouge, but that was a charge that could not be sustained for long; Kiernan has since been recognised as one of the world's foremost critics of the Pol Pot regime. In 1995, in response to his many years of research exposing the atrocities of the Khmer Rouge (including a catalogue of works that have appeared in fourteen languages), a Khmer Rouge court indicted, tried and sentenced Kiernan to death *in absentia*.

Although Kiernan had already published lengthy works on Cambodia in the early 1980s, his first major study was *How Pol Pot Came to Power: Colonialism, Nationalism, and Communism in Cambodia, 1930–1975* (1985). This incisive and thoroughly researched work examined how it was that Pol Pot rose to power from obscurity in a poor French colony to becoming leader of the country prior to one of the most dramatic and destructive periods of social engineering ever witnessed.

The book examined Cambodian history from 1930 to 1975, tracing the origins and trajectory of the Cambodian communist movement as well as providing a detailed profile of the life of Saloth Sar, who took the revolutionary name of Pol Pot in the early 1950s. Kiernan located the origin of the Khmer Rouge's success within the context of the conflict between French colonialism and a developing Cambodian nationalism, in which the communist movement saw its chance of freeing Cambodia and at the same time establishing a progressive socialist order.

Pol Pot focused his activities in the jungle, and built there a communist ideology based on returning Cambodia to an idealised, pristine peasant society, in which the 'corruption' of modern life would be eliminated. His rise to power could be fixed squarely within the Cold War environment of the 1960s and 1970s, and particularly the Vietnam War. Taking advantage of the weakness of the US-backed government of Lon Nol and the political vacillation of King Norodom Sihanouk, Pol Pot and the Khmer Rouge waged an effective guerrilla war that saw the defeat of the old regime by 17 April 1975.

Kiernan's study unravelled many of the intricacies of how this was all played out, and placed the Khmer Rouge's efforts to achieve power alongside other communist struggles in Asia, particularly in Indonesia, Thailand, Burma and India. Though at the same time engaged in a number of other projects, it was logical that he should follow this up with an analysis of what followed after the communists took over, which he did in *The Pol Pot Regime: Race, Power, and Genocide in Cambodia under the Khmer Rouge, 1975–79* (1996). This was the first definitive account of the Khmer Rouge revolution, and Kiernan showed how their ideological preoccupation with racist and totalitarian policies led Pol Pot's communists to impose a genocidal reign of terror on their own country.

Given his facility with the Khmer language, Kiernan could not only work closely with Cambodian written sources; he was also able to draw on more than 500 interviews with survivors, as well as written 'confessions' obtained under torture and duress from the Khmer Rouge in places such as Tuol Sleng prison. One of the key characteristics of the book was the quality and degree of its detail. While undertaking a vast amount of original research of his own (in which he uncovered much newly available archival material), Kiernan also synthesised much of the existing research that had already been undertaken. Quite simply, he asked the question, What was the nature of the regime that turned Cambodia into a succession of killing fields and murdered or starved to death 1.7 million of the country's eight million inhabitants? This book was his answer to that question.

Kiernan depicted the horrific nature of Pol Pot's rule clearly and intelligently, leaving little room for doubt that this was one of the most destructive of all twentieth-century regimes. One-fifth of the population lost their lives through state-induced starvation, disease, torture and murder. Kiernan meticulously examined Pol Pot's killing machine and cleared up many misconceptions found in earlier studies. He detailed how Pol Pot, obsessed with notions of ethnic Khmer purity and a return to 'Year Zero' – a fantasy time of past national grandeur – then exterminated ethnic Chinese, Vietnamese, Thai and Lao minorities, as well as Buddhist monks and Muslim Chams throughout Cambodia. Besides chronicling the nature of the brutal totalitarian government of the Khmer Rouge and its atrocities, Kiernan also made a singular contribution to the scholarship by highlighting the extent of internal resistance faced by Pol Pot, and how this resistance played an important role in bringing about the collapse of the regime after the country was invaded by Vietnam in early 1979.

While Kiernan's reputation as one of the foremost writers on the Cambodian Genocide had long been assured, it was his book *Blood and Soil: A World History of Genocide and Extermination from Sparta to Darfur* (2007b) that propelled him into the vanguard of writers on genocide as defined more broadly. It was a major contribution to Genocide Studies. Ambitious in scope, it was nothing less than an attempt to tell the history of genocide from ancient times to the present day, though it focused specifically on the past six centuries, that is, from 1492 onwards and the European encounter with the New World.

The core of the book was divided into three parts: 'Early Imperial Expansion', 'Settler Colonialism' and 'Twentieth-Century Genocides'. In view of the huge nature of his task, Kiernan explained at the outset what he considered to be central to his theme, namely, a list of 'four recurring ideological preoccupations of the perpetrators of genocide, extermination, and genocidal massacres'. These were, in turn, 'racism, expansionism, agrarianism, and antiquity' (Kiernan, 2007b: 38). The rest of his study was really an unpicking of the themes thrown up by these 'preoccupations', 'which often seem sufficient for genocidal violence'. This way, Kiernan was able to identify connections, patterns and features that almost always gave prior indication of the catastrophe to come: prejudice based on race or religion, the quest to physically expand boundaries, or fixations on past golden ages or a return to peasant roots.

Kiernan was then at pains – almost apologetically so – to explain why he could not include all cases of genocide, mass murder and peoplehood destruction, though the very scope of his work was a sufficient illustration of just how difficult (if not impossible) it would be under any circumstances for justice to be done to every such case. It is a task no author could achieve in a single volume, though Kiernan came closer than anyone else had to date. *Blood and Soil* was a thoroughly researched and highly detailed account of many instances of genocidal violence and extermination, and sought, in an original and stimulating way, to provide reasons for such behaviour. It provided new insights and a new approach to achieving an understanding of genocide and why it occurs.

In the same year as *Blood and Soil* Kiernan also produced *Genocide and Resistance in Southeast Asia: Documentation, Denial, and Justice in Cambodia and East Timor* (2007c). Here he sought to trace the trajectory of two cases of genocide and extermination that began in Southeast Asia at about the same time: Pol Pot's Khmer Rouge war of annihilation in search of the Year Zero, and Indonesia's occupation and subjugation of the former Portuguese colony of East Timor. Both began in 1975, both led to death on a massive scale, and most of the deaths in each case occurred between 1975 and 1980.

Kiernan examined the consequences of actions from two diametrically opposite political regimes, Cambodian communist revolutionaries and Indonesian right-wing militarists, and showed how both regimes exterminated ethnic minorities as well as political dissidents. The goals were different in each, however: in East Timor the Indonesians were seeking conquest, while in Cambodia, as he had shown previously, the Khmer Rouge's ambition was the achievement of a radical revolution the likes of which the world had never before seen. Kiernan brought to his analysis a new approach to the use of historical documentation and the study of the politics and mechanisms of genocide. He showed that Cambodia and East Timor not only shared the experience of genocide, but also that of civil war, international vacillation followed (eventually) by intervention, and the inadequacy of UN conflict-resolution instruments in the face of sovereign integrity. And – building on a theme introduced by Kiernan in his earlier works on Cambodia – on this occasion he again acknowledged the existence and impact of indigenous resistance to genocide and extermination, an often-overlooked aspect of the equation (particularly with regard to Cambodia). As he wrote:

> Resistance movements that inflict casualties on perpetrator regimes ... are of course not the only forms of resistance worth studying. In various cases, organized non-violent or passive

resistance has also obstructed mass repression and rescued targeted victims. At an individual level, more everyday forms of resistance have also enabled victims to survive, including by enabling them to maintain their dignity and self-respect. These other kinds of resistance are not the focus of this book, but deserve equal attention.

(Kiernan, 2007c: 3–4)

It was a sentiment that would surely find assent from other genocide scholars such as (among others) **Terrence Des Pres, Yehuda Bauer** and **Jacques Sémelin**.

Ben Kiernan is one of the leading genocide intellectuals in the world today. Unquestionably he is the leading scholar of the Cambodian Genocide, and has played a key role in unearthing confidential documentation of the atrocities committed by the Khmer Rouge. His writings have transformed our understanding not only of Cambodia in the twentieth century, but also of the historical phenomenon of genocide. While known primarily for his work on Cambodia and the Khmer Rouge rather than as a comparative scholar, however, his recent work has clearly broadened his status, and has certainly extended his influence throughout the field of Genocide Studies overall.

Kiernan's major writings

(with Serge Thion) *Khmers Rouges! Matériaux pour l'histoire du communisme au Cambodge*, Paris: J.-E. Hallier/A. Michel, 1981.

(with Chanthou Boua) *Peasants and Politics in Kampuchea, 1942–1981*, London: Zed Books, 1982.

(Ed. with David P. Chandler) *Revolution and Its Aftermath in Kampuchea: Eight Essays*, New Haven: Yale University Press, 1983.

How Pol Pot Came to Power: Colonialism, Nationalism, and Communism in Cambodia, 1930–1975, New Haven (CT): Yale University Press, 1985.

Cambodia: The Eastern Zone Massacres, New York: Columbia Center for the Study of Human Rights, 1986a.

(with Camille Scalabrino, Steve Heder et al.) *Cambodge: Histoire et enjeux*, Paris: L'Harmattan, 1986b.

(Ed.) *Burchett: Reporting the Other Side of the World, 1939–1983*, New York: Quartet Books, 1986c.

(Trans. and ed. with David P. Chandler and Chanthou Boua) *Pol Pot Plans the Future: Confidential Leadership Documents from Democratic Kampuchea, 1976–1977*, New Haven: Yale Center for International and Area Studies, 1988.

(Ed.) *Genocide and Democracy in Cambodia: The Khmer Rouge, the United Nations, and the International Community*, New Haven: Yale University Southeast Asia Studies, 1993.

The Pol Pot Regime: Race, Power and Genocide in Cambodia under the Khmer Rouge, 1975–1979, New Haven (CT): Yale University Press, 1996.

Le Génocide au Cambodge, 1975–1979: Race, idéologie, et pouvoir, Paris: Editions Gallimard, 1998.

(Ed. with Robert Gellately) *The Specter of Genocide: Mass Murder in Historical Perspective*, Cambridge: Cambridge University Press, 2003.

(Ed.) *Conflict and Change in Cambodia, New York: Routledge*, 2007a.

Blood and Soil: A World History of Genocide and Extermination from Sparta to Darfur, New Haven (CT): Yale University Press, 2007b.

Genocide and Resistance in Southeast Asia: Documentation, Denial, and Justice in Cambodia and East Timor, New Brunswick (NJ): Transaction Publishers, 2007c.

LEO KUPER (1908–94)

Leo Kuper was a Professor of Sociology at the University of California, Los Angeles who wrote extensively on race relations and genocide. Born into a religiously observant Lithuanian Jewish family in Johannesburg, South Africa in 1908, he studied law at the University of the Witwatersrand, from which he graduated in 1931. He practiced law in Johannesburg until 1940, often acting in human-rights cases for African clients, and representing one of the first non-racial trade unions. Soon after the Second World War broke out he joined the South African army, and served as an intelligence officer in Kenya, Egypt and Italy until 1946, when he returned to South Africa. After the war he organised the National War Memorial Health Foundation, which helped to provide social and medical services for those who were disadvantaged – at first Africans, Coloureds and Indians, and, later, whites. In 1947 he undertook an MA degree in Sociology at the University of North Carolina, returned briefly to South Africa, and moved on to work as a lecturer in Sociology at the University of Birmingham. In 1953 Kuper returned to South Africa as Professor of Sociology at the University of Natal, where he remained until 1961.

During the 1950s Kuper was an active member of the Liberal Party of South Africa (he was a founder and chairman of the Natal branch of the party), and published a number of works on the subject of race relations. In 1961 he moved to the University of California, Los Angeles as a professor of Sociology, where he would remain until his retirement in 1976. The murder of his brother (a judge in South Africa) in 1963 strengthened Kuper's commitment to finding ways to achieve peaceful social change, and his published works began more and more to demonstrate what he saw as an obligation to the future. While other works showed where he was heading in this regard – in particular, *Race, Class and Power: Ideology and Revolutionary Change in Plural Societies* (1974) – it was his study *The Pity of It All* (1977) that stamped Kuper as a scholar determined to look into the forces leading to social and political violence and how these could be met.

Kuper's interest related to pluralistic societies in which a number of different ethnic and/or racial groups lived side by side – not always harmoniously. All too often, he saw, social and political circumstances in such societies make the possibility of non-violent reformist transitions difficult if not impossible to achieve. He focused on the accompanying process of polarisation that can take place in such societies, and how reform all too frequently fails as a result. Polarisation, he saw, is rarely determined by the structure of society, and need not necessarily take a violent form when it is the consequence of political change. He felt that reform is possible even in plural societies that are dominated by a minority and established as a result of conquest.

The Pity of It All considered four main case studies: Algeria, Rwanda, Burundi and Zanzibar. Kuper concluded that they all failed in the reform process, and that polarisation ensued leading to genocidal violence. Looking carefully at these situations, he deemed that the reform process in such societies was a case of missed opportunities which could have had another outcome if circumstances had been different – most specifically, that the many points of conflict to be found in plural societies can be inflamed by externally driven events or domestic leaders with a divisive or sectarian agenda. Once polarisation becomes entrenched in a plural society groups can organise increasingly on the basis of exclusive and (often mutually) antagonistic relations, which can lead to violent outcomes that intensify in escalating cycles.

The 'pity' to which the book's title referred lay in the fact that all too often alternatives exist that are not tried. The best option, he saw, would be if dominant societies voluntarily cooperated in the creation of stability and peace through surrendering part of their ascendancy in favour of shared power with other members of their plural society, and if, likewise, minority groups in society became more organised so they could transcend the narrowness of their separate identity. Critical reception for this book was not wholly positive, and it was viewed in some quarters as being unrealistic, but this did not deter Kuper from continuing to examine the sources of social disharmony and violence.

Kuper was a founding member of the Council of the Institute on the Holocaust and Genocide, Jerusalem, established by **Israel Charny**, Shamai Davidson and **Elie Wiesel** in 1979. In 1985 he and

Michael Young, Baron Young of Dartington, established International Alert, a forum on ethnic conflict, genocide and human rights. Its main concern related to anticipating, predicting and preventing genocide and other mass killings. Its twin interests were, first, in conflict resolution and conflict avoidance in accordance with international standards, and, second, as its name implies, to work to 'alert' international attention to situations of ethnic violence that are assuming genocidal proportions. Kuper's own work proceeded apace during this time; it was when writing on the massacres of Tutsis and Hutus in Rwanda and Burundi in the 1960s and 1970s that he came to the conclusion that poor (and non-) intervention from international agencies and governments had previously done more harm than good, and that this could be addressed through the greater provision of information and consciousness-raising among the broader population.

Kuper's efforts became more sustained during the early 1980s. His most important book, *Genocide: Its Political Use in the Twentieth Century* (1981), was the first in a run of three key works that placed him at the forefront of influence over the direction that Genocide Studies would take. He began with a discussion of the very definition of the word genocide. Whereas many subsequent arguments would turn on definitions of genocide – more often than not because commentators did not like that of the 1948 UN Convention on Genocide that made genocide a crime – Kuper's book followed precisely that description. As he wrote, explaining his position:

> I shall follow the definition of genocide given in the Convention. This is not to say that I agree with this definition. On the contrary, I believe a major omission to be in the exclusion of political groups from the list of groups protected. In the contemporary world, political differences are at the very least as significant a basis of massacre and annihilation as racial, national, ethnic or religious differences. Then too, the genocides against racial, national, ethnic or religious groups are generally a consequence of, or intimately related to, political conflict. However, I do not think it helpful to create new definitions of genocide, when there is an internationally-recognized definition and a Genocide Convention which might become the basis for some effective action, however limited the underlying conception.
>
> (Kuper, 1981: 39)

What followed was a thorough dissection of the various intricacies of genocide, in which he extended the definition to include political groups through an analysis that showed how politics was at the base of so much of the persecution of the four groups mentioned in the Convention. He provided a broad historical background in order to undertake a theoretical examination of the question of genocide, providing case studies of the Armenians in Turkey, the Jews in Europe and the Hutus in Burundi, among others. He considered atrocities committed by Asians and Africans as well as by Nazis and Soviets, and assessed the record of the UN up to that time.

Among many pathbreaking innovations in the book, one that came to be axiomatic of Kuper's approach related to localised massacres that, while not necessarily appearing as part of a state-wide policy of group destruction, might nonetheless destroy a given population within a region or defined territory. Noting that the annihilation of a section of a group in a contained situation (for example, in the wiping out of a whole village of men, women and children) contains some of the elements of genocide, Kuper sought to find a way to give such massacres their proper place within a model of genocide while recognising that such events did not, *by themselves*, constitute genocide. He introduced the notion of 'genocidal massacre' to deal with such situations, finding the concept especially useful in describing colonial situations. The large number of massacres accompanying colonial acquisition, he concluded, pointed clearly to an affinity between colonialism and genocide. While even an aggregation of genocidal massacres did not necessarily connote a policy of genocide, nonetheless the motives which underlay them were, in their time-and-place circumstances, motivated by a genocidal intent. For Kuper, therefore, the genocidal massacre, while not equating with genocide, was a device for explaining the many examples of destruction that took place during territorial acquisition, maintenance and decolonisation (Kuper, 1981: 10).

All in all, *Genocide* was a book that arguably articulated the issues and the history of genocide more completely than any previous published work. It was, moreover, recognised as such by Kuper's peers. Sociologist **Eric Markusen** described it as 'perhaps the definitive social scientific analysis of genocide currently available' (Markusen in Charny, 1999: 378), while **Israel W. Charny** considered it to be Kuper's 'major and seminal work' (Charny, 1999: 374).

Kuper's second key piece on genocide in the early 1980s was a pamphlet entitled *International Action against Genocide* (1982). This essentially distilled many of the main points about non-intervention that had been made in *Genocide*, but here he also succinctly summarised the history of the major genocidal outbreaks of the twentieth century and offered some suggestions 'which may contribute to an international movement for the eradication of this most horrifying crime against humanity' (Kuper, 1982: 17). It was an excellent introductory essay on its topic, and prepared the groundwork for Kuper's third discourse on genocide from this period, *The Prevention of Genocide* (1985).

Here he divided the crime of genocide into two categories: domestic genocides, which he referred to as those arising out of internal divisions within a society; and genocides arising out of international warfare. Kuper analysed critically the major obstacles holding back effective UN action, while assessing realistically the prospects of such action in the future. He considered past failures with regard to punishment, lamenting the impunity that had for so long allowed perpetrators to engage in their murderous acts. The book combined discussions of philosophy and morality (covering such issues as the right to life, ideology and self-determination) with discussions of politics and the law (looking at the past records of individual states against a context of domestic and international regulations). Ultimately, he concluded, the refusal of the international community to live up to the promises of the UN Convention on Genocide was a major contributor to the high incidence of genocidal outbreaks in recent times.

As a sociologist, Leo Kuper's work on race relations and inter-group dynamics showed where the breakdown of social stability could lead. His work was characterised by a thoughtful examination of his topics based on meticulous research. His pioneering work in Genocide Theory, and the lead he gave to younger scholars searching for ways into the subject, made him one of the foremost thinkers in the field – perhaps, it could be said, the successor *par excellence* to the founder of the field of Genocide Studies, **Raphael Lemkin**. His major concern was always that a means could be found to bring effective international action to bear in order to stop what he referred to as 'the odious scourge', but that genocide should also be understood more fully by informed, educated people in the broader sphere as well – and it was to achieving these twin objectives that he dedicated his work and his thinking.

Kuper's major writings

Passive Resistance in South Africa, London: Jonathan Cape, 1956.
(with Hilstan Watts and Ronald Davies) *Durban: A Study of Racial Ecology*, London: Jonathan Cape, 1958.
Race, Class and Power: Ideology and Revolutionary Change in Plural Societies, London: Duckworth; 1974.

The Pity of It All: Polarisation of Racial and Ethnic Relations, Minneapolis: University of Minnesota Press, 1977.

Genocide: Its Political Use in the Twentieth Century, New Haven (CT): Yale University Press, 1981.

International Action against Genocide, London: Minority Rights Group, pamphlet no. 53, 1982.

'Types of Genocide and Mass Murder', in Israel W. Charny (ed.), *Toward the Understanding and Prevention of Genocide*, Boulder (CO): Westview Press, 1984, 32–47.

The Prevention of Genocide, New Haven (CT): Yale University Press, 1985.

'Other Selected Cases of Genocide and Genocidal Massacres: Types of Genocide', in Israel W. Charny (ed.), *Genocide: A Critical Bibliographic Review*, London: Mansell Publishing, 1988, 155–71.

'The Prevention of Genocide: Cultural and Structural Indicators of Genocidal Threat', *Ethnic and Racial Studies*, 12, 2 (1989), 157–73.

'Reflections on the Prevention of Genocide', in Helen Fein (ed.), *Genocide Watch*, New Haven (CT): Yale University Press, 1992, 135–61.

'Theoretical Issues Relating to Genocide: Uses and Abuses', in George Andreopoulos (ed.), *Genocide: Conceptual and Historical Dimensions*, Philadelphia: University of Pennsylvania Press, 1994, 31–46.

Reference

Charny, Israel W., 'Kuper, Leo', in Israel W. Charny (editor in chief), *Encyclopedia of Genocide*, vol. 2, Santa Barbara (CA): ABC-Clio, 1999, 373–76.

BEREL LANG (b. 1933)

Berel Lang is an American philosopher and ethicist. Born in 1933 in Norwich, Connecticut, he received his PhD from Columbia University in 1961. He taught at the University of Colorado, the State University of New York at Albany, and Trinity College, Connecticut, and is currently a Visiting Professor at Wesleyan University, Connecticut.

Like **Zygmunt Bauman** in the field of Sociology and **Alexander Laban Hinton** in Anthropology, Lang is concerned that his own academic discipline, Philosophy, has not addressed the Holocaust frontally, or, in his words, the 'challenge of the event to philosophy [is] to take history seriously'. As he sees it, his arguments fall into four categories. In a private communication to the authors, Lang articulated his stance as follows:

1. Against the 'uniqueness' claim for the Holocaust on the grounds that even if it were true, the question would remain of why it

was important; also that the term 'uniqueness' implies limits on the future as well as the past and that it leads easily, if not necessarily into claims that the Holocaust is unspeakable – beyond representation as well as beyond understanding, the latter being, as I argue it, no more applicable to the Holocaust than to any other complex historical event.

2. Arguing that evil or wrongdoing can be, and in the Holocaust was, committed knowingly; that is with an awareness that wrong was being done (not, to be sure, in all instances, but often). There is much evidence of this – at least sufficient to make it a plausible thesis and thus worth debating.

3. That 'artistic' representation of the Holocaust is intrinsically dependent on and thus subordinate to historical representation – and that, aside from this dependence, artistic representation opens the way to subjective articulation that becomes a danger insofar as it may involve rejection of the limits of historical representation. Artistic representation may avoid this danger, but often it does not, and when this is put together with the general pitfalls of subjective expression (sentimentality, kitsch, hyperbole, cliché), the subordinate role of artistic representation becomes more evident still.

4. That the Holocaust was contingent historical fact, neither unavoidable nor necessary, and thus its occurrence depended on an historical sequence of acts and omissions that might have been different from what they were. These acts and omissions are both 'macro-cosmic' [as in large-scale political decisions] and micro-cosmic, a much more neglected source; that is, acts or omissions that occurred in crevices of everyday life in Germany and occupied Europe that were not blatant atrocities but that contributed to the atmosphere that made them possible – e.g. such small-scale events as taking the place of a professional (lawyer, professor) who had been dismissed because he was a Jew, or occupying the apartment of a deported family.

(Lang, personal correspondence, September 2009)

It is in two of his works – *The Future of the Holocaust: Between History and Memory* (1999) and *Post-Holocaust: Interpretation, Misinterpretation, and the Claims of History* (2005) – that we find the best summary explorations of Lang's thinking.

The Afterword to *The Future of the Holocaust* is entitled 'Lessons to Learn, or What Future for the Holocaust?' Concerned with historical realities, Lang situated the event within the sites of both Jewish and

German history, realising that the two are now and forever inextricably bound to one another. However, he addressed (and dismissed) simplistic religious-theological attempts at 'understanding' the Holocaust (such as punishment for transgression either of victims or others, appeal to human freedom, withdrawal of God from human concern, and so on), but, instead, suggested 'the conclusive question of how, in the face of God's beneficence and omnipotence, he would yet find sufficient reason to acquiesce in, if not to cause, such an occurrence' (Lang, 1999: 176). Lang's silence on the matter, in response, suggested that there is none. This question of silence as statement is central to Lang's argument in *Heidegger's Silence* (1996), wherein he argues that philosopher Martin Heidegger's silence regarding Nazism, whether before, during or after the Second World War, was loud evidence of his assent to Nazism, and was therefore, ultimately, reflected in his philosophy.

Equally, Lang rejected the all-too-common notion that the Holocaust is the most horrifyingly dramatic contemporary example of 'man's inhumanity to man', by reminding his readers that the Nazi agenda was not a universal attempt to annihilate the human race, but, quite pointedly, a specific group within the human community – the Jews (and, to a somewhat lesser extent, though counting as genocide nonetheless, the Sinti-Roma peoples).

For Lang, the first true 'lesson' of the Holocaust is its *incredible* aspect, 'the sense that what in the Holocaust became actual was viewed, as it unfolded, as impossible – that it simply could not be happening ... The eyes that saw and understood in ordinary circumstances did not, in *those* circumstances, see and understand, not even what was happening immediately before them or to them' (Lang, 1999: 178, emphasis in original). Thus, by implication and extension, 'If the Holocaust happened once, it can happen again' (Lang, 1999: 180), not as an exactly repeatable historical event (because by definition no two events can be identical), but in the broadest parameters, as the post–Second World War genocides in Cambodia, Bosnia, Rwanda and Darfur give eloquent testimony. As a result of the Holocaust, therefore, the spectre of genocide haunts the human community; it remains at the forefront of human consciousness and awareness.

The second 'lesson' of the Holocaust for Lang is that neither so-called high culture, with which Germany was associated at the beginning of the twentieth century, nor the rule of law proved to be an impediment to the implementation of the these horrors. Moreover, the similar codes of conduct of the professional classes (doctors, lawyers, academics, clergy), as well as the institutions with which they themselves were associated (universities, churches) proved to be of little help. A subtext here is Lang's comment that 'nominal historical circumstances – and personal decisions – are capable of overcoming even deep-rooted and valued foundations of "enlightenment"' (Lang, 1999: 181), which further opens the door to discussions of education, psychological construction and ethics within the human community.

A third 'lesson' Lang derives from his study of the Holocaust – which is to say, from its very historicity – and one applicable to genocide also – is its *incrementality*. While preferring to avoid the historical debate between the so-called Functionalists and Intentionalists, he notes that prior to 1941 the Nazi agenda was calculatingly directed towards forced emigration rather than extermination. Thus, by implication, ethical intervention at various steps along the way, while not necessarily preventing the Holocaust, might have curbed somewhat its excesses, possibly resulting in fewer deaths.

As an ethicist, Lang could thus conclude that:

> where genocide is concerned, there are no bystanders – supposed disinterested parties who as onlookers may choose or not, with equal justice, to maintain their neutrality ...
>
> But if any one implication emerges from the incremental development of the Nazi genocide, it is that the individuals and groups who at the time or even afterward regarded themselves as bystanders have discovered that they did indeed have a role and thus a measure of responsibility in this mechanism. ... This includes ... the governmental institutions and individual citizens of the Allied powers (even among Jewish groups outside Europe, in the United States and the then Palestine) who at times acted as though they too were bystanders, as if they had a choice – with something to be said on either side – between remaining disengaged and becoming involved. The point here is that anyone close enough to see such a 'choice' is by that fact implicated. A decision at that juncture to be 'disengaged' is already an engagement, with determinate, and in this case severe, consequences. It might be argued that where genocide occurs in the new 'global village,' there simply are no bystanders.
>
> (Lang, 1999: 185)

For Lang, the bottom line regarding lessons to be learned from any examination of the *Shoah* is its factuality as both its 'primary and most concrete lesson' (Lang, 1999: 190).

In his book *Post-Holocaust* (2005), Lang began with the following critique: '"professional" philosophers ... have contributed relatively little, in quantity or significance, to Holocaust Studies in its now more than half-century history', arguing that 'the loss to philosophy' becomes clear 'when the neglect that I have alleged in relation to the Holocaust is viewed in the context of the indifference or even antagonism in much contemporary philosophy to the relevance of history *as such*' (Lang, 2005: 173). This lack of engagement thus results from a negative relationship between those who 'do' Philosophy and those who 'do' History. Lang continued by outlining 'a number of issues ... central to Holocaust Studies that also involve substantive considerations of continuing philosophical importance'. These are: (1) The Concept of Genocide, (2) Corporate and Individual Intentions, (3) Classical Ethics, and (4) Holocaust Representation.

With regard to the first, he considered issues of 'the structural and moral character of genocide, the definition of the groups and types of action to which the term is applicable; the role of intention in those actions; the place of genocide in moral history' (Lang, 2005: 178). The second dealt with issues relating to 'the extent and nature of responsibility on the parts of individuals and groups; the differentiated relation of such responsibility to intentional and non-intentional acts' (Lang, 2005: 179). With regard to the third, he examined issues of 'whether ethical practice in extreme situations bears on ethical decisions in everyday (non-extreme) life' (Lang, 2005: 180). Finally, he dealt with issues of 'the possibility or necessary limits of artistic representation' (Lang, 2005: 180–81).

Even here, however, Lang cautioned that because it is in the nature of philosophical thought and discourse, abstraction is necessarily part of the process. Despite this, in relation to the Holocaust philosophers must remain grounded in the historical reality of the event itself, and focus on its specificity rather than perceive it as one among a series of similar or dissimilar events – and thus lessen its significance. Indeed, in his influential reflection *Act and Idea in the Nazi Genocide* (1990), Lang made much of the interrelationship between acts and ideas, specifically focusing on the *Shoah* itself. Particularly relevant for Lang was the term 'Nazi Genocide' to categorise this historical event (Lang, 1990: 81–102), according to which he was adamant that what happened to the Jews of Europe under the Nazis was a clear act of genocide and not a simple case of persecution, pogrom or oppression.

Berel Lang's importance to the field of Holocaust Studies, and, by extension, the study of genocide, lies in his willingness to critique his own discipline – Philosophy – for its glaring omissions in addressing what he understands to be among the central historical realities of the twentieth century and beyond. The precision of his language and his readiness to offer suggestions not only of the large philosophical questions that need to be engaged, but also to seriously and straight-forwardly confront whatever lessons may be derived from such an examination, form a vital part of his seminal contributions to Holocaust thought.

Lang's major writings

(Ed.) *Writing and the Holocaust*, New York: Holmes and Meier, 1988.

Act and Idea in the Nazi Genocide, Chicago: University of Chicago Press, 1990.

Heidegger's Silence, Ithaca (NY): Cornell University Press, 1996.

The Future of the Holocaust: Between History and Memory, Ithaca (NY): Cornell University Press, 1999.

Holocaust Representation: Art within the Limits of History and Ethics, Baltimore: Johns Hopkins University Press, 2000.

Post-Holocaust: Interpretation, Misinterpretation, and the Claims of History, Bloomington: Indiana University Press, 2005.

(Ed. with Simone Gigliotti) *The Holocaust: A Reader*, London: Basil Blackwell, 2005.

Philosophical Witnessing: The Holocaust as Presence, Waltham (MA): Brandeis University Press, 2009.

LAWRENCE L. LANGER (b. 1929)

Lawrence L. Langer is Alumnae Chair Professor of English Emeritus at Simmons College, Boston, where he was a faculty member between 1958 and his retirement in 1992. Born in New York City in 1929, he was educated at the City College of New York and Harvard University. He is perhaps the most important critic, and leading interpreter, of Holocaust literature in English. His works have been highly influential in shaping the ways in which literary analysis of the *Shoah* has developed over the past four decades.

In an early essay, for instance, Langer noted that for future gen-erations the task of imagining the Holocaust will be challenging, as the survivors who set down their accounts of what happened to them do not ask us to try to 'imagine' their experiences; for the most part, that is not what they are attempting to achieve. Addressing the issue, Langer observed that:

> The challenge of imagining the Holocaust – not the anti-Semitic tactics which led up to it, but its apocalyptic end in the gas

chambers and crematoria of the death camps – is a permanent one, and will indeed grow more difficult for future generations who will lack the advantage of hearing living voices confirm the details of the ordeal they survived. The only evidence we will have available then is the kind we depend on increasingly today: verbal and visual accounts which inspire the imagination to conjure up an unimaginable world.

(Langer, 1980: 312–13)

In this instance, Langer's major interest was to consider testimonial accounts not as historical documents, but as triggers for the imagination:

the ultimate focus, the one requiring our constant collaboration, must be unambiguous – such art is deceptive and unfaithful if it does not bring us closer to the worst, and beyond the worst – to the unthinkable. Not in tribute to the dead, not to redeem them – but in agonizing confirmation of the catastrophe that consumed them.

(Langer, 1980: 322)

Most importantly, this confirmation must be recognised and understood by the generations of the future, which will have only published survivor testimonies from which to learn what happened. As he was to write later in *Admitting the Holocaust* (1995), the discussion can be broadened:

The implications of the Holocaust are so bleak that we continue to wrestle with the desperate issue of how best to represent it. That problem still needs to be solved. Literature, history, testimony, commentary, theological speculation – many avenues exist for entering its vestibule, but no two approaches offer identical visions to those who cross the threshold into the landscape of the Holocaust itself.

(Langer, 1995b: 180)

For many survivors, the issue is not so clear-cut. Often, it is sufficient simply to tell the story, to record, to bear witness, to show that the world through which they lived was in fact all too real. The challenge is less one of 'imagining the Holocaust' than of conveying to the world an understanding of what they went through, of explaining the essence of the evil that one group of people inflicted upon another, as seen from the perspective of someone who was there as a participant-observer-victim. If there is, in short, nothing mysterious about the Nazis or the Holocaust they perpetrated, neither is there anything mysterious about the testimonies the survivors have written. They do not attempt to make magic, nor do they attempt to imagine the unimaginable. They simply try to tell the story from their own individual perspectives.

Initially, Langer's interest was with literature. One of the earliest contributions to the topic was *The Holocaust and the Literary Imagination* (1975), which dealt with the major genres of Holocaust literature as they had then developed, through an investigation of how the texts of the Holocaust could be interpreted. It was a pioneering work of criticism that addressed a fundamental paradox: how, in light of the Holocaust, can literature continue to play the same roles it had before Auschwitz – of delighting, of alerting, of adapting humanity to a series of contrived situations – when that humanity has since been witness to the Holocaust? Langer considered the range of possible stylistic approaches to the subject, guiding his readers through a huge mass of 'the literature of atrocity' and meticulously examining the literary style devised by each of the authors he examined. His study was a detailed account of some of the most powerful texts to have emerged from the Holocaust, in which he argued that that experience had created a new kind of literature. Indeed, its newness has forced readers to redefine pre-Holocaust notions of theme, character and structure. Of particular importance was how authors have been able to represent the Holocaust; put simply, of whether or not it is actually the function of literature to do so in a post-Auschwitz environment, and, if it is, how such literature should characterise the extreme events it seeks to address.

In short, Langer focused on the special problem of the writer who seeks to communicate the reality of the Holocaust to a world in which that event was possible. His book was an attempt at interpreting the efforts of authors (both Jewish and non-Jewish) to shape the reality of the Holocaust and make it accessible for a readership unaccustomed to such horror. As an original work of substantial creativity, it was listed as a Finalist for a United States National Book Award in the Arts and Letters category for 1976. A follow-up volume, *The Age of Atrocity* (1978), extended many of the themes first introduced in the earlier work.

In *Versions of Survival* (1982), Langer began to move away from the *literature* of the Holocaust in favour of investigating *survivor accounts* of that experience. Some survivors, it is true, had already been developing their narratives through literary genres, but Langer was now more interested in the ways in which survivors sought to tell their own stories through the written form. While acknowledging that 'every survivor memoir must be read, at least partially, as a work of the imagination, which selects some details and blocks out others for the purpose of shaping the reader's response' (Langer, 1982: xii), he admitted that his choice of title did not mean 'to question the accuracy, so far as that accuracy is within the author's control, of accounts of the deathcamp experience'. The book, rather, was an exploration of how survivors seek to convey their story, and how it is that the very process of the telling can thereby be both therapeutic and artistic at the same time.

Langer's study *Holocaust Testimonies: The Ruins of Memory* (1991) examined the nature and uses of survivor accounts in even greater depth. He was at this time a member of the Honorary Board of Consultants of the Fortunoff Video Archive, a collection housed at Yale University of over 4,300 videotaped interviews with witnesses and survivors of the Holocaust. He was instrumental in conducting interviews and interviewer-training sessions for the Archive, and the book, based on 300 of the Archive's more than 1,400 taped interviews with survivors, was listed by the editors of the 100th Anniversary Issue of the *New York Times Sunday Book Review* in December 1996 as one of thirteen 'books of particular permanent interest' published during the century.

Holocaust Testimonies explored the pain survivors were still experiencing decades after the event. Instead of searching for examples of heroism in the face of horror, Langer allowed the survivors to tell their own stories of the emotional and physical trauma of finding ways to stay alive. Survivors, he found, related their accounts of daily dread in the face of extreme hunger, brutal treatment and the confrontation with death and assault for which their life beyond the wire could never possibly have prepared them. He showed not only their Holocaust experience; he also drew attention to their post-Holocaust efforts at reintegration into some sort of normal life, noting that such efforts were often impossible to achieve. A highly influential work, *Holocaust Testimonies* made an important contribution to Holocaust scholarship by its focus on the impact of the experience on the lives of those remaining after the days of terror and destruction had passed.

In *Art from the Ashes* (1995a), Langer continued to examine the nature of Holocaust testimony, but here he compiled a huge anthology of survivor testimonies and literature. He sought to create through these works a composite portrait of survival, amalgamating art, drama, poetry and prose about the Holocaust in order to create a sense of what the victims lived through. It comprised works by men and women, Jews and non-Jews, well-known and unknown figures, those who were there and those who were not a direct part of the event. In his Introduction he wrote:

> We may never know what the Holocaust *was* for those who endured it, but we do know what has been said about it and ... the varied ways writers have chosen to say it. If the Holocaust has ceased to seem an event and become instead a theme for prose narrative, fiction, or verse, this is not to diminish its importance, but to alter the route by which we approach it.
>
> (Langer, 1995a: 3)

His title, he wrote, should be seen as though the Jews were not 'a phoenix reborn from the mutilation of mass murder, redeeming that time of grief', but, instead, 'to suggest a symbiotic bond linking art and ashes into a seamless kinship'.

In *Admitting the Holocaust* (1995b), Langer revisited some of his earlier thoughts on the destruction wrought by the Holocaust, presenting a series of essays that came to grips with the human dimension of the *Shoah* as an assault on human values. He explored the ways in which various approaches to understanding the Holocaust (for example, in History, Literature, Film and Theology) have provided insights into how the experience can be understood, through extending the boundaries of the human mind: as he wrote, the book was 'my attempt over nearly a decade to wrestle with the rupture in human values as it really was – a rupture that after the war left stunned minds staring blankly at alien modes of living and dying in the monstrous milieu of ghettos and camps' (Langer, 1995b: 3). His essential purpose was summed up in his Introduction, and in some respects it could be viewed as a defining perspective on where all his work had been leading up to that time:

> the valuable lessons of history collapse into pretentious evasions of the grim legacies that twentieth-century reality has left us: the Holocaust above all, but only as the chief example of companion forms of mass dying through war, revolution, famine, repression, and genocide. The challenge before us is to rewrite the internal scenario of our lives to include the deaths of others – the victims of our violent time. Through their skirmish with the Holocaust,

survivors have been forced to do this, and their testimony becomes a model for our own efforts.

(Langer, 1995b: 12)

Admitting the Holocaust presented a perspective on the *Shoah* affirming that survivor testimonies and other Holocaust literature should still be the place to visit when seeking to achieve some measure of comprehension as to what the experience represented at the most intimate, human level.

Preempting the Holocaust (1998) was a second collection of essays Langer had previously written about literary and artistic treatments of the Holocaust. He ranged widely; one of his themes, for example, compared women's and men's experiences of the Holocaust (here his work complemented that of **Joan Ringelheim** and **Adam Jones**), while another related to the appropriate language needed to describe the Nazis and their genocidal campaign against the Jews (he decried against those who used terms that depersonalised the Nazis as 'monsters', or the killing process as a 'killing machine', as this tended to deprive the Nazis of human responsibility for their actions). The purpose of the collection, he asserted, was to make a contribution to the ongoing question of how modern civilisation can confront the Holocaust and still keep going ahead in a positive manner.

A further collection of essays was *Using and Abusing the Holocaust* (2006). Here, Langer undertook an analysis of intellectual and personal responses to the Holocaust in literature, film and art. In a range of penetrating essays, he considered some of the ways in which writers, artists and filmmakers use, and at times misuse, the Holocaust. He noted that as the event itself recedes in time, 'it grows more and more difficult to recapture the way it was for those who faced it: everything has come to depend on who tells the tale, and how' (Langer, 2006: xi). Given that, he assessed various literary efforts to establish a place in modern consciousness for those victimised by the Nazis. It is never an easy task, he asserted, because 'The ghastly details of the Holocaust are a constant reminder of the abyss separating the lived experience of those who endured it from the language that seeks to describe it' (Langer, 2006: xi).

In recent times Langer has developed his ideas further, through an ongoing and insightful series of explorations of the life and work of Holocaust survivor and surrealist painter Samuel Bak. In these, too, he has shown that the voice of the survivor (in this case, through art) is an authentic voice that cuts to the heart of the Holocaust experience in ways that stretch the imagination and adds to understanding for those who were not there.

179

The essence of Lawrence L. Langer's thinking has been that the Holocaust is best approached by those who experienced it in their flesh. He has sought both to examine the core of memory and to understand the nature of the encounter being remembered. Over a long period, we see that his interest has undergone change. Initially, as he tried to make sense of the Holocaust, he employed literature as the means to approach some measure of understanding; as his focus sharpened he began to examine more and more the nature of memory – not in the same sense as other literary scholars like **James E. Young**, but rather through the medium of survivor testimony. Looking deeply into the abyss, Langer has identified that what the Holocaust was really about was human violence and horror. He cannot find any profound human truths within it, and has not sought to find some higher meaning. For Lawrence L. Langer, the Holocaust was unmitigated human evil, a fact that has to be acknowledged and confronted for what it was. Recognition of this, though it sounds so obvious to twenty-first-century readers, is perhaps Langer's abiding contribution to the field.

Langer's major writings

The Holocaust and the Literary Imagination, New Haven (CT): Yale University Press, 1975.

The Age of Atrocity: Death in Modern Literature, Boston: Beacon Press, 1978.

'The Writer and the Holocaust Experience,' in Henry Friedlander and Sybil Milton (eds), *The Holocaust: Ideology, Bureaucracy, and Genocide*, Millwood (New York): Kraus International, 1980, 309–322.

Versions of Survival: The Holocaust and the Human Spirit, Albany (NY), SUNY Press, 1982.

Holocaust Testimonies: The Ruins of Memory, New Haven (CT): Yale University Press, 1991.

Art from the Ashes: A Holocaust Anthology, New York: Oxford University Press, 1995a.

Admitting the Holocaust: Collected Essays, New York: Oxford University Press, 1995b.

Landscapes of Jewish Experience: Paintings by Samuel Bak. Essay and Commentaries by Lawrence L. Langer, Lebanon (NH): University Press of New England, 1997.

Preempting the Holocaust, New Haven (CT): Yale University Press, 1998a.

'Gendered Suffering? Women in Holocaust Testimonies', in Dalia Ofer and Lenore J. Weitzman (eds), *Women in the Holocaust*, New Haven (CT): Yale University Press, 1998b, 351–63.

The Game Continues: Chess in the Art of Samuel Bak, Bloomington: Indiana University Press, 1999.

'Damaged Childhood in Holocaust Fact and Fiction', in Michael A. Signer (ed.), *Humanity at the Limits: The Impact of the Holocaust Experience on Jews and Christians*, Bloomington: Indiana University Press, 2000, 329–42.

In a Different Light: The Book of Genesis in the Art of Samuel Bak, Seattle: University of Washington Press, 2001.

Samuel Bak: New Perceptions of Old Appearances, Syracuse (NY): Syracuse University Press, 2005.

Using and Abusing the Holocaust, Bloomington: Indiana University Press, 2006.

Return to Vilna in the Art of Samuel Bak, Syracuse (NY): Syracuse University Press, 2007.

RAPHAEL LEMKIN (1900–59)

Raphael Lemkin was a Polish-born refugee from Nazi tyranny, Professor of Law at Duke University and Yale University, Adviser to United States Justice Robert H. Jackson at the International Military Tribunal in Nuremberg at the conclusion of the Second World War, and author of the monumental study *Axis Rule in Occupied Europe: Laws of Occupation, Analysis of Government, Proposals for Redress* (1944). Twice nominated for – though never awarded – the Nobel Peace Prize (in 1950 and 1952), Lemkin is best remembered as the motivating and energising presence behind the United Nations Convention on the Prevention and Punishment of the Crime of Genocide 1948, and as the 'father' of the academic discipline of Genocide Studies. Ironically, he has only recently been accorded the recognition he deserves for his contributions to the promotion of human rights on an international scale within the context of international law. This is despite the ratification of the Convention by his adopted country of the United States in 1988, his voluminous correspondence in a multiplicity of languages, his several unpublished manuscripts and his output of published articles, newspaper accounts of his work, interviews, and the like.

Lemkin was born on 24 June 1900, in the town of Bezwodne, eastern Poland, in an area of restricted Jewish residence commonly known as the 'Pale of Settlement'. He was one of three children, all boys: his brothers were named Elias and Samuel. Elias survived the Holocaust, while Samuel and his parents did not. Some time during his teenage years, Lemkin came across a copy of the book *Quo Vadis*, by the Polish writer Henryk Sienkiewicz. This novel described the nearly successful attempt by the Roman Emperor Nero to exterminate all the Christians in his realm. The effect upon Lemkin of this graphic account of those horrors, even though fictionalised, was electric. He was simply unable to conceive how it was that human beings could engage in such massively destructive behaviour towards other human beings. He asked his mother, 'Why did the Christians permit

181

themselves to be thrown to the lions without calling the police?' Her response, which clearly stimulated further reflection from her son, was 'Do you think the police could help them?'

It was this initial confrontation with horror that led Lemkin, already a voracious reader, to search out other equally devastating accounts of what he would later term 'genocide' – the Huguenots by the French; the Catholics by the Japanese; the Muslims by the Spanish; the Armenians by the Turks; his own people by the Russians, and so on. Ultimately, it impelled him towards his chosen profession of Law, and to work for the passage of an international legal convention against genocide itself.

Next to nothing is known of Lemkin's life during the years of the First World War, other than his own admission of following closely the increasing revelations of the Turkish genocide of the Armenians (1915–23), and the release of more than 150 British-interned Turks from the island of Malta (where they had been held on charges of 'war criminality'). In 1926 he obtained his Doctorate of Laws from Lvov University just as another incident claimed his attention.

On 25 May of that year, in Paris, Sholom Schwartzbard assassinated Symon Petlyura, a Ukrainian socialist politician, statesman and leader of the Ukrainian fight for independence from the Soviet Union. Brought to trial for his crime, Schwartzbard's defence was that he had been avenging the deaths of fifteen members of his family, including his parents, murdered in a series of pogroms in the Ukraine, for which he felt Petlyura had not done enough either to prevent them from happening or to punish those responsible during his brief term as President of the Ukraine Republic. The French jury found him not guilty. Lemkin's response to the Schwartzbard trial was to publish an article applauding both the act and the acquittal, but noting that no such law and process existed for addressing such tragedies on a larger scale of national, racial or religious groups.

In 1929 Lemkin was appointed Deputy Public Prosecutor in Warsaw, and Secretary of the Penal Section of the Polish Committee on Codification of Laws, in addition to representing Poland at the annual meeting of the International Bureau for the Unification of Penal Law and serving as Secretary-General of the Polish Group for the Association of Penal Law. In 1933, an international conference on penal and criminal law met in Madrid, Spain, and Lemkin used the opportunity to present his idea of an international law addressing two crimes: 'barbarity' and 'vandalism'. The former he defined as destroying a national or religious collectivity, the latter as destroying works of culture representative of the genius of such groups.

Lemkin was ultimately prevented from attending by the Polish Minister of Justice, who evidently agreed with the anti-Semitic *Gazeta Warszawska* which, in a series of articles, saw Lemkin's work as being a Jewish issue only. Between 1933 and 1939 Lemkin continued to sharpen his thinking about the legal implications and ramifications of such violence against groups.

On 1 September 1939 Germany invaded Poland; two days later, the Second World War began. As Warsaw experienced destruction first hand, Lemkin's first thoughts were to flee to safety to either Lithuania or Sweden, and then move on to America, places where he had already established good friends and contacts. After journeying across Russia, he reached Seattle, Washington, in early 1941. Lemkin then went to Chicago, on his way to Duke University, North Carolina, where friends had secured for him an academic appointment at the Duke Law School.

One year later, in June 1942, Lemkin received a letter from the Board of Economic Warfare in Washington DC, inviting him to serve as its Chief Consultant. He accepted the offer immediately. The Chairperson of that Board was Henry Wallace, at the time Vice President of the United States. Through this and other contacts, Lemkin was able to submit to President Franklin Delano Roosevelt a one-page brief *vis-à-vis* his proposal for an international treaty banning 'vandalism and barbarity'. Roosevelt responded affirmatively, but, due to the exigencies of the war itself, such work would have to come later. At the same time, Lemkin worked hard on his massive 674-page book *Axis Rule in Occupied Europe,* published in 1944 by the Carnegie Endowment for International Peace in Washington DC. During this same period, rumours were rife through the nation's capital regarding Nazi atrocities against Jews that paralleled Germany's military successes. In *Axis Rule*, Lemkin devoted the entirety of Chapter 9 to a discussion of 'genocide' – a 'new term and new conception for destruction of nations'. As he wrote at the beginning of that chapter:

> New conceptions require new terms. By 'genocide' we mean the destruction of a nation or of an ethnic group. This new word, coined by the author to denote an old practice in its modern development, is made from the ancient Greek word *genos* (race, tribe) and the Latin *cide* (killing), thus corresponding in its formation to such words as tyrannicide, homicide, infanticide, etc. Generally speaking, genocide does not necessarily mean the immediate destruction of a nation, except when accomplished by mass killings of all members of a nation. It is intended rather to signify a coordinated plan of different actions aiming at the

destruction of essential foundations of the life of national groups, with the aim of annihilating the groups themselves. The objectives of such a plan would be disintegration of the political and social institutions, of culture, language, national feelings, religion, and the economic existence of a national group, and the destruction of the personal security, liberty health, dignity, and even the lives of the individuals belonging to such groups. Genocide is directed against the national group as an entity, and the actions involved are directed against individuals, not in their individual capacity, but as members of the national group.

(Lemkin, 1944: 79)

Prior to the start of the Nuremberg War Crimes Trials on 20 November 1945, Lemkin had already joined the staff of Chief Prosecutor United States Justice Robert H. Jackson, and was able to have the word genocide inserted into the overall indictment. It would ultimately be removed, however, as the jurists themselves opined that they were bound by the Statute of the International Military Tribunal, which did not contain such a charge, and that those brought to trial could only be so for crimes committed during or in connection with the recent war of Nazi aggression.

Before the conclusion of the trials on 1 October 1946, Lemkin was already hard at work writing and publishing a number of articles in a wide variety of locations, advocating an international law banning genocide. Upon his return to the United States, he refocused his energies towards achieving recognition from the newly established United Nations.

Much of Lemkin's autobiography *Totally Unofficial Man* was devoted to the various political and other intrigues necessitated by the ultimate passage of what was then both a controversial and revolutionary legal change of direction for the international community. He also detailed the day-to-day work of writing and rewriting the text and the necessity of going one-on-one with the various official UN nation-state representatives, winning them to his cause as one who had no *official* status whatsoever (hence the title of his autobiography). By this time, he was already teaching at Yale Law School. At the same time that he was working tirelessly towards the passage of the Convention on the Prevention and Punishment of the Crime of Genocide, others were working equally tirelessly for the passage of the Universal Declaration of Human Rights. Lemkin saw them as separate and distinct, and, in some ways, working against each other: the Convention was to have the force of law; the Declaration was not, and thus, while opposed to the latter's passage at the time, Lemkin was careful not to give too strong a voice to that disagreement.

Finally, on 9 December 1948, the General Assembly of the United Nations, now with the support of both its Legal Committee and the Security Council, began its deliberations. It passed unanimously, and two days later, on 11 December 1948, Twenty-two member states signed the declaration to proceed to ratification by their own home governments. Lemkin was jubilant. the following day found him in hospital in Paris, suffering from complete and total exhaustion, or, in his own words, 'genociditis, exhaustion from working on the Genocide Convention'. He would never regain his full vigour.

Several weeks later, Lemkin returned to the United States and took up his professorial duties at Yale University. He was determined to work on US ratification, which he was to do, frustratingly, and in concert with others, until his death in 1959. With every other signatory state successfully ratifying the Genocide Convention, Lemkin redoubled his efforts, seemingly to no avail. The Convention on the Prevention and Punishment of the Crime of Genocide went into effect by the United Nations on 21 January 1951. It was only ratified by the United States on 14 October 1988, and signed into law by President Ronald Reagan on 4 November 1988.

On 28 August 1959, Raphael Lemkin died of a heart attack in New York City. Just seven people attended his funeral.

In a speech entitled 'The Legacy of Raphael Lemkin' delivered on 13 December 2000 at the United States Holocaust Memorial Museum, Michael Ignatieff, then Carr Professor of Human Rights Practice at Harvard University, made the following comments:

> [Lemkin] was one of those tragic Polish patriots never allowed membership in the nation he actually claimed as his own ...
>
> He was also a prisoner of the past – this faith in an international legal order that in some sense was, in my view, quite possibly a delusional one ...
>
> Lemkin remained trapped by the hopeful optimism of a civilization in twilight, just as he was trapped, I think, by another delusion, which is that Western Civilization is universal.
>
> (Ignatieff, 13 December 2000)

'Tragic', 'delusional', 'trapped' are, indeed, strong words to describe a singularly unique individual who, largely by virtue of his own prodigious intellect and energies, changed the way nation-states regard collective violence both internally and across their borders. Prior to

Lemkin and the Second World War, there were no significant international human-rights conventions (apart from those regarding the status of prisoners of war addressed in the various Geneva and Hague Conventions of 1864, 1907, 1929 and 1949), though the crimes themselves were by then already part of world history.

Lemkin's vision was truly pioneering. His work in bringing to the world's stage the concept of genocide, having himself no official status whatsoever, and his own driven personality to 'make it happen' in memorial tribute to his own family and to other victims, celebrates his contribution. Proper historical and other analyses do not insist on what *should* have been the case (that is, what Lemkin *should* have included or excluded or rewritten or rephrased in his writings, thinking, definitions, and so on), but, rather, focus on what Lemkin *did* accomplish in initiating a series of conversations in the international arena regarding the most heinous of crimes against humanity and the venue for those conversations, that of international law. That individuals, scholars and other professionals in the international community continue to debate these issues, their nuances and their implications, even as states persist in engaging in genocide, is the ultimate tribute to Lemkin's success.

Lemkin's major writings

Axis Rule in Occupied Europe: Laws of Occupation, Analysis of Government, Proposals for Redress, Washington DC: Carnegie Endowment for International Peace, 1944.
'Genocide – A Modern Crime', *Free World*, 4 (1945), 39–43.
'Genocide as a Crime under International Law', *American Journal of International Law*, 41, 1 (1947), 145–51.
'Totally Unofficial Man', in Samuel Totten and Steven Leonard Jacobs (eds), *Pioneers of Genocide Studies*, New Brunswick (NJ): Transaction Publishers, 2002, 365–99.

Reference

Ignatieff, Michael, 'The Legacy of Raphael Lemkin', paper delivered at United States Holocaust Memorial Museum, Washington DC, 13 December 2000, at http://www.ushmm.org.

MARK LEVENE (b. 1953)

Mark Levene is a Reader in Comparative History, and member of the Parkes Centre for Jewish/non-Jewish relations (of which he was Director in 2005–6) at the University of Southampton, UK. Born in

London in 1953, he was educated at the University of Warwick and Wolfson College, Oxford, where he received his DPhil in 1981.

Levene's path to Genocide Studies was far from being a 'standard' progression through academia. After the completion of his DPhil he became concerned about what he saw as the imminence of nuclear apocalypse owing to NATO's cruise-missile deployment in Europe, and throughout the 1980s he was fully immersed in peace campaigning. Over time, however, he became intellectually dissatisfied with tendencies within the peace movement to see the world in terms that were often too simplistic – as though 'getting rid of the bomb' would somehow, magically, create peace. Given this start, it could not be said that Levene's graduate work would necessarily lead to the study of anti-Semitism, the Holocaust or genocide.

While engaged in these activities, he became a lecturer at the Spiro Institute for the Study of Jewish History and Culture, London, where at the beginning of the 1990s a colleague, Ronnie Landau, invited him to help broaden out a pedagogic work then being compiled on the Holocaust that would include other cases of genocide. Without realising it, this would be the start of what would ultimately become Levene's magnum opus many years later, a projected four-volume global history of genocide. Soon after this, and well into his thirties, he decided to embark on an academic teaching career, first at the University of Warwick, then at the University of Southampton.

Levene's initial interests saw him trying to develop an understanding of wider concerns relating to the phenomenon of genocide. His first major project in this regard resulted in a book he co-edited with a colleague, Penny Roberts, in 1999. The result, *The Massacre in History*, was in some respects a pathbreaking work, in that it addressed an issue that had seen surprisingly little academic treatment up to that time. Earlier, in 1995, Levene and Roberts had convened a conference in which the groundwork for a study of massacre was laid. Placing massacre as an area of study within the context of both History and contemporary events, the conference sought to introduce new ways of viewing the phenomenon. The resultant book explored the nature of massacre from a variety of different social, historical, political and cultural perspectives. In his Introduction, Levene sought a way to identify why it was that historians had so far given massacre such a wide berth, and concluded that the notion was essentially one that was inconvenient:

Perhaps some of the problems inherent in this discussion may indicate why historians sometimes fight shy of the subject.

> Ugly, vicious events, often appearing to lack clear delineation of logic, massacres throw off course where they do not completely skewer any project which seeks to chart through precise information and data the long-term transformation of societies, economies and polities. Nor do apparently pathological, even sado-masochistic tendencies obviously complement the historian's penchant for the 'objective' fact or rational deduction. Yet history, after all, involves empirical observation of societies more often than not in conflict and crisis. It is, among other things, about relationships of power and unequal ones at that. Ensuing tensions, frequently leading to violence, cannot be ignored or sidestepped; on the contrary they are absolutely integral to understanding how history 'works.' As such, charting the incidence or, obversely, avoidance of massacre, may indeed throw light on a town, or region, or country's political, social, or economic development. The way such developments are either rationalized, justified or condemned may tell us much about the *mentalité* of a people – or peoples – as may the manner in which 'the massacre' becomes embedded and depicted within their respective cultures.
>
> (Levene and Roberts, 1999: 4)

In short, Levene was attempting to draw the attention of his discipline to an area that had hitherto not yet been addressed satisfactorily, signalling that the notion of massacre, thus far largely overlooked, was to a significant degree often central to the course of human development and social change, and that its relative omission until now pointed to a reluctance to engage with what should otherwise be a very important element of scholarly focus.

In subsequent studies, Levene engaged with a variety of topics relating to the Holocaust and genocide which suggested that he was searching for an appropriate vehicle in order to articulate his thinking. At this time he was working, largely in isolation, on his own independent genocide research; in some respects it was idiosyncratic, as he was not at that stage part of any academic network or circle, and he did not even have a central thesis from which to operate – other than a general intuition that studying the Holocaust as the be-all and end-all of the phenomenon of genocide was unsatisfactory. His articles ranged widely, from Jewish history, to the Armenian Genocide, to the Holocaust, to Genocide Theory. Specific projects even found him investigating the Chittagong Hill Tracts in Bangladesh, Greek Jewish history before the First World War, and Romanian Jewish history during the Second. During this time, however, he was refining his thinking to the point where he could envisage a central project that would expand and express his thoughts on the history of genocide, thereby providing answers to the questions that had been of most concern to him regarding the motive forces behind the phenomenon.

It took him some time to develop the singularity of argument for which he was searching, very much by reading through (and engaging with) a wide range of existing arguments. To take but one example, the notion that genocide was a by-product not simply of modernity, as advocated by **Zygmunt Bauman**, needed to be further developed, such that a range of dynamic processes, *including* 'modernisation', out of which the modern globalising and globalised international system/political economy was emerging, had to be dealt with more comprehensively.

Levene saw that he would be forced to eschew both the path of primary research and specialisation in a specific area study, becoming, rather, a generalist with a precise focus. His justification for doing this was that he was trying to obtain a broad overview of historical development through the prism of a particularly disturbing but persistent by-product, namely, genocide. For Levene, this phenomenon could not be viewed as a series of isolated aberrations, but rather as evidence of a much more serious systemic dysfunction in the nature of Western-led international society as it has emerged in the last two to three hundred years. His major study, *Genocide in the Age of the Nation State*, was the outcome of these reflections.

It was intended that this study would become a four-volume study examining the subject of genocide from within an extensive global and historical framework. In attempting to write as complete a history of genocide as had yet been written, Levene began by establishing a conceptual framework in which to situate it, and this was to form the content of the first volume, *The Meaning of Genocide* (2005). He held that studying genocide requires the recognition that all examples being examined are to be valued for their uniqueness, or, as he put it, 'all genocides need to be treated with regard (and respect) to their particular dynamic, their peculiar, necessarily individual and unrepeatable features' (Levene, 2005: 32). This perspective runs counter to that of some other authors, in particular Steven T. Katz, who had earlier been unequivocal in his argument that the Holocaust was a singular event in human history, the only true case of genocide ever to have taken place (Katz, 1994; see also Rosenbaum, 1996). For Levene,

> The challenge, implicit in this study ... is the degree to which we
> can successfully stand back from the fray in order to see the wood

for the trees. Our premise remains that genocide is not so much a series of isolated, aberrant and essentially unconnected events but is at the very heart of modern historical development. Paradoxically, this is why, while maintaining a rigorous definition of genocide, we have so much subject matter with which to engage. Doubly paradoxically, part of our intrinsic challenge will also be to delineate – as far as possible – the degree to which we are dealing with an identifiably discrete phenomenon within a much broader and, indeed, unremittingly scarred landscape of mass exterminatory violence, a consideration which, instead of extracting it into an entirely separate category of its own, might demand some additional effort in framing its specific morphology, as well as in locating its more particular psycho-social and political, etiology.

(Levene, 2005b: 32)

Levene was fully conscious that there might be some who would not agree with him: indeed, he acknowledged that 'the appearance of fuller data may, in time, change the specific contours of this investigation, just as rigorous counter-analysis may challenge or undermine its basic conception' (Levene, 2005b: 32).

Volume 2 of *Genocide in the Age of the Nation State – The Rise of the West and the Coming of Genocide* (2005) – considered an area that was beginning to build momentum in the field of Genocide Studies: the question of colonial genocides of indigenous peoples in the lands of recent European settlement. Earlier, when Levene was working independently on amassing his materials and developing his thinking in the early 1990s, he was not aware that some others were beginning to also think along similar lines. Yet the sort of material he was gathering turned out to have a major synergy with an emerging field of colonial emphasis, especially with regard to an Australian historian, A. Dirk Moses (see Moses, 2004; Moses, 2008a; Moses, 2008b). The two were working quite separately and independently, each unaware of the other's existence.

Levene's work in *The Rise of the West* was a meticulous examination of the relationship between the expansion of Europe, the development of the modern nation-state, and the extreme state violence that is prevalent in the contemporary world. He took a long-term view, considering not only colonial situations in North America, Asia, Africa and Australia, but also the clash between the modern state and ideology in Europe itself – specifically, through an investigation of the French Revolution's attempts to coerce the people of the Vendée region of western France into accepting the new state and the ideas it espoused. By itself, Western expansion need not have instigated a series of genocidal eruptions. However, when conflicts emerged as a result of invasion, subjugation and subordination, and these were coupled with the insistence that a distinctly Western (and modern) model of humanity be imposed upon the non-Western (and therefore, non-modern) societies thereby conquered, massive violence on a genocidal scale was much more likely to take place than at any previous time. Genocide, seen from this perspective, was thus a Western phenomenon, coincident with modernity and the impress of the European blueprint on the rest of the world.

As his project developed, Levene found that he could not escape from modes of thinking he had encountered in an earlier phase of his life as an environmental and peace activist – which is not to suggest that he had ever abandoned his stance as an environmentalist or peace activist. Rather, he began trying to find ways of melding the academic and the activist into one. This enabled him to see beyond the specificity of genocide, to the wider underpinnings of conflict and crisis in the modern world. Here, his interests were informed by more than just the field of History. What this has since led to is a reconsideration of the bases upon which writing about the nature of mass violence leading to massacre and genocide can take place, and into an intellectually stimulating area that considers the impact of climate change on society's propensity for fragmentation and disintegration. The work he has done beyond his scholarly writing, therefore, must also be taken into account when considering the development and articulation of his thoughts on genocide.

Thus, as the founder of *Rescue! History*, Levene has sought to draw the attention of those working in the Humanities to the reality and urgency of human-created climate change. His key concern is with the impact of climate change on the world in its entirety; where this has its most dire consequence on the fabric of human society, he asks:

> should 'lessons' on averting our own Nemesis lead to historical consideration of much more instrumental efforts aimed at technological breakthroughs, or forms of political and social restructuring, which arguably have also been responses to resource depletion, environmental degradation and, indeed, past climate change? What human 'collateral damage,' however, has been the by-product of such often Herculean efforts? Have not attempts to overcome limitations on what was humanly possible simply led to ever more lethal tendencies towards destruction and

self-destruction, exacerbating into the bargain not only fraught power relationships between man and nature but also between man and man? Are indeed, our own worst tendencies in recent times, imperial and colonial subjugation, total war, Auschwitz, genocide, ethnic cleansing, Hiroshima and the 'exterminist' thrust of the nuclear arms race, not to say contemporary efforts by hegemonic powers, lesser states and corporate cartels to monopolistically control and determine the remaining, dwindling hydrocarbon reserves and other key resources worldwide, been simply harbingers of where we are heading?

(http://rescue-history-from-climate-change.org)

Further developing this thinking, Levene is also a co-founder of Crisis Forum, a consciousness-raising body that believes humankind is in serious trouble due to an economic and political system that is destroying its ability to sustain its existence. The Forum is founded on the premise that the interlocking series of political, economic, environmental, social and epidemiological dangers facing humanity are unprecedented in human existence, requiring a drastic change to all existing global political and economic practice if the human species is to survive into the foreseeable future. Seen in this light, the problem has been until now characterised by a head-in-the-sand approach which has been interpreted in a very narrowly focused and tunnel-visioned manner. Thus, global warming, Third World starvation, resource wars, a spiralling decline in biodiversity, AIDS, the risk of global economic meltdown, the threat of terrorism, forms of religious fundamentalism, and so on, are far from individual crises, but are instead symptomatic of an all-encompassing systemic dysfunctionality (http://www.crisis-forum.org.uk). Where this new thinking seems to be taking Levene is into an area of investigation that considers the future prospects for genocide in light of the interrelationships within a changing world brought about by accelerating anthropogenic climate change. He explores general contours of likely violence in the present and future, and how genocide may have to be seen as one of very many likely outcomes of climate change.

It could not be said that Mark Levene has followed an orthodox path towards his current position as a leading scholar of genocide. While he embraces large projects in his own right, he is also willing to work with others in developing new initiatives, such as an undertaking with the University of Edinburgh's **Donald Bloxham**, *Zones of Violence*, a ten-volume monograph series, in which each study is authored by a specialist, examining different regions of the globe that have been subjected to repeat instances of genocide and related violence in modern history. In some respects, a project such as this provides a useful summary of Levene's approach. Together with the four volumes of his own *Genocide in the Age of the Nation State* (of which two have already appeared) and the *Rescue! History* and *Crisis Forum* projects, it illustrates work that is expansive, ambitious and at the cutting edge. In the work of Mark Levene we see a breadth of thinking and a concern for humanity that is both influential and highly original.

Levene's major writings

War, Jews and the New Europe: The Diplomacy of Lucien Wolf, 1914–1919, Oxford: Oxford University Press, 1992.

'Frontiers of Genocide: Jews in the Eastern War Zones, 1914 to 1920 and 1941', in Panikos Panayi (ed.), *Minorities in Wartime*, Oxford: Berg, 1993, 83–117.

'Yesterday's Victims, Today's Perpetrators? Considerations on Peoples and Territories within the Former Ottoman Empire', *Terrorism and Political Violence*, 6 (Winter 1994a), 444–61.

'Is the Holocaust Simply Another Example of Genocide?', *Patterns of Prejudice*, 28, 2 (1994b), 3–26.

'Creating a Modern "Zone of Genocide": The Impact of Nation and State Formation on Eastern Anatolia, 1878–1923', *Holocaust and Genocide Studies*, 12, 3 (Winter 1998), 393–433.

'Connecting Threads: Rwanda, the Holocaust and the Pattern of Contemporary Genocide', in Roger W. Smith (ed.), *Genocide: Essays Toward Understanding, Early Warning and Prevention*, Williamsburg (VA): Association of Genocide Scholars, 1999, 27–64.

(Ed. with Penny Roberts), *The Massacre in History*, Oxford: Berghahn Books, 1999.

'Why is the Twentieth Century the Century of Genocide?', *Journal of World History*, 11, 2 (2000), 305–36.

'The Changing Face of Mass Murder: Massacre, Genocide and Post-Genocide', *International Social Science Journal*, 174 (2002), 443–52.

'A Dissenting Voice; or How Current Assumptions of Deterring and Preventing Genocide May be Looking at the Problem through the Wrong End of the Telescope', *Journal of Genocide Research*, 6, 2–3 (2004), 153–66, 431–45.

'Rescue! History, A Manifesto for the Humanities in the Age of Climate Change', *Viewpoint*, 447 (16 November 2005a), 1–5, at http://www.viewpoint.soton.ac.uk/Viewpoint/447/

Genocide in the Age of the Nation State, vol. 1, *The Meaning of Genocide*, London: I. B. Tauris, 2005b.

Genocide in the Age of the Nation State, vol. 2, *The Rise of the West and the Coming of Genocide*, London: I. B. Tauris, 2005c.

(Ed. with David Cromwell) *Surviving Climate Change: The Struggle to Avert Global Catastrophe*, London: Pluto Press, 2007a.
'David Sheffer's "Genocide and Atrocity Crimes," A Response', *Genocide Studies and Prevention*, 2, 1 (2007b), 81–90.
'Empire, Native Peoples, and Genocide', in A. Dirk Moses (ed.), *Empire, Colony, Genocide, Conquest, Occupation and Subaltern Resistance in World History*, Oxford: Berghahn Books, 2008, 183–204.

References

Katz, Steven T., *The Holocaust in Historical Context*, vol. 1, *The Holocaust and Mass Death before the Modern Age*, New York: Oxford University Press, 1994.
Landau, Ronnie S., *The Nazi Holocaust*, London: National Book Network, 1994.
Moses, A. Dirk (ed.), *Genocide and Settler Society: Frontier Violence and Stolen Indigenous Children in Australian History*, New York: Berghahn Books, 2004.
Moses, A. Dirk (ed.), *Colonialism and Genocide*, New York: Routledge, 2008a.
Moses, A. Dirk (ed.), *Empire, Colony, Genocide: Conquest, Occupation and Subaltern Resistance in World History*, New York: Berghahn Books, 2008b.
Rosenbaum, Alan S. (ed.), *Is the Holocaust Unique? Perspectives on Comparative Genocide*, Boulder (CO): Westview Press, 1996.

PRIMO LEVI (1919–87)

Primo Levi was an Italian-Jewish Holocaust survivor and author, best known for his insightful memoirs, short stories, poems, essays and novels. A chemist by training, he was born in Turin, Italy, in 1919 to non-observant Jewish parents. As a child he developed a voracious appetite for reading, and was encouraged in his educational interests by his parents. In October 1937 he enrolled at the University of Turin to study Chemistry, and, despite the difficulties placed upon Jewish students by Mussolini's racial legislation, he managed to graduate in the summer of 1941. In October 1943 Levi joined the liberal Giustizia e Libertà partisan movement, but was captured by the Fascist militia and told he would be shot as a partisan. To save his life, he confessed to being Jewish in order for his 'crime' to be recategorised, and was sent to an internment camp for Jews at Fossoli, near Modena, in central Italy. When Fossoli fell into the hands of the Germans, they began deporting the camp's Jews to Auschwitz. On 21 February 1944 Levi arrived there and had the number 174517 tattooed on his left forearm. He was liberated by the Russians in January 1945. His survival was in large part due to his contracting scarlet fever, which prevented him from becoming part of the infamous and deadly Auschwitz death marches. He returned to Turin 10 months after the liberation, his long journey home having taken a circuitous route from Poland, through Byelorussia, Ukraine, Romania, Hungary, Austria and Germany. This trip he later chronicled in his book *La Tregua* (*The Truce*, or, in its American version, *The Reawakening*).

In 1947 he published his first book, *If This is a Man* (US title, *Survival in Auschwitz: The Nazi Assault on Humanity*). This was Levi's account of his time in Auschwitz, and became his best-known work. In 1958 the book was translated into English, followed by German and several other languages. Eventually, it was accepted as a classic of Holocaust literature, as it remains today.

Levi set out systematically to remember his experiences, thinking through what had happened and how he was able to survive, and rendering his time in Auschwitz comprehensible in a prose style that would be understandable to all. He was impelled to write the book in order to bear witness to the horrors of the Nazis; without sentimentality, he recounted his experience with powerful words that described the fear, the endless hunger and the everyday pain of life. At the same time, he was also able to show examples of affection, generosity, and even, from time to time, humour. The book was a masterpiece about the survival of the human spirit in a place designed to destroy it. Its strength lay in how Levi was able to show the ways in which prisoners dealt with ongoing moral dilemmas and challenges to their physical endurance, and provided insight into how they viewed their hopes for the future – in so far as they could think of such things in Auschwitz.

In 1948 Levi began working as an industrial chemist, which he would remain for the next 30 years. At the same time, he continued to write, and most of his works were translated into English and other languages. The most important of these were *The Truce* (1963), two collections of fantasy stories, *Natural Histories* (1966) and *The Sixth Day* (1971), *The Periodic Table* (1975), The *Monkey's Wrench* (1978), *If Not Now, When?* (1981), *Collected Poems* (1984), *Other People's Trades* (1985) and *The Drowned and the Saved* (1986). Having experienced the pain of writing his Auschwitz and post-Auschwitz memoirs (which have often since been republished together in a single-volume format), Levi preferred to be known also as a writer about other subjects. He became a regular contributor of newspaper commentaries and articles, wrote science fiction and poetry, and even a novel.

Levi retired in 1977 to devote himself full-time to writing, but on 11 April 1987 he fell to his death from his third-story apartment in

Turin. (It was, to add to the tragedy, the same multi-story apartment where he had been born in 1919.) The question of whether his death was in fact suicide (he had been under a doctor's care for depression, having already suffered from this affliction both after the war and in the early 1960s) or a loss of balance as a result of his medications remains unresolved. (Gambetta, n.d.)

Collectively, according to scholar Robert S. C. Gordon, Levi's works address some of the most challenging questions facing twentieth-century modernity: the risks and rewards of science; the nature of historical responsibility; the limits of the human; the workings of language; and the ethics of everyday life (Gordon, 2007: xviii). Indeed, Levi's writings are those of one who witnessed first-hand the events about which he writes, who cannot escape such responsibilities, but in so doing asks the most uncomfortable of questions to which even he himself cannot fully present answers. As Marco Belpoliti, editor of Levi's complete works in Italian, has written:

> he has exposed himself in the role of witness, he has faced the problem of not wishing to forget ... in his persistence in asking himself questions that have no certain answers or which, if they have them, undermine received opinions, whether of individuals or groups of people.
>
> (Belpoliti, 2005: xiii–xiv)

Author Steve Lipman has related the following much-quoted incident, taken from *If This is a Man*, as an example of the difficulties inherent for Levi – and this is certainly also the case for many others who wish to 'make sense' of the events which they themselves experienced:

> To describe the nihilistic condition of daily existence in Auschwitz, Levi told the story of being locked in a hut and, wracked with thirst, leaning out of a window to break off an icicle. A guard snatched the icicle away.
>
> 'Warum?' Levi asked in his basic German. 'Why?'
>
> 'Hier ist kein Warum,' the guard answered, pushing Levi back inside – 'Here there is no why.'
>
> (Lipman, 2006: 7)

One such example of this quest for understanding was Levi's addressing of what he called 'The Grey Zone'. That zone, as he described it, is the space between absolute good and absolute evil, where moral choices are made for the purpose of survival rather than death, where the desire to live surmounts the desire to be honourable. Levi recognised that we should hold back from any condemnation of those who collaborated with the Nazis – the *Sonderkommando* men in the death camps were the example he used – for abetting the killing process of their fellow Jews. As he wrote, 'one is never in another's place. Each individual is so complex an object that there is no point in trying to foresee his behavior, all the more so in extreme situations; and neither is it possible to foresee one's own behavior' (Levi, 1989: 43). Levi discussed this most fundamental of moral dilemmas without condemnation, and with the dispassionate objectivity that was a hall-mark of his writing. He wrote of 'the motives that impelled some prisoners to collaborate to some extent with the Lager [that is, the camp] authorities', and 'the extreme case of collaboration' represented by the *Sonderkommando* men. Ever the humanist, and aware of the fragility of the human person, he concluded with the recognition that 'Willingly or not we come to terms with power, forgetting that we are all in the ghetto, that the ghetto is walled in, that outside the ghetto reign the lords of death, and that close by the train is waiting' (Levi, 1989: 69).

Building on this further, while he reserved his condemnations for the actual perpetrators of the crimes, he could not exonerate the cow-ardice of the German people as a whole, in particular their failure to align themselves with their past. In the Preface to *The Drowned and the Saved* he wrote of the greatest crime in the history of humanity, namely,

> [T]he failure to divulge the truth about the Lager. ... [This] represents one of the major collective crimes of the German people and the most obvious demonstration of the cowardice to which the Hitlerian terror had reduced them. ... Without this cowardice the greatest excesses would not have been carried out, and Europe and the world would be different today.
>
> (Levi, 1989: 14–15)

Not afraid to confront the controversial, he also addressed the contentious issue of the 'uniqueness' of the Holocaust, writing that

> the Nazi concentration camp system remains a *unicum* [that is, a stand-alone example], both in its extent and its quality. At no other place or time has one seen a phenomenon so unexpected and so complex: never have so many human lives been extin-guished in so short a time, and with so lucid a combination of technological ingenuity, fanaticism, and cruelty.
>
> (Levi, 1989: 21)

The Drowned and the Saved also addressed several other important topics, as indicated by the titles of the various chapters – 'The Memory of the Offense', 'Shame', 'Communicating', 'The Intellectual in Auschwitz', 'Stereotypes' – but arguably none were more important than the article 'Useless Violence', which Levi defined as 'an end in itself, with the sole purpose of inflicting pain, occasionally having a purpose, yet always redundant, always disproportionate to the purpose itself' (Levi, 1989: 106). Such violence could take numerous forms in the camps, and Levi, perhaps subconsciously aligning himself with **Terrence Des Pres**, cited the examples of 'excremental coercion' (both the lack of proper facilities and the need for permission, frequently denied, for visiting the latrines) and its assault upon modesty, the daily *Appel* or 'roll call' which must always be balanced no matter how long it took, *Bettenbauen* (the invented German term for 'making beds' in the barracks – a daily torture that frequently resulted in beatings if even a single crease was out of place), the degrading tattooing in Auschwitz of both men and women (and a direct violation of Orthodox Jewish religious tradition), and the absurdity of so-called work – in reality mindless repetition of hard labour such as the continuous relocation of sand piles – which bore no relation whatsoever to furthering the war effort. While for the most part having no discernible purpose or logic, Levi concluded that 'before dying the victim must be degraded, so that the murderer will be less burdened by guilt. This is an explanation not devoid of logic but it shouts to heaven: it is the sole usefulness of useless violence' (Levi, 1989: 126).

As a thinker, Primo Levi brought together the rational objective insights of the scientist and the literary skills of the writer, and forced his readers to look at events not through coloured lenses but as they truly were: ugly, ignoble, neither the work of demi-gods nor of demi-satans, but of ordinary human beings capable of extraordinary evil. He argued for the necessity of a new approach to philosophy, and to understanding the world, after the Holocaust. In his work he found the unrelenting eye of the objectivist who focused his own lens unremittingly on the Holocaust – the result of his own personal and tragic experiences – and that, combined with his skilled literary talents, has left a legacy not only of descriptive accuracy, recording what actually transpired, but of memory that will simply not allow us to forget the event itself. By raising the most uncomfortable questions, and allowing the questions themselves to lead towards answers, he ensured that the search for answers will continue for many years to come.

Levi's major writings

Se questo è un uomo (1947) (*If This Is a Man* – US title, *Survival in Auschwitz*)
La tregua (1963) (*The Truce* – US title, *The Reawakening*)
Storie naturali (1966) (*The Sixth Day and Other Tales*)
Lilìt e altri racconti (1971) (Part 1 can be found in *Moments of Reprieve*; some stories from Parts 2 and 3 are in *A Tranquil Star*)
Vizio di forma (1971) (*The Sixth Day and Other Tales*; some stories are also in *A Tranquil Star*)
Il sistema periodico (1975) (*The Periodic Table*)
L'osteria di Brema (1975) (*Shema: Collected Poems*)
La chiave a stella (1978) (*The Wrench* – US title, *The Monkey's Wrench*)
La ricerca delle radici (1981) (*The Search for Roots: A Personal Anthology*)
Se non ora, quando? (1982) (*If Not Now, When?*)
Ad ora incerta (1984) (in *Collected Poems of Primo Levi*)
L'altrui mestiere (1985) (*Other People's Trades*)
I sommersi e i salvati (1986) (*The Drowned and the Saved*)
Racconti e Saggi (1986) (*The Mirror Maker*)
The Drowned and the Saved, London: Sphere Books, 1989.
Conversazioni e interviste 1963–1987 (1997) (*Conversations with Primo Levi*)
The Voice of Memory: Interviews, 1961–1987, New York: The New Press, 1990.
The Black Hole of Auschwitz, London: Polity Press, 2005.
Auschwitz Report, London: Verso, 2006.
A Tranquil Star: Unpublished Stories of Primo Levi, London: Penguin Books, 2007.

References

Belpoliti, Marco Belpoliti (ed.), *The Black Hole of Auschwitz* (Malden: Polity Press, 2005), xiii–xiv.
Gambetta, Diego, 'Primo Levi's Last Moments', *Boston Review: A Political and Literary Forum*, at http://www.bostonreview.net
Gordon, Robert S. C. (ed.), *The Cambridge Companion to Primo Levi*, Cambridge: Cambridge University Press, 2007, xviii.
Lipman, Steve, 'Turin's Witness', *The New York Jewish Week*, 24 February 2006.

ROBERT JAY LIFTON (b. 1926)

Robert Jay Lifton is an American psychiatrist known chiefly for his studies of the psychological causes and effects of war and political violence, and for his theories regarding thought reform. Born in Brooklyn, New York, in 1926, his early education was at Cornell University, followed by medical studies at New York Medical College and an internship at the Jewish Hospital of Brooklyn. From 1951 to 1953 he served as a US Air Force psychiatrist in Japan and Korea, and was a Research Associate in Psychiatry at Harvard University from 1956 to 1961. In a long and varied career, he has been a professor and researcher in such settings as the Washington School of Psychiatry, Harvard University and the John Jay College of Criminal Justice (where he helped to found the Center for the Study of Human Violence).

During the late 1950s and early 1960s, Lifton investigated the 'thought reform' procedures used against captured American soldiers during the Korean War, leading to a broader area of interest relating to brainwashing in wartime. His book *Thought Reform and the Psychology of Totalism: A Study of 'Brainwashing' in China* (1961) came from this interest. Taken at its broadest, Lifton's interest thus focused on the ways in which oppressive regimes impacted upon people's minds (and therefore their lives). In several of his subsequent works he would investigate this further, examining the manner in which people adapted to the stresses of life under the intense pressures of wartime. Three such studies were highly influential, in which he took three very different cases (one looking at survivors of nuclear war, one looking at soldiers under traumatic wartime conditions, and one looking at perpetrators of genocide), and assessed the psychological adaptations each required in order to accommodate themselves to the new life that circumstances had thrust upon them.

In *Death in Life: Survivors of Hiroshima* (1968a), Lifton attempted to explain both the physical and psychological effects of the 1945 nuclear attack on Hiroshima, discussing the survivors and their feelings of guilt that they had survived while others around them had been consumed. Survivors, called *hibakusha*, or 'explosion affected persons', were victims of the blast, the heat and the effects of radiation. Lifton's major concern was with the psychological effects on the survivors. *Hibakusha*, he found, developed several theories to cope with their experience:

1. Why us? Ours was a small city of limited military importance.
2. We were guinea pigs. The Americans wanted to test their new bomb. We were their lab rats.
3. We were the victims of racial bias. They only use weapons like that on the coloured races.
4. The people responsible will suffer divine retribution for their actions.
5. We, the survivors, have a mission to explain the horrors of nuclear war to the world.

Lifton's analysis of *hibakusha*, and his subsequent consideration of Vietnam veterans in *Home from the War: Vietnam Veterans – Neither*

Victims nor Executioners (1973), was telling. In both situations he was looking at highly traumatised populations, in many instances ostracised by those around them with little appreciation of what they had been through.

The contrast between this situation and that of the third group Lifton studied – medical professionals in Germany during the Third Reich – drew some highly significant conclusions about how otherwise seemingly humane and caring people can rationalise their participation in morally reprehensible acts such as mass murder. *The Nazi Doctors: Medical Killing and the Psychology of Genocide* (1986), far from being a book that looked specifically at atrocity-producing trauma, sought to learn more about the nature of human evil. Lifton wrote at the outset that 'I had no doubt about the reality of Nazi evil', but he saw a need to probe it nonetheless; to avoid doing so would be 'a refusal to call forth our capacity to engage and combat it' (Lifton, 1986: xi). His study, however, was not meant to be a comprehensive historical study of the medical profession in general during the Third Reich. Rather, he was interested in 'the relationship of specific groups of Nazi doctors, and particular individuals, to mass murder – as well as the broader "healing" claim of the [Nazi] regime' which held that through killing groups of unwanted human beings the German people could survive (Lifton, 1986: xii). As he saw it,

> Much has been said about relationships of perpetrators and victims, and such relationships had considerable importance in Auschwitz and elsewhere. But I have found it essential to make the sharpest differentiation between the moral and psychological situation of members of the two groups. Whatever the behavior of either, prisoners were in the situation of being threatened inmates while Nazi doctors were threatening victimizers. This clear distinction must be the beginning of any evaluation of medical behavior in Auschwitz. Jews were the main objects of Nazi genocide and therefore the main victims of Nazi doctors. But my concerns in this book also include non-Jewish inmates such as Poles and political prisoners and Russian prisoners of war; and also mental patients in Germany and occupied areas victimized even more directly by Nazi doctors.
>
> (Lifton, 1986: xiii)

Lifton also noted a broader issue that had to be dealt with: 'the relationship of Nazi doctors to the human species'. Talking to an Auschwitz survivor with first-hand experience of the Nazi doctors,

Lifton was asked, 'Were they *beasts* when they did what they did? Or were they *human beings*?' The survivor 'was not surprised by my answer: they were and are men, which is my justification for studying them; and their behavior – Auschwitz itself – was a product of specifically *human* ingenuity and cruelty' (Lifton, 1986: 4, emphasis in original).

Lifton's project built on a wide range of interviews with former Nazi medical professionals and those who survived them, noting that many of the doctors were in fact careerists with little compunction about murdering for the sake of racist 'health'. He showed that medically supervised killing in the camps had its origin in the so-called euthanasia programme before the Second World War, when the Nazi eugenics campaign forced the sterilisation and state-sanctioned murder of those deemed to be 'life unworthy of life' – German citizens who were mentally retarded, physically handicapped and/or emotionally disturbed. From here, it was but a short step to systematic murder of larger groups of people (such as the Jews), in which the medical profession played an important technical role.

Of course, the very idea of doctors taking part in the business of mass murder seems contradictory, and Lifton traced the ineluctable reasoning that could allow the notion of medical healing to be so corrupted. Ultimately, he asked how it was that doctors could rationalise becoming mass murderers while at the same time taking extraordinary professional care to ensure that their medical techniques were not compromised. Lifton's study provided a new and intimate look at how genocide can be validated, not by wild-eyed psychopaths, but by highly educated professionals who very often sincerely believed that they were applying their skills in the best possible way for the good of all. His work, in this sense, was both profound and disturbing.

Lifton's research was in part facilitated by one of his protégés, a sociologist from Minnesota named **Eric Markusen**. As the two worked more and more closely, their relationship developed into one of direct collaboration, and as the 1980s proceeded they began analysing the twin notions of a 'genocidal mentality' and the relationship between modern war and genocide. It was Lifton's work with survivors of Hiroshima that led him to becoming opposed to the spread, testing and use of nuclear weapons, as he rationalised that the nuclear option in international affairs made global genocide a possibility. Lifton and **Markusen**, who was just as concerned as Lifton about such matters, later collaborated in co-authoring a book examining these issues, *The Genocidal Mentality: Nazi Holocaust and Nuclear Threat* (1990). This was a study of the thinking that impels military planners to seek the death of vast numbers of people when strategies of nuclear confrontation are being formulated. They examined the role played by the Holocaust in shaping modern-day consciousness of the nuclear threat, and one of their key arguments was that the human sense of right and wrong has been dulled as a result of the Holocaust – indeed, of the whole war experience of the twentieth century. Accordingly, events involving mass death and destruction are no longer met with a sense of horror or indignation. More than that, they also posited that those most likely to bring about such death and destruction – military and bureaucratic elites, politicians and highly educated technical experts – have been offered a precedent by the Nazi experience that exonerates them from any sense of personal responsibility for the damage they cause. This is, they argued, 'the genocidal mentality'.

Lifton and **Markusen**'s purpose with this book was to look at the moral question of to what extent men and women in the modern state should, or can, obey orders – including those which might result in the death of millions. It was thus both an extension of Lifton's earlier work on perpetrators, and a commentary on where the twentieth century – the century of genocide – had been inexorably leading up to.

It is difficult to summarise Lifton's overall contribution to the field of Holocaust and Genocide Studies. His substantial scholarly output for nearly half a century has had an enormous impact on the ways in which people approach the subject of humans' psychological propensity for evil, as well as their adaptability and resilience in the face of monstrous adversity. His work, moreover, has been inspirational for other scholars in unexpected places. **Lawrence L. Langer**, for example, perhaps the foremost literary critic of the Holocaust, credited Lifton's book *Death in Life* as the one which 'inspired me to ask some of my own questions about the effect of the Holocaust on the literary imagination' (Langer, 1975: xiii). As a psychologist, Lifton's realm is the mind and how it functions, much like another leading Genocide Studies scholar, **Israel W. Charny**. Both seek to penetrate very dark places in the human psyche; both have done so by looking at how those places function during equally dark times. Lifton has concluded that the inner workings of the human temperament are not innately cruel, and that only genuine sociopaths are able to undertake truly evil anti-human acts without suffering lasting emotional harm. Nonetheless, in his view the commission of such acts does not require any unusual degree of personal evil or mental illness, and can surface in anyone if the appropriate timing and circumstances present themselves.

Robert Jay Lifton's work is a constant reminder that the human inclinations to do evil and do good are split by only a very fine line of conscience, and that that line is constantly under pressure. While not a moral philosopher, Lifton's scientific approach has brought to light some highly moral issues regarding the nature of being human, and as a result of his exertions our understanding of the deepest motive forces behind mass killing, victimhood and survivorship has been enhanced.

Lifton's major writings

Thought Reform and the Psychology of Totalism: A Study of 'Brainwashing' in China, New York: Norton, 1961.

Death in Life: Survivors of Hiroshima, New York: Random House, 1968a.

Revolutionary Immortality: Mao Tse-Tung and the Chinese Cultural Revolution, New York: Random House, 1968b.

History and Human Survival: Essays on the Young and the Old, Survivors and the Dead, Peace and War, and on Contemporary Psychohistory, New York: Random House, 1970.

(with Richard A. Falk and Gabriel Kolko) *Crimes of War: A Legal, Political-Documentary, and Psychological Inquiry into the Responsibilities of Leaders, Citizens, and Soldiers for Criminal Acts of War*, Random House, 1971.

Home from the War: Vietnam Veterans – Neither Victims nor Executioners, New York: Simon and Schuster, 1973.

(with Shuichi Kato and Michael Reich) *Six Lives/Six Deaths: Portraits from Modern Japan*, New Haven (CT): Yale University Press, 1979.

(with Richard A. Falk) *Indefensible Weapons: The Political and Psychological Case against Nuclearism*, New York: Basic Books, 1982.

(with Nicholas Humphrey) *In a Dark Time: Images for Survival*, Cambridge (MA): Harvard University Press, 1984.

The Nazi Doctors: Medical Killing and the Psychology of Genocide, New York: Basic Books, 1986.

(with Eric Markusen) *The Genocidal Mentality: Nazi Holocaust and Nuclear Threat*, New York: Basic Books, 1990.

Destroying the World to Save It: Aum Shinrikyo, Apocalyptic Violence, and the New Global Terrorism, New York: Owl Books, 2000.

Reference

Langer, Lawrence L., *The Holocaust and the Literary Imagination*, New Haven: Yale University Press, 1975.

FRANKLIN H. LITTELL (1917–2009)

Franklin Hamlin Littell may rightly be called the 'father' of Holocaust Studies in the United States, having taught the first graduate seminar on the Holocaust at Emory University, Georgia, in 1959. In addition, together with Hubert Locke, then of Wayne State University, Michigan, he co-founded the Annual Scholars' Conference on the Holocaust and the Churches in 1970, which remains today the longest ongoing conference of its kind in the world.

Littell was born in Syracuse, New York in 1917. He received his Master of Divinity from Union Theological Seminary (New York) in 1937, and his PhD from Yale University in 1946. A minister of the United Methodist Church, Littell taught at a number of colleges before joining Temple University, Philadelphia, where he retired in 1986. In 1976 he established the first doctoral programme in Holocaust Studies in the United States. Later, he became the Ida E. King Distinguished Professor of Holocaust and Genocide Studies at Richard Stockton College (Pomona, New Jersey), in the MA programme he and his wife, Marcia Sachs Littell, co-founded.

Littell was also a prolific author, whose best-known book remains *The Crucifixion of the Jews: The Failure of Christians to Understand the Jewish Experience* (1975). This was reissued in a new format 30 years later, for an entirely new audience of younger readers. Littell argued that 'the cornerstone of Christian Antisemitism is the superseding or displacement myth, which already rings with the genocidal note'. He continued:

> The murder of six million Jews by baptized Christians, from whom membership in good standing was not (and has not yet been) withdrawn, raises the most insistent question about the credibility of Christianity. The existence of a restored Israel, proof positive that the Jewish people is not annihilated, assimilated or otherwise withering away, is substantial refutation of the traditional Christian myth about their end in the historic process.
>
> (Littell, 1975: 2)

A profoundly theological work, *The Crucifixion of the Jews* was Littell's attempt to deal with the predicament in which Christian integrity found itself as a result of both the Holocaust and its historic anti-Semitism; the ongoing survival of the Jews; the rebirth of the Third Jewish Commonwealth in the State of Israel; and the God celebrated by both Jews and Christians. Realising the provocative nature of his title, Littell noted that 'the crucifixion and resurrection of the Jewish people are the most important events for Christian history in centuries' (Littell, 1975: 6). As a Protestant clergyman highly critical of his religious tradition's past, Littell's work and thought complemented that of leading 'post-Auschwitz' Catholic thinker **Harry**

James Cargas, who shared much Christian fellowship with Littell in the 1970s and 1980s.

For Littell, it was the experience of attending a Nazi Party rally in Nuremberg, Germany, early in the 1930s, and later serving for a decade as Chief Protestant Adviser for the US Military High Command in Germany after the Second World War, which began his intellectual journey. From these experiences, he came to the conclusion that, first, the ground of Nazism had been prepared by 2,000 years of Christian anti-Semitism; and second, that the Holocaust itself presented what he termed a 'credibility' crisis' for religious Christianity and its theology. Almost all his scholarship examined individual responsibility in a free society, and sought to encourage interfaith dialogue – mainly between Christians and Jews, but in the last years of his life extended to Muslims, as well.

A consistent theme running through Littell's work was the 'lessons to be learned' from the Holocaust for both Christians and Jews. For Littell, ever the pragmatist,

> Our first task, to be sure, is to continue to tell the story as accurately as our several methodologies and disciplines make possible. ... Another immediate but major task which confronts us as we consider the lessons of the Holocaust is the reconstruction of Christian theology. ... A third major task is the reconstruction of higher education.
>
> (Littell, 2003: especially 263–84)

Taking his own agenda seriously, Littell's 'tasks' became translated into the very framework by which the Annual Scholars' Conference on the Holocaust and the Churches then operated for the next four decades:

1. The study of the Nazi assault on its enemies – the Jewish people and those Christians who held fast to their faith – must be carried on by *interfaith* teams.
2. Our subject must be *interdisciplinary*, bringing into focus the varied vernaculars and methodologies of the camps; and
3. Our teams for research, writing and discussion must be *international*, bringing together scholars who are citizens of those countries most concretely concerned in searching out the lessons of the Church Struggle and the Holocaust – especially Israel, the German Federal Republic and the USA.

> (Littell, 2003: 355, emphasis added)

Of equal importance for Littell, reflected in both his early and later work, was his concern with the creation of a Genocide Early Warning System as a concrete, preventative measure against the forces of extremism that could lead to another Holocaust. In his 7 November 1996 Ida E. King Lecture at Richard Stockton College, he most fully articulated the various components of such a system, which he had previously addressed in a number of other pieces (Littell, 2003: 1–6, 133–43, 252; see also Jacobs, 2010).

In that lecture, 'Creating an Early Warning System: The 20th Century Confrontation with Terrorist Movements', he framed his analysis by addressing three crises: whether or not the 'cancer' afflicting Christianity is terminal; the moral and vocational confusion in higher education (i.e. the collapse of moral and ethical discipline in the professions); and the too-easy assault on freedoms hard-won by the manipulation of men and women in the political arena. He postulated a sixteen-point 'grid' by asking the question, What then are some of the points ('stars') to look for in fashioning a 'grid' at this level? His list, in summary form, read as follows:

1. Is there a rise in the number of terrorist movements, inadequately resisted by those entrusted with the maintenance of order and public safety?
2. Is there a lack of leaders of high profile and high quality, to give confidence to the mature and serve as role models for the young?
3. Is a language of polarisation, extreme emotion and violence becoming acceptable in the public form?
4. Are people restless, anxious and insecure because of military defeat, economic loss, social insecurity, violence in the streets?
5. Is there a developing failure to distinguish between military and police actions in managing internal affairs?
6. Are branches of government usurping by misuse of power the constitutional prerogatives of other centres of power and responsibility, thereby jeopardising the checks and balances by which the executive, the legislative branch and the judiciary are restrained from the arrogance of power?
7. Are the offices of government responsible for the clandestine use of authority, sliding from civilian control and on the way to becoming loose cannons?
8. Is the power of government being misused to save not the general welfare but special interests (corporate, communal, religious, racial, sectional)?
9. Can government offices be relied upon to tell the truth?

10. Is there a lively network of free associations and civic forums at the local level in which public issues are openly and adequately debated?
11. Are there adequate and functioning lines of communication through which the discussions and conclusions of face-to-face local groups are channelled to the highest levels of such sub-political associations and made to impact upon the instruments of government?
12. Is the political forum free of religiously and ideologically exclusive language?
13. Is there an alienated youth generation, the product of shattered families and a moral collapse of society?
14. Are there private armies, attached to political parties or warlords, training an alienated youth to usurp the functions of the state?
15. Is there evidence of a collapse of professional ethics, with doctors, business executives, lawyers, theologians, journalists, and others serving extremist politics and/or movements disloyal to the general welfare?
16. Are there universities training only technically competent barbarians, or are they also educating patriotic citizens of disciplined ethics and commitment to the common good?

(Littell, 2003: 104–6)

For Littell, Germany's Nazi Party 'was a terrorist, potentially genocidal movement for years before it became an illegitimate regime with the power to commit genocide' (Littell, 2003: 106–8). Thus to answer any of these questions in the affirmative is to signal from the outset the potential for the rise of a terrorist movement or movements committed to potentially genocidal violence and moving in that direction.

From this baseline, Littell then posited a second grid of fifteen points, by which to further confirm the identity of such movements, and applied this knowledge to a practical preventative implementation of his ideas. The first of these was a list of 'What Is to Be Done Now':

1. Legislation is enacted banning the training of private individuals in the use of anti-personnel weapons.
2. Legislation is enacted forbidding the sale of weapons to private individuals, with the exception of registered sales of equipment to registered hunters and sports clubs.
3. All manufactured shells are required to include taggants [that is, chemical or physical markers added to materials to allow various forms of testing].
4. The recruitment and training of private armies is forbidden.

5. No uniformed public marches or demonstrations are permitted, except by units under police or military control.
6. 'Hate speech' and other expressions of the Language of Assault against targeted minorities are prosecuted as crimes.
7. Double penalties are enacted for 'ordinary' crimes (for example, bank robberies or counterfeiting) planned and committed by terrorist groups.

(Ibid.: 110)

The second of set of initiatives, building on this, was entitled 'New Legislation Needed':

1. A National Office of Defense against Terrorism shall be created with professional staff and adequate budget.
2. Procedures are developed for applying the Early Warning System to potentially genocidal ('terrorist') movements and banning them from public life.
3. Public demonstrations, recruitment activities and membership in a banned group are defined as crimes against the republic.
4. No newspapers, magazines, radio or television stations may be owned or controlled by a member of a banned group.
5. No business or non-profit organisation may be incorporated by an individual member or the banned group itself.
6. An individual convicted of membership in a banned association is found guilty of war against the USA and his [sic] civic liberties are cancelled.
7. A systematic and stringent set of sanctions against regimes promoting terrorism and supporting terrorist movements is adopted and declared.
8. Close cooperation with other legitimate governments in the suppression of terrorism is made a priority policy.

(Ibid.: 111)

Significantly, and unfortunately, neither Littell's analyses nor his system have been subject to intense analysis or conversation in any academic or governmental venue. Thus, his proposal remains on the table, though in the aftermath of the 9/11 tragedy in the United States the Department of Homeland Security was established with a cabinet-level position and a mandate to 'prevent terrorist attacks within the United States; reduce America's vulnerability to terrorism; and minimize the damage and recover from attacks that do occur'.

It was Franklin H. Littell's experience of Nazism close up, together with the aftermath of the Holocaust, coupled with his profound religiosity as a committed and believing Christian and his personal integrity and intellectual awareness as an academic, that undoubtedly formed his enduring steadfastness to finding ways in which the curse of Christian anti-Semitism could be brought to an end. That commitment was annexed to a further belief that the Christian churches had to face up to their moral and theological failings during the time of the Third Reich. Given this, his work, across a lifetime of committed effort, profoundly influenced not only the shape of Holocaust and Genocide Studies in the United States and internationally, but also inspired and affected a large range of Christian clergy and lay thinkers as well.

Littell's major writings

NOTE: Franklin H. Littell was the author of more than two dozen books, and over a thousand articles. A lengthy 'Bibliography of Franklin H. Littell' is to be found in Sharon Gutman Lightner and Marcia Sachs Littell (eds), *A Modern Prophet: Letters to Franklin H. Littell on His 80th Birthday June 20, 1997*, Merion (PA): Westfield Press International, 1998, 258–300.

(Ed. with Hubert G. Locke) *The German Church Struggle and the Holocaust*, Detroit: Wayne State University Press, 1974.

The Crucifixion of the Jews: The Failure of Christians to Understand the Jewish Experience, New York: Harper and Row, 1975.

'Fundamentals in Holocaust Studies', *Annals of the American Academy of Political and Social Science*, no. 450 (July 1980), 213–17.

'The Credibility Crisis of the Modern University', in Henry Friedlander and Sybil Milton (eds), *The Holocaust: Ideology, Bureaucracy, and Genocide*, Millwood (NY): Kraus International, 1980, 271–83.

(Ed.) *Hyping the Holocaust: Scholars Answer Goldhagen*, Merion Station (PA): Merion Westfield Press International, 1997.

'Priorities in Unfinished Business', in Harry James Cargas (ed.), *Holocaust Scholars Write to the Vatican*, Westport (CT): Greenwood Press, 1998, 57–65.

A Christian Response to the Holocaust: Selected Addresses and Papers (1952–2002), Merion (PA): Westfield Press International, 2003.

Reference

Jacobs, Steven Leonard, 'Franklin H. Littell and Israel W. Charny: Comparing/Contrasting Two Genocide Early Warning Systems', *Challenges: The Online Journal of the Zachor Society* (forthcoming, 2010).

MAHMOOD MAMDANI (b. 1947)

Mahmood Mamdani is the Herbert Lehman Professor of Government, and a member of the departments of Anthropology, Political Science and Middle East and Asian Languages and Cultures in the School of International and Public Affairs at Columbia University, New York. Born in Kampala, Uganda, in 1947, Mamdani is a third-generation East African of Indian origin. He was educated at the University of Pittsburgh, Tufts University (Massachusetts) and Harvard University.

After completion of his studies in the United States he returned to Uganda, but was forbidden to remain. As a Ugandan of Indian origin, he was a victim of dictator Idi Amin's expulsion order of 1972, in which the entire Indian population of Uganda had been given 90 days to leave the country. The exiled Mamdani lived as a refugee in Britain, but returned to Uganda after Amin's overthrow and joined Uganda's largest university, Makerere, in Kampala. He joined Columbia University in 1999, and in May 2008 he was named as one of the world's top 100 public intellectuals by the influential United States quarterly *Foreign Policy*.

Mamdani is recognised as a major voice on African affairs throughout the world, and for his views regarding Western colonialism. Where genocide is concerned, his main contribution rests on two important works: *When Victims Become Killers: Colonialism, Nativism, and Genocide in Rwanda* (2001) and *Saviors and Survivors: Darfur, Politics, and the War on Terror* (2009).

The first of these was written essentially in order to address the question of why it was that in 1994 Rwanda exploded in such a fireball of destruction, and how it came to be that so many in the Hutu population participated in the killing. Mamdani did not see the genocide as some sort of mysterious evil force unleashed as if by accident, but, rather, viewed the underlying factors of the genocide in terms of a reckoning with the tensions embedded in post-colonial Africa, according to which colonially inspired differences between so-called subject races came to the fore and spilled over as the ultimate expression of identity politics. Arguing its case strongly, the book sought to situate the Rwandan tragedy in its proper, post-colonial, context. Mamdani provided an intellectual history of the divisions between Hutus and Tutsis, and articulated a series of historical, geo-graphic, regional, theoretical, moral and political forces that prevailed even before the genocide seemed possible. Looking at the nature of political identities generated during German and Belgian colonial rule, he considered that the failures of the Rwandan Hutu nationalist revolution of 1959 transcended these identities, extending their reach to a regional demographic well beyond Rwanda itself. This way, Mamdani was able to develop further his critique of colonialism, showing how artificial and fragile many post-colonial national identities actually are – the legacy of Western priorities rather than African needs or preferences.

What made *When Victims Become Killers* such an important work was that it attempted to create a genuine understanding of the social dynamics that made the horror of 1994 possible. Mamdani's analysis of the differences between Hutu and Tutsi, as historically grounded and incessantly changing political identities, broadened previous understandings of citizenship and political identity in post-colonial Africa, and his analysis of Rwandan society was particularly acute. He held no less a view than that the Hutu killers saw themselves as victims who feared losing out in the struggle for power with the same Tutsis who had for so long ruled them in the past, supported by their European colonialist masters. It was this that made it possible for so many of the Hutus to turn on their neighbours; given this, the book posited a view that the Tutsis were really caught between a much deeper conflict between colonists and natives – with the Tutsis neither one nor the other, though representative of the former in the eyes of the latter.

The Hutus form a numerical majority in Africa's Great Lakes region, significantly larger than their neighbours the Tutsis. Before the genocide they numbered about 87 per cent of Rwanda's population. Traditionally, Hutu life was founded on a clan basis in which small kingdoms prevailed, but after the arrival of the Tutsis sometime in the fifteenth century a feudal system was established in which the Hutus were reduced to vassal status. Upon establishing hegemony over the other peoples of the region, the Tutsis built an order that placed them at the head of society as a wealth elite (based on cattle-raising), an aristocracy and, at the head of society, a king (*mwaami*). The fundamental division between Hutus and Tutsis was therefore based more on a form of class difference than on ethnicity, particularly as a great deal of intermarriage took place. While the relationship between the two peoples prior to the 1950s had been essentially one based on hierarchy and dominance, interactions were, for the most part, peaceful. Hutu dissatisfaction, where it existed, was expressed non-violently.

Under Belgian colonial rule, more overt divisions were introduced into Rwandan society. Identity cards bearing an individual's ethnic group and place of residence were introduced in 1933, and the cardholder could not relocate to another address without approval from the colonial authorities. After Rwanda's independence in 1961, the identity cards were retained as a means of positive discrimination in favour of the Hutu majority. This was a complete turnaround from the previous Belgian policy, which had been to elevate the Tutsi minority to positions of social, political and economic hegemony. With the ascent to power of the regime of Juvenal Habyarimana in 1973, Tutsis were segregated, persecuted and, on occasion, massacred on account of the group labelling impregnated on their identity cards.

It was measures such as these that Mamdani saw as being at the root of the genocide of 1994, and in this sense he could argue that the genocide was in fact a direct consequence of Belgian imperialism. The Belgians reconstructed Hutu and Tutsi identity, highlighting *racial* rather than *ethnic* (and even less, class) difference, and in so doing politicised those same identities. In developing his theory of this new 'identity politics', Mamdani posited the view that the genesis of Hutu–Tutsi violence could be traced back to the period of Belgian colonialism, in which the former were constructed as indigenous and the latter as alien. Much of the book in fact focused on the colonial era, as Mamdani sought to tell the story of a constructed race formation that started in the colonial period and continued through independent Rwanda.

Quite clearly, what Mamdani set out to do was to create an understanding of the political nature of the crimes of 1994, and locate them in their appropriate historical context. He showed successfully just how difficult it can be to explain genocide. Facile interpretations of 'Hutus following orders', or of population pressure on the land, or of some sort of mysterious genocidal malaise overtaking the population, cannot stand without taking into account the type of construct Mamdani offered in this work, and that this analysis came from a scholar of African background only served to underscore the importance of his perspective. The answers he posited were based on a rejection of Western imperialist-imposed models of democracy, which would simply restore the majority Hutus to power in the same manner as before. Instead, he sought the acceptance of both Hutus and Tutsis within a political, rather than a cultural or class, model. Here we see the theorist offering a radical and new direction for the reformation of political identity, with the ambition of preventing future catastrophes such as that of 1994.

In 2009 Mamdani published his second major contribution to genocide thought, *Saviors and Survivors*. (This was also his second offering on the nature of terrorism within the context of the post 9/11 War on Terror. He had earlier produced *Good Muslim, Bad Muslim: America, the Cold War, and the Roots of Terror* (2004), which had argued against the Western perception that 'bad' Muslims are all extremist Islamic fundamentalist terrorists hating freedom, while 'good' Muslims are modern, Western-oriented, secular and support US foreign policy – and that when 'terrorism' takes place it is as a response to foreign, usually Western, oppression.) Mamdani's views on Darfur were certainly expressed through his opposition to the Save Darfur Coalition in the USA.

The Save Darfur Coalition is a grouping of over 180 religious, political and human-rights bodies that seeks to achieve international intervention to stop the killing in Darfur. While sounding admirable in terms of its goals, some non-Western critics have labelled it a biased organisation that does not present an even-handed view of what is happening in the region. Others have been critical of the movement because the funds it raises do not go on to assist the Darfuris themselves, but are instead used for lobbying the United States government to intervene. Critics such as Mamdani look at this as a form of hidden imperialism, and of unconstitutional meddling in the internal affairs of a sovereign state. Instead, they argue, the con-flict in Darfur is essentially about land, power and the environment, with issues concerning race running far behind. *Saviors and Survivors* was a radical re-evaluation of the tragedy of Darfur that challenged the premises upon which liberal support for humanitarian intervention was (and is) based.

Mamdani traced the path to the current situation in the region through its historical and colonial roots, looking at the crisis in Darfur within the context of the broader history of Sudan's colonial and post-colonial experience. He examined the history of Sudan and the origins of the current conflict back to the tenth century CE, and through this was able to demonstrate how the divide between Arab and non-Arab ethnic groups is political rather than racial in nature. Proceeding from this, he examined more contemporary events, where drought and desertification have led to conflict over land among local tribes, rebellion and, attempting to address this, involvement from the forces of the state. Mamdani explored a number of factors contributing to the early twenty-first century's worst man-made disaster. He showed that the conflict in Darfur began as a civil war between nomadic and peasant tribes over fertile land, triggered by the drought; how British colonial officials had earlier artificially tribalised Darfur, dividing its population into 'native' and 'settler' tribes and creating reservations for the former at the expense of the latter – and in this sense, created antagonisms where none had previously existed; and how the civil war intensified in the 1990s when the Sudanese government tried unsuccessfully to address the problem by creating homelands for tribes which at that stage did not have any land of their own. His argument continued with the assertion that political parties opposed to the central government in Khartoum then intervened in Darfur, such that by 2003 two rebel movements had been created, leading to a brutal insurgency and a terrible, government-directed counter-insurgency.

By far the most contentious part of the book related to Mamdani's argument that the word genocide is an inappropriate description for what has been happening in Darfur. Examining the world's response, he maintained that old assumptions, from earlier eras, have influenced current geopolitical viewpoints. Put simply, Western declarations of 'genocide' in Darfur have been made prematurely, almost as if to make up for having waited too long to react to the genocide in Rwanda. Moreover, while acknowledging the scale of the violence being committed in the region, Mamdani contended that Darfur is not a site of genocide but rather a site where the *language* of genocide has been used for political purposes by the West in order to further demonise the Arabs as perpetrators of murderous violence, within the context of the global War on Terror. Calling for military intervention under the guise of 'humanitarian intervention' was thus another form of colonialism – in which organisations such as the Save Darfur Coalition were simultaneously complicit and, for those carried along by the hype, duped by a much more insidious neo-colonialist lobby.

Overall, Mamdani's position was that the situation in Darfur should be viewed from within the paradigm of the West's historic colonial encounter with Africa, and not from within a model that automatically sees all African conflicts as genocidal and therefore seemingly beyond help – and requiring, as a result, renewed Western intervention. He did not consider the situation in Darfur as a case of genocide requiring foreign military intervention, and made a case that the conflict is a political problem, with a historical basis, requiring a political solution. This solution, furthermore, should be African in origin – not dictated by the UN or great external powers acting unilaterally, but instead by the African Union. The most urgent need, in Mamdani's view, is not to punish those responsible for the mass killings of 2003–4 (and beyond) through indictments at the International Criminal Court. It is, rather, to arrive at a political solution that will reform the land system in Darfur and political power in Sudan.

Mahmood Mamdani is a passionate advocate of African affairs, and an important alternative voice on the question of genocide in Africa. Fervently opposed to colonialism in all its forms, he sees humanitarianism as a variety of neo-imperialism in much the same manner as he views allegations of genocide as a Western rush to judgement, based on ulterior motives. His core interest has always been rooted in colonial and post-colonial Africa, with a fundamental concern for the colonially crafted identities – often created quite artificially – prevalent throughout the continent. It is this concern with the definition of citizenship in the post-independence period that has led to many misunderstandings in the past (in this he would find agreement from another genocide scholar to have addressed the issue, **Leo Kuper**), misunderstandings that have generated communal violence, rebellions, civil wars and international conflicts. From here it can be but a short step to genocide, a state of affairs Mamdani contends could be avoided if Africa is left to its own devices without the continued foreign intervention that has proven so destructive as a result of the past two centuries of exploitation.

Mamdani's major writings

From Citizen to Refugee: Uganda Asians come to Britain, London: Francis Pinter, 1973.

Imperialism and Fascism in Uganda, Trenton (NJ): Africa World Press, 1983.

Citizen and Subject: Contemporary Africa and the Legacy of Late Colonialism, Princeton (NJ): Princeton University Press, 1996.

When Victims Become Killers: Colonialism, Nativism, and Genocide in Rwanda, Princeton (NJ): Princeton University Press, 2001.

Good Muslim, Bad Muslim: America, the Cold War, and the Roots of Terror, New York: Pantheon/Random House, 2004.

'The Politics of Naming: Genocide, Civil War, Insurgency', *London Review of Books*, 29, 5, 8 March 2007.

Saviors and Survivors: Darfur, Politics, and the War on Terror, New York: Pantheon, 2009.

'The Genocide Myth', *Guernica: A Magazine of Art and Politics*, 9 May 2009, at http://www.guernica.com/spotlight/1031/the_genocide_myth.

ERIC MARKUSEN (1946–2007)

Eric Markusen was a Senior Researcher in the Department of Holocaust and Genocide Studies at the Danish Institute for International Studies, Copenhagen and Professor of Sociology and Social Work at Southwest Minnesota State University, Marshall, Minnesota. Born in Detroit in 1946, he was interested in the study of Sociology from an early age, and undertook graduate study at the University of Washington and the University of Minnesota. Throughout his career he combined his professional areas of Sociology and social work. For most of his teaching life he was based at Southwest Minnesota State, until in 2001 he went on extended leave in order to take up a position as Research Director at the Danish Centre for Holocaust and Genocide Studies, Copenhagen. From 2002 until his death in 2007 he served in his role at the Danish Institute for International Studies.

After a long period studying issues relating to the threat of nuclear war, Markusen turned his attention to Genocide Studies in the 1980s. Inspired by the work of his colleagues and mentors **Robert Jay Lifton** and Robert Fulton, he began analysing the twin notions of a 'genocidal mentality' and the relationship between modern war and genocide. Ultimately, these would lead him in a wholly new direction, and to a number of pathbreaking publications. Indeed, it was in 1981, while studying nuclear weapons issues at Princeton University's Center for Energy and Environmental Studies, that Markusen first met **Lifton**, and worked with him as he undertook research for his own book *The Nazi Doctors* (Lifton, 1986). The relationship between the two would prove to be a lasting and productive one, as Markusen and **Lifton** would later collaborate in co-authoring *The Genocidal Mentality: Nazi Holocaust and Nuclear Threat* (1990).

This was a study of the thinking that impels military planners to make an allowance for the deaths of vast numbers of people when strategies of nuclear confrontation are being formulated – what the authors referred to as 'nuclear omnicide'. Markusen and **Lifton** examined the role played by the Nazi Holocaust in shaping modern-day consciousness of the nuclear threat. A key argument they put forward was that the human sense of right and wrong has been dulled as a result of the Holocaust, so that events involving mass death and destruction are no longer met with a sense of horror or indignation. They also posited that those most likely to bring about such death and destruction – military and bureaucratic elites, politicians and highly educated technical experts – have been offered a precedent by the Nazi experience, which exonerates them from any sense of personal responsibility for the damage they cause. This is, they argued, 'the genocidal mentality'.

They defined such a mentality as 'the willingness, under certain conditions, to take steps that could kill hundreds of millions of people' (Lifton and Markusen, 1990: 37). It has, they wrote, become 'both an everyday matter and part of the various structures of society', and they looked at the moral question of how far men and women in the modern state should, or can, obey orders – including those which might result in the death of millions. Where Markusen had already signalled his interest in mass death as generated by the threat of nuclear war – in an earlier edited volume, *Nuclear Weapons and the Threat of Nuclear War* (1986) – he now articulated his thinking about mass death in a much more sustained manner. Finding a way to stop genocide was henceforth to be his primary scholarly pursuit.

In attempting to understand genocide, Markusen realised that he would need to travel to places that were the sites of the events he was studying, and his research between the mid-1980s and his death in early 2007 took him around the world on a multitude of trips. His preference was to undertake field research wherever possible, as a result of which he visited the scene of innumerable atrocities. He was renowned for his willingness to go into risky situations to get evidence, and his quest to understand the genocidal mentality took him to death camps, former Soviet satellites, the killing fields of Cambodia, bombed villages of Croatia and Bosnia, the border of Ethiopia/Eritrea, and Darfur. He also sought to speak with those directly affected by the atrocities he was studying, whether as victims or helpers. As a speaker and teacher, he was equally busy, trying to fathom how perpetrators and their accomplices could act as they did; he also sought to learn why governments were willing – often eagerly – to engage in the mass killing of innocent people.

Beginning in February 1994, Markusen began to undertake field research on genocide in the former Yugoslavia. What followed were more than two dozen visits to the region, including Sarajevo, Belgrade, Zagreb, Mostar, Kosovo, Vukovar and Dubrovnik. During the Bosnian War he visited Pale, the capital of the Bosnian Serbs – where he interviewed close aides to Radovan Karadzic – and the besieged city of Sarajevo, which he accessed through the tunnel that had been cut under Sarajevo airport and was the city's only lifeline during the war. From 1995 onwards, he began to consult with the Office of the Prosecutor at the International Criminal Tribunal for the Former Yugoslavia, making dozens of visits to The Hague to discuss his research and participate in dialogue on the nature of genocide. The level of his knowledge about genocide, and the authority he brought to the subject, was honoured not only in this way, but also through his being engaged as a consultant to the Swedish Prime Minister's Office, to the Legal Advisor to the President of Eritrea, to the National University of Rwanda, to the Institute for Research on Crimes against Humanity and International Law at Sarajevo University, and to the Home Office of the United Kingdom.

Direct experience of war gave Markusen reason to think that perhaps the very destructiveness to be found therein was itself genocidal. In this, his thoughts were at the cutting edge of where some others had been heading at the same time. Towards the end of the twentieth century – the most destructive in history – genocide was most frequently seen as having something to do with brutal death, massive of type and uncompromising in its choice of victim; more often than not, armies in war were seen as the major vehicles · through which this killing was to take place. In *The Holocaust and Strategic Bombing* (1995), an important study regarding the relationship between genocide, war and strategic bombing during the Second World War, Markusen and a colleague from the University of Minnesota, David Kopf, concluded that war can create a variety of dispositions leading to genocide, whereby massive human destruction is facilitated through such features as depersonalisation, social violence, extensions of government power, and alienation of victim groups. They argued that 'war in general, and total war in particular, create psychological, social, and political conditions conducive to genocidal killing'. While under many conditions this should be taken as a given, Markusen and Kopf used this basic truth in order to develop a broader position on the relationship:

> [These conditions] do so in a number of ways: by exacerbating fears and anxieties that can be directed against a scapegoat group either within the society or in an enemy society; by reducing democratic checks and balances or reinforcing totalitarian tendencies; by utilizing trained and often brutal professional killers in the military to hunt down and slaughter internal and external enemies; by increasing the vulnerability of the victims in a variety of ways; and by creating a climate of psychological numbing and desensitization among members of the society that is engaged in the genocidal killing.
>
> (Markusen and Kopf, 1995: 243)

In the case of massive strategic bombing during the Second World War, they asked, what was the goal which underlay the killing? They concluded that it was in effect a means to an end, 'that is, surrender, rather than an end in itself' (Markusen and Kopf, 1995: 246). On the other hand, they disagreed strongly with those who would otherwise regard war and genocide as separate phenomena. Returning to the conditions conducive to creating a genocidal mentality, they identified noticeable parallels in the factors necessary both to wage war and commit genocidal killing. Further, they found that the majority of those engaging in the two activities could not only be described as emotionally 'normal' and stable, but also as good citizens undertaking justifiable duties for the good of their country or society. Put simply, in *The Holocaust and Strategic Bombing* Markusen and Kopf sought to draw their readers' attention to the need to be aware of just how disposed modern-day governments are to the planning, preparation and annihilation of vast numbers of non-combatants (see also Bartrop, 2002).

In 2001, Markusen was appointed as Research Director for the newly formed Danish Centre for Holocaust and Genocide Studies in Copenhagen. The objective of this body was to introduce the field of Genocide Studies to Denmark, and Markusen embraced his role enthusiastically. He travelled throughout Europe giving lectures about genocide, helping to organise conferences, and meeting with other researchers and students interested in genocide. His intention was to build a Genocide Studies network, and as part of this initiative he co-founded the Nordic Network of Genocide Scholars, comprising researchers from Norway, Sweden, Denmark and Holland.

Then, in 2004, he was appointed a member of the Atrocities Documentation Team (ADT) organised by the Coalition for International Justice and the American Bar Association, to interview refugees from Darfur who had fled to Chad. This mission comprised twenty-four investigators, and was established to enable the US State Department to determine whether or not genocide was occurring (or had occurred) in Darfur. For Markusen, the mission inspired hope that genocide scholarship could perhaps make a difference to the overall situation, and the work of the ADT was used by the US State Department. In September 2004 US Secretary of State Colin Powell, proceeding from the ADT study, addressed the United Nations and concluded that 'genocide has been committed in Darfur and that the government of Sudan and the *Janjaweed* bear responsibility – and genocide may still be occurring' (*Washington Post*, 10 September 2004: A01). It was the first time that any government had officially and publicly accused another government of genocide. Markusen's disillusionment over the subsequent failure of the United States to follow up this announcement with concrete action led him to focus his energy even more on stopping the genocide. He taught university courses covering Darfur, wrote articles, spoke at rallies, engaged with the media, co-edited a special issue of *Genocide Studies and Prevention* and, with another genocide scholar (and fellow-member of the ADT), Samuel Totten, co-edited a book about the US Government's investigation and confirmation of allegations of genocide in Darfur.

Entitled *Genocide in Darfur: Investigating the Atrocities in the Sudan* (2006), this book brought together essays from contributors who were involved in the ADT, as well as genocide scholars, international lawyers, and officials from the US government and non-governmental organisations. In line with Markusen's approach over many years, the book put forth a view dear to the hearts of many scholars working in the field of Genocide Studies:

> *What can be done to halt the killing, raping, and dying? The simple but profound answer is to apply much more pressure, pressure that is systematic, ongoing, and relentless, all aimed at prodding the United Nations, regional organizations, and individual nations to act and to act now.* Quite frankly, it is not enough to simply sign a petition, write a single letter, give some money, wear a wristband, or write a single article. Each and every individual who detests the thought of genocide must attempt to keep pressure on the powers that be, and that means not being satisfied or complacent by carrying out a single action or two.
>
> (Markusen and Totten, 2006: 236, emphasis in original)

Here we see Markusen and Totten desperately keen to assist the people of Darfur and stop the killing, but immensely frustrated at being unable to do so. It might be said that the language employed is an elegy for Markusen himself; the book was released shortly before his death, at a time when he was already planning to return to Chad in order to meet more Darfuris and obtain further documentation about their situation. Indeed, Markusen travelled to Addis Ababa a little over a month before he died, to meet with European Union and African Union officials working to solve the Darfur crisis.

Eric Markusen held that the danger of victimisation was ongoing, that modern warfare was itself genocidal, and that it created the necessary social and psychological conditions that permitted genocide to occur. He abhorred the state of affairs that could lead to vast numbers of innocent people being deliberately targeted for destruction simply because of their membership in a group deemed unacceptable by members of another group. As he saw it, both the idea of mass killing and its scale represented the defining moral issue of our time, and his commitment to education, research, networking and activism led him to the only conclusion possible: that new generations of students and citizens must be encouraged to appreciate just how serious the epidemic of genocidal destruction had become. When he died he was at the peak of his energy and influence as a thinker and educator about genocide, and in his honour the 2007 conference of the International Association of Genocide Scholars, held in Sarajevo, was dedicated to his memory.

Markusen's major writings

(with Robert Jay Lifton and Dorothy Austin) 'The Second Death: Psychological Survival after Nuclear War', in Jennifer Leaning and Langley Keyes (eds), *The Counterfeit Ark: Crisis Relocation For Nuclear War*, Pensacola (FL): Ballinger, 1984, 285–300.

(Ed. with John Harris) *Nuclear Weapons and the Threat of Nuclear War*, San Diego: Harcourt Brace Jovanovich, 1986.

'Genocide and Total War: A Preliminary Comparison', in Isidor Wallimann and Michael Dobkowski (eds), *Genocide and the Modern Age: Etiology and Case Studies Of Mass Death*, Westport (CT): Greenwood Press, 1987, 97–123.

(with Robert Jay Lifton) *The Genocidal Mentality: Nazi Holocaust and Nuclear Threat*, New York: Basic Books, 1990.

'Comprehending the Cambodian Genocide: An Application of Robert Jay Lifton's Model of Genocidal Killing', *The Psychohistory Review*, 20, 2 (1992), 145–70.

'Genocide and Modern War', in Michael Dobkowski and Isidor Wallimann (eds), Genocide *in Our Time*, Ypsilanti (MI): Pierian Press, 1992, 117–48.

(with David Kopf) *The Holocaust And Strategic Bombing: Genocide and Total War in the Twentieth Century*, Boulder (CO): Westview Press, 1995.

(with Roger Smith and Robert Jay Lifton) 'Professional Ethics and the Denial of the Armenian Genocide', *Holocaust and Genocide Studies*, 9, 1 (1995), 1–22.

'Genocidal Dimensions of the Atomic Bombs?', in Henry Knight and Marcia Littell (eds), *Uses and Abuses of Knowledge*, Lanham (MD): University Press of America, 1997, 189–206.

'Reflections on the Holocaust and Hiroshima', *Bridges: An Interdisciplinary Journal of Theology, Philosophy, History, and Science*, 5, 1–2 (1998), 47–64.

'My Path to Genocide Studies', in Samuel Totten and Steven Leonard Jacobs (eds), *Pioneers of Genocide Studies*, New Brunswick (NJ): Transaction Publishers, 2002, 295–311.

(with Martin Mennecke) 'The International Criminal Tribunal for the Former Yugoslavia and the Crime of Genocide', in Steven L. B. Jensen (ed.), *Genocide: Cases, Comparisons and Contemporary Debates*, Copenhagen: Danish Center for Holocaust and Genocide Studies, 2003, 293–359.

(with Martin Mennecke) 'Genocide in Bosnia and Herzegovina', in Samuel Totten, William S. Parsons and Israel W. Charny (eds), *Century of Genocide: Critical Essays and Eyewitness Accounts*, second edition, New York: Routledge, 2004, 415–47.

(Ed. with Samuel Totten), *Genocide in Darfur: Investigating the Atrocities in the Sudan*, New York: Routledge, 2006.

References

Bartrop, Paul R., 'The Relationship between War and Genocide in the Twentieth Century: A Consideration', *Journal of Genocide Research*, 4, 4 (December 2002), 519–32.

Lifton, Robert Jay Lifton, *The Nazi Doctors: Medical Killing and the Psychology of Genocide*, New York: Basic Books, 1986.

ROBERT MELSON (b. 1937)

Robert Melson is an American political scientist who has written extensively about how revolution and war have served, in various situations, as key factors in creating contexts that lend themselves to the creation of genocidal policies whose aims are to transform societies. Born in 1937 in Warsaw, Poland, he and his parents survived the Holocaust by camouflaging their Jewish identity and successfully overlaying it with a Christian one. And not just any Christian identity; the Mendelsohn family, as they were, assumed a fictitious role as the family Zamojski, a branch of an aristocratic Polish family with a highly respected position as leaders in society and a pedigree stretching back for generations. Along the way, 'Count' and 'Countess' Zamojski (Melson's parents, Willy and Nina), and their son 'Count Bobi' (Melson himself), were able to save additional members of the family and other Jews who were also caught up in their masquerade.

Later in life, Melson interviewed his parents, using the oral recording techniques of a historian. This cannot have been an easy task, as all manner of personal baggage intruded into his interviews: the parent–child relationship, the passage of time, and the fact that the interviewer was himself an actor in the drama. Nonetheless, he managed to combine his roles as researcher and participant-observer by trying to remain as true to his parents' responses as possible, by 'neither denying nor embellishing my parents' exploits nor suppressing incriminating or embarrassing moments' (Melson, 2000: 6).

Throughout the period of Nazi rule, Melson's parents kept up their charade as Polish aristocrats, entertaining Nazi officers in their home, establishing business enterprises trading with the Reich, celebrating Christian festivals, and enjoying a well-to-do 'Aryan' existence. Whenever any indiscretion had even the tiniest potential to give away their identity, the family would go into a frenzy of worry and apprehension, fearful of deliberate denunciation by those who knew them, or of accidental exposure stemming from their own legitimate anxieties. Ultimately, the deception worked. Melson and his parents survived the war, though most of their wider family perished at the hands of the Nazis.

In 1947, the family moved to the United States. Melson attended Massachusetts Institute of Technology for his undergraduate degree before moving to graduate study at Yale University and then back to MIT to complete a PhD in Political Science. In the spring of 1964 Melson undertook field research which formed an important part of his doctoral work in Nigeria as a Foreign Area Fellow of the Ford Foundation. The 15 months he spent there gave him first-hand experience of the circumstances leading to the breakdown of the state, and he witnessed the preconditions to what has been called – questionably, for some – genocide.

During his research, Melson observed how thousands of Igbo people – those who made up the majority of Nigeria's breakaway state of Biafra – had migrated to the Muslim-dominated north of the country in search of work. Here, they lived in communities that were strictly segregated from the Muslim majority. Later, in early 1966, the Igbo were collectively held responsible by the Nigerian government for the murder of several military officials, resulting in a series of murderous riots. Violence escalated throughout the year and the deaths rose from hundreds to thousands, provoking a wholesale flight of Igbo back to their traditional home in the southeast. Because the central government seemed unable to curb anti-Igbo violence, in May 1967 the Eastern State seceded, and created an Igbo majority state called Biafra. War rapidly escalated from the summer of 1967 onwards. One weapon employed by the Government of Nigeria – and acknowledged openly by ministers and military figures alike – was to cut off food supplies to the civilian population of Biafra. Igbo leaders, both in Biafra and abroad, labelled the deaths as genocide, and unheeded appeals were made to the UN to recognise Biafra and to intervene in order to save the population. It was the first time the charge of genocide had been made in the international environment since the term entered international law in 1948. The Biafran War lasted from June 1967 until the sudden collapse of Biafran resistance in January 1970, and took a terrible toll on the Igbo people, with the deaths of up to a million people, including vast numbers of children.

Melson's experiences in pre–civil war Nigeria led not only to his dissertation, but also to his first book, *Nigeria: Modernization and the Politics of Communalism*. As a survivor of the Holocaust, Melson could not help but make the connections between his own experience and those of the Igbo of Biafra, as he later wrote: 'The Biafran war taught me that the slaughter of innocent people based on their identity was not limited to the Holocaust, and it prompted me to use my scholarly training for the purpose of understanding ethnic conflict and genocide' (Melson, 2002: 142). From this start, Melson's major areas of teaching and research have remained focused on the nature of ethnic conflict and genocide.

His most important work relating to the study of genocide is *Revolution and Genocide: On the Origins of the Armenian Genocide and the Holocaust*, which in 1993 won the highly prestigious PIOOM Award in Human Rights from Amnesty International in the Netherlands. In this work, Melson highlighted a number of ways in which revolutionary situations have led to international or civil conflict, leading further towards persecution then genocide. He argued that by redefining what the political community will be in the post-revolutionary environment, revolutionaries can cast certain groups (ethnic, occupational, sexual-preference) or classes (feudal, middle, working) in the role of enemies of the new society. When such negatively categorised groups are then linked to real or potential foreign enemies, the prospect of those maligned groups becoming targeted for repression – or even genocide – is heightened. For Melson, several infamous cases from history showed that, in a revolutionary situation, war or internal conflict proved decisive for enabling ideological motivations to be translated into policies of genocide. Melson focused on the Armenian Genocide and the Holocaust, but by extension he was also able to include other cases such as the Soviet man-made terror-famine in Ukraine (1932–33) and the Cambodian Genocide (1975–79). Quite simply, as he saw it, 'By redefining the political community, revolutions cast certain classes and communal groups into the role of the enemies of society and the revolutionary state'; when these groups are then somehow linked to foreign enemies in wartime, 'the chances of their becoming targets of repression and even genocide are considerably increased'. He identified three reasons for this:

1. Wartime aggravates feelings of vulnerability and/or intensifies feelings of invincibility. In both cases it contributes an essential psychological element to the radical phases of revolutions that turn genocidal.
2. Wartime permits states to become more autonomous and independent of domestic and foreign public opinion, thereby encouraging radical solutions to social and political 'problems.'
3. Wartime conditions may close off other policy options, leaving genocide as a strong choice for an already radicalized regime.

(Melson, 1992: 273)

Thus, where the Armenian Genocide and the Holocaust are concerned, certain commonalities can be detected that help to answer the essential question of Melson's work: 'Why did genocide happen in these two instances, and why does it happen at all?' (Melson, 1992: xv)

By examining the Committee of Union and Progress in Turkey and the National Socialist Party in Germany, Melson carefully evaluated the revolutionary nature of the two regimes as the major motif underlying their transformation into governments capable of committing genocide. Here, his work identified four main points characterising the two regimes:

1. Both the Committee of Union and Progress and the Nazis were revolutionary vanguards that were motivated by ideologies of revolutionary transformation.
2. Both movements came to power during a revolutionary inter-regnum after the fall of an old regime.
3. Both Armenians and Jews were ethnoreligious communities that had occupied a low or pariah status in traditional society, and both had experienced rapid progress and social mobilization in the modern world.
4. Both genocides followed revolutions and wars.

(Melson, 1992: 17)

And, he might have added, both genocides also took place during a war, after a period in which the societies in which they occurred had been prepared for genocide by a lengthy period of conditioning by the respective perpetrator regimes.

Melson's argument concerning the relationship between revolution and genocide was unprecedented, and, while filling an important gap in the literature, nonetheless led to additional questions. As he pointed out, not all revolutions lead to genocide, the American Revolution of 1776 and the English Revolution of 1688 being important illustrations of this. He contended that the character of revolutionary ideology plays a crucial role in determining the direction a revolution will take; and that this, of course, plays an immense role when it comes to the question of genocidal violence either during or after the revolutionary changes have taken place. Put succinctly, Melson stated that 'it was ideology in the context of revolution and war that had produced genocide' in the case of Armenia and the Holocaust (Melson, 2002: 144).

A later argument, again from a comparative dimension, and once more employing the examples of Armenia and the Holocaust, was equally forceful in its conclusion. In an article published in 1996, he considered the paradigmatic nature of the two cases relative to Genocide Theory. His contention was a strong one:

> The Armenian Genocide, rather than the Holocaust, may serve as a closer prototype for current mass murders in the postcolonial Third World and in the contemporary post-Communist world. In Nigeria and Yugoslavia, for example, as in the Armenian case and unlike the Holocaust, minorities were territorial ethnic groups, aiming at some form of autonomy or self-determination while the perpetrators were driven by a variant of nationalism, and the methods of destruction involved massacre and starvation. In the Holocaust, the victims were not a territorial group; the ideology was a variant of a global racism and antisemitism, not nationalism; and the characteristic method of destruction was the death camp. Indeed, in the contemporary world, only the Cambodian genocide perpetrated by the Khmer Rouge bears a closer resemblance to the Holocaust than to the Armenian Genocide.
>
> (Melson, 1996b: 167)

The argument that the Armenian Genocide bears a greater similarity to modern genocides than the Holocaust performed two tasks: first, it reinforced the often-stated notion of Holocaust uniqueness by demonstrating its incomparability with other experiences, while at the same time stressing its ideological and global nature; and second, it broke new ground conceptually by identifying in the Armenian case a new paradigm for understanding contemporary genocides. While the second point has yet to be taken up by other scholars, the first tapped into a pre-existing discourse that has not yet been exhausted.

Given the originality of his contributions, Robert Melson's influence has served to stimulate discussion and debate within the fields of both Holocaust Studies and Genocide Studies over a lengthy period. In September 2000, in recognition of his authority in the areas of comparative genocide and the Armenian Genocide, he testified before the United States House of Representatives Subcommittee on International Operations and Human Rights – just at the time he was beginning to turn his thoughts to another case of genocide thus far untouched in his scholarly considerations, Rwanda. Once more, he set his reflections against a backdrop of genocide relative to revolution, and drew the conclusion that 'the Rwandan genocide was a product both of the revolution of 1959 and the war against the RPF

[Rwandan Patriotic Front] that the revolution spawned' (Melson, 2003: 336). His academic treatment of the issue strengthened his earlier positions regarding revolution and genocide, and extended the discussion further. In the early part of the twenty-first century his thinking began to move in the direction of genocide prevention, and to question why it is that humanity has seemingly not learned from the experiences of the past. With this we see an underscoring of both the intellectual energy and the creativity of this important scholar of Holocaust and Genocide Studies.

Melson's major writings

(Ed. with Howard Wolpe) *Nigeria: Modernization and the Politics of Communalism*, East Lansing (MI): Michigan State University Press, 1971.
'On the Dictinctiveness of the Armenian Genocide and the Holocaust', in Alan Berger (ed.), *Bearing Witness: 1939–1989*, Lewiston (NY): Edwin Mellen Press, 1991, 55–69.
Revolution and Genocide: On the Origins of the Armenian Genocide and the Holocaust, Chicago: University of Chicago Press, 1992.
On the Uniqueness and Comparability of the Holocaust: A Comparison with the Armenian Genocide, Sydney: Centre for Comparative Genocide Studies, Macquarie University, 1995.
'The Armenian Genocide as Precursor and Prototype of Twentieth Century Genocide', in Alan S. Rosenbaum (ed.), *Is the Holocaust Unique?*, Boulder (CO): Westview Press, 1996a, 87–100.
'Paradigms of Genocide: The Holocaust, the Armenian Genocide, and Contemporary Mass Destructions', *Annals of the American Academy of Political and Social Science*, no. 548 (November 1996b), 156–68.
False Papers: Deception and Survival in the Holocaust, Urbana (IL): University of Illinois Press, 2000.
'My Journey in the Study of Genocide', in Samuel Totten and Steven Leonard Jacobs (eds.), *Pioneers of Genocide Studies*, New Brunswick (NJ): Transaction Publishers, 2002, 139–51.
'Modern Genocide in Rwanda: Ideology, Revolution, War, and Mass Murder in an African State', in Robert Gellately and Ben Kiernan (eds), *The Specter of Genocide: Mass Murder in Historical Perspective*, Cambridge: Cambridge University Press, 2003, 325–38.

HANS MOMMSEN (b. 1930)

Hans Mommsen is an Emeritus Professor of Modern History at the Ruhr University, Bochum, Germany. A leading expert on Nazi Germany and the Holocaust, he is one of Germany's pre-eminent historians. He was born into an academic family in Marburg in 1930.

His twin brother, the late Wolfgang Mommsen, was a leading historian of late-nineteenth-century German foreign policy; his father, Wilhelm Mommsen, was a historian of nineteenth-century Germany; and his great-grandfather, Theodor Mommsen, was a Nobel Prize–winning historian of ancient Rome. Hans studied at the Universities of Heidelberg, Tübingen and Marburg, arriving at Bochum in 1968.

A social democrat by conviction, Mommsen's political leaning was a contributing factor to how he shaped his historical perspectives. A member of the German Social Democratic Party since 1960, his writing shows him as one who is resolutely anti-Nazi and committed to democratic ideals. Most of Mommsen's writing has looked at the Weimar and Nazi periods in German history. His books in English focus particularly on the transition between Weimar democracy and the onset of Nazism, as well as on the Nazi period itself. Three of these, in particular, can be discussed here.

First, *From Weimar to Auschwitz: Essays in German History* (1991), took a broad view of the crisis of the Weimar Republic and the rise of Nazism, tracing the role of the bourgeoisie in late-nineteenth-century Germany and building a perspective on how it was that the expectations of victory during the First World War, having been dashed through Germany's defeat and descent into revolution, led to resentment and disillusionment with the Weimar Republic. The book considered why middle-class disenchantment with the imperial regime led to the November 1918 revolution, and then, when the republic was established, it was again the middle class that sought its destruction. Mommsen was thereby also forced to deal with more open-ended questions relating to the nature of democracy and totalitarianism (and, in particular, Nazi totalitarianism).

In *The Rise and Fall of Weimar Democracy* (1998), Mommsen again examined the Weimar period in Germany between 1919 and 1933. Considering the period from a political and economic perspective, he explored the complexities of the time but resisted the temptation to project what this would mean for the future; in other words, he looked at the period in its own terms, rather than forecasting the 'inevitable' onset of Nazism that lay within that history. As a result, he was able to trace Germany's path through the aftermath of revolution, through parliamentary democracy and its attendant political and economic crises, and show how its internal structural weaknesses were no match for the two parties (communism and Nazism) that were dedicated to its destruction.

Finally, in *Alternatives to Hitler: German Resistance under the Third Reich* (2003), Mommsen traced the complex history of German resistance to Hitler and the Nazis, from their ascent to power in January 1933 through to the attempted assassination of Hitler and the aborted assumption of power by a clique of army officers – 'Operation Valkyrie' – in July 1944. Mommsen considered the full range of opposition, from small acts of political disobedience and statements of resentment or antipathy, to wholesale attempts to overthrow the government. For some this was a controversial book, as Mommsen did not hold back from passing what he saw to be appropriate judgements; thus, in examining the resisters' motives, he found that not all were inspired by the highest humanitarian impulses. While there were certainly those who operated out of a sense of principled commitment, some were not convinced that democracy should follow Hitler, and were interested only in exchanging the Nazi form of the totalitarian state for another version; others operated from pragmatic self-interest, while yet others were thoroughly indifferent or ambivalent towards the Nazi 'Final Solution to the Jewish Question' (*Endlösung der Judenfrage*). Recognising that resistance to Nazism was itself commendable and virtuous, Mommsen's considera- tion of the varied motives of those opposed to Nazism showed that there was little to be achieved in painting a purely black-and-white picture of such behaviour.

Mommsen is perhaps best known, overall, for his position in the debate over the Holocaust which occurred during the 1980s, and which was known in Germany as the *Historikerstreit* ('historians' quarrel'). As a historiographical debate about the origins of the Holocaust, the main issues revolved around two fundamental questions: first, did Hitler possess a master plan for the annihilation of the Jews that could be traced to an earlier time? And second, was the Final Solution ordered directly by Hitler, or did the decision 'evolve' over time through the actions of the German bureaucracy and military? A number of historians on both sides participated in the debate, with prominent Functionalists including Mommsen himself, his brother Wolfgang, **Raul Hilberg**, **Christopher Browning**, Götz Aly, Karl Schleunes, Martin Broszat and **Zygmunt Bauman**. Among the leading Intentionalists were Andreas Hillgruber, Karl Dietrich Bracher, Daniel Jonah Goldhagen, Klaus Hildebrand, Eberhard Jäckel, Richard Breitman and **Lucy S. Dawidowicz**. Moreover, not all Functionalists or Intentionalists advocated their points equally; there were moderates and radicals on both sides.

Mommsen was a classic Functionalist who viewed the onset of the Final Solution as part of a process of increasing escalation within a bureaucracy beset with internal rivalries. These rivalries saw various government departments competing with one another in escalating rounds of mounting anti-Semitic regulations between 1933 and 1941, culminating in the latter year. Hitler himself, in all this, played a relatively minor role, notwithstanding that he was an extreme anti-Semite who wanted to do *something* (though he was unclear as to what that might be) with the Jews. It was essentially the political conditions Hitler had created that led to the destruction of a normal orderly governmental process, and prevented the political system from re-establishing some internal balance in the aftermath of the chaotic later Weimar years. Instead, what Mommsen described as a 'cumulative radicalisation process' formed (Interview, Shoah Resource Center, 1997). This made itself felt primarily in the field of racial (that is, anti-Semitic) politics. As Mommsen outlined it, 'Hitler, by destroying the inherited governmental structure and replacing it by the socio-darwinist struggle between competing institutions and satraps, created the preconditions for the acceleration of violence and inhumanity.' He did not, however, act by himself: 'The driving force were people like Himmler, Heydrich, Globocnik, and Eichmann, as well as the leading generals and diplomats, who pressed for the implementation of what hitherto had been predominantly a propagandistic target' (Interview, Shoah Resource Center, 1997).

Interviewed in 1997, Mommsen stated that the years following the *Historikerstreit* had seen something of a convergence between the two positions, though there seemed to have emerged 'a divergence between the younger generation and the generation to which I belong, which makes itself felt in the realm of Holocaust research, while the conflict between the functionalists and the intentionalists is vanishing'. Given this, Mommsen held that the main issue in the debate was still related to the question of when the Holocaust was set in motion, but that now it was being asked with more science and less passion.

The role of Hitler, in Mommsen's view, was far from crucial. While Hitler was important on an ideological level – given that his insatiable hatred against the Jews formed the basis upon which the continuous escalation of anti-Jewish measures took place – his public utterances with respect to the so-called Jewish Question avoided any direct allusion to the ongoing annihilation process and were restricted to metaphors. Mommsen noted that Hitler

> scrupulously avoided becoming personally identified with the Final Solution, which, as he knew very well, was extremely unpopular among the German population. ... Even before the war, Hitler tried to avoid any direct responsibility for the 'Jewish

Question,' as can be shown with respect to the November pogrom in 1938, when he did not openly support the anti-Jewish excesses. ... [Further,] it is a matter of fact that Hitler did not want to identify himself with the murderous process either publicly or privately, ... [and that his] role was always ambivalent.

(Interview, Shoah Resource Center, 1997)

The notion that Hitler was therefore a relatively weak dictator who reacted to various social pressures, rather than acting as a strong totalitarian leader, caught many critics by surprise. Moreover, Mommsen reinforced his assertions regarding the weakness of the Nazi state through the view that Nazi disorganisation did not allow for a truly totalitarian dictatorship.

As to the root cause of the Holocaust – anti-Semitism – Mommsen has posited that the Nazi version did not differ significantly from its forerunners in the late nineteenth century. That being the case, something was necessary in order to give it the push needed to transform it into a genocidal ideology. What changed, in Mommsen's view, were the intensity and the circumstances under which it became virulent:

Already **Hannah Arendt** pointed out that a new quality arose in the way in which the slaughter was performed, because it was regarded as an ordinary job and no longer as an exceptional act. The pseudo-rational character of the persecution was the main difference from the historical pogroms that were driven by spontaneous, uncontrolled, and undisciplined emotions. Hence, it was a tragic phenomenon that the eastern Jews expected that they could bypass the onslaught of the Germans by being resilient and behaving according to historical pogrom situations. They were certainly wrong in doing this, because there was a specific difference between the former way of mobilizing Jew-hatred and deliberately implementing mass murder, as the Nazis did.

(Interview, Shoah Resource Center, 1997)

The Holocaust, therefore, was not the result of any ideological decision on the part of the Nazi hierarchy, and least of all on the part of Hitler. It was, rather, 'a political process which eventually led to the conclusion that there was no way out but to kill the Jews in Auschwitz and elsewhere' – and even this did not come into being before the second half of 1941, a point on which Mommsen and other prominent Functionalists, such as **Christopher Browning**, agree.

Mommsen has argued that the Holocaust was a unique event in many respects. He identifies these as including 'the moral dimension, the cruelty of the perpetrators, the systematic implementation, and so on'. As he sees it, however, this uniqueness does not create some form of exclusivity that ranks the Holocaust higher than other atrocities. A comparative view is both possible and necessary, with the Holocaust as an extreme example of the decline of Western civilisation and its descent into barbarity. He holds that it is crucial for future generations to learn from the complexity of the experience of Nazi Germany in order to prevent the appearance of similar circumstances under which phenomena like the Holocaust might reappear. Comparative analysis and interdisciplinary historical research, in this sense, is more than useful; it is the responsible thing to do. While some elements of the Holocaust were certainly unique, one should not approach it as if it were incomprehensible. The Holocaust was not, Mommsen concludes, 'a black box'.

Finally, if we are to assess Mommsen's overall contribution to the scholarship of the Holocaust, we need to consider how he has approached the task of researching the period and drawing his conclusions. Across an academic lifetime of reflecting on early twentieth-century German history, Mommsen has tried to demystify the Nazi period by pointing to the regime's very real inadequacies and failings. For Mommsen,

> The methodological challenge [has] consist[ed] in analysing the relation between different factors contributing to the deliberate murders [of the Jews]. In this respect, I tend to put more weight upon the systemic factors, as represented in bureaucratic mechanisms and political interrelations. This viewpoint may be influenced by the deliberation that we are analysing the Nazi regime last but not least from the viewpoint of preventing the emergence of similar political and psychological constellations in the future, which, however, will not reappear on the same scale. From this perspective, the ideological factor seems to be less relevant than others if similar events like the anti-Jewish genocide might come into being again. According to my conviction, it is primarily structural determinants that produce situations in which the rule of the civil law is endangered and the inherited institutions get undermined, which is the precondition for a reign of terror and of mass murder. Every potentate will produce a more or less convincing ideological justification for the use of violence.
>
> (Interview, Shoah Resource Center, 1997)

In short, Mommsen's overall perspective is that political and bureaucratic systems literally *create* genocides, while leaders establish the climate conducive to their realisation and direct the activity while it is taking place. Such an approach is light years away from the view voiced by many during and immediately after the Second World War, which tended to demonise Hitler and portray him as something extra-human (thereby exonerating the German people themselves).

Hans Mommsen's contribution to the study of the Holocaust has been extensive. By showing how the agencies of the state can become perverted, unstructured, mistrustful and inefficient, he has highlighted an important matter for concern in a contemporary environment that has become more bureaucratic than ever before. Far from seeing the Third Reich as a freak one-off phenomenon, Mommsen has demonstrated how it is that Germany's experience six and seven decades ago has real relevance for the world today, and why constant attention to that time must be maintained as a warning for future generations.

Mommsen's major writings

Beamtentum im Dritten Reich. Mit ausgewahlten Quellen zur national sozialistischen Beamtenpolitik, Stuttgart: Deutsche Verlags-Anstalt, 1966.

Arbeiterbewegung und nationale Frage, Göttingen: Vandenhoeck and Ruprecht, 1979.

Herrschaftsalltag im Dritten Reich: Studien und Texte, (Ed. with Susanne Willems), Düsseldorf: Schwann, 1988.

Die verspielte Freiheit: der Weg der Republik von Weimar in den Untergang, 1918 bis 1933, Berlin: Propyläen, 1989.

From Weimar to Auschwitz: Essays in German History, Cambridge: Polity Press, 1991.

Der Nationalsozialismus und die deutsche Gesellschaft, Hamburg: Rowohlt, 1991.

Widerstand und politische Kultur in Deutschland und Österreich, Vienna: Picus, 1994.

(with Manfred Grieger) *Das Volkswagenwerk und seine Arbeiter im Dritten Reich*, Düsseldorf: ECON, 1996.

Aufstieg und Untergang der Republik von Weimar 1918–1933, Ullstein: Berlin, 1997.

The Rise and Fall of Weimar Democracy, Durham (NC): University of North Carolina Press, 1998.

Von Weimar nach Auschwitz: Zur Geschichte Deutschlands in der Weltkriegsepoche, Stuttgart: Deutsche Verlags-Anstalt, 1999.

Alternative zu Hitler: Studien zur Geschichte des deutschen Widerstandes, Munich: Beck, 2000.

Der Erste Weltkrieg und die europäische Nachkriegsordnung: Sozialer Wandel und Formveränderung der Politik, Cologne: Böhlau, 2000.

(Ed.) *The Third Reich between Vision and Reality: New Perspectives on German History, 1918–1945*, Oxford: Berg, 2001.

Alternatives to Hitler: German Resistance under the Third Reich, Princeton (NJ): Princeton University Press, 2003.

Germans against Hitler: The Stauffenberg Plot and Resistance Under the Third Reich, London: I.B. Tauris, 2008.

Reference

'An Interview with Prof. Hans Mommsen', Shoah Resource Center, Yad Vashem, 12 December 1997, Jerusalem, at http://www.yadvashem.org.

NORMAN M. NAIMARK (b. 1944)

Norman M. Naimark is the Robert and Florence McDonnell Professor of History and East European Studies at Stanford University, California. He is also a Senior Fellow at the Hoover Institution and at the Freeman-Spogli Institute of International Studies at Stanford. Born in Suffern, New York in 1944, Naimark was educated at Stanford University, prior to moving to Massachusetts to teach at Boston University and serve as a fellow at Harvard University's Russian Research Center. In 1988 he returned to Stanford as a member of the faculty, and he has remained there ever since.

Naimark's early research focused on the problems associated with radical and other politics in both the Russian Empire and Soviet Eastern Europe. His edited and documentary volumes have addressed such topics as nationality issues in the former Soviet Union, the Soviet campaign against the Nazis on the Eastern Front, history and politics in the former Soviet Union, communism in Eastern Europe, and the Soviets in Austria and the former Yugoslavia.

Increasingly, however, he has turned his attention to the problems associated with ethnic cleansing and genocide, particularly as expressed in his seminal work *Fires of Hatred: Ethnic Cleansing in Twentieth Century Europe* (2001), as well as in a number of shorter writings. For Naimark, the distinction between the two notions is critical yet far from clear-cut.

Fires of Hatred was an in-depth analysis of five case studies: the Turks against the Armenians (1915) and against the Anatolian Greeks (1921–22); the Nazis against the Jews (1941); the Soviets against the Chechen-Ingush and Tatars (1944); the Poles and Czechs against the Germans (post-1945); and the Serbs primarily against Bosnian Muslims (1992–95). Prior to commencing his investigation, however,

Naimark made two substantive points central to his overall arguments: first, that both ethnic cleansing and genocide as they have been practiced in the twentieth century are, essentially, *modern* phenomena; and second, that the Holocaust remains the paradigmatic and most well-documented example of genocide in all recorded history, and as such serves as the critical standard by which to examine all other cases.

With regard to the first point, he wrote that 'the impetus to homogenize is inherent to the twentieth-century state ... The drive toward ethnic cleansing comes in part from the modern state's compulsion to complete policies and finish with problems *but also in part from its technological abilities to do so*' (Naimark, 2001: 8–9, emphasis added). Thus, modern ethnic cleansing takes place not only because of the state's desire for homogenisation, but also because of the very modern abilities of such nation-states.

Considering the Holocaust, he wrote that it was 'the paradigmatic genocide of the twentieth century' (Naimark, 2001: 35) and, as such,

> the Holocaust has become the dominant historical metaphor of our time. ... Especially in the early 1960s, the Holocaust has been ubiquitous in our intellectual, moral, and spiritual universe; and indeed if the lessons of the Holocaust are applied with restraint and subtlety, they can approvingly serve as signposts for action in the contemporary world. ... The discourse of the Holocaust is unavoidable; the task is to apply its lessons – when appropriate – to our understanding of the past and future.
>
> (Naimark, 2001: 58)

Definitionally, however, care must be taken to distinguish between ethnic cleansing and genocide based not on the horrors, pain and needless deaths inflicted upon the innocent victims, but, rather, on the objectives associated with each. The term 'ethnic cleansing' is not an easy one to pin down. In the 1990s, a former senior Pentagon analyst, Norman F. Cigar, offered his judgement of events as they were being played out in Bosnia, concluding that 'The Muslim community of the former Yugoslav republic of Bosnia–Herzegovina has been the victim of what can be termed, by any accepted legal and moral measure, genocide' (Cigar, 1995: 3). Developing his case further, Cigar argued that:

> the genocide – or ethnic cleansing, as it has been commonly known – that befell the Muslims of Bosnia–Herzegovina was not simply the unintentional and unfortunate by-product of combat

or civil war. Rather, it was a rational policy, the direct and planned consequence of conscious policy decisions taken by the Serbian establishment in Serbia and Bosnia-Herzegovina. This policy was implemented in a deliberate and systematic manner as part of a broader strategy intended to achieve a well-defined, concrete, political objective, namely, the creation of an expanded, ethnically pure Greater Serbia.

(Cigar, 1995: 4)

Cigar considered that the notion of ethnic cleansing, a term that was new to most observers in the 1990s, equates with genocide. For some, this would appear a thoroughly acceptable linkage of themes. Without defining what ethnic cleansing actually is, many would look at the images coming out of the Bosnian conflict – long lines of civilian refugees having been forced out of their homes by intimidation, coercion or outright force; busloads of these same people arriving at border crossings; roadsides littered with the bodies of those who had been massacred – and conclude that the terms ethnic cleansing and genocide are quite clearly synonymous. Indeed, Cigar's very title proclaims this merging of the two concepts: *Genocide in Bosnia: The Policy of 'Ethnic Cleansing'*. It is of interest that while he looked carefully into the definitional and conceptual elements of the term genocide, he did not see a need to do so regarding the term ethnic cleansing, other than to say that the two terms effectively mean the same thing.

Elsewhere, **Eric Markusen**, in the *Encyclopedia of Genocide*, wrote in 1999 that ethnic cleansing is 'the deliberate, systematic, and forced removal of a particular ethnic group from a specified territory', though he added, after Andrew Bell-Fialkoff, that 'cleansing' in the past has not been limited to ethnic groups and should rightly be referred to as 'population cleansing' (Markusen, 1999: 215). In similar vein, Roger Cohen refers to ethnic cleansing as 'the use of force or intimidation to remove people of a certain ethnic or religious group from an area', the purpose of which is to ensure 'through killing, destruction, threat, and humiliation that no return is possible' (Cohen, 1999: 136).

Given such thinking, the question has to be asked: are genocide and ethnic cleansing really different manifestations of the same thing – peoplehood destruction – or are they quite unlike phenomena? Clearly, Cigar sees nothing to distinguish the two, yet Naimark was unambiguous in declaring the opposite:

ethnic cleansing and genocide are two different activities, and the differences between them are important. ... Genocide is the intentional killing off of part or all of an ethnic, religious, or national group; the murder of a people or peoples ... is the objective. The intention of ethnic cleansing is to remove a people and often all traces of them from a concrete territory. The goal, in other words, is to get rid of the 'alien' nationality, ethnic, or religious group and to seize control of the territory they had formerly inhabited.

(Naimark, 2001: 3)

Conceding that people, sometimes numbering millions, can be killed during ethnic cleansing (either murdered deliberately, or through brutal treatment, lack of food, or in myriad other ways), Naimark acknowledged that ethnic cleansing can 'bleed' (his term) into genocide, but emphasised nonetheless that the two terms are quite distinct from each other – and that, moreover, the distinction can have a number of useful applications (Naimark, 2001: 4).

Further, while ethnic cleansing may very well 'bleed' into genocide (and it often has), and forced relocation/removal has often been accompanied by genocide, they are not, for Naimark, to be understood as identical terms, nor can the events they embrace be considered the same. Others have been influenced by Naimark's assertions. Indeed, as noted by Columbia University History Professor István Deák in a review of *Fires of Hatred* published in 2002,

Hitler at first practiced the ethnic cleansing of the Jews, wanting them to remove themselves as far as possible from Europe. Later, however, the cleansing of the Jews turned into genocide, with the aim, unique in the history of human extermination, of killing all those whom the Nazis saw as Jews, irrespective of their geographic location, age, gender, nationality, citizenship, and religion.

(Deák, 2002: 49)

In an even lengthier review in March 2004 by Manchester University's Nick P. Barron, an additional argument by Naimark was succinctly outlined – namely, that modernity itself carries within it the potential for both ethnic cleansing and genocide. Barron identified four essential points from Naimark's overall argument:

Firstly, the late-nineteenth century witnessed the spread of 'racialist nationalism' which asserted an 'essentialist view of nations, a view that that excluded the "other" and foreswore assimilation' ... Secondly, as European imperial territories fragmented in the early twentieth century, there emerged a new form of state, defining itself in ethnic terms and striving to 'homogenize' society to meet its own 'needs for order, transparency, and responsiveness' ... Thirdly, the new states' capacity to intervene in society and effect their desired social and spatial reordering would have been impossible without modern innovations in communications, transportation, and the means of killing ... Finally, Naimark directs attention to the role of political elites in instigating ethnic cleansing, and of bureaucrats and technical professionals in organizing its implementation.

(Barron, 2004)

Beyond this, Naimark continues to bring to our attention the violence inherent in the process of ethnic cleansing which, when intensified owing to the need for urgency, or local conditions, or a radicalisation of the process from the centre, all too easily leads to genocide. The cases of both the Armenians and the Jews support his central thesis. Contextually and additionally, for Naimark these so-called cleansing activities, no matter how violent, always seem to occur within the parameters of war or its chaotic aftermath. Naimark goes even further and suggests strongly that the governments responsible for this 'dirty work' of ethnic cleansing attempt, as part of their overall plan, the complete obliteration of the cultural and material evidence of the very peoples they are trying to relocate (including robbing their victims of their personal and familial possessions), with the cases of both the Armenians and the Bosniaks (Bosnian Muslims) quite clearly providing evidence of this.

Finally, Naimark considers the misogynistic nature of both ethnic cleansing and genocide, which becomes manifest not only through the murderous destruction of children (the next and ensuing generations) but the violence of rape (and impregnation) by the perpetrators against women (and even underage girls) of all ages. That rape has been part and parcel of soldiers' conduct in war through human history is nothing new. That we continue to see – in Bosnia, in Rwanda, in Darfur, among other recent locations – its use not as a by-product of wartime violence but as one tactic among many connected to ethnic cleansing and/or genocide lends an immediacy to Naimark's work that places his thinking in the forefront of genocide theory – and highlights a development which international case law has been addressing through such courts as the International Criminal Tribunal for Rwanda (see, for example, *Prosecutor v. Jean-Paul Akayesu, Case No. ICTR-96-4-T*).

In the academic tradition of sound scholarship, Norman M. Naimark is most concerned over the issue of loose usage and terminological imprecision. He would have all those who address the concerns he raises sharpen their intellectual foci through a rigorous questioning of whether the events being discussed are genocide or ethnic cleansing, democide (see **R. J. Rummel**), politicide (see **Barbara Harff**), mass murder or massacre. His issue here is that this should be done not to complicate discussion, but, rather, for the purposes of clarification and isolation of the various factors by which some communities continue to engage in murderous, destructive and/or extreme violence against others.

Naimark's major writings

The Russians in Germany: The History of the Soviet Zone of Occupation, 1945–1949, Cambridge (MA): Harvard University Press, 1995.

Fires of Hatred: Ethnic Cleansing in Twentieth Century Europe, Cambridge (MA): Harvard University Press, 2001.

'Remembering Genocide in Srebrenica', *Hoover Daily Report* 13 July 2005, at http://www.hoover.org.

'Totalitarian States and the History of Genocide', *Telos*, Vol. 136 (2006), pp. 10–25.

(Ed. with Paul R. Gregory) *The Lost Politburo Transcripts: From Collective Rule to Stalin's Dictatorship*, New Haven: Yale University Press, 2008.

References

Barron, Nick P., H-Net Review of *Fires of Hatred*, March 2004, at http://webmail.aol.com.

Bell-Fialkoff, Andrew, *Ethnic Cleansing*, New York: St Martin's Press, 1996.

Cigar, Norman F., *Genocide in Bosnia: The Policy of 'Ethnic Cleansing'*, College Station (TX): Texas A & M University Press, 1995.

Cohen, Roger, 'Ethnic Cleansing', in Roy Gutman and David Rieff (eds), *Crimes of War: What the Public Should Know*, New York: Norton, 1999.

Deák, István, 'The Crime of the Century', *New York Review of Books*, 26 September 2002.

Markusen, Eric, 'Ethnic Cleansing and Genocide', in Israel W. Charny (Editor-in-Chief), *Encyclopedia of Genocide*, Vol. 1, Santa Barbara (CA): ABC-Clio, 1999.

SAMANTHA POWER (b. 1970)

Samantha Power is the Anna Lindh Professor of Global Leadership and Public Policy at Harvard University, and Founding Director, also at Harvard, of the Carr Center for Human Rights Policy. Born in Ireland in 1970 and emigrating to the United States in 1979, she grew up in Pittsburgh, Pennsylvania and Atlanta, Georgia. Though originally aspiring to become a newspaper sports reporter, upon her graduation from Yale University her journalistic career took her down a different path. She began covering genocidal conflicts and gross human-rights violations in a number of the world's hot spots, including Bosnia, Burundi, Darfur, East Timor, Kosovo, Rwanda and Zimbabwe. Seeing at first hand the frequent impotence of international efforts to combat genocide, particularly those of the United States, led in 2002 to her Pulitzer Prize–winning book 'A Problem from Hell': America and the Age of Genocide – for which she also received the 2003 National Book Critics Circle Award for general non-fiction, and the 2003 Council on Foreign Relations Arthur Ross Prize for the best book on US foreign policy. She followed this up with an article in The New Yorker in August 2004 entitled 'Dying in Darfur: Can the Ethnic Cleansing in Sudan be Stopped?', which won the 2005 National Magazine award for best reporting.

As a working journalist as well as a scholar, Power continues to write on foreign policy issues for a number of major periodicals syndicated throughout the world. In 2000 she also co-edited, with Graham Allison, Realizing Human Rights: Moving from Inspiration to Impact. Her most recent project is a biography of Sergio Vieira de Mello, the UN envoy killed by a suicide bomber in Iraq along with fourteen others in 2003. Entitled Chasing the Flame: Sergio Vieira de Mello and the Fight to Save the World, this study appeared in early 2008.

Prior to the release of A Problem from Hell, Power wrote 'Bystanders to Genocide' in The Atlantic Monthly, which in many ways summarised the arguments that would follow in the larger work. In this lengthy article – the result of a three-year investigation – she criticised the United States government under then-President Bill Clinton for its ongoing failures to do anything substantive to halt the genocide in Rwanda in 1994, which saw the slaughter of at least 800,000 of its Tutsi minority, and substantial numbers of less radical (or 'moderate') Hutus, by the Hutu majority. In that piece, Power asked a range of questions that would frame her investigation regarding the lack of US involvement in previous cases of genocide. These included: Why did the United States not do more for the Rwandans at the time of the killings? Did the President really not know about the genocide, as marginal comments in his memoranda suggested? Who were the people in Clinton's Administration who made the life-and-death decisions that dictated US policy? Why did they decide (or decide not to decide) as they did? Were any voices inside or outside the US government demanding that the United States do more? If so, why were they not heeded? And most crucially, what could the United States have done to save lives? In response to such concerns, Power would later admit that her own moral passion, both at the time of her early articles and at the time of the appearance of '*A Problem from Hell*', reflected her own naiveté with regard to political realism and affairs of state.

Rejecting claims of ignorance over what was happening in Rwanda, of a lack of compassion, or a lack of concrete action as to what could have been accomplished, Power's research conclusively showed that an absence of US involvement was *not* a case of inactive 'bystanderism' (hence the ironic title of the piece), but, rather, the result of *active non-involvement*:

> In reality the United States did much more than fail to send troops. It led a successful effort to remove most of the UN peacekeepers who were already in Rwanda. It aggressively worked to block the subsequent authorization of UN reinforcements. It refused to use its technology to jam radio broadcasts that were a crucial instrument in the coordination and perpetuation of the genocide. And even as an average 8,000 Rwandans were being butchered each day, US officials shunned the term 'genocide,' for fear of being obliged to act. The United States in fact did virtually nothing 'to try to limit what occurred.' Indeed, staying out of Rwanda was an explicit U.S. policy objective.
>
> (Power, 2001)

The scenario of 'active non-involvement', in fact, was consistent with what Power regarded as the 'major findings' of '*A Problem from Hell*' relating to US policy responses to genocide, which were, she wrote, 'astonishingly similar across time, geography, ideology, and geopolitical balance'. Her arguments were several: 'Despite graphic media coverage, American policy makers, journalists, and citizens are extremely slow to muster the imagination needed to reckon with evil'; 'It is in the realm of domestic politics that the battle to stop genocide is lost'; 'The US government not only abstains from sending its troops, but takes very few steps along a continuum of intervention to deter genocide'; and 'US officials spin themselves (as well as the American public) about the nature of the violence in question and the likely impact of an American intervention' (Power, 2002: xvi–xviii).

Though her conclusions throughout '*A Problem from Hell*' were essentially negative with regard to the lack of positive American involvement in all past cases of genocide – the Armenian Genocide, the Holocaust, Cambodia, Bosnia, Rwanda and even Iraq – in an online interview, also in *Atlantic Monthly* (14 March 2002), Power was much more positive regarding her reasons for writing the book and what needs be done in the future if US policy is to be more effective.

She wrote the book, she said, for 'the screamers', those persons in positions of responsibility who choose to speak out against government policies, often at great personal and professional cost (a number of whose stories are told throughout the book), as well as in the hope that the learning curve concerning what is and what is not genocide – and what can and cannot be done in the future – will prove far less difficult to surmount than it has been in the past. Further, still reflecting her earlier uncertainties about how change could be accomplished, she asked: (a) How can we get cases of genocide taught in diplomatic history classes? (b) How can we get the Foreign Service Institute to talk to its diplomats about the perils of negotiating for too long? (c) How can we develop a toolkit of unconventional means to deal with this unconventional crime? And (d) How can we get people to be looking out for this so that we can steepen the grade of that learning curve and shorten the distance that people have to move between 'not knowing' to 'knowing' and then to 'really knowing' – that different, transcendent kind of knowledge that takes people forever to acquire? (Power, 2002)

Power's post-9/11 fears, however, reflected in her subsequent work, remain whether the United States will denounce genocide, and/or use the word appropriately. It should be noted that in the case of Darfur since 2003, former US Secretaries of State Colin Powell and Condoleezza Rice, and former US President George W. Bush, all used the word genocide from an early date, though doing so has not yet resulted in significant intervention on the part of the United States – neither unilaterally nor in concert with African and non-African nation-states. Nor has the United States threatened prosecution, used American military or other technology, frozen foreign assets, lifted or imposed arms or other embargoes, rallied multilateral troop deployments under UN auspices, or generally taken the lead as the true political superpower that it is.

As a result of such considerations, therefore, in a 2006 article in *Harvard Magazine* entitled 'Fixing Foreign Policy: Overcoming Bipartisan Blindness about America's Interest Abroad', Power suggested four reasons why America's foreign policies have failed, and four solutions. Here, she argued that American foreign policy is continuing at an all-time low because

1. 'the United States is nowhere near as powerful as it was five years ago, or as many within the Bush administration believe it to be';
2. 'the United States is more isolated internationally than it has ever been';
3. there is a major problem regarding presidential 'accountability' and/or the lack thereof; and
4. 'citizens are so overwhelmed by the complexity of the challenges around the world – and by our perceived ham-handedness in tackling them – that many are falling prey to the temptation to retreat'.

(Power, 2006: 26–29)

Her solutions, replete with examples throughout, are, equally, fourfold: first, before the United States will be welcomed again as a team captain in the international community, it must prove itself able to be a team player; second, if the burdens of global security are to be shared, other countries must accept their portion of international responsibility; third, in promoting democracy, the United States typically stands more for what might be called 'electocracy' than it does for what individuals crave, which is 'human security' – and that must be changed, as even President Bush acknowledged that 'human rights and national-security policies are linked'; and finally, curing US foreign policy of its defects will require engaging the American people in the enterprise (Power, 2006: 26–29, 88–89).

Overall, it can be said that Samantha Power is an important critical voice in Genocide Studies. She continues to bring to the table the intellect and insights of a scholar, the eye and talents of a journalist, and the moral passion of a human being truly concerned about her fellow human beings caught in the grip of a crime which shows few signs of abating. She has not been without her detractors, some of whom have argued that her reliance on an idealised vision of 'political will' as a way to stop genocide does not take into account the actuality of a world system that is still founded on political realism. Her influence, however, has been widespread, with a broad readership in the non-specialised general community embracing her ideas and taking her theoretical perspectives on international action to a new level of direct action when meeting with their elected representatives.

Power's major writings

(Ed. with Graham Allison) *Realizing Human Rights: Moving from Inspiration to Impact*, New York: Palgrave Macmillan, 2000.

'Bystanders to Genocide', *Atlantic Monthly* (September 2001), at http://www.theatlantic.com.

'Never Again Again', *Atlantic Monthly* (14 March 2002), at http://www.theatlantic.com.

'A Problem from Hell': America and the Age of Genocide, New York: Basic Books, 2002.

'Dying in Darfur: Can the Ethnic Cleansing in Sudan be Stopped?', *New Yorker* (30 August 2004), at http://www.newyorker.com.

'Fixing Foreign Policy: Overcoming Bipartisan Blindness about America's Interests Abroad', *Harvard Magazine* (July–August 2006), 26–29, 88–89.

Chasing the Flame: Sergio Vieira de Mello and the Fight to Save the World. New York: Penguin, 2008.

JOAN RINGELHEIM (b. 1939)

Joan Ringelheim is a former Director of Oral History at the United States Holocaust Memorial Museum, and one of the world's foremost scholars concerned with the remembrance of Jewish women during the Holocaust. Her interest in this area was first brought to a broader audience in 1983, with a conference she organised based on that theme. Since then, she has written, taught and lectured extensively on the subject, legitimising the topic and propelling it into the forefront of inquiry about the Holocaust.

Ringelheim was born in Brooklyn, New York in 1939, and educated at Boston University. After receiving her PhD, she taught philosophy for the next 13 years. During this period two major foci emerged in her teaching and research, the Holocaust and feminist theory. Together, these two fields opened up a new area of investigation, specifically, women and the Holocaust. In 1982–83 she received an American Council of Learned Societies Fellowship and a Kent Fellowship from the Center for Humanities at Wesleyan University, as well as a grant from the New York Council for the Humanities to produce the first conference on women and the Holocaust.

At the seminal 1983 conference entitled 'Women Surviving: The Holocaust', in which Ringelheim and other scholars really began to define the field, she laid out very specifically what needed to be done in order to develop a wholly new approach to the study of the *Shoah*:

What I would like to do is go from right to left with the conference title, 'The Holocaust: Surviving Women' and talk a little bit about what's wrong with the title. First, The Holocaust. It is a little bit like trying to change the Ten Commandments. It is a term that seems written in stone and which can't be changed (and perhaps one doesn't want to). However, I would like to suggest that there is no such thing as 'The Holocaust.' What men, women and children experienced was not one event, but a myriad of events which we've tied into an analytical knot so we can speak about it with ease and with single breaths. The Holocaust is made up of individual experiences. They may have been momentous experiences for some, but it seems to me that the momentousness often occurs after we've identified what the event is. There was no such language for those experiences when people were going through them.

(Ringelheim, in Ringelheim and Katz, 1983: 23–24)

It was also important for Ringelheim that not everyone experienced the event in the same way. One of the things she sought to explore was not just the commonalities, but the differences between men's and women's experiences and the differences in experience among women.

Building on her theme of acknowledging difference when studying the destruction of the European Jews, she continued that:

We need to be able to listen to those who experienced the Holocaust, to understand the differences in those experiences and to hear the silences ... the silences of the survivors who have not been allowed to speak or haven't had a place to speak to those of us who have had questions. It is important for us to share, to listen to each other, to realize the extent to which we don't know about each other's lives.

(Ringelheim, in Ringelheim and Katz, 1983: 24)

Her concern was about more than just how the Holocaust should be interpreted; she extended her ideas by considering the nature of survivorship, at that time a burgeoning topic within the broader field of Holocaust interpretation (see Bartrop, 2000; Bettelheim, 1980; Des Pres, 1976). Quite simply, for Ringelheim 'no one was a survivor until after the event ... one only knew one was a survivor when it was all over'. In the meantime, 'what women were doing was *trying to survive*', and it was this that led her to advocate that more focus be placed on the quest for survival 'so we don't simply talk about the ones who got through, but also all of the people, all of the women who tried to survive but didn't make it … ' Indeed, the conference itself, in Ringelheim's view, was 'an attempt to see how women, even those who can no longer speak, *try* to get through. We need to reclaim the history of all those who are here, as well as all those who are not here' (Ringelheim, in Ringelheim and Katz, 1983: 25, emphasis in original). Thus, it is important to move beyond looking at big-picture issues (as she stated, 'we too often talk about the Holocaust in sacred terms and this can sometimes be dangerous because that kind of language silences those who experienced it in other ways'), and consider also those that could lead women to 'transform … situations of death and impoverishment into possibilities for life' (Ringelheim, in Ringelheim and Katz, 1983: 26).

In 1985, Ringelheim affirmed her belief that women experienced the Holocaust differently to men, citing examples from her interviews with twenty Jewish women survivors who 'spoke of their sexual vulnerability: sexual humiliation, rape, sexual exchange, pregnancy, abortion, and vulnerability through their children – concerns that men either described in different ways or, more often, did not describe at all' (Ringelheim, 1985: 743). Her project, as she stated it, was 'to make graphic the complexity of these Jewish women's lives because of the connections between biology and sexism' (Ringelheim, 1993: 378).

She extended her approach by moving away from her earlier cultural feminism which had essentialised women's culture, and had argued for the worthiness of the study of women in the Holocaust on this basis, as well as acknowledging the political implications that a liberal ideology brings (Ringelheim, 1985: 753–57, Note 6). She warned against the development of a theory of women surviving better than men owing to some sort of innate set of female behaviours, as this could lead to the trap of glorifying an inherent women's culture. Moreover, she claimed, it is not enough simply to say that women behaved differently to men, without acknowledging the various subject categories within that broader category of 'woman', and without referring to the very specific historical context within which these women were operating. As Ringelheim explained in a later work, it is necessary to examine the situation of Jewish women in the Holocaust because 'if in the gas chambers or before the firing squads all Jews seemed alike to the Nazis, the path to this end was not always the same for women and men. The end – namely annihilation or death – does not always describe or explain the process' (Ringelheim, 1998: 350).

This notwithstanding, she cautioned that the point should not be to celebrate women's culture, but rather to interrogate how women endured the Holocaust (Ringelheim, 1993: 756). Her assertions demonstrate the existence of what she called a 'split memory', between 'traditional versions of the Holocaust' and women's individual experiences which do not fit into those narratives (Ringelheim, 1998: 344). This split between genocide and gender-specific trauma, she held, 'exists not only in the memories of witnesses but also in the historical reconstruction by scholars'. She made clear how the narratives of the Holocaust have been constructed to avoid women's experiences, and thereby argued for a broadening of the nature of Holocaust narratives.

In an essay written in 1990, Ringelheim spelled out the core of her position in terms that would become simultaneously definitive and pioneering:

> For the Nazis, the *functions* of Jewish and Aryan women were the same (reproduction and nurturance of family). However, the *value* of each was different. Simply, when Aryan and considered biologically superior, they were valued as women; when Jews, they were not. It is impossible that the deeply held sexism within the Nazis' ideology did not affect their beliefs about and treatment of Jewish women. If the Nazis identified women by their reproductive functions, then Jewish women cannot be allowed to be Jews because they are *women*. Jewish men cannot be allowed to be Jews because they are *Jews* – the authentic Jews. The lives of women became more precarious than those of men because of sexism, not only because of anti-semitism. If anti-semitism were all that mattered, men and women would have been similarly endangered and victimized. Thus, the question is not whether being male or female mattered during the Holocaust. The real question is: How did it matter? It is blind, if not malicious, to subsume and hide women's experiences under those of men when there are significant differences.
>
> (Ringelheim, 1990: 146–47, emphasis in original)

Ringelheim noted that

> there was a direct link in Nazi policy between anti-semitism and sexism. Jewish women suffered both as Jews and as women from anti-semitism and sexism in their genocidal forms. More women were deported than men. More women were killed than men. Women's chances for survival were simply not equivalent to those of men.
>
> (Ringelheim, 1990: 147)

Joan Ringelheim has been described as 'the founding mother of women's Holocaust studies' (Rittner and Roth, 1993: 373). Overall, her contribution to the field of Holocaust Studies – and, by extension, to the study of genocide overall – has been profound. While she has not produced any major book-length studies in the areas covered by her thinking, her many articles and unpublished papers have nonetheless had a major impact on how Holocaust Studies can and should be viewed, and not just by partisan scholars. In a similar manner to **Adam Jones** regarding the experience of men in genocidal situations, Joan Ringelheim has focused attention on the singular nature of women's experiences during the Holocaust, and for this her work should be recognised widely for its originality and insightfulness.

Ringelheim's major writings

(Ed. with Esther Katz) *Proceedings of the Conference on Women Surviving the Holocaust*, New York: Institute for Research in History, 1983.
'The Unethical and the Unspeakable: Women and the Holocaust', *Simon Wiesenthal Center Annual*, 1 (1984), 69–87.
'Women and the Holocaust: A Reconsideration of Research', *Signs*, 10, 4 (Summer 1985), 741–61.
'Thoughts about Women and the Holocaust', in Roger S. Gottlieb (ed.), *Thinking the Unthinkable: Meanings of the Holocaust*, New York: Paulist Press, 1990, 141–49.
'Verschleppung, Tod und Überleben: Nationalsozialistische Ghetto-Politik gegen jüdische Frauen und Männer im besetzten Polen', in Theresa Wobbe (ed.), *Nach Osten: Verdeckte Spuren nationalsozialistischer Verbrechen*, Frankfurt am Main: Neue Kritik, 1992, 135–60.
'Women and the Holocaust: A Reconsideration of Research', in Carol Rittner and John K. Roth (eds), *Different Voices: Women and the Holocaust*, New York: Paragon House, 1993, 373–418.
'Genocide and Gender: A Split Memory', in Ronit Lentin (ed.), *Gender and Catastrophe*, London: Zed Books, 1997, 18–33.
'The Split between Gender and the Holocaust', in Dalia Ofer and Lenore J. Weitzman (eds), *Women in the Holocaust*, New Haven (CT): Yale University Press, 1998, 340–50.

References

Bartrop, Paul R., *Surviving the Camps: Unity in Adversity during the Holocaust*, Lanham (MD): University Press of America, 2000.
Bettelheim, Bruno, *Surviving and Other Essays*, New York: Random House, 1980.
Des Pres, Terrence, *The Survivor: An Anatomy of Life in the Death Camps*, New York: Oxford University Press, 1976.

Rittner, Carol and John K. Roth, 'Introduction to Chapter 26', in Rittner and Roth (eds), *Different Voices: Women and the Holocaust*, New York: Paragon House, 1993.

CAROL RITTNER, RSM (b. 1943)

Carol Rittner is the Dr Marcia R. Grossman Professor of Holocaust Studies at Richard Stockton College, Pomona, New Jersey. A member of the Roman Catholic Religious Sisters of Mercy, she was born in 1943 and educated at universities in Pennsylvania, Maryland and Michigan. She received her doctorate in Education from Penn State University. Before joining the faculty at Richard Stockton College, Rittner was the first Director of the Elie Wiesel Foundation for Humanity, New York, where she organised three international conferences in Paris (1988), Boston (1989) and Haifa (1990). At Stockton, she has held the positions of Distinguished Professor of Religious Studies (1995), and Distinguished Professor of Holocaust and Genocide Studies (1999). Between 2006 and 2008 she was the Interim Director of the MA Program in Holocaust and Genocide.

Concerned with inter-religious dialogue, Rittner has involved herself with issues related to Jews and Christians in the United States, Catholics and Protestants in Ireland, and Israelis and Palestinians in Israel. Her concern with the *Shoah* has focused primarily on two areas: the story of the 'righteous gentiles', and women's experiences (like **Joan Ringelheim**, she recognises that a male-told story is only half a story). Beyond the Holocaust itself, she has also broadened her thinking to address the plight of women in post–Second World War genocides, in particular looking at the horrors of genocidal rape. A further interwoven thread throughout her work has been the interface of the religious communities and religious and spiritual issues in the aftermath of the *Shoah* (specifically) and genocide (generally).

It is as an educator that Rittner has most frequently done her best work. Together with Mary Johnson of Facing History and Ourselves, for example, Rittner has written 'a framework for teaching about the "mosaic of victims" in the Third Reich', suggesting some 'questions and activities to help students think about how issues of the Nazi era have relevance today' (Johnson and Rittner, 1996: 123–37). In an unpublished presentation in the early 2000s to the Stockholm International Forum on the Holocaust, entitled 'Teaching in a Contemporary Context: The Banality of Good and Evil', she stated:

What interest me are questions about human behavior during the Holocaust. Hundreds of books have been written about the Holocaust, but they have not diminished what **Primo Levi** called 'the grey zone,' that region of haunting questions about human behavior that cannot be answered with certainty. True, we know a great deal about what happened during the Holocaust, about who was responsible, and who was victimized – what we don't know is why so many Germans and their collaborators throughout Nazi-occupied Europe so willingly became one of Hitler's 'willing executioners,' to borrow Daniel Goldhagen's phrase.

How could ordinary human beings, people presumably raised to distinguish right from wrong, people with families of their own, participate in the vicious slaughter of powerless men, women and children? Why didn't the structures of civil society – education, law, religion, diplomacy – stop this evil? Where did moral and religious education flounder? Why did moral and religious education fail to create more resistance to evil and encourage more doing of good? Why did the teaching of good and evil in organized societal and religious institutions fail to prevent the Holocaust?

(Rittner, in Rittner, Smith and Steinfelt (eds), 2000: 2)

Summarising her list of questions, she continued: 'What kind of education can help students grapple with such questions?' She concluded that 'More than ever we need a critical education that will address why we make wars, destroy lives, brutalize and devalue others, and put national interests above humanness. We need an education that will do more than provide students with the capacity to work in a post-industrial economy'. Thus, the story of the Holocaust must not only encompass that which is already known, but also meet the challenge of that which is only now beginning to be assessed, specifically, women's voices as well. In a talk given at Sonoma State University on 16 March 1993, entitled 'Different Voices: Women during the Holocaust', Rittner stated:

Remembering the Holocaust is an incomplete act if the only voices we hear, the only silences we commemorate are those of men. That women felt compelled to write, to bear witness, to leave a record for future generations should not be overlooked, nor should it be forgotten. The challenge is to let women speak for themselves, to attune our ears to what has been overlooked or taken for granted in their experience of the Holocaust, to try and learn more about how women responded to their circumstances; how they took on new responsibilities; what relationships were seen as crucial; whether they were old relationships or newly created ones. We should try to discover what was most important to women living under abnormal conditions of deprivation, humiliation, and terror; try to find what personal and perhaps gender-related resources they called upon to sustain hope as well as life; and conversely, try to discover what vulnerability exposed them to suffering or ultimately to death.

For Rittner it is not only women's voices that complete the story, but the complicated role of non-Jewish rescuers who, while decidedly a very small part of the overall population of countries overrun by the Nazis, exhibited courage in the face of extreme adversity while not perceiving themselves as heroic, but, rather, as ordinary human beings doing what came naturally to them. In an untitled address of 12 February 2003, she stated:

The story of the rescuers frequently is not simply the tale of a single noble act of letting a Jew into their home, but of repeated choices and of a continuous struggle against enormous odds in order to save a person or persons ... On the whole, neither gender, nor age, nor nationality, nor education, nor profession, nor economic class, nor religious leaning, nor political persuasion play a determining role as to who would be a rescuer. Whereas most people surrender personal responsibility for their actions when these actions are dictated by an authority figure, the rescuers of Jews obviously did not. Why not? Most studies indicate that, as children, in a very significant number of cases, the rescuers were raised in homes where love was in abundance, where parents were altruistic and tolerant and where children were disciplined by reason and explanation, and where they were taught five essential principles: that human beings are basically the same and differences between them are to be respected; that the world is not divided into 'us and them' but rather contains a common bond of humanity; that they should have a clear sense of right and wrong, should stand up for their beliefs, have moral integrity, self confidence, and self-worth; that kindness and compassion toward others should be practiced, and that they should be of independent mind, self-sustaining, and never follow the crowd.

(see also Rittner and Myers, 1986)

An uncomfortable corollary to this understanding of the rescuers is Rittner's assessment of the complicated role of Pope Pius XII during the Holocaust:

> Was Pope Pius XII concerned that more lives would be lost? Did he feel personally responsible for the deaths of Catholics that might result from his statements? We shall probably never know for sure. What I do know is that it seems hideous to me to think that his life, even the life of 'the Church as such,' was, or is, more valuable than the life of *any* being. It pains me to say it, but I think this is the message that is being communicated by those in the Roman Catholic Church who want to have Pope Pius XII beatified. Institutions, however, no matter how sacred, are not more sacred than human beings.
>
> Pope Pius XII should have, and I believe *could have*, done more, been more explicit in his defense of the Jewish people and in his condemnation of the Holocaust. Doing so might have cost him his life. But then, 'What kind of life does one lead to be able to pray, "My God, if sacrifice of life is needed, let them kill us rather than those with families?"'
>
> (Rittner and Roth, 2002: 271–72)

Ever the religiously committed Roman Catholic, Rittner took both the rescuers and the Pope into consideration in examining her own faith in an essay written in 2001:

> Is despair the last word? No, I do not think so. I believe God's last word about human history will not be a word of condemnation or anger but a word of mercy and liberation. This is what provides the basis for lasting hope. ...
>
> Does my belief about God make sense in the presence of burning children? ... I can only hope that God will hold in eternal memory all we human beings have done, all we have become. I can only hope that God's eternal faithfulness – even in the face of radical evil – is God's refusal to abandon us – even in the face of 'disgust' – will draw forth, in this world and in the world to come, a greater, finer potential – a healing, mending potential for all creation.
>
> (Rittner and Roth, 2001: 126, 128)

Further addressing the topic 'Spirituality after the Shoah' on 17 June 2007, Rittner suggested that

Any religious tradition that holds that certain values or certain teachings are morally superior to others has the capacity to create 'enemies of God,' 'enemies of the good,' or both, by demonizing those who follow a different value system or a different set of teachings from their own.

Christian spirituality after the Shoah must be a spirituality of recognition: recognition that every human being is God's image in this fragile world of ours. What must inspire and motivate us Christians as we live our lives in relationship with others is the recognition that every human being, without exception, is unique, equal, and of infinite value. This is the true glorification of God in an age when there has been such a serious assault on the credibility of faith because of the great destruction of human life during the Shoah, and, indeed, during the entire twentieth century.

(Rittner, unpublished paper, 2007)

Finally, Rittner's concern with the plight of women in genocide has led her to address directly the question of rape and sexual violence, and, more specifically, the failure of the male leadership of her own church to find concern for the disastrous situation in which trauma-tised and assaulted women all too frequently find themselves after the fact. Arguing that rape itself is a weapon against vulnerable popula-tions, she is seriously critical when it comes to what she regards as the failure of her church in both Rwanda and the former Yugoslavia:

I do not think that just because there are large numbers of Roman Catholics in a country, the leadership of the Roman Catholic Church will concern itself with issues I or others may think are important, such as the use of rape as a weapon of war and genocide. But, given that the leadership of the Catholic Church often speaks out on issues involving sex and sexual morality, I think it is reasonable to ask if the Vatican, that is, the pope, his cardinals, archbishops and bishops, took notice of the widespread sexual violence during the genocides in former Yugoslavia and Rwanda during the 1990s.

(Rittner, 2009: 298)

While fully acknowledging that her church did, indeed, address the overall tragedies in both cases of genocide, she asked:

What is one to make of this silence? What is one to make of these men of the Church who are so vocal about abortion, sterilization, birth control, and euthanasia, but so silent about rape and the men who use their penises as weapons of war and genocide? What should one make of such an unholy silence?

I can only conclude that the leadership of the Roman Catholic Church ... failed to witness the affliction of God's people (women) in Yugoslavia and Rwanda, failed to hear the cry of complaint God's people (women) uttered against the men who used rape as a weapon of war and genocide in Rwanda and Yugoslavia, and failed, failed utterly to know well what God's people (women) were suffering in the 1990s and still suffer today.

I still wait for the 'great voice ... in Rome' to speak out and condemn the evil of rape as a weapon of war and genocide.

(Rittner, 2009: 298)

In 1991, after her time as Director of the Elie Wiesel Foundation, Rittner began a lasting and highly productive relationship with **John K. Roth**, a Professor of Philosophy from Claremont McKenna College in California. Across a number of edited volumes, the two amassed an impressive listing of publications, dealing with a wide range of the topics mentioned here: commentaries on the relationship between Pope Pius XII and the Holocaust; the nature of Christian faith in the aftermath of the *Shoah*; the Auschwitz convent controversy; the position of women in the Holocaust; how religious scholars have undertaken their research about the Holocaust; the role of religion in the Rwanda Genocide; and the future of genocide in the modern world.

For Carol Rittner, wrestling with such topics points the way towards how some sort of an understanding can be created concerning why people have behaved the way they have in the past (and, all too frequently, also in the present). Her energies have been directed towards the plight of the vulnerable, most specifically women, not only in the Holocaust but also those traumatised by the evils of rape in the genocides of the former Yugoslavia and Rwanda. In trying to understand the Righteous Gentiles during the *Shoah*, moreover, she has also found a model of hope with which to address the darkness. In all these ways she has made an impressive contribution to the scholarship of the Holocaust and genocide, for which the field is both richer and more developed.

Rittner's major writings

NOTE: In addition to the following, Carol Rittner has also produced a vast number of addresses and unpublished papers, many of which she was kind enough to provide the authors with, and which cannot fit comfortably into a listing of published works.

(Ed. with Sondra Myers) *The Courage to Care: Rescuers of Jews during the Holocaust*, New York: New York University Press, 1986.

(Ed.) *Elie Wiesel: Between Memory and Hope*, New York: New York University Press, 1990.

(Ed. with John K. Roth) *Memory Offended: The Auschwitz Convent Controversy*, Westport (CT): Praeger, 1991.

(Ed. with John K. Roth) *Different Voices: Women and the Holocaust*, New York: Paragon House, 1993.

(with Mary Johnson) 'Circles of Hell: Jewish and Non-Jewish Victims of the Nazis', *Annals of the American Academy of Political and Social Science*, 548 (1996), 123–37.

(Ed. with John K. Roth) *From the Unthinkable to the Unavoidable: American Christian and Jewish Scholars Encounter the Holocaust*, Westport (CT): Greenwood Press, 1997. See also Rittner's own essay in that collection, 'From Ignorance to Insight', 125–36.

(Ed.) *Anne Frank in the World: Essays and Reflections*, Armonk (NY): M. E. Sharpe, 1998.

(Ed. with Stephen D. Smith and Irina Steinfeldt) *The Holocaust and the Christian World: Reflections on the Past, Challenges for the Future*, London: Kuperard, 2000.

(Ed. with John K. Roth) *'Good News' After Auschwitz? Christian Faith within a Post-Holocaust World*, Macon (GA): Mercer University Press, 2001.

(Ed. with John K. Roth) *Pope Pius XII and the Holocaust*, London: Leicester University Press, 2002.

(Ed. with John K. Roth and Stephen D. Smith) *Will Genocide Ever End?* St. Paul (MN): Paragon House, 2004a.

(Ed. with John K. Roth and Wendy Whitworth) *Genocide in Rwanda: Complicity of the Churches?* St. Paul (MN): Paragon House, 2004b.

'Rape, Religion, and Genocide: An Unholy Silence', in Steven Leonard Jacobs (ed.), *Confronting Genocide: Judaism, Christianity, Islam*, Lanham (MD): Lexington Books, 2009, 291–305.

JOHN K. ROTH (b. 1940)

John K. Roth is the Edward J. Sexton Professor Emeritus of Philosophy, and Founding Director (in 2003) of the Center for the Study of the Holocaust, Genocide and Human Rights, at Claremont McKenna College, California. Born in 1940 in Grand Haven, Michigan, Roth was educated at Pomona College, Yale University Divinity School and Yale University. In 1966 he joined Claremont McKenna, where he remained for the rest of his career until his retirement in 2006. In 1988 he was named United States National Professor of the Year by the Council for Advancement and Support of Education (CASE) and the Carnegie Foundation for the Advancement of Teaching for his work on the Holocaust and the American Experience.

Roth's scholarly work on the *Shoah* began with the 1979 publication of *A Consuming Fire: Encounters with Elie Wiesel and the Holocaust*. This explored **Elie Wiesel**'s impact on the post-Holocaust theological work of one of Roth's close friends and intellectual soul mates, Michael Berenbaum, focusing on **Wiesel**'s theme of protest against God in light of the destructiveness of the Holocaust. Writing the book helped Roth to examine more closely his understanding of his own Christian tradition. Over the next few years this saw him become closely involved with post-Holocaust theology, such that in 1986 he and **Richard Rubenstein**, a Jewish scholar from Florida, produced *Approaches to Auschwitz: The Holocaust and Its Legacy*, a study exploring the continuing theological significance of the Holocaust and the various ways in which it has been studied. The book sought to clarify the political, historical and economic roots of the *Shoah* without losing sight of the complexities of its history, and in so doing analysed the Holocaust's definitive impact on human civilisation and its unparalleled importance in determining the fate of the world. Intended as a text for students, the book was a thought-provoking study of the Holocaust from a number of different disciplinary perspectives.

Roth then teamed up with Berenbaum in order to edit *Holocaust: Religious and Philosophical Implications* (1989), a student textbook of theological and reflective sources on the Holocaust. It was a compilation of what are now considered classic pieces of Holocaust literature, written by such authors as **Raul Hilberg**, **Hannah Arendt**, **Primo Levi**, George Steiner, **Richard Rubenstein**, **Elie Wiesel**, **Emil Fackenheim**, Eliezer Berkovits**, Lucy S. Dawidowicz**, **Terrence Des Pres**, **Lawrence Langer**, **Yehuda Bauer**, Tadeusz Borowski, **Robert Jay Lifton** and Irving Greenberg, as well as including essays from Berenbaum and Roth themselves. Many of the pieces came from books and journals that had by then gone out of print, and were organised around what Roth and Berenbaum found to be the most frequently asked questions by their students: (1) Is the Holocaust unique? (2) What really happened in the ghettos and death camps? (3) Who knew what was going on? (4) How could people do the things they did? And (5) What about God? The book was a comprehensive introduction to the most fundamental – though complex – issues raised by the Holocaust, and was an important compendium of religious and analytical accounts regarding that experience.

In 1991 Roth began a lasting and highly productive relationship with Sister **Carol Rittner**, a Roman Catholic nun who until recently had been Director of the Elie Wiesel Foundation for Humanity in New York. *Memory Offended: The Auschwitz Convent Controversy* (1991), which the two co-edited, was an examination of the furore that had emerged over the presence of a Carmelite convent at the site of the Auschwitz extermination camp. The book was a collection of fifteen essays written from eminent Christian and Jewish perspectives, along with an appendix of relevant documents and official statements regarding the convent. As a work dealing with a very current and divisive issue in Christian–Jewish relations, the book attempted to create an understanding of what the controversy was all about, and how the rancour it fostered could be overcome.

Then, in 1993, **Rittner** and Roth again collaborated to edit a groundbreaking volume, *Different Voices: Women and the Holocaust*. Their intention was to demonstrate the degree to which women had been voicing their experiences about the Holocaust since 1945, and in this regard the book was a worthwhile addition to an area that had been pioneered by such scholars as **Joan Ringelheim** slightly earlier. In *Different Voices* Roth and **Rittner** brought together twenty-eight pieces, some long out of print and some written specifically for the volume, which reinforced the dimensions of women's experience during the Holocaust, as well as offering commentary on the nature of scholarly reflection about this dimension of *Shoah* scholarship.

In 1999 Roth collaborated with Stephen R. Haynes, Professor of Religious Studies at Rhodes College, Tennessee, to edit *The Death of God Movement and the Holocaust: Radical Theology Encounters the Shoah*. The book evaluated the religious and cultural legacy of the 'Death of God' movement and its relationship to the Holocaust, surveying the subject from a variety of angles. The so-called Death of God theologians of the late 1960s both influenced and responded to the challenges of theodicy at a time of intellectual ferment, during which the discipline of theology underwent revolutionary change. Several of these thinkers, foremost among whom were the Christians Thomas Altizer, William Hamilton and Paul Van Buren, and the Jew **Richard L. Rubenstein**, were inspired in their thinking by treating the Holocaust as a major and cataclysmic challenge to Christian and Jewish faith. Up to three decades after they were writing, the American Academy of Religion organised a symposium revisiting the issue, in which these four theologians were invited to reflect on how awareness of the Holocaust had affected – and, if appropriate, continued to affect – their thinking. Roth and Haynes's volume brought together their essays, along with responses by other noted scholars who offered critical commentary on the movement's impact, legacy and relationship to the Holocaust.

One of Roth's most important volumes, *Ethics after the Holocaust: Perspectives, Critiques, and Responses*, also appeared in 1999. Based on a series of ongoing discussions undertaken at the biennial Pastora Goldner Holocaust symposium at Wroxton College, England, the book was comprised of a series of discussions between six influential Holocaust scholars – Leonard Grob, Peter J. Haas, David H. Hirsch, David Patterson, Didier Pollefeyt and Roth himself – from the fields of Literature, Philosophy, Religious Studies and Theology. Dealing with the moral and ethical implications of the Holocaust in the same year that produced the crises in Kosovo and East Timor, the issues they explored had an immediacy that was at once as important as it was topical. The discussions were diverse in tone, with interpretations reflecting the nature of the different disciplines and modes of thinking from which the various contributors came. It was a volume that promoted investigation and discussion about moral failures during and after the Holocaust, and its discursive style headed towards a conclusion that interpreted the Holocaust as an attack both on its victims and on moral goodness itself. In the aftermath of Auschwitz, the book asserted, a new ethics must be formulated to take into account the fact of the Holocaust's assault on morality. The simple reaffirmation of pre-Holocaust ethics would henceforth be inappropriate owing to the recently exposed failures of Western religious, philosophical and ethical traditions. Far from preventing the Holocaust, they may indeed have been seriously implicated in it. (In this regard, those engaged in the dialogue reflected the thinking of other leading theological thinkers, such as **Harry James Cargas** and **Franklin H. Littell**, to name but two.)

In 1998 Roth made national news when he was chosen to direct the Center for Advanced Holocaust Studies at the United States Holocaust Memorial Museum in Washington DC. When appointed, he faced vociferous opposition from both Jewish and Christian conservatives. Viewed as a liberal who had in the past relativised the Holocaust alongside other humanitarian tragedies, he was attacked by those who doubted his capacity to put the Holocaust in its 'proper' place in the global hierarchy of atrocity. After much personal anguish, and with immense regret, he declined the appointment, even though the US Holocaust Memorial Council had voted overwhelmingly to reaffirm his appointment and unanimously passed a resolution repudiating the attacks it said were being waged against him.

To avoid distracting from the Museum's work, and despite much support from his academic colleagues around the world, Roth withdrew from the position.

In 2001 he published his account of what had happened, *Holocaust Politics*. This deep reflection considered such matters as who owns or controls public memory and how it should be interpreted, the nature of divisions among Holocaust scholars, and disputes over projects commemorating the victims of Nazi genocide. Holocaust politics, as Roth defined the issue, involved

> the ways – often conflicting – in which the Holocaust informs and affects human belief, organization, and strategy, on the one hand, and in which human belief, organization, and strategy inform and affect the status and understanding of the Holocaust, on the other. Its existence unavoidable, Holocaust politics, like all politics, is not an end in itself but a means to achieve higher goods. Our attitudes and priorities determine its all-important quality.
>
> (Roth, 2001a: 5)

Roth's chapters included titles such as 'Who Owns the Holocaust?', 'What Can and Cannot be Said about the Holocaust?' and 'How is the Holocaust Remembered?' He also included chapters on ethics after Auschwitz and the role of the Catholic Church during the Holocaust.

Following this experience, Roth again teamed up with **Rittner** to co-edit '*Good News' After Auschwitz?: Christian Faith within a Post-Holocaust World* (2001b), a volume that brought together a number of essays asserting that God's embodied presence through Jesus provides life and hope that even the Holocaust cannot destroy. It was a book with a positive message that offered hope in the face of Christianity's massive failures during the *Shoah*.

A year later, Roth and **Rittner**, together with James M. Smith of England's Aegis Trust, moved into the arena of Genocide (as distinct from Holocaust) Studies to produce *Will Genocide Ever End?* This comprised twenty-nine short essays from genocide scholars examining problems relating to genocide definition, political and psychological aspects of the issue, and the nature of legal mechanisms and other instruments that can be employed for the purpose of genocide prevention. Roth, **Rittner** and Smith assembled a cohort of distinguished specialists in Genocide Studies, among them Roger W. Smith, Steven Leonard Jacobs, **Stephen C. Feinstein**, **Helen Fein**, **Richard L. Rubenstein**, **Mark Levene**, **Robert Melson**, **Eric Markusen**,

Ervin Staub, Henry R. Huttenbach, **Barbara Harff**, **Herbert Hirsch**, **Ben Kiernan**, Samuel Totten and Hubert Locke, all for the purpose of providing an insight into the vexed subject of how to prevent genocide. As in Roth's previously edited volumes, these contributors came from a variety of disciplines and areas of professional expertise, and provided a series of very different approaches to the key issues and how they can be resolved.

In subsequent projects, Roth edited other works, including (with **Carol Rittner**) *Pope Pius XII and the Holocaust* (2002b), (with David Patterson) *After-Words: Post-Holocaust Struggles with Forgiveness, Reconciliation, Justice* (2004a), (with **Carol Rittner** and Wendy Whitworth) *Genocide in Rwanda: Complicity of the Churches?* (2004b) and *Genocide and Human Rights: A Philosophical Guide* (2005a).

In *Gray Zones: Ambiguity and Compromise in the Holocaust and its Aftermath* (2005b), which Roth co-edited with Jonathan Petropoulos of the Gould Center for Humanistic Studies at Claremont McKenna College, highly skilled Holocaust scholars, including **Raul Hilberg**, Gerhard L. Weinberg, **Christopher Browning**, Peter Hayes and Lynn Rapaport, considered the deep and dark place identified by Holocaust survivor **Primo Levi** as 'the grey zone' – the space between absolute good and absolute evil, where moral choices are made for the purpose of survival rather than death, where the desire to live surmounts that to be honourable. **Levi** recognised that those who had not been there should hold back from condemnation of those who were: as he wrote, 'one is never in another's place. Each individual is so complex an object that there is no point in trying to foresee his behavior, all the more so in extreme situations; and neither is it possible to foresee one's own behavior' (Levi, 1989: 43). The book provided an insight into the world of what many Holocaust scholars have tried to achieve – namely, to explore and understand the history and implications of the murder of the Jews of Europe for the world today. Roth and Petropoulos brought an interdisciplinary focus to the subject of this moral ambiguity as experienced by people living under the intense stress of the extreme situation provoked by the Holocaust, and the essays in the book, taken together, showed that the closer we come to reaching conclusions about the Holocaust, the more complex that event turns out to be. The overwhelming logic of the Holocaust – a thoroughly illogical event, by definition – is that the moral compromises it forced provide us with a clearer understanding of what it is that makes up the complexity of the human psyche. And in many instances, this is far from pleasant.

An examination of John K. Roth's output of edited works, books and articles reveals a deep sensitivity to the Jewish people, but also more than that. He has always been faithful to the historical truths of the Holocaust in order to expose the dreadful potential it carries for contemporary society. He has sought at every opportunity to unite Christians and Jews in a healing understanding of that event, while at the same time he has been a passionate critic of the failures of Christianity. And in the philosophical study of ethics relative to the Holocaust – an area he pioneered in the face of a dearth of such material – he has sought to provide ways of understanding that have been highly influential in extending discussion and exposing others to issues of which they might otherwise have been unaware.

Roth's major writings

A Consuming Fire: Encounters with Elie Wiesel and the Holocaust, Atlanta: John Knox Press, 1979.

(with Richard L. Rubenstein) *Approaches to Auschwitz: The Holocaust and Its Legacy*, Atlanta: John Knox Press, 1987.

(Ed. with Michael Berenbaum) *Holocaust: Religious and Philosophical Implications*, St. Paul (MN): Paragon House, 1989.

(Ed. with Carol Rittner) *Memory Offended: The Auschwitz Convent Controversy*, New York: Praeger, 1991.

(Ed. with Carol Rittner) *Different Voices: Women and the Holocaust*, St. Paul (MN): Paragon House, 1993.

(Ed. with Carol Rittner) *From the Unthinkable to the Unavoidable: American Christian and Jewish Scholars Encounter the Holocaust*, Westport (CT): Praeger, 1997.

(Ed. with Stephen R. Haynes) *The Death of God Movement and the Holocaust: Radical Theology Encounters the Shoah*, Westport (CT): Greenwood Press, 1999a.

Ethics after the Holocaust: Perspectives, Critiques, and Responses, St. Paul (MN): Paragon House, 1999b.

Holocaust Politics, Louisville (KY): Westminster John Knox Press, 2001a.

(Ed. with Carol Rittner) *'Good News' After Auschwitz? Christian Faith within a Post-Holocaust World*, Macon (GA): Mercer University Press, 2001b.

(Ed. with Carol Rittner and James M. Smith) *Will Genocide Ever End?*, St. Paul (MN): Paragon House, 2002a.

(Ed. with Carol Rittner) *Pope Pius XII and the Holocaust*, Leicester: Leicester University Press, 2002b.

(Ed. with David Patterson) *After-Words: Post-Holocaust Struggles with Forgiveness, Reconciliation, Justice*, Seattle: University of Washington Press, 2004a.

(Ed. with Carol Rittner and Wendy Whitworth) *Genocide in Rwanda: Complicity of the Churches?* St. Paul (MN): Paragon House, 2004b.

(Ed.) *Genocide and Human Rights: A Philosophical Guide*, New York: Palgrave Macmillan, 2005a.

(Ed. with Jonathan Petropoulos) *Gray Zones: Ambiguity and Compromise in the Holocaust and its Aftermath*, New York: Berghahn Books, 2005b.

(Ed. with Jennifer L. Geddes and Jules Simon) *The Double Binds of Ethics after the Holocaust*, London: Palgrave Macmillan, 2010.

Reference

Levi, Primo, *The Drowned and the Saved*, London: Sphere Books, 1989.

RICHARD L. RUBENSTEIN (b. 1924)

One of the doyens of philosophical and theological reflection on the question of God in light of the Holocaust, Richard Lowell Rubenstein has, in large part, helped to define the agenda of post-Holocaust theology. President Emeritus and Distinguished Professor of Religion at the University of Bridgeport, Connecticut, and Lawton Distinguished Professor Emeritus of Religion at Florida State University, he was born in New York City in 1924, the eldest son of an assimilated Jewish family. In 1942 he began his academic education at Hebrew Union College, Ohio, but became disillusioned with the nature of the curriculum. Finishing his undergraduate studies at the University of Cincinnati, he moved to the Conservative movement's Jewish Theological Seminary (New York), from which he obtained his rabbinic ordination in 1952. He then studied at Harvard Divinity School, where he was awarded a Master of Sacred Theology, and obtained his PhD with a dissertation on the psychoanalytic understanding of rabbinic legends. Rubenstein's roles throughout this period included the position of pulpit rabbi of two congregations in Massachusetts, and as Jewish chaplain at Harvard University, Radcliffe and Wellesley Colleges, and Director of the B'nai B'rith Hillel Foundation and chaplain to the Jewish students at the University of Pittsburgh, Carnegie-Mellon University and Duquesne University. In 1970 he moved to Florida State University, where he remained until 1995, when he took up the position of President of the University of Bridgeport.

In 1966 Rubenstein published a work that was simultaneously to change the nature of Holocaust thought and alter the future direction of his own life. *After Auschwitz: Radical Theology and Contemporary Judaism* explored radical theological frontiers in Jewish thought and was a significant discussion on the meaning and impact of the

Holocaust for Judaism. For Rubenstein, the Holocaust exploded the traditional Judaic concept of God, especially the God of the Covenant with Abraham. He asserted that 'We stand in a cold, silent, unfeeling cosmos, unaided by any purposeful power beyond our own resources'; in view of that, he asked, 'After Auschwitz, what else can a Jew say about God?' (Rubenstein, 1966: 152). He adjudged that not many of those around him had thus far realised that the Holocaust – which he encapsulated within the paradigmatic image of Auschwitz – had altered, even destroyed, the basis upon which Jewish faith had hitherto always rested. In the simplest of terms, he asked, 'How can Jews believe in an omnipotent, beneficent God after Auschwitz?' (Rubenstein, 1966: 153). The classical Jewish explanations for the conundrum of undeserved suffering in light of an omnipotent, omnipresent and Covenantal God had, until the *Shoah*, always been able to address this through reference to forms of interpretation that put the onus back on the Jewish people themselves, usually through divine retribution for sin. But here was an experience that was so immense, and caused the death and suffering of so many people, that punishment for sin could not possibly have explained it all. Further, its very magnitude had elevated it into a category of evil that stood alone when compared to all other catastrophes that had befallen the Jewish people. The thought that a benevolent and compassionate God could send Hitler was 'too obscene' for Rubenstein to accept (Rubenstein, 1966: 153). In the biblical Book of Job, the protagonist, a virtuous man who still believed in God no matter what sufferings he endured, had the truth of his ordeal revealed to him by God through a discourse that effectively explained that the magnitude of God's ultimate purpose could not be understood by mere humans; they could only view their own small part in the overall picture, but the ultimate reward, for all humanity, would be worth it in the end (Job, 42: 1-6). For Rubenstein, what happened to European Jewry during the Holocaust, by contrast, 'cannot be likened to the testing of Job' (Rubenstein, 1966: 153), as the evil of the German death camps seemed so purposeless that to see God's hand in it defies credulity. To portray what happened as an expression of God's will, therefore, would be to maintain that God *wanted* Auschwitz, a notion that for Rubenstein was utterly repugnant.

Rubenstein argued that the Holocaust overturned traditional Jewish teaching regarding the God of History, and a void now existed where previously the Jewish people experienced God's presence. In the original Covenant between God and Israel, an omnipotent deity would look to the interests of the Jewish people in exchange for their fidelity to His laws. The God of Israel was the God of History, but Rubenstein argued that as a result of the *Shoah* Jews could no longer advocate the notion of an omnipotent God at work. Further, the Covenant was now irretrievably broken, and no more could the Jews see themselves as the Chosen People. In the wake of the Holocaust, life had to be lived on its own terms; there was no ultimate meaning, no hidden truth waiting to be revealed at the End of Days.

This 'death of God' notion did not, however, mean that Rubenstein abandoned the idea of divinity. The God of History might no longer exist, and the Covenant might be broken forever, but Rubenstein did not replace God with atheism:

> When I say we live in the time of the death of God, I mean that the thread uniting God and man, Heaven and earth, has been broken. We stand in a cold, silent, unfeeling cosmos, unaided by any powerful power beyond our own resources.
>
> (Rubenstein, 1966: 151–52)

In short, Rubenstein's revolutionary book attacked belief in the God of History, the notions of Covenant and divine election, and the idea embedded in theodicy that God's goodness and justice, in the face of the existence of evil, could be defended. It was as much controversial as it was fascinating; no theologian, Jewish or Christian, had ever before attacked these beliefs with such passion or vehemence. *After Auschwitz* was an innovative, controversial work, suggesting that the bases upon which all previous belief had rested for the past three millennia were in fact fatally flawed. The book caused outrage in many circles, though Rubenstein's thinking was appropriate for its time, coming a generation after the Holocaust itself and in a decade when questions were being asked about all manner of existential realities which had previously been unchallenged. Its influence was considerable, and generated intense debate within theological and philosophical circles. It is generally agreed today that *After Auschwitz* initiated most future discussion on the implications of the Holocaust for Jewish religious thought, and for many this led to a re-evaluation of the meaning of belief. Jewish thinkers such as Irving Greenberg, **Emil Fackenheim** and Arthur A. Cohen, and Christian scholars such as **A. Roy Eckardt**, **Harry James Cargas**, **Franklin H. Littell** and **John K. Roth** (among many others) were all influenced or in some way affected by Rubenstein's arguments. *After Auschwitz* took the Jewish community by storm, and established Rubenstein's name as a major thinker. It also outraged many among the Jewish religious establishment, and shunted Rubenstein into something of a theological wilderness for the rest of his career.

Within the academy, however, he was considered an original thinker and iconoclast worthy of respect. *After Auschwitz* was such a profound piece of writing that his next few books, though attracting notice, were not received with anything like the same degree of critical acclaim as his first. It was to be several years before the appearance of his next important book. *The Cunning of History: Mass Death and the American Future* (1975) drew him back to his earlier arguments about the Nazi Holocaust, this time looking at the nature of the society created by man rather than by God. In what was a profound argument, Rubenstein concluded that the *Shoah* was a supreme expression of modernity, and of how Enlightenment reason and industrial knowledge could lead to mass murder – the ultimate articulation of secularisation, modern planning, bureaucracy and technical development in the service of national and racial cohesion. In short, the onset of modernity laid the foundation, and the realisation of the modern bureaucratic state provided the means. As he explained, accompanying these developments was a trend in the unfolding European story towards viewing certain segments of a given population as expendable. Unwanted people could henceforth be 'processed' in the same manner as any other unwelcome commodity, and it was here that Rubenstein's title – the *cunning* of history – became most clearly apparent. History, he asserted, is cunning because it deceives us; offered the best the world had to offer, that 'best' proved to be a chimera when corrupted in unscrupulous hands.

Rubenstein developed some of these ideas in *The Age of Triage: Fear and Hope in an Overcrowded World* (1983), which was an examination of the history of the destruction of unwanted populations. It looked at events as diverse as the Holocaust, the Irish Famine of the 1840s, the Enclosure Movement in Tudor England in the sixteenth century, and the Vietnamese Boat People in the 1970s. The study proceeded from an examination of so-called surplus humans, those people in any modern society who 'for any reason can find no viable role in the society in which [they are] domiciled' (Rubenstein, 1983: 1). Once more, the idea was that modernity had a lot to answer for, and that the march of 'progress' was not always linear and upwards. The book provided a highly original way in which to account for the preconditions for genocide, and offered Rubenstein to a broader audience as an important contributor to secular ideas, as distinct from the theological dimension for which he was already well known.

In the years that followed, Rubenstein was in demand as a writer of scholarly articles in anthologies and edited works, and he appeared at academic conferences all over the world as a featured speaker.

In 1987, together with a Christian scholar from California, **John K. Roth**, he produced *Approaches to Auschwitz*, a study exploring the continuing significance of the Holocaust and the various ways in which it has been studied. It sought to clarify the political, historical and economic roots of the *Shoah* without losing sight of the complexities of its history, and in so doing it analysed the Holocaust's definitive impact on human civilisation and its unparalleled importance in determining the fate of the world. Intended as a text for students, the book was a thought-provoking study of the *Shoah* from a number of different disciplinary perspectives.

The book's penultimate chapter, 'God and History: Philosophical and Religious Responses to the Holocaust', took Rubenstein back to his original ideas from *After Auschwitz*, through a quick survey of some other authors who had since considered the same issues he had back in 1966. Rubenstein described the personal and academic experiences he had undergone as a young scholar and rabbi that had led him to conclude that the God of History must be denied owing to the Holocaust. Here, he again argued that notions of Covenant and divine election are destructive theologies, and reaffirmed the statements about the death of the Covenantal God that he had made more than two decades before.

In 2010 – at an age when many authors would otherwise have ceased writing – Rubenstein produced *Jihad and Genocide*, a work he considered to be his most important since *After Auschwitz*. Here he examined the historic relationship between radical Islamist *jihad* and genocide, looking closely at the many violent expressions of *jihad* that have occurred over the past century, from the Armenian Genocide to current genocidal threats to Israel from Iran, with much in between. In a carefully researched examination, he considered the potential for radical Islamists to initiate targeted – indeed, genocidal – violence justified by the religious obligation for *jihad*. Again, Rubenstein showed himself prepared to court controversy, this time when the raising of such issues was accompanied by a sense of urgency throughout the world.

Richard L. Rubenstein has been an innovative thinker whose approach to Judaism and religion in light of the most destructive period of human history and arguably the most murderous sustained assault any people has faced shook the religious tradition he addressed and from which he came. His books and articles, which have been translated into languages as diverse as French, German, Russian, Japanese, Korean, Italian, Hungarian, Dutch, Swedish, Polish and Hebrew, have been at once vilified and praised, dismissed and embraced. His notions about 'surplus people', moreover, have shown him to be a multi-dimensional thinker who is as much at ease in discussing history and sociology as he is with theology. As one of the tiny number of those who were at the cutting edge of serious philosophical and theological reflection on the Holocaust at its inception, Rubenstein's overall contribution to the field has been (and remains) creative, powerful, controversial and highly profound.

Rubenstein's major writings

After Auschwitz: Radical Theology and Contemporary Judaism, Indianapolis: Bobbs-Merrill, 1966.
Morality and Eros, New York: McGraw-Hill, 1970.
Power Struggle: An Autobiographical Confession, New York: Scribner, 1974.
The Cunning of History: Mass Death and the American Future, New York: Harper and Row, 1975.
The Age of Triage: Fear and Hope in an Overcrowded World, Boston: Beacon, 1983.
(with John K. Roth), *Approaches to Auschwitz: The Holocaust and Its Legacy*, Atlanta: John Knox Press, 1987.
Jihad and Genocide, Lanham (MD): Rowman and Littlefield, 2010.

RUDOLPH J. RUMMEL (b. 1932)

Rudolph J. Rummel is an Emeritus Professor of Political Science at the University of Hawaii-Manoa. Born in 1932 in Cleveland, Ohio, he was educated at the University of Hawaii and Northwestern University, Illinois, where he obtained his PhD in Political Science in 1963. In 1966 he returned to the University of Hawaii, where he remained until his retirement in 1995. In 1996 he became Professor Emeritus in the Department of Political Science there.

As a scholar and writer, Rummel has produced a lengthy list of influential publications on war, mass murder and destructive regimes. His earlier work, while providing an indication of where his interests lay, was not so much concerned with genocide as with research methods and quantitative-statistical analysis. His ongoing contribution to the field of Genocide Studies, however, has concerned the relationship between totalitarian regimes, genocide and democracy. Throughout his career he has devoted himself to assembling data on collective violence and war, and has consistently drawn the conclusion that states that are governed on well-established principles of democracy do not engage in mass collective violence towards their own citizens or those of other states. According to Rummel, knowledge of this fact, and its dissemination, is the major means by which genocidal violence can be eliminated. Democracy, in this schema, is thus the form of government least likely to kill its own (or others') citizens, and in a series of case studies appearing in the 1990s Rummel demonstrated the extent to which this fundamental premise of his work could be verified.

Rummel is perhaps best known for coining the term 'democide' as a way to extend the definition of genocide to embrace other examples of mass killing not otherwise covered as criminal acts in international law. His term designates the murder of any person, or group of people, by government. This can include genocide, mass murder or what Rummel refers to as politicide, that is, government-sponsored killings for political reasons. Rummel also considers any deaths caused through intentional governmental neglect or disregard of the lives of its citizens, with some kind of ultimate destructive objective in mind. Capital punishment, civilian deaths in a war zone and military deaths in combat are excluded from his definition. Rummel has two kinds of mass killing in mind. The first is the product of nuclear warfare, which entirely eliminates the distinction between combatant and civilian by the scope of the destructive violence it unleashes. (In this regard, he is in agreement with other scholars such as **Robert Jay Lifton** and **Eric Markusen**.) The same can be said of the potential of chemical and biological weapons, as any future war resorting to these weapons would likely claim untold millions of casualties, dead and wounded. Democide has the potential of thoroughly disrupting urban and rural life to the point that the survivors will be left with no basic society or culture to salvage. It is destruction well beyond that wreaked by genocide or other forms of political, social and cultural devastation.

A second application of the term democide characterises the massive collective destruction that took place throughout the twentieth century. Between 1900 and 2000 there was a huge increase in what Rummel refers to as 'megadeaths' by human hands. Colonial wars, the two World Wars, civil wars and revolutions collectively killed scores of millions, as if the human race were at war with itself. Yet while these events all had genocidal attributes, they need not in every situation be considered as genocide per se, but are more accurately trans-genocidal, that is, something *more* than genocide. The 1994 Rwandan Genocide had certain aspects of this phenomenon: not only were Tutsis targeted for annihilation, but so were the Hutus belonging to the political opposition. Hence, democide considers the idea of 'genocide plus', that is, genocide with an additional dimension to mass killing. The term *megacide* has served as a substitute for democide: the former focuses on quantity, whereas the latter brings to mind the human quality of killing humankind to the point of extinction. Democide, in Rummel's view, is far less likely to occur in democratic states than in those that are authoritarian, totalitarian or absolute. He argues strongly that political power and democide are intimately connected, such that the more absolute a regime, the greater its propensity for democide. Thus, he concludes, truly democratic regimes should be encouraged at all costs if democide is to be reduced (and, hopefully, eradicated).

Although Rummel's prodigious scholarly output has continually emphasised the key point that totalitarian polities are more likely to kill their own and others' citizens, the fundamental studies he produced in the 1990s saw the clearest articulation of his arguments. These can be addressed briefly in turn here.

In *Lethal Politics: Soviet Genocides and Mass Murders 1917–1987* (1990), Rummel's first foray into a dedicated area study dealing with genocide/democide, he revealed that every Soviet leader, from Lenin to Gorbachev, waged war of some sort against their own population. Atrocities were carried out against entire populations, whether through massacre, state-induced famine (as in the *Holodomor*, or terror-famine, in Ukraine in the 1930s), or through the slave-labour horrors of the gulag. In order to underscore his argument, Rummel introduced a comprehensive statistical analysis to reach a conclusion as to the number consumed by the Soviet state across its seven-decade-plus duration. His chilling deduction reached a figure of nearly 62 million killed as a result of state actions since 1917.

Rummel followed up *Lethal Politics* with a second book on communist destructiveness, *China's Bloody Century: Genocide and Mass Murder Since 1900* (1991). A much longer book than *Lethal Politics*, it showed that no people in the twentieth century had experienced as much mass killing at the hands of their own government as had the Chinese. Such killing took many forms: murdered by rebels conniving with their own rulers; defeated in wars against a variety of imperial powers; killed by warlords who ruled various parts of China in the 1920s and 1930s; or put to death by Nationalists or

Communists for political reasons. He broke down the number of those killed, and the different regimes under which their lives were lost, as follows:

1. Transformation and the Nationalist Struggle, 1900 to September 1949
   105,000 victims: Dynastic and Republican China
   632,000 victims: Warlord China
   2,724,000 victims: The Nationalist Period
   10,216,000 victims: The Sino-Japanese War
   3,949,000 victims: Japanese Mass Murder in China
   4,968,000 victims: The Civil War
2. The People's Republic of China
   8,427,000 victims: The Totalisation Period
   7,474,000 victims: Collectivisation and 'The Great Leap Forward'
   10,729,000 victims: The Great Famine and Retrenchment Period
   17,731,000 victims: The 'Cultural Revolution'
   874,000 victims: Liberalisation

(http://www.hawaii.edu/powerkills)

The grand total was 62,829,000. Subsequently, he revised two of these figures upwards. For the period of the Great Famine (1958–62), he recalculated a figure of 38,000,000, resulting in a further overall revision for the People's Republic of China era (1928–87) from 38,702,000 to 76,702,000. The result was a staggering total combined death figure, across the twentieth century, of 104,296,000.

How can such a massive death rate across less than a century be explained? It transcended the lines of ideology and politics, and took place during times of both peace and war. In Rummel's view, the one constant factor was the arbitrary use of unchecked power without accountability. He argued that whenever such power is centralised and irresponsible, the likelihood exists that it will be corrupted – often violently – so as to enable the leaders to achieve their own ends. It was the first time anyone had attempted in a systematic fashion to assess the nature of Chinese governments' destructiveness vis-à-vis their own people, and it was a damning indictment of how unaccountable power without redress can act according to utterly devastating (and frequently inexplicable) norms.

While in dealing with the Soviet and Chinese situations Rummel was addressing himself to the perceived commonalities of communism, in *Democide: Nazi Genocide and Mass Murder* (1992) Rummel turned to the Nazis in Germany between 1933 and 1945. This book documented in great detail a long list of estimates in order to look at the mass killing of civilians under the Third Reich. Rummel offered a mid-estimate that for him seemed the most plausible, totalling 20,946,000 deaths caused through direct Nazi actions. The huge number represented deaths which took place in a variety of ways: the murder of hostages; reprisal raids; medical experiments under inhuman conditions; deaths while at forced labour; so-called medical killing during the 'Euthanasia' or 'T-4' campaign; forced starvation in ghettos and camps; exposure owing to Nazi methods of incarceration or during death marches in 1944–45; terror bombing of civilian centres during the war; and, of course, deaths in concentration camps of all kinds, including extermination camps. Rummel employed a similar statistical method as he did for the books on the Soviet Union and China. Where the Holocaust was concerned, he took every credible estimate he could find and assessed them in order to compute a low, middle and high estimate for the number of Jews killed. His mid-range estimate came out at 5,291,000.

The books mentioned above specifically detailed governmental mass murder in three of the leading totalitarian states. In *Death by Government: Genocide and Mass Murder in the Twentieth Century* (1994), Rummel took his task one step further by summarising the overall effect of government on the world during this time. He focused in detail on those governments around the world which have killed 1,000,000 or more people, and in a follow-up volume, *Statistics of Democide: Estimates, Sources, and Calculations on Twentieth Century Genocide and Mass Murder* (1997), he presented the evidence for his conclusions.

The very first words of *Death by Government* stated what Rummel referred to as the new Power Principle: 'Power kills; absolute Power kills absolutely' (Rummel, 1994: 1). From this, he introduced the notion of states or regimes that committed 'megamurders', that is, 'those states killing in cold blood, aside from warfare, 1 million or more men, women and children'. His deduction was alarming: 'These fifteen megamurders have wiped out over 151 million people, almost four times the almost 38,500,000 battle dead from all this century's international and civil wars up to 1987' (Rummel, 1994: 3). Four totalitarian regimes, furthermore, were responsible for *dekamegamurders*, that is, were each responsible, *on their own*, for over ten million deaths. For the statistically minded, these were the USSR (1917–87), 61,911,000; Communist China (1949–87), 35,236,000; Nazi Germany (1933–45), 20,946,000; and Nationalist China (1928–49), 10,076,000. He followed these up with a list of what he referred to as the 'lesser megamurdering states': Japan (1936–45), 5,964,000; Cambodia (1975–79), 2,035,000; Turkey (1909–18), 1,883,000; Vietnam (1945–87), 1,678,000; North Korea (1948–87), 1,663,000; Poland (1945–48), 1,585,000; Pakistan (1958–87), 1,503,000; Mexico (1900–20), 1,417,000; Yugoslavia (1944–87), 1,072,000; Tsarist Russia (1900–17), 1,066,000.

Rummel then proceeded with a series of chapters on each of these megamurdering states, examining how it was that mass murder could take place there. His conclusion reaffirmed his earlier statements:

> The more power a government has, the more it can act arbitrarily according to the whims and desires of the elite, and the more it will make war on others and murder its foreign and domestic subjects. The more constrained the power of governments, the more power is diffused, checked, and balanced, the less it will aggress on others and commit democide. At the extremes of Power, totalitarian communist governments slaughter their people by the tens of *millions*; in contrast, many democracies can barely bring themselves to execute even serial murderers.
>
> (Rummel, 1994: 1–2, emphasis in original)

There was only one possible conclusion that could be drawn from this: 'The way to end war and virtually eliminate democide appears to be through restricting and checking Power, i.e., through *fostering democratic freedom*' (Rummel, 1994: 27, emphasis in original).

The notion of the 'democractic peace' was not new, though Rummel was (and remains) one of its strongest supporters. The idea was first put forth by an American sociologist and criminologist, Dean Babst, who in 1964 wrote the first academic paper employing statistical data arguing that democracies do not fight among themselves. Rummel, for his part, had studied all international conflicts resulting in a toll of at least a thousand deaths, and found that in the period between 1816 and 2005 there were 205 wars between non-democracies, 166 wars between non-democracies and democracies, and no wars between well-established democracies (http://www.hawaii.edu/powerkills). Inescapably, no judgement could lead in any other direction than that democracy has to be considered the most effective force for deterring the emergence of violent and genocidal situations. Rummel's hypothesis, cultivated over nearly four decades of careful research, was abstracted in his summative volume *Power Kills: Democracy as a Means of Nonviolence* (1997b). He articulated five essential points in order to establish his core arguments:

1. well-established democracies do not make war on and rarely commit lesser violence against each other;
2. the more two nations are democratic, the less likely war or lesser violence between them;
3. the more a nation is democratic, the less severe its overall foreign violence;
4. the more democratic a nation, the less likely it will have domestic collective violence; and
5. the more democratic a nation, the less its democide, that is, all and any murders committed by official agencies when acting under state instructions.

(Rummel, 1997b: 4–5)

By confining his analysis to 'well-established democracies', Rummel was able to dismiss regimes that either (a) refer to themselves as democracies, but are in fact dictatorships (as with the so-called communist People's Democracies of the Cold War era); or (b) are still in the process of becoming democratic, with sectional aggression and violence still playing a part in the public culture of the state.

The idea of the democratic peace thus clearly feeds directly into concepts concerning genocide prevention; put succinctly, the more democracies exist in the world, the less likely both war and genocide are to occur. This theory of the democratic peace has its detractors, particularly from those of the political left, and criticisms have been put on two basic levels: first, that democracies such as the United States, Canada, Australia and the like are founded on genocidal dispossession of indigenous populations; and second, that so-called First World nations such as those previously mentioned, as well as many European states, have engaged (and still engage) in genocidal practices against other, less developed nations. What such critics miss, however, is the fact that the essential relationship in such instances is never between states which all are well-established democracies, which is what the democratic peace idea requires.

The twentieth century was the most murderously violent in history. Over the last four decades, it might be argued, no scholar has done more to promote understanding about the true causes of that violence than Rudolph J. Rummel. Mobilising every resource available to him, he has not only traced its contours and the statistical devastation it has wrought; he has also offered a convincing argument as to what is for him the only possible solution and hope for the future, namely, that democracy, as a method of non-violence, must be valued, fought for and nurtured at every turn. As an inescapable reflection on the world in which we live, this conclusion – which might seem obvious – exists largely as a result of Rummel's indefatigable labours, and the influence his thinking has had on a large number of other scholars and teachers, whether directly or vicariously.

Rummel's major writings

Understanding Conflict and War, vols. 1–5, Beverly Hills (CA): Sage, 1975–81:
Vol. 1: *The Dynamic Psychological Field*, 1975.
Vol. 2: *The Conflict Helix*, 1976.
Vol. 3: *Conflict in Perspective*, 1977.
Vol. 4: *War, Power, Peace*, 1979.
Vol. 5: *The Just Peace*, 1981.
Lethal Politics: Soviet Genocides and Mass Murders 1917–1987, Rutgers (NJ): Transaction Publishers, 1990.
China's Bloody Century: Genocide and Mass Murder since 1900, Rutgers (NJ): Transaction Publishers, 1991.
Democide: Nazi Genocide and Mass Murder, Rutgers (NJ): Transaction Publishers, 1992.
Death by Government: Genocide and Mass Murder in the Twentieth Century, New Brunswick (NJ): Transaction Publishers, 1994.
'Democracies ARE less warlike than other regimes', *European Journal of International Relations*, 1 (December 1995), 457–79.
Statistics on Democide, Charlottesville (VA): Center on National Security and Law, University of Virginia, 1997a.
Power Kills: Democracy as a Means of Nonviolence, New Brunswick (NJ): Transaction Publishers, 1997b.
Saving Lives, Enriching Life: Freedom as a Right, and a Moral Good, at http://www.hawaii.edu/powerkills/htm, 2001.
'From the Study of War and Revolution to Democide – Power Kills', in Samuel Totten and Steven Leonard Jacobs (eds), *Pioneers of Genocide Studies*, New Brunswick (NJ): Transaction Publishers, 2002, 153–77.
The *Never Again* series (http://www.hawaii.edu/powerkills):

War & Democide Never Again, Book 1.
Nuclear Holocaust Never Again, Book 2.
Reset Never Again, Book 3.
Red Terror Never Again, Book 4.
Genocide Never Again, Book 5.
Never Again?, Book 6.

Never Again: Ending War, Democide, and Famine through Democratic Freedom (non-fiction supplement to the *Never Again* series, 2006).

WILLIAM SCHABAS (b. 1950)

William Schabas is Director of the Irish Centre for Human Rights at the National University of Ireland, Galway, where he holds the chair in Human Rights Law. A prolific author in the areas of international criminal and human-rights law, he is perhaps the world's most authoritative expert on the international law of genocide, as well as on international human rights law and the death penalty.

Born in Cleveland, Ohio in 1950, he was educated at the Universities of Toronto and Montréal. Between 1985 and 2005 he was a lawyer serving as a member of the Québec Bar. He acted as counsel in litigation before the Supreme Court of the United States, the Supreme Court of Canada, the United Nations Human Rights Committee and the Inter-American Commission of Human Rights, as well as in various Canadian courts. In 1995–96 he was Senior Policy Advisor at the International Centre for Human Rights and Democratic Development, Montréal, and between 1996 and 2000 an Assessor at the Québec Human Rights Tribunal. In May 2002, the President of Sierra Leone appointed Schabas to that country's Truth and Reconciliation Commission. A university academic as well as a human-rights lawyer of international repute, he taught at the Université du Québec à Montréal between 1991 and 2001, and in 2000 was appointed Professor of Human Rights Law and Director of the Irish Centre for Human Rights at the National University of Ireland, Galway.

From the outset, Schabas showed an interest in human-rights affairs, and as a jurist his initial concern lay with both the morality and the legality of the death penalty. In *The Abolition of the Death Penalty in International Law* (1993), he outlined how the movement towards the abolition of the death penalty in international law developed, and discussed not only how the UN network of human-rights instruments operates, but also the intricacies of international humanitarian law, European human-rights law, and Inter-American human-rights law. The book stamped Schabas as one who was thorough and sensitive not only to issues, but also to both the letter and spirit of the law. While never departing from his concerns regarding the death penalty – the book would subsequently appear in a second, then third, edition, and spin off into a number of other related projects – by the end of the 1990s Schabas turned his attention to the question of genocide in international law, and to how an international anti-genocide legal regime could be (indeed, already was being) created.

The key to understanding Schabas's views on genocide lies in his definitive perspective that genocide is first and foremost a criminal act. In his imposing study *Genocide in International Law* (2000) – an authoritative guide to the interpretation and application of genocide in international law – Schabas did more than just review the processes accompanying the drafting of the 1948 United Nations Convention on Genocide and its interpretation, as might be expected in most legal texts. He also considered the many additional definitions that have arisen regarding the term, as well as how the crime is committed, how alleged perpetrators have offered defences for their actions, and what responsibilities states have with regard to processes of extradition and their obligations as signatories to the Convention. Schabas focused on the judicial interpretation of the Convention, relying on debates in the International Law Commission and political statements in bodies like the UN General Assembly, as well as the growing body of case law that has emerged in the years since the end of the Second World War. He also gave attention to the groups protected under the UN Convention on Genocide; to problems of criminal prosecution; and to issues of international judicial cooperation such as those relating to extradition. In the second edition of the book, published in 2009, he also dealt with the international duty to prevent genocide, particularly with regard to the much newer doctrine known as 'the responsibility to protect'.

Among the many features of genocide discussed by Schabas were acts not covered in the Genocide Convention that are often confused with it in more popular interpretations. Hence, he discussed the notions of cultural genocide, 'ethnic cleansing', ecocide, apartheid and nuclear killing (what **Robert Jay Lifton** and **Eric Markusen** referred to in their own analysis as 'nuclear omnicide'). He was particularly critical of the term 'ethnic cleansing', then in current usage owing to the war horrors that had taken place in Bosnia between 1992 and 1995. The United Nations General Assembly (A/RES/47/121), on 18 December 1992, had concluded that 'mass expulsions of defenceless civilians from their homes' had taken place, alongside 'the existence in Serbian and Montenegrin controlled areas of concentration camps and detention centres in pursuit of the abhorrent policy of "ethnic cleansing," *which is a form of genocide*' (http://www.un.org/documents/ga/res/47/a47r121/htm, emphasis added). Schabas took issue with this from a strictly legal point of view, noting that the UN's perspective was 'troublesome'. He commented that as 'there is no generally recognised text defining ethnic cleansing, the various attempts by jurists, diplomats and scholars concur that it is aimed at displacing a population in order to change the ethnic composition of a given territory, and generally to render the territory ethnically homogeneous or "pure." Plainly, this is not the same thing as genocide, which is directed at the destruction of the group'. Thus, he concluded, 'it is incorrect to assert that ethnic cleansing is a form of genocide, or even that in some cases, ethnic cleansing amounts to genocide. Both, of course, may share the same goal, which is to eliminate the persecuted group from a given area.' That said, however, 'While the material acts performed to commit the crimes may often resemble each other, they have two quite different specific intents. One is intended to displace a population, the other to destroy it.' In his view, 'the issue is one of intent and it is logically inconceivable that the two agendas coexist.' This is not to say that there is no relationship between the two; rather, he argued, ethnic cleansing can be viewed as a possible portent of genocide to come, particularly if the targeted population refuses to move or does not relocate fast enough. Under such circumstances, perpetrators may well decide to remove their victims through killing, such that 'Genocide is the last resort of the frustrated ethnic cleanser' (Schabas, 2000: 199–201).

Against this context, Schabas was able to bring legal perspectives to a number of individual cases of massive human-rights violations in Bosnia, Cambodia, Ukraine, Latin America and elsewhere. The necessity of establishing a legal determination was, as he saw it, vital; after all, in the first instance genocide is a crime, and, as such, if responsibility is to be ascribed, the crime must first be proven to the highest possible standards and in accordance with the legislation – in this case, the UN Genocide Convenion – that proscribes it. For Schabas, this is more than just a matter of academic convenience; it is at the core of how genocide is to be prevented and punished.

Schabas followed up his study of genocide law with a pathbreaking investigation of the International Criminal Court (ICC), created on 17 July 1998 after 120 UN member states became parties to the Rome Statute that authorised its establishment. In *An Introduction to the International Criminal Court* (2001) Schabas described a number of important aspects of the new court: the historical context of prosecutions for massive human-rights violations, from the ancient Greeks to the present day; the nature of the crimes that would be prosecuted by the ICC; how trials would be conducted; what the appeals procedure would be; the nature of punishment for those found guilty; the rights of victims; and – a vital consideration in view of the court's international composition – how the court would be administered. Schabas reflected on the three categories of crime over which the

ICC would preside, namely, crimes against humanity, war crimes and genocide. He noted that in the UN Genocide Convention the General Assembly had recognised back in 1948 the first two categories, particularly crimes against humanity, as violations that were most likely to take place during periods of armed international conflict. The UN preference at that time was instead to elevate genocide to a distinct category, and recognise that it would still constitute an international crime even if committed during a period of peace. By 1998, on the other hand, 'the recognized definition of crimes against humanity has evolved and now unquestionably refers to atrocities committed in peacetime as well as in wartime'; given this, today, 'genocide constitutes the most aggravated form of crime against humanity' (Schabas, 2001: 30). Hence we see, especially in the aftermath of Rwanda in 1994 and Bosnia between 1992 and 1995, the close attention paid by the ICC to this specific crime.

Schabas was also interested in clarifying another issue current at the time of the court's establishment, namely, the questioned need for such a tribunal in light of the prior existence of the International Court of Justice (ICJ). For Schabas, there was no difficulty here:

> The ICJ is the court where States litigate matters relating to their disputes as States. The role of individuals before the ICJ is marginal, at best. ... [N]ot only does the ICC provide for prosecution and punishment of individuals, it also recognizes a legitimate participation for the individual as victim. In a more general sense, the ICC is concerned, essentially, with matters that might generally be described as serious human rights violations. The ICJ, on the other hand, spends much of its judicial time on delimiting international boundaries and fishing zones, and similar matters.
>
> (Schabas, 2001: viii)

Despite the fact that 'the ICJ finds itself increasingly involved in human rights matters', it is because of its state-to-state focus, and because of the large number of *non*-human rights issues with which it has to deal, that the ICJ could not be transformed into a tribunal to preside over the same issues as the new International Criminal Court.

In *War Crimes and Human Rights* (2008), Schabas collected together a number of his essays and articles on human-rights law and international criminal law, in particular relating to a wide variety of topics among which were the death penalty, genocide and crimes against humanity, the establishment and operation of the ICC and the International Criminal Tribunals for the former Yugoslavia and

Rwanda, the scope and effectiveness of truth and reconciliation commissions, terrorism and the implementation of international human-rights norms in domestic law. Once more, he showed that questions of jurisprudence, to be effective, had to be rooted in the law, and that when criticism of that law was needed, it should be made.

Prior to William Schabas's work on genocide, the majority of academic research in the area had been undertaken by historians, political scientists or (less frequently) philosophers. Most scholarship, as he saw it, 'frequently ventured onto judicial terrain, not so much to interpret the [Genocide Convention] and to wrestle with the legal intricacies of the definition as to express frustration with its limitations' (Schabas, 2000: 7). It was the state of the world towards the end of the twentieth century that changed this, as people saw an urgent need both to clarify how the Convention was to be used, and then to put it into concrete operation. Schabas's own recognition was that 'The issue is no longer one of stretching the Convention to apply to circumstances for which it was never meant, but rather one of implementing the Convention in the very cases contemplated by its drafters in 1948' (Schabas, 2000: 8–9). The crux of his huge output has been that when there is a need for justice, the law should be understood and invoked, and that, moreover, it should be the appropriate law relevant to the crime. And in view of the fact that there *is* a law directly relevant to genocide, there should be no equivocation over when and how it should be applied. That such equivocation has all too often prevailed demonstrates, in Schabas's view, that there is a greater need than ever for education about the law relating to genocide. He recognises that the legal term 'genocide' is loaded, and that it does not always fit every situation involving massive human-rights abuses. That does not, however, mean to suggest that the term should be placed into the 'too-hard' basket and never used. It is Schabas's ongoing contribution to addressing the need for this awareness that has placed him among the first rank of legal thinkers on the subject of genocide in the modern world.

Schabas's major writings

The Abolition of the Death Penalty in International Law, Cambridge: Grotius Publications, 1993 (2nd edn, 1997; 3rd edn, 2002).

(Ed. with Flavia Lattanzi) *Essays on the Rome Statute of the ICC*, vol. 1, Rome: Editrice il Sirente, 2000.

Genocide in International Law, Cambridge: Cambridge University Press, 2000 (2nd edn, 2009).

Introduction to the International Criminal Court, Cambridge: Cambridge University Press, 2001 (2nd edn, 2004; 3rd edn, 2007).

(with Michael Scharf) *Slobodan Milosevic on Trial: A Companion*, New York: Continuum, 2002.

(Ed. with Gideon Boas) *International Criminal Law Developments in the Case Law of the ICTY*, The Hague: Martinus Nijhoff Publishers, 2003.

(Ed. with Flavia Lattanzi) *Essays on the Rome Statute of the ICC*, vol. 2, Rome: Editrice il Sirente, 2004.

(Associate Editor with Dinah Shelton, Howard Adelman, Frank Chalk and Alexandre Kiss) *Encyclopedia of Genocide and Crimes against Humanity* (3 vols), Detroit: Thomson Gale, 2004.

The UN International Criminal Tribunals: the Former Yugoslavia, Rwanda and Sierra Leone, Cambridge: Cambridge University Press, 2006.

(Ed. with Ramesh Thakur and Edel Hughes) *Accountability for Atrocity*, Tokyo: UN University, 2007.

War Crimes and Human Rights: Essays on the Death Penalty, Justice and Accountability, London: Cameron May Publishers, 2008.

JACQUES SÉMELIN (b. 1951)

Jacques Sémelin is a French historian and political scientist at Sciences Po, Centre d'Etudes et de Recherches Internationales (CERI) (the Centre for International Studies and Research), and Research Director at Centre National de la Recherche Scientifique (CNRS) (the National Centre for Scientific Research). CERI-CNRS are located in Paris, where Sémelin has been a Research Fellow in Political Science since 1990.

Born in 1951 in Le Plessis Robinson (a suburb of Paris), Sémelin was educated at La Sorbonne Paris V, La Sorbonne Paris IV and the Institut d'Etudes Politiques de Paris. At the age of 16, owing to a genetic condition, he learned that the day would come some time in the future when he would lose his sight. Determined to utilise the time he had available in order to be able to pursue a fulfilling career doing something about which he cared, he sought to complete his higher education. His PhD topic considered civilian resistance in Nazi-occupied Europe, and in July 1985, as part of his research, he embarked upon a study trip to Poland in order to investigate the underground education movement there between 1941 and 1945. By that stage, his eyesight had already declined considerably.

On this trip, he visited Auschwitz for the first time. It was not initially intended that he would do so on this trip, but finding himself in Kraków for research, he felt that his close proximity to Auschwitz obligated him to go there. The visit had an unexpected consequence, in that it led him permanently to reconsider the way he looked at his own condition. As he wrote later:

> I found reasons to fight instead of complain. ... I came back from Auschwitz with newfound energy, with an even fiercer determination to defy the fate that I was promised. Who was I to complain thus about my fate, compared to everything all those unfortunate people, all those innocent human beings, had to go through, stripped bare before being herded into the gas chambers? Sure, I too could consider myself an innocent victim of the evil that had been silently attacking my eyes from birth. But I had neither been beaten, nor tortured, nor tattooed, nor shaven, nor starved, nor gassed nor burned. By comparison, my own condition suddenly appeared to me terribly insignificant.
>
> (Sémelin, 2009: 133–36; Sémelin, 2007)

Intellectually, this revelation affected the direction of all Sémelin's future work. While continuing to engage in his research on civilian resistance in wartime, he would henceforth devote his energies to the study of violence and genocide.

In 1989, he published his first major study, *Sans armes face à Hitler. Le Résistance civile en Europe (1939–1943)*, a version of his doctoral work. Published in English in 1994 as *Unarmed Against Hitler: Civil Resistance in Nazi Europe (1939–1943)*, it was more than a simple historical outline of resistance in Nazi Europe. Instead, it sought to define the basic principles that underlay civilian resistance. Addressing the question of what Europeans attempted in the quest to obstruct the Nazis as they sought to impose their ideology on European society, Sémelin examined the nature of such concepts as resistance, non-cooperation and legitimacy, as well as discussing their wider implications – not only with regard to developments during the Second World War, but also in relation to the implications of such behaviour for future proponents of non-violence in the face of aggression.

The relative success of this volume notwithstanding, by this time much of Sémelin's actual interest had moved on, to issues relating to violence, massacre and genocide. In an early consideration of this new topic, published in both French and English in 2001, he delved into the issue of massacres as a way into approaching broader questions about genocide, and this was to remain the keystone of his subsequent work in the area. He noted that:

research by political scientists on the subject of massacre is still too limited. To be sure, the subject may be treated as part of a general analysis of the political situation of a country in which one or several massacres may have taken place. However, rarely ... is 'massacre' as an object of research in and of itself taken into consideration and even less so in a comparative perspective.

(Sémelin, 2001b: 377)

It was this perceived deficiency in the literature of his own discipline that Sémelin saw a need to correct.

Prior to launching himself headlong into the area, however, Sémelin was still concerned with the general issue of social violence. Examining non-violent action and civil resistance – his preference was for the second expression – he sought a way to answer one simple question: how can ordinary people accomplish extraordinary acts by resisting without weapons, when confronted by the need to fight back? He found the answer, not in libraries or academic symposia, but at home. In response to a wide range of questions from his daughters about the challenges of day-to-day life, Sémelin developed a pedagogy for dealing, non-violently, with violent or potentially violent situations. In *Nonviolence Explained to my Children* (2002a), Sémelin addressed questions relating to general annoyances, bullying at school, sexual assault, youth violence and racism (among other issues), responding to conflict situations from an ethical and historical perspective. He explained that non-violence is not the same as passivity, but instead a means of acting that seeks to resolve conflicts, fight injustice and build lasting peace. Utilising his professional skills, he illustrated his responses with historical examples, such as from within the US Civil Rights struggle, Poland's Solidarity trade union movement and the students of Tiananmen Square in China in 1989, as well as with non-violent role models such as Martin Luther King, Jr. and Mahatma Gandhi.

Building on this, Sémelin then turned his interests more fully to genocide research. The question that most concerned him was one that had already been the focus of pioneers in the field such as **Raphael Lemkin** and **Hannah Arendt**, namely, how is it possible that ordinary people can commit extraordinary crimes? How, indeed, can we comprehend the socio-political processes that give rise to extreme violence, ethnic cleansing and genocide?

In 'Toward a Vocabulary of Massacre and Genocide' (2003b), he began to establish his ground as an authority on the concept and realities of the notion of massacre. Here, he recognised that massacre is a complex topic, requiring analysis along two main lines: first, by way of a thorough historical grounding in order to appreciate how massacres took place in the past; and second, through a consideration of what he referred to as 'trans-disciplinary openness', that is, that 'the phenomenon of massacre is in itself so complex that it calls for the contributions of several disciplines, particularly sociology, anthropology and psychology' (Sémelin, 2003b: 193–94). In a solid introductory analysis on the topic, Sémelin demonstrated the various ways in which the idea of massacre had been addressed in the past, and the areas requiring deeper treatment today. His conclusion was that much more remains to be done:

> Social science must be able to provide a better understanding of all [the points I have raised]. Having said this, these elements are still limited in their capacity to make sense of these often astonishing phenomena [i.e., genocides]. Undoubtedly the social sciences could provide a better analysis of the nature of this black hole and could surely even estimate its elementary structure. But an unknown dimension shall always remain: an implacable zone of darkness.
>
> (Sémelin, 2003b: 209)

Sémelin's subsequent work was, in effect, devoted to trying to penetrate that zone.

The main question directing him, and which he would address persistently from now on, was 'How can we comprehend the socio-political processes that give rise to extreme violence, ethnic cleansing or genocide?' Through a number of important articles, in French and English, he examined definitional issues relating to massacre and genocide, seeking at each stage to bring clarity to concepts while at the same time motivating the disciplines he was addressing – always with the hope that they would push the boundaries of understanding a little bit further. As a historian, Sémelin was at all times stimulated by the words of the renowned French historian Marc Bloch, who had earlier written that 'when all is said and done, a single word, under-standing, is the beacon light of our research', but that, despite this, 'we are never sufficiently understanding' (Bloch, 1944: 143). (In this regard, Sémelin took the same inspiration from Bloch as another important thinker on the Holocaust and genocide, **Robert Skloot**, who came from a very different discipline area.)

Sémelin's most important work up to this time was *Purify and Destroy: The Political Uses of Massacres and Genocides* (2007), in which he carefully and systematically worked through the reasons behind mass killing during the twentieth century, and attempted to locate its sources – both within society at large and within the human psyche. Adopting his interpretation of the conception of genocide – 'that particular process of civilian destruction that is directed at the total eradication of a group, the criteria by which it is defined being determined by the perpetrator' (Sémelin, 2007b: 340) – he demonstrated that it is possible do so through comparative analysis, comparing the Holocaust, the Rwandan Genocide and ethnic cleansing in Bosnia-Herzegovina, while at the same time acknowledging and respecting the specific differences of each. Based on the essential distinction between massacre and genocide, the book identified the main steps of a general process of destruction, both rational and irrational (which Sémelin called delusional rationality), in which people and societies respond in particular ways to fear, resentment and the search for a utopia, and remodelling the social body in response by eliminating the enemy. He also identified the main stages that can lead to a genocidal process, in which ordinary people become perpetrators. He presented a general overview of mass violence both before and during the twentieth century, based upon three models of the destruction process:

- *Destroying to subjugate*, in which the goal is to annihilate a group partly in order to force the rest into total submission;
- *Destroying to eradicate*, in which the goal is to eliminate a community 'from a more or less extensive territory controlled or coveted by a state', a process involving the 'cleansing' or 'purifying' of the area of another's presence; and
- *Destroying to revolt* (usually committed by non-state actors), in which the aim is to strike a target group in a single blow to provoke an intense traumatic shock likely to influence its leaders' policies.

(Sémelin, 2007b: 324–61)

Throughout his analysis, Sémelin made thorough use of historical examples to illustrate his propositions, positing an argument regarding the multidisciplinary and variegated nature of genocide against which all allegations of the crime must be benchmarked.

Sémelin's commitment to clarity, explanation and understanding took a new course in April 2008, with the launch of his most important project to date, the Online Encyclopaedia of Mass Violence (http://www.massviolence.org). As founder and Editor-in-Chief, Sémelin presided over a global endeavour that took four years even to launch. The gradual construction of the website was the result of extraordinary teamwork on the part of computer specialists and scholars, who coordinated a variety of technical, scientific and pedagogical criteria established by a team of genocide and human-rights specialists. The information content on the website is not provided by an interested public in the manner of Wikipedia; rather, academic authorities of relevant historical and theoretical issues are invited to contribute on specific issues germane to their subject areas. Each submission is peer reviewed before being uploaded onto the system, and it is expected that the Encyclopedia will become the premier international online reference site for the diffusion of knowledge on mass violence (inclusive of genocide, ethnic cleansing, massacres, and so on). Consistent with Sémelin's own approach to research, it was held that the foremost responsibility of the Online Encyclopaedia would be to build up knowledge and share it, free of charge.

In his most recent published work, *La Résistance aux Génocides. De la pluralité des actes de sauvetage* (2008), which he co-edited with Claire Andrieu and Sarah Gensburger, Sémelin returned to his earlier investigations on resistance, this time looking at resistance to genocide (with a focus, though not exclusively, on the Holocaust). Here, he argued that such resistance can take not one but several forms, which acquire various shapes as micro-social forms of opposition to curb the process of destruction. He also considered the nature of rescue from genocidal situations, noting that, aside from a handful of ground-breaking studies, scholarly research has taken little interest in such behaviour. It was intended that this book would be innovative in that, while it examined research on the rescue of Jews in Nazi Europe, it also broadened out to consider efforts to protect victims of other mass murders, such as in Armenia and Rwanda. The scholarly ambition of such a work was also to lay the foundation for a possible comparative analysis, with the hope that it could stimulate further reflection and thereby enable more work to be done in the future. Such comparison could then suggest new analytical perspectives, and propose cross-disciplinary questions for the case studies under examination.

Jacques Sémelin is a scholar dedicated to the idea that respect should be paid to words. Specialist terms must be used correctly, lest they lose their effectiveness. He is, for example, sceptical about the tendency among some people to define genocide as any kind of massacre, preferring a more limited and rigorous approach to the use of the genocide notion. However, he acknowledges the importance of the 1948 UN Convention on the Prevention and Punishment of the Crime of Genocide. For Sémelin, this document represents a fundamental contribution to international law, bearing witness to the emergence of a universal conscience which is attempting to oppose the outrageousness of mass crimes. Nevertheless, the most important factor in analysis, for Sémelin, is to understand the social and political processes that produce such deadly events through comparative research and interdisciplinary analyses. In this, perhaps, we see his major contribution to the thought processes that are only now starting to accompany mainstream scholarship in genocide studies.

Sémelin's major writings

Pour sortir de la violence, Paris: Éditions Ouvrières 1983.
(with Christian Mellon and Jean-Marie Muller) *La dissuasion civile*, Paris: Fondation pour les Études de Défense Nationale, 1985.
Sans armes face à Hitler. Le Résistance civile en Europe (1939–1943), Paris: Payot, 1989.
'Le totalitarisme à l'épreuve de la résistance civile (1939–89)', *Vingtième Siècle* (July 1993), 79–90.
'Qu'est-ce que résister?', *Esprit*, 198 (January 1994a), 50–63.
Unarmed Against Hitler: Civil Resistance in Nazi Europe (1939–1943), Westport (CT): Praeger, 1994b.
(with Christian Mellon) *La non-violence*, Paris: Presses universitaires de France (in the series 'Que sais-je?'), 1994c.
La non-violence expliquée à mes filles, Paris: Le Seuil, 2000.
'Penser les massacres', *Revue Internationale de Politique Comparée*, 8, 1 (Spring 2001a), 7–22.
'In Consideration of Massacres', *Journal of Genocide Research*, 3, 3 (November 2001b), 377–89.
Nonviolence Explained to my Children, Cambridge (MA): Da Capo Press, 2002a.
'From Massacre to the Genocidal Process', *International Social Science Journal*, 174 (December 2002b), 429–42b.
'Analysis of a Mass Crime: Ethnic Cleansing in the Former Yugoslavia (1991–99)', in Robert Gellately and Ben Kiernan (eds), *Specter of Genocide: Mass Murder in Historical Perspective*, Cambridge: Cambridge University Press, 2003a, 353–70.
'Toward a Vocabulary of Massacre and Genocide', *Journal of Genocide Research*, 5, 2 (June 2003b), 193–210.
Purifier et détruire. Usages politiques des massacres et génocides, Paris: Le Seuil, 2005.
J'arrive là où je suis étranger, Paris: Éditions du Seuil, 2007a.
Purify and Destroy: The Political Uses of Massacres and Genocides, London: Hurst, 2007b.

(Ed. with Claire Andrieu and Sarah Gensburger) *La Résistance aux Génocides. De la pluralité des actes de sauvetage*, Paris: Presses de Sciences Po, 2008.

'On Visiting the Auschwitz Museum', in Adam Jones (ed.), *Evoking Genocide: Scholars and Activists Describe the Works that Shaped their Lives*, Toronto: Key Publishing House, 2009, 133–36.

(Ed. with Claire Andrieu and Sarah Gensburger) *Resisting Genocide: The Multiple Forms of Rescue*, London: Hurst, 2010.

Reference

Bloch, Marc, *The Historian's Craft*, Manchester: Manchester University Press, 1944.

ROBERT SKLOOT (b. 1942)

Robert Skloot is an Emeritus Professor of Theatre and Drama at the University of Wisconsin-Madison. Born in 1942 in Brooklyn, New York, he was educated at Union College (New York), Cornell University and the University of Minnesota, where he earned his PhD in 1968. He arrived at the University of Wisconsin as an Assistant Professor in 1968, and remained there for the rest of his career, directing approximately forty plays by all manner of play-wrights, including Albee, Beckett, Feiffer, Goldoni, Howe, Kopit, Molière, Odets, Pirandello, Rabe, Shepard, Stoppard and Vogel, among others. Before his retirement he directed seminars for high-school teachers that were funded by the National Endowment for the Humanities on the subject of 'The Theatre and the Holocaust'. Highly decorated for his work in the teaching of theatre, he has lectured all over the world on the Holocaust and genocide relative to the theatre.

Skloot's principal teaching area involved theatre literature. This involved a focus on contemporary drama, especially on the subjects of the Holocaust and genocide. His interest in the Holocaust came from his Jewish identity and an abiding sense of humanity, not from any direct connections with that experience. As he wrote in a short memoir, 'Our family lost no one in the Holocaust, and I cannot recall the subject ever coming up in my childhood save for the oblique references to my grandmother's sponsorship in America of two Polish couples whose families were destroyed in the catastrophe' (Skloot, 2004: 192). Yet the Holocaust 'revealed an attraction impossible to resist' (Skloot, 1987: 337). He became convinced from an early time that his chosen field of drama was a site in which the most human of situations could be explored, and in which the major moral issues of his time – and, perhaps, their resolution – could be exposed. He was 'attracted to the Holocaust for the ethical, cultural, and aesthetic problems it encompasses', and was 'less concerned with the theological or political issues it subsumes under its insatiable shadow' (Skloot, 1987: 337). Thus, 'the arts can, and should, contribute to the public discourse on serious subjects, the Holocaust among them'. Moreover, this was not something for which artists should feel that they have to take a back seat to historians or political scientists. As he wrote on another occasion, 'Because the theatre is essentially a showplace of humanity using real people on stage to confront real people in audiences (whatever style this takes), I find it the best way to make my case. Others have their tools, and that's OK – with the proviso that they keep focus on the actual, permanent loss of [life] and to the human spirit' (Skloot, personal correspondence, 7 August 2008). Skloot considered artists to be 'the first among equals in the company of Holocaust investigators', a position upon which 'my own work is based and has been based since the 1970s' (Skloot, 2004: 190).

One of the primary issues motivating Skloot as a director and teacher of theatre was how to find ways of understanding and preventing genocide and creating a world that is simultaneously less violent and more protective and supportive of human life. Throughout his career he saw serious possibilities for the arts to play a role in preparing or creating social change, and specifically how the art of theatre can be used in furthering this goal. As his thoughts in the area developed, he came more and more to the view that the theatre of the Holocaust is a site in which 'the hardest part of researching the field' – namely, 'the problem of hope' (Skloot, personal correspondence, 7 August 2008) – can be explored and, perhaps, enabled. With hope comes the possibility of survival, providing significant avenues of exploration on stage. In an article published in 1987 he advanced these views as follows:

> The images of survival we confront in Holocaust drama ultimately influence and are influenced by what we believe about the issue at the heart of the Holocaust experience: the nature and possibility of choice. That subject, and the hope it arouses or defeats in us, is the lasting and continuing focus of the theatre of the Holocaust, and the inquiry which will shed light on the darkness we all carry.
>
> (Skloot, 1987: 348)

Of course, the issue of survival is imperative in any discussion of genocide; it is as important as genocidal motive, execution and rescue. It is little surprise, therefore, that Skloot devoted another of his articles to the issue of dramas that choose survival as their theme, and in this he interwove his discussion of plays with a discussion of the work of non-playwrights who have similarly wrestled with the question of survival from a different perspective, such as Bruno Bettelheim and **Terrence Des Pres**, among others (Skloot, 1987: 348). Clearly, Skloot has confidence in the role of theatre to help in making the world a less violent place, in which suffering can decrease and the common traits of humanity can be understood by all. As he would write in the Introduction to his 2006 play *If the Whole Body Dies: Raphael Lemkin and the Treaty against Genocide*, 'plays do things to people. What the theatre can provide uniquely is a connection between human beings and among groups through the creation of empathy. It is a connection that, however brief, creates visible, remarkable humane possibilities that differ from the violent and terror-filled world too many know, even though many others are, with luck and resources, seemingly exempt from danger' (Skloot, 2006a: 6–7). What, therefore, does the theatre of genocide actually do? As Skloot sees it, theatre manages to 'extend the limits of our language and imagination' (Skloot, 2008: 9), through an audience's exposure to features typifying genocidal situations, such as fear, endurance, resistance, despair, grief, confusion, courage and cowardice. Thus,

> The theatre in performance contains an inexhaustible supply of images and words, created in the *present* (not like the *pastness* of a photograph) that can in an important way add to the process of instruction. The dramatized stories of terror from Armenia, Cambodia, Bosnia and Rwanda lock the pictures of genocide in our minds, and with them in place, they become a stimulus for encouraging and sustaining purposeful, humane action in response to what is revealed on stage.
>
> (Skloot, 2008: 22, emphasis in original)

In other words, theatre enables audience members to visualise, through their own imagination as well as those of actors, designers, playwrights and directors, a glimpse of what genocide can be like, as replicated for them on stage. In this way, the theatre fulfils an educational function, exercising its power (as well as its obligation) to work against evil tendencies. For Skloot, it can do this in two ways: first, by raising issues of history, no matter how painful; and second, by revealing images of the varieties of goodness that can confront a genocidal environment.

In some respects, Skloot sees himself as carrying on a tradition already pioneered by those in the theatre long ago. As he wrote in 2006, 'Writers, from the ancient Greeks to present-day poets, are rarely silent when presented with the opportunity to discuss the sufferings brought by war and atrocity. The themes they engage – life and its destruction, justice and injustice, belief and betrayal, purity and corruption, goodness and evil, and so on – are the subjects of great literature in every age' (Skloot, 2006b: 59). Placing himself as part of a continuum, he questions why there are some in academia and elsewhere who deny the arts what he sees as their rightful place in helping to create a genocide-free world:

> The (antiwar) work of artists … tends to be overlooked by many in politics and academe who carry a negative bias toward things freighted with idealism and emotion. The work is greeted as soft and starry-eyed, depressing and irrelevant, distractive and untrustworthy, and a host of other dismissive pejoratives. But artists know better, and so do the millions who over time have seen *Guernica*, heard the *Requiem* or stood in the confounding, earthly courtyard of the Berlin Jewish Museum.
>
> (Skloot, 2006a: 6)

His ongoing hope is that those in the social sciences will see that knowledge can be obtained in ways grounded as much in feeling as in fact, and that the power of insight communicated through theatre can be just as legitimate as the work they do themselves. That said, he has respect

> for *any* scholarly discipline or personal background that can lead to taking up the Holocaust as a subject of serious study: wherever on the margin we begin will soon take us to the black hole at the centre. Historians, sociologists, political scientists, doctors and lawyers, scholars of ethnic or women's studies, novelists, poets, and (to my purpose) playwrights, have all made substantial contributions to our understanding of an event which, defiantly, eludes complete understanding.
>
> (Skloot, 1987: 337, emphasis in original)

Skloot's view is that theatre can assist understanding through commenting on and influencing public discourse. This can take place through a number of strategies that describe the victims' suffering and assertion of their essential worthiness; discussing the perpetrators' motivations; presenting images of healing and compassion; evoking empathy; questioning the proper use of historical knowledge; and the expansion and dissemination of what the critic Susan Sontag called a 'collective instruction' of culture (Skloot, 2008: 5).

Skloot's thinking demonstrates that such plays are not only extensive, but also immensely useful. There are a large number awaiting production, from artists and theatres committed to staging stories and images of human barbarity and human courage. These plays inquire into the behaviour of victims, perpetrators and bystanders, attending to the legacy left to the generations that have come after the catastrophe. Some critics – and Skloot cites the historian Peter Novick as one of them – doubt that engaging with these texts can do anything to move the world to a less violent, more peaceful place. Others, on the other hand, argue that exposure to anti-genocidal works can make a difference, especially in educational curricula devoted to reducing conflict and advocating human rights. Skloot counts himself among these latter, holding to a belief in theatre's transformational possibilities and dedicating his professional work to bringing the theatre arts to the table of discussion when the issue of the Holocaust and/or genocide is raised.

Reflecting on these matters, Skloot has concluded that a number of lessons can be extracted from his teaching and directing at the University of Wisconsin. In an article in 1987 he listed five objectives of playwrights who are drawn to this topic: honouring the victims; teaching history to audiences; evoking emotional responses; discussing ethical issues; and suggesting solutions to universal contemporary problems (Skloot, 1987: 342). To these worthy points he added, in a later reflection, the following ideas:

- Universities have an obligation to address the issues of violence and atrocity, including the Holocaust and genocide, throughout the curriculum;
- The victims of violence, often anonymous in death, need recognition and remembrance;
- The Holocaust is not 'a Jewish problem', but is part of Western history. Representing the Holocaust can involve exploitation and commercialisation, which must be resisted;
- It is correct and necessary to acknowledge that we are all capable of doing terrible things;
- Some of us may be better prepared to resist the easy path to doing harm by learning about the sorrowful history of humanity in recent times;
- Hope is hard to hang on to.

(Skloot, 2006b: 61)

Recently, he has added the idea that the theatre is also a crucial element in confronting and contradicting the phenomenon of Holocaust and genocide denial.

As something of a personal manifesto, these thoughts have been complemented by the added realisation that 'plays are ineffective in bringing about *immediate* changes in societies no matter how intelligent or powerful they may be' (Skloot, 2008: 6, emphasis in original), and that, moreover, 'their effectiveness in reducing violence is impossible to ascertain but has been dispiritingly small in light of the seemingly ineradicable outbreak of war and genocide' (Skloot, 2006b: 59) in the twentieth century.

Despite this, however, plays can help to provide a better understanding of the violent world in which we live, creating images that, in the long run, may make the world more peaceful and just. As Skloot sees it, such images can prepare the ground for changes in official policies (and certainly for the ways in which people think). Skloot sees his work, and that of the theatre, as one of raising awareness about genocide, with the aim of facilitating its prevention. He seeks to provoke empathy for peoples whose lives are vulnerable and endangered, and thereby bring audiences closer to understanding the historical and cultural forces that create the lethal conditions for mass murder. He is fully conscious of the fact that genocide is still a powerful force in the world, and recognises that in our time the prevention or postponement of wholesale slaughter has not been avoided, whether by individual behaviour or state actions. 'Certainly,' he has written, the cry of 'Never again!' that was heard first in the aftermath of the Holocaust has come to seem little more than a hollow slogan today: 'Always, everywhere!' would be a more accurate description of world events (Skloot, 2008: 4).

Robert Skloot has devoted himself to ridding the world of the scourge of genocide through the medium of theatre. To do so, he has sought at every turn to raise consciousness of the human dimension of that experience, emphasising its tragedy and encouraging empathy from those who write, act in, produce, direct and watch plays. If the seeming attractiveness of genocide is to be reduced, if its horrible potential is to be averted, Skloot's unwavering line has always been – and remains – that the pressure to work towards the ultimate goal must involve all disciplines and professions, including artists from the theatre and elsewhere. In so far as he has been able to encourage and develop this vitally important understanding within his own discipline, it can be said that he has to a large degree succeeded.

Skloot's major writings

(Ed.) *The Theatre of the Holocaust: Four Plays*, vol. 1, Madison (WI): University of Wisconsin Press, 1982 (reprinted 1999).

'We Will Never Die: The Success and Failure of a Holocaust Pageant', *Theatre Journal*, 37, 2 (1985), 167–80.

'The Drama of the Holocaust: Issues of Choice and Survival', *New Theatre Quarterly*, 3, 12 (November 1987), 337–48.

The Darkness We Carry: The Drama of the Holocaust, Madison (WI): University of Wisconsin Press, 1988.

'Stage Nazis: The Politics and Aesthetics of Memory', *History & Memory*, 6, 2 (1994), 57–87.

(Ed.) *The Theatre of the Holocaust: Six Plays*, vol. 2, Madison (WI): University of Wisconsin Press, 1999.

'The Heft of Useful Things: The Hard Work of Holocaust Theatre', in Samuel Totten, Paul R. Bartrop and Steven Leonard Jacobs (eds), *Teaching About the Holocaust: Essays by College and University Teachers*, Westport (CT): Praeger, 2004, 189–204.

If the Whole Body Dies: Raphael Lemkin and the Treaty Against Genocide, Madison (WI): Parallel Press, 2006a.

'The Theatre of the Holocaust: Lessons of an Ongoing Journey', *Wisconsin People and Ideas*, Summer 2006b, 57–61.

(Ed.) *The Theatre of Genocide: Four Plays about Mass Murder in Rwanda, Bosnia, Cambodia and Armenia*, Madison (WI): University of Wisconsin Press, 2008.

'Staying Ungooselike: The Holocaust and the Theatre of Choice', in Edna Nahshon (ed.), *Jewish Theatre: A Global View*, Leiden (Netherlands): Brill Academic Publishers, 2009, 241–55.

ELIE WIESEL (b. 1928)

Elie Wiesel is a Romanian-born American writer, thinker and teacher, world-renowned for his work in raising awareness of the Holocaust and its meaning for contemporary society. For many, he is the conscience and expression of all Holocaust survivors. A prolific author, his written work has dealt with Judaism, the Holocaust and the moral responsibility of all people to fight hatred, racism and genocide.

Wiesel was born in 1928 in the town of Sighet, in Transylvania, when it was still part of Romania prior to its occupation by Hungary in 1940. As a child his world essentially revolved around family, religious study, community and God, but with the Nazi invasion of Hungary in the spring of 1944 this all changed. His entire village was first incarcerated in two ghettos in Sighet, and then deported to Auschwitz. At the age of 15, Wiesel was crammed into a freight car along with his parents and three sisters and sent to Auschwitz, where he was tattooed with the number A-7713. He and his father were separated from his mother and sisters, and were sent on slave labour to the Bunawerke, a sub-camp of Auschwitz. He and his father remained together for a year, surviving a death march to Buchenwald in the winter of 1944–45, until his father died just a short time before the camp was liberated by the Americans in April 1945. Both of Wiesel's parents, and one of his sisters, perished during the Holocaust.

After liberation, Wiesel was taken to Paris where he lived in an orphanage. Between 1947 and 1950 he studied Talmud, Philosophy and Literature at the Sorbonne, attending lectures by Jean-Paul Sartre and Martin Buber. Working as a teacher of Hebrew and a choirmaster in order to supplement his income, he then became a journalist. He steadfastly refused to write about or discuss his Holocaust experiences. A meeting with the 1952 Nobel Laureate for Literature, François Mauriac, however, convinced him of the need to begin writing about his experiences, and this was to lead him on an altogether unexpected path as the recognised voice of Holocaust survivors everywhere.

His best-known work is his Holocaust memoir, *Night*. This was first written in Yiddish, Wiesel's native language. In its initial incarnation, it ran to more than 800 pages. A version of this, published in 1956 in Argentina, *Un di velt hot geshvign* (*And the World Remained Silent*), was substantially shorter at 245 pages. Wiesel then halved the manuscript further in French, finally publishing it in 1958 as *La Nuit*. The book was then translated into English as *Night*, and published in 1960. The success of this edition of the book has been nothing less than phenomenal. It has been translated into thirty languages, and by March 2006 some six million copies had been sold in the United States alone. On 13 February 2006 *Night* ranked first on *The New York Times* bestseller list for paperback non-fiction.

Night is a work of considerable linguistic power, proceeding from a style that is at once stripped of all extravagance and consisting of a multitude of memorable phrases. Nearly every line, it seems, is quotable. Wiesel, the religiously pious teenager from a country village, appears as an anguished soul tortured by having survived an experience that took his parents, sister and so many others. The book witnesses the death of his innocence, and the death of his belief in God. Recurring themes are his increasing disgust with mankind and his loss of faith. A single question gnaws at him and does not allow him to rest: how can a loving God, the same God in whom he had once placed his very being, have allowed the Holocaust to occur? While the book is filled with descriptions and reflections that are inspirational and worthy of citation, his description of his first night at Auschwitz provides an excellent example of his writing style and the challenge that has ruled his personal world ever since:

> Never shall I forget that night, the first night in camp, that turned my life into one long night seven times sealed.
> Never shall I forget that smoke.
> Never shall I forget the small faces of the children whose bodies I saw transformed into smoke under a silent sky.
> Never shall I forget those flames that consumed my faith forever.
> Never shall I forget the nocturnal silence that deprived me for all eternity of the desire to live.
> Never shall I forget those moments that murdered my God and my soul and turned my dreams to ashes.
> Never shall I forget those things, even were I condemned to live as long as God Himself.
> Never.
>
> (Wiesel, 1958 (new translation, 2006): 34)

It was from this moment, perhaps, that any personal future – and, at that time, his life was far from assured – would be dedicated to ethical issues and the will to bear witness to the Nazi horror. *Night*, in recording Wiesel's experience, came to be a symbolic recording of the experience of all Jews, and as a result he has since dedicated himself to ensuring that no-one can forget what happened. For Wiesel, 'Never Again!' is more than a phrase; for five decades it has been his life's mission to inform all of the reality of what he has tried to convey, so that none can say they 'didn't know'.

In 1955 Wiesel moved to the United States, and made his home in New York, becoming an American citizen in 1963. From here he became known as one of the world's most powerful voices – if not *the* most powerful voice – in Holocaust consciousness. From 1972 to 1976 he was the Distinguished Professor of Judaic Studies at the City University of New York, and in 1976 he was appointed Andrew W. Mellon Professor in the Humanities at Boston University. Wiesel's work received recognition from the United States government in

1978, when he was appointed Chair of the Presidential Commission on the Holocaust established by President Jimmy Carter. In 1980 the Commission was renamed the US Holocaust Memorial Council, and Wiesel remained in this position until 1986. In further acknowledgement of his contribution to the betterment of society, Wiesel was awarded the US Congressional Gold Medal of Freedom in 1985, the Nobel Peace Prize in 1986, and an honorary knighthood in recognition of his advocacy work for Holocaust education in the United Kingdom.

Wiesel's many writings show an author possessing a highly diverse range of skills. He has made compelling and profound contributions to literature and theology, and it might be said that his Holocaust writing has been among the most important ever composed. In an interview with journalist David Yonke in 2008, Wiesel summed up much of the philosophical essence conveyed through all his writing with the following statement:

> 'I was fighting indifference. All my work is against indifference,' he said. 'I believe really it is true that the opposite of love is not hate but indifference. But also the opposite of education is not ignorance but indifference. The opposite of beauty is not ugliness but indifference. The opposite of life is not death but indifference to life and death. So the indifference is what permits evil to be strong, what permits injustice to win, what permits catastrophe to go and kill and not stop'.

> (Yonke, 2008)

It is this opposition to indifference, and his quest to try to ensure that 'Never Again' becomes the guiding principle directing the actions of everyone, that has led Wiesel to repeat, over and over again, one of the most powerful and renowned statements made by any writer on the Holocaust: 'to remain silent and indifferent is the greatest sin of all' (http://xroads.virginia.edu/~CAP/HOLO/ElieBio.htm). Putting his own words into practice, one of the first things Wiesel and his wife, Marion, did after he won the Nobel Peace Prize in 1986 was to establish a foundation to promote peace and human rights throughout the world: the Elie Wiesel Foundation for Humanity. The Foundation's mission, rooted in the memory of the Holocaust, is to combat indifference, intolerance and injustice through international dialogue and youth-focused programmes that promote acceptance, understanding and equality, and in fulfilment of this mission it runs multiple programmes domestically and around the world.

Projecting his commitment even more forthrightly, in November 1992, during the Bosnian War, Wiesel went to Belgrade, Sarajevo, Banja Luka and the Manjaca concentration camp. Upon his return, he publicly urged US Secretary of State Lawrence Eagleburger to speak out against the genocide that was then occurring. He was not successful. Eighteen months later, at the opening of the United States Holocaust Memorial Museum in Washington DC, he made a further public plea to President Bill Clinton on the necessity of addressing the Bosnian Genocide, but again he was unsuccessful. Such initiatives were not isolated; for decades Wiesel's has been an imposing voice in speaking out against injustice and genocide around the world, notably with regard to apartheid in South Africa, the so-called Disappearances in Argentina, the treatment of dissidents in the Soviet Union, Serb actions in Bosnia-Herzegovina, Saddam Hussein's actions against the Kurds in northern Iraq, and the genocide of black Africans in Darfur at the hands of the government of Sudan. In 2007 the Wiesel Foundation issued a letter condemning Armenian Genocide denial by the Turkish government and its supporters, signed by fifty-three Nobel laureates including Wiesel himself. He has, moreover, been a major advocate for Jewish rights around the world, and in earlier times was an outspoken critic regarding the respective difficulties faced by Soviet and Ethiopian Jewry.

Wiesel has been credited with giving the very term 'Holocaust' its existing currency, though he does not feel that the word adequately describes the totality of the Nazi horror against the Jewish people. His preference is for it to be employed less, in order to avoid it becoming overused, and for the term – and the subject in general – to be treated with much more respect than it has been so far. As a word, 'Holocaust' is derived from the Greek *holokauston*, and is understood to be a Hebrew biblical reference to a sacrifice that is totally consumed by fire. In the Hebrew Bible, for example, I Samuel 7:9 refers to 'a burnt offering to God', the Hebrew term for which is *olah*. The term continues to be problematic because of its religious and theological associations; the vast majority of Jews and Christians do not affirm that the deaths in the *Shoah* were intended as offerings to God. Equally problematic in English is the linking of the word with both Jews and Nazis to describe the event, where one continues to find writers using the expression 'Jewish Holocaust' as well as those who use the term 'Nazi Holocaust'.

As a devout youth, Wiesel found immense difficulty aligning his belief in a just and compassionate God with the senseless injustice and destruction of the *Shoah*. The brutality surrounding him in

Auschwitz, Gleiwitz and Buchenwald forced him to question and get angry at God. Yet he did not deny God's existence or stop believing in Him, even though 'I doubted His absolute justice' (Wiesel, 1958 (new translation, 2006): 45). In his interview with David Yonke in 2008, he said that even today he cannot understand how such horrors ever existed, though 'even at the lowest points he never doubted the existence of God'. As he said at that time, 'Of course I never stopped believing in God. The things I say in *Night*, both to God and against God, I stand by every word. But the moment I said that, the next day I went on praying to God' (Yonke, 2008). This presents a complicated theological picture of Wiesel's thinking that connects to other discussions by such authors as **Richard L. Rubenstein**, **John K. Roth** and Michael Berenbaum. Much of Wiesel's writing, in fact, is devoted directly to dealing with the conundrum of belief in God in a post-Auschwitz universe, as an answer to this forms a major part of how the ethical underpinnings of modern society will be established in the future. Thus far, he would contend, not only has the issue not been dealt with satisfactorily, there have been far too many influences working actively against its achievement.

At his Nobel Lecture the day after he accepted the Peace Prize in 1986, Elie Wiesel referred to the incredulity being experienced by his generation at the state of the world four decades after the liberation of the camps:

> If someone had told us in 1945 that in our lifetime religious wars would rage on virtually every continent, that thousands of children would once again be dying of starvation, we would not have believed it. Or that racism and fanaticism would flourish once again. Nor would we have believed there would be governments that would deprive men and women of their basic rights merely because they dared to dissent. Governments of the Right and of the Left still subject those who dissent – writers, scientists, intellectuals – to torture and persecution. How is one to explain all this unless we consider the defeat of memory?
>
> (Wiesel, 1990b: 246)

Wiesel's major concern was that in the decades since the end of the Second World War nothing substantial had been learned as a result of that terrible conflict. All the cries of 'Never Again!', so frequently uttered at the time of the liberation of the camps, had amounted to nothing more than hot air. No-one seemed to care about the suffering of others anymore; everyone, it appeared, was out for themselves at the expense of their fellows. While none of this was new for Wiesel by 1986, it saddened him to look at the world around him and constantly draw the same conclusion. After a cataclysm such as the Holocaust, everyone should be looking out for the welfare and safety of everyone else, but this was not happening. Wiesel, in a later statement, was forced to ask: 'How can I expect a man to have compassion for humanity if he has none for the individual who lives alongside him?' (Wiesel, 1990c: 138). Having survived the Holocaust, Elie Wiesel has ever since done all in his power to foster the kind of understanding that will enable people to see the necessity of developing this compassion – to defeat indifference – and thus to prevent more atrocities and other genocides.

Wiesel's major writings

Un di velt hot geshvign, Buenos Aires: Tsentral-Farband fun Poylishe Yidn in Argentine, 1956.
Night, New York: Hill and Wang, 1958 (new translation, Harmondsworth (Middlesex): Penguin Books, 2006).
Dawn, New York: Hill and Wang, 1961.
The Accident, New York: Hill and Wang, 1962.
The Town beyond the Wall, New York: Atheneum, 1964.
The Gates of the Forest, New York: Holt, Rinehart and Winston, 1966a.
The Jews of Silence, New York: Holt, Rinehart and Winston, 1966b.
Legends of our Time, New York: Holt, Rinehart and Winston, 1968.
A Beggar in Jerusalem, New York: Random House, 1970a.
One Generation After, New York: Random House, 1970b.
Souls on Fire, New York: Random House, 1972a.
Night Trilogy, New York: Hill and Wang, 1972b.
The Oath, New York: Random House, 1973a.
Ani Maamin, New York: Random House, 1973b.
Zalmen, or the Madness of God, New York: Random House, 1974.
Messengers of God, New York: Random House, 1976.
A Jew Today, New York: Random House, 1978a.
Four Hasidic Masters and Their Struggle against Melancholy, Notre Dame (IN): University of Notre Dame Press 1978b.
The Trial of God, New York: Random House, 1979.
Images from the Bible, New York: The Overlook Press, 1980.
The Testament, New York: Summit Books, 1981a.
Five Biblical Portraits, Notre Dame (IN): University of Notre Dame Press 1981b.
Somewhere a Master, New York: Summit Books, 1982.
The Golem, New York: Summit Books, 1983.
The Fifth Son, New York: Summit Books, 1985.
Twilight, New York: Summit Books, 1988a.

(with Albert Friedlander) *The Six Days of Destruction*, Mahwah (NJ): Paulist Press, 1988b.
A Journey into Faith, New York: Donald I. Fine, 1990a.
From the Kingdom of Memory: Reminiscences, New York: Summit Books, 1990b.
Evil and Exile, Notre Dame (IN): University of Notre Dame Press 1990c.
Sages and Dreamers, New York: Summit Books, 1991.
The Forgotten, New York: Summit Books, 1992.
A Passover Haggadah, New York: Simon and Schuster, 1993.
All Rivers Run to the Sea: Memoirs, vol. I, *1928–1969*, New York: Knopf, 1995.
(with François Mitterrand) *Memoir in Two Voices*, New York: Arcade, 1996.
And the Sea is Never Full: Memoirs, vol. II, *1969–*, New York: Knopf 1999a.
King Solomon and his Magic Ring, New York: Greenwillow, 1999b.
Conversations with Elie Wiesel, New York: Schocken Books, 2001.
The Judges, New York: Knopf, 2002.
Wise Men and Their Tales, New York: Schocken Books, 2003.
The Time of the Uprooted, New York: Knopf, 2005.
A Mad Desire to Dance, New York: Random House, 2009a.
Rashi, New York: Schocken Books, 2009b.

Reference

Yonke, David, 'Holocaust Survivor Elie Wiesel, Who Will Speak at UT, is Dedicated to Ethical Issues', *Toledo Blade*, 19 October 2008, at http://www.toledoblade.com/apps/pbcs.dll/article?AID=/20081019/ART16/810180319.

JAMES E. YOUNG (b. 1951)

James E. Young is Professor of English and Judaic Studies at the University of Massachusetts Amherst, where he has taught since 1988. Born in 1951 in San Jose, California, he was educated at the University of California, Berkeley and the University of California, Santa Cruz. Young joined the University of Massachusetts Amherst in 1988. From an early point in his scholarly career, he seemed set on the path of literary criticism and the interpretation of original memoir, particularly Holocaust testimony. With an interest in the ways in which memory is constructed, over time he developed a specific expertise in Holocaust memorialisation and the projection of that memory through the development of dedicated specialist monuments and museums. Young should not, however, be labelled a scholar of Museum Studies; as a scholar of Literature, Judaic Studies, Literary Criticism and (above all) the nature of memory transmission, Young's interests range widely across the various ways in which the experience of the Holocaust can be (and has been) recalled – and to what end such recollection is to be directed.

Young's first major work in this regard was *Writing and Rewriting the Holocaust: Narrative and the Consequences of Interpretation* (1988), which sought to provide a new approach to the critical appreciation of Holocaust literature and historiography. Here, he attempted to apply modern literary theory to the study and remembrance of the Holocaust through its texts, and produced one of the earliest critical analyses of Holocaust narrative. Young considered the many forms in which the Holocaust has been dealt with by a range of authors, engaging with the multifaceted nature of memory and how it has been expressed.

He identified, in the book's very first lines, precisely what he saw as the major issues involved in assessing the state of Holocaust literature:

> To a great extent, Holocaust studies have always been inter-disciplinary: historical inquiry provokes political and sociological questions, while philosophical and religious inquiry inevitably entail larger literary issues. With the rise of contemporary literary and historical theory, scholars of the Holocaust have come increasingly to recognize that interpretations of both the texts and events of the Holocaust are intertwined. For both events and their representations are ultimately beholden to the forms, language, and critical methodology through which they are grasped. Religious meaning and significance, historical causes and events, are simultaneously reflected and generated in Holocaust narrative – as well as in the names, periodization, genres, and icons we assign this era. What is remembered of the Holocaust depends on how it is remembered, and how events are remembered depends in turn on the texts now giving them form.
>
> (Young, 1988: 1)

Young considered a fundamental question: is there any discernible distinction between Holocaust literary testimony and historical reality? While Holocaust literature might often be mistaken for fiction, he asked, is this really the case in every situation? Such considerations alert us to a type of memoir which needs to be read differently from other forms of historical documentation. Published survivor accounts are quite clearly subjectively true, in that they chronicle events either directly witnessed by their authors or told to them by others at the time of their incarceration. It is this truth, and these events, which the survivors attempt to impart to their readers, and it was this that most concerned Young in *Writing and Rewriting the Holocaust*. For his effort, he was awarded a *Choice* Outstanding Academic Book Award in 1989.

The Texture of Memory (1993), Young's next book, extended his work on how the memory of the Holocaust has been constructed, through a reflection on Holocaust memorials in Europe, the United States and Israel. The book was a groundbreaking study of the fusion of Holocaust memory and public art in contemporary life. It took a broad-based approach to analysing monuments to the Holocaust, and the histories they possess. Young considered how four different countries – Poland, Germany, the United States and Israel – recall the same events (for instance, Auschwitz or the Warsaw ghetto uprising), and found that the different sites of memory emphasise different aspects of each. Young analysed the ways in which the various countries 'remember' the events being considered, and concluded with an analysis of how memory is constructed and interpreted. The differences were carefully explored: for the Germans and Austrians, memorialising the Holocaust has required public recognition of their crimes; for the Jews, on the other hand, it has required public expression of their suffering. Young showed how each monument is charged with the often highly problematic struggle between collective memory and national self-image, self-interest and aspirations for the future. In this way, the meaning of the Holocaust continues to be redefined in each new generation in the countries under examination.

Young was keen to emphasise that this process is not a generalised one in which all those beholding memorials will necessarily respond the same way. Indeed, one of his stated aims was 'to break down the notion of any memorial's "collective memory" altogether'. Instead, he wrote,

> I prefer to examine 'collected memory', the many discrete memories that are gathered into common memorial spaces and assigned common meaning. A society's memory, in this context, might be regarded as an aggregate collection of its members' many, often competing memories. If societies remember, it is only insofar as their institutions and rituals organize, shape, even inspire their constituents' members. For a society's memory cannot exist outside of those people who do the remembering – even if such memory happens to be at the society's bidding, in its name.
>
> (Young, 1993: xi)

Young's intention, therefore, was to 'reinvigorate otherwise amnesiac stone settings with a record of their own lives in the public mind, with our memory of their past, present, and future' (Young, 1993: ix).

Doing this would not only examine the memorials themselves; Young's study would also serve 'as a broad critique of the memorialisation process at large' (Young, 1993: xiii). In this way, Young felt, he could move beyond the confines of Holocaust Studies – as important as that was – and 'also heighten critical awareness of all memorials, of the potential uses and abuses of officially cast memory, and ultimately of the contemporary consequences that past events hold for us in their memorial representations'.

Ultimately, Young sought to address the issue of to what end the Holocaust is remembered. Given the turbulent world of the late twentieth century, he argued that the question should be 'how do we respond to the current moment in light of our remembered past?'

> This is to recognize that the shape of memory cannot be divorced from the actions taken in its behalf, and that memory without consequences contains the seeds of its own destruction. For were we passively to remark only the contours of these memorials, were we to leave unexplored their genesis and remain unchallenged by the recollective act, it could be said that we have not remembered at all.
>
> (Young, 1993: xi)

Young articulated – perhaps for the first time – the purposes behind memorialisation, and focusing on an issue that needed to be tackled both within the existing literature (of which there was, to that point, surprisingly little) and within the realm of public discourse.

Building on this experience, in 1994 he was invited to act as Guest Curator of an exhibition entitled 'The Art of Memory: Holocaust Memorials in History' at the Jewish Museum in New York City. The exhibition ran from March to August of that year, following which it travelled to Berlin and Munich. The exhibition catalogue, which Young edited, was published in Germany as *The Art of Memory: Holocaust Memorials in History* (1994). A volume of essays from leading authors including Nathan Rapaport, Claudia Koonz, **Saul Friedländer**, Peter Novick and **Primo Levi** (among others), the book was a carefully constructed investigation of how public memory of the Holocaust was at that point being shaped in museums and memorials in North America, Europe and Israel, and why it was taking those forms. Once more Young was concerned with issues relating to the motives behind memorial design, the impact of memorials on public consciousness, and the degree to which memorials reflect the ideals, myths and political needs of the societies for which they are designed. Considering memorial and museum design as a form of art, Young's work here both complemented and added another dimension to the contemporaneous work of Holocaust art historian **Stephen C. Feinstein**. The essential difference was that Young focused his attention on matters relating to memory, while **Feinstein** was more concerned with the development of awareness and understanding.

Young followed this up with another monograph, *At Memory's Edge: After-Images of the Holocaust in Contemporary Art and Architecture* (2000). This was an ambitious work that delved deeply into the heart of an extremely sensitive issue: the manner in which Germany, the perpetrator nation, commemorates the Holocaust. In 1997 Young had been appointed by the Berlin Senate to the five-member *Findungskommission* for Germany's national 'Memorial to Europe's Murdered Jews'. He was the only foreigner and the only Jew on the committee, which ultimately selected a design by Peter Eisenman for a memorial that was finished and dedicated in May 2005. The experience placed Young in a unique position to write with authority as a 'participant-observer' of German approaches to memorialisation, and *At Memory's Edge* was the result: a collection of essays with topics ranging from Art Spiegelman's *Maus* books to Daniel Libeskind's Jewish Museum in Berlin, and much in between. Young's personal observations of the Berlin Memorial's evolution provided an informative perspective of how the city of Berlin remembers formerly despised people who are no longer at home there, and how Germany can – and should – remember the extermination of Jews once committed in its name.

Young's work on memorials and memory has recently been extended beyond that of the Holocaust. He has also consulted with Argentina's government on its memorial to the *desaparacidos*, as well as with numerous city agencies on their memorials and museums. He was appointed by the Lower Manhattan Development Corporation to the jury for the World Trade Center Site Memorial competition, won by Michael Arad and Peter Walker in January 2004, and now under construction.

The primary issue motivating Young in *At Memory's Edge* related to memory for the next generation – how people deal with what he termed a 'vicarious past'. The book's very first words outlined the problem:

How is a post-Holocaust generation of artists supposed to 'remember' events they never experienced directly? Born after

Holocaust history into the time of its memory only, a new, media-savvy generation of artists rarely presumes to represent these events outside the ways they have vicariously known and experienced them. This postwar generation, after all, cannot remember the Holocaust as it occurred. All they remember, all they know of the Holocaust, is what the victims have passed down to them in their diaries, what the survivors have remembered to them in their memoirs. They remember not the actual events but the countless histories, novels, and poems of the Holocaust they have read, the photographs, the movies, and video testimonies they have seen over the years. They remember the long days and nights in the company of survivors, listening to their harrowing tales until their lives, loves, and losses seem grafted onto their own life stories.

(Young, 2000: 1)

As he was thinking about this, Young found himself drawn to the necessary task of engaging with the question of how the next generation of a perpetrator society understands such a tragedy as genocide, when first-hand memories of that event are fading. Where Germany is concerned, the issues that other societies might face are compounded by its role as the country that gave the world Hitler and the Final Solution:

Memorial artists in Germany ... are both plagued and inspired by a series of impossible questions: How does a state incorporate shame into its national memorial landscape? How does a state recite, much less commemorate, the litany of its misdeeds, making them part of its reason for being? Under what memorial aegis, whose rules, does a nation remember its barbarity? Where is the tradition for memorial mea culpa, when combined remembrance and self-indictment seem so hopelessly at odds? Unlike state-sponsored memorials built by victimized nations and peoples to themselves in Poland, Holland, or Israel, those in Germany are necessarily those of former persecutors remembering their victims.

(Young, 2000: 7)

This of course presents major points of departure for Germany relative to other European countries, but there is more to it than just that. In view of the issues, Young wrote, 'it is little wonder that German national memory of the Holocaust remains so torn and convoluted'; moreover, these concerns raise two further questions:

'How do former persecutors mourn their victims? How does a nation reunite itself on the bedrock memory of its crimes?' (Young, 2000: 7)

None of these questions are easy to answer, nor are the issues simple to address. James E. Young's approach has been to ask the questions as he sees them, and thereby to stimulate further discussion. Further, while he would not arrogate to himself the position of final arbiter of any of these matters, his is nonetheless one of the most authoritative views regarding memory and memorialisation, as his work over the past three decades, in a variety of settings, attests.

Young's major writings

'Memory and Monument', in Geoffrey Hartman (ed.), *Bitburg in Moral and Political Perspective*, Bloomington: Indiana University Press, 1986, 103–13.

Writing and Rewriting the Holocaust: Narrative and the Consequences of Interpretation, Bloomington (IN): Indiana University Press, 1988.

The Texture of Memory: Holocaust Memorials and Meaning, New Haven (CT): Yale University Press, 1993.

(Ed.) *The Art of Memory: Holocaust Memorials in History*, Munich: Prestal Verlag, 1994.

'Memory and the Politics of Identity: The U.S. Holocaust Memorial Museum', in Linda Nochlin and Tamar Garb (eds), *The Jew in the Text*, London: Thames and Hudson, 1995, 292–304.

'America's Holocaust: Memory and the Politics of Identity', in Hilene Flanzbaum (ed.), *The Americanization of the Holocaust*, Baltimore: Johns Hopkins University Press, 1999, 68–82.

At Memory's Edge: After-Images of the Holocaust in Contemporary Art and Architecture, New Haven (CT): Yale University Press, 2000.

'The Uncanny Arts of Memorial Architecture', in Barbie Zelizer (ed.), *The Holocaust in Visual Culture*, New Brunswick (NJ): Rutgers University Press, 2001, 179–97.

'Holocaust Museums in Germany, Poland, Israel, and the United States', in Konrad Kwiet and Jurgen Matthaus (eds), *Contemporary Responses to the Holocaust*, Westport (CT): Praeger, 2004, 249–74.

'The Memorial Process: A Juror's Report from Ground Zero', in John Mollenkopf (ed.), *Contentious City: The Politics of Recovery in New York City*, New York: Russell Sage Foundation, 2005, 140–62.

'The Stages of Memory at Ground Zero', in Oren Baruch Stier and J. Shawn Landres (eds), *Religion, Violence, Memory, and Place*, Bloomington: Indiana University Press, 2006, 214–34.

'Mandating the National Memory of Catastrophe', in Austin Sarat and Lawrence Douglas (eds), *Law and Catastrophe*, Stanford (CA): Stanford University Press, 2007, 131–58.

INDEX

Note: Page references in **bold** refer to the main discussion relating to each author